WITHDRAWN
LIBRARY.CEDARMILL.ORG
CEDAR MILL LIBRARY

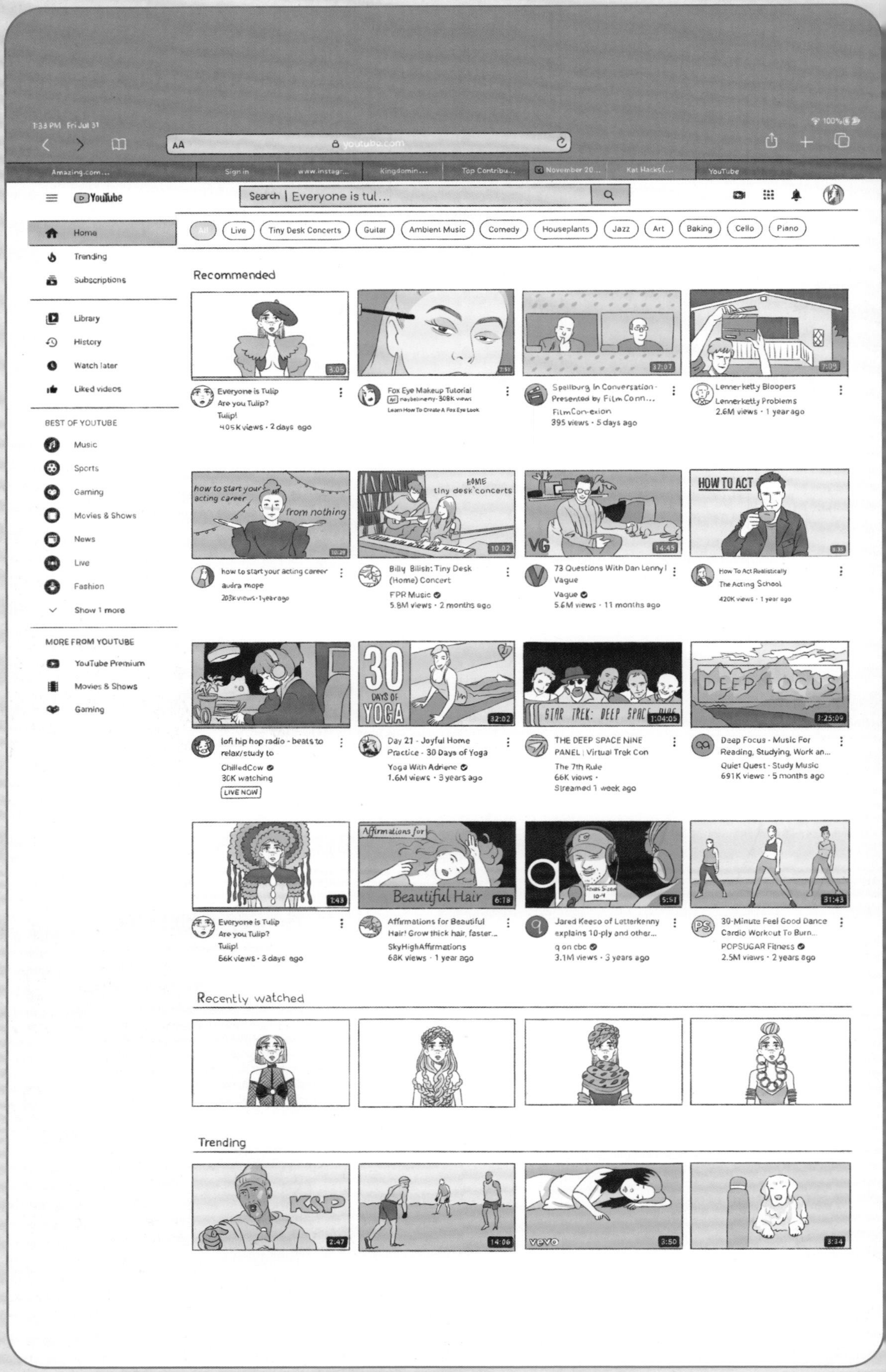
1:33 PM Fri Jul 31
100%
AA
youtube.com
Amazing.com...
Sign in
www.instagr...
Kingdomin...
Top Contribu...
November 20...
Kat Hacks(...
YouTube
YouTube
Search | Everyone is tul...
Home
Trending
Subscriptions
Library
History
Watch later
Liked videos
BEST OF YOUTUBE
Music
Sports
Gaming
Movies & Shows
News
Live
Fashion
Show 1 more
MORE FROM YOUTUBE
YouTube Premium
Movies & Shows
Gaming
All
Live
Tiny Desk Concerts
Guitar
Ambient Music
Comedy
Houseplants
Jazz
Art
Baking
Cello
Piano
Recommended
3:05
Everyone is Tulip
Are you Tulip?
Tulip!
405K views · 2 days ago
7:51
Fox Eye Makeup Tutorial
Learn How To Create A Fox Eye Look
37:07
Spellburg In Conversation - Presented by Film Conn...
FilmCon-exion
395 views · 5 days ago
7:09
Lennerketty Bloopers
Lennerketty Problems
2.6M views · 1 year ago
how to start your acting career
from nothing
10:29
how to start your acting career
audra mope
203K views · 1 year ago
HOME
tiny desk concerts
10:02
Billy Bilish: Tiny Desk (Home) Concert
FPR Music
5.8M views · 2 months ago
VG
14:45
73 Questions With Dan Lenny | Vague
Vague
5.6M views · 11 months ago
HOW TO ACT
How To Act Realistically
The Acting School
420K views · 1 year ago
lofi hip hop radio - beats to relax/study to
ChilledCow
30K watching
LIVE NOW
30 DAYS OF YOGA
32:02
Day 21 - Joyful Home Practice - 30 Days of Yoga
Yoga With Adriene
1.6M views · 3 years ago
STAR TREK: DEEP SPAC
1:04:05
THE DEEP SPACE NINE PANEL | Virtual Trek Con
The 7th Rule
66K views · Streamed 1 week ago
DEEP FOCUS
3:25:09
Deep Focus - Music For Reading, Studying, Work an...
Quiet Quest - Study Music
691K views · 5 months ago
1:43
Everyone is Tulip
Are you Tulip?
Tulip!
56K views · 3 days ago
Affirmations for
Beautiful Hair
6:18
Affirmations for Beautiful Hair! Grow thick hair, faster...
SkyHighAffirmations
68K views · 1 year ago
q
5:51
Jared Keeso of Letterkenny explains 10-ply and other...
q on cbc
3.1M views · 3 years ago
31:43
30-Minute Feel Good Dance Cardio Workout To Burn...
POPSUGAR Fitness
2.5M views · 2 years ago
Recently watched
Trending
K&P
2:47
14:06
vevo
3:50
3:34

EVERYONE IS TULIP

WRITTEN BY

DAVE BAKER

ART AND LETTERING BY

NICOLE GOUX

COLORS BY

ELLIE HALL
with NICOLE GOUX

DARK HORSE BOOKS

Publisher
MIKE RICHARDSON

Editor
KONNER KNUDSEN

Designers
SARAH TERRY and NICOLE GOUX

Digital Art Technician
SAMANTHA HUMMER

EVERYONE IS TULIP, June 2021. Everyone is Tulip™ & © 2021 Nicole Goux and Dave Baker. Published by Dark Horse Comics LLC, 10956 SE Main Street, Milwaukie, Oregon 97222. All rights reserved. Dark Horse Comics® and the Dark Horse logo are trademarks of Dark Horse Comics LLC, registered in various categories and countries. All rights reserved. No portion of this publication may be reproduced or transmitted, in any form or by any means, without the express written permission of Dark Horse Comics LLC. Names, characters, places, and incidents featured in this publication either are the product of the authors' imaginations or are used fictitiously. Any resemblance to actual persons (living or dead), events, institutions, or locales, without satiric intent, is coincidental.

Published by Dark Horse Books
A division of Dark Horse Comics LLC
10956 SE Main Street | Milwaukie, OR 97222

DarkHorse.com

First edition: June 2021
Ebook ISBN 978-1-50672-230-6
ISBN 978-1-50672-229-0

10 9 8 7 6 5 4 3 2 1
Printed in China

Neil Hankerson Executive Vice President • Tom Weddle Chief Financial Officer • Randy Stradley Vice President of Publishing • Nick McWhorter Chief Business Development Officer • Dale LaFountain Chief Information Officer • Matt Parkinson Vice President of Marketing • Vanessa Todd-Holmes Vice President of Production and Scheduling • Mark Bernardi Vice President of Book Trade and Digital Sales • Ken Lizzi General Counsel • Dave Marshall Editor in Chief • Davey Estrada Editorial Director • Chris Warner Senior Books Editor • Cary Grazzini Director of Specialty Projects • Lia Ribacchi Art Director • Matt Dryer Director of Digital Art and Prepress • Michael Gombos Senior Director of Licensed Publications • Kari Yadro Director of Custom Programs • Kari Torson Director of International Licensing • Sean Brice Director of Trade Sales

Library of Congress Cataloging-in-Publication Data

Names: Baker, Dave (Comic book writer), writer. | Goux, Nicole, artist. | Hall, Ellie, colourist.
Title: Everyone is Tulip / script, Dave Baker ; art and letters, Nicole Goux ; colors, Ellie Hall with Nicole Goux.
Description: First edition. | Milwaukie, OR : Dark Horse Books, 2021. | Summary: "Follow the journey of Becca, a young would-be actress, as she attempts to navigate the seedy underworld of Hollywood. What she doesn't know is that she is about to be conscripted into the even more sinister ecosystem of internet performance art videos. This woman's dreams of making it on the Big Screen rapidly evolve into something decidedly stranger"-- Provided by publisher.

Identifiers: LCCN 2020045870 | ISBN 9781506722290 (trade paperback)
Subjects: LCSH: Graphic novels.
Classification: LCC PN6727.B3266 E94 2021 | DDC 741.5/973--dc23
LC record available at https://lccn.loc.gov/2020045870

CHAPTER 1

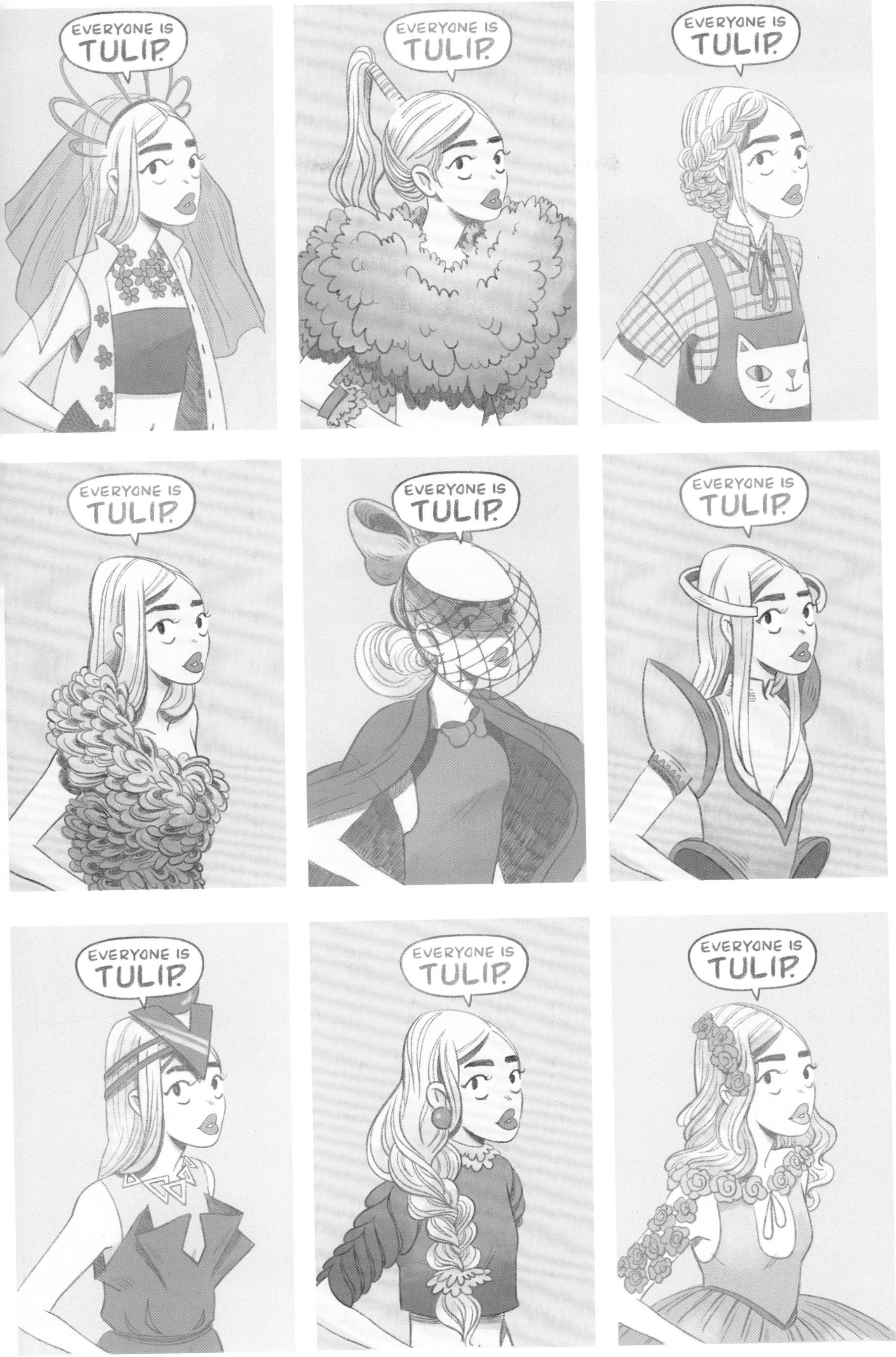
EVERYONE IS TULIP.
EVERYONE IS TULIP.
EVERYONE IS TULIP.
EVERYONE IS TULIP.
EVERYONE IS TULIP.
EVERYONE IS TULIP.
EVERYONE IS TULIP.
EVERYONE IS TULIP.
EVERYONE IS TULIP.

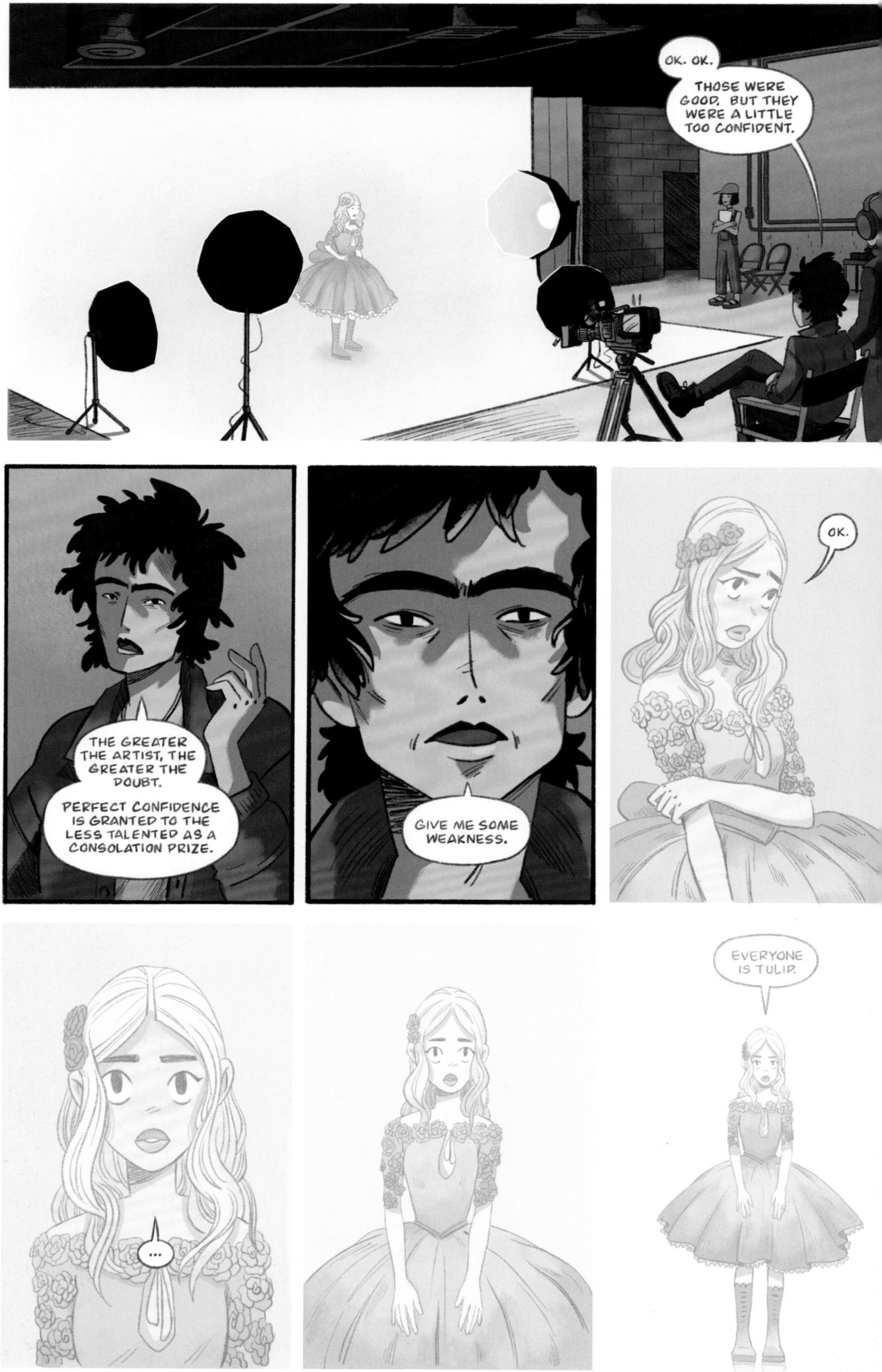
OK. OK.
THOSE WERE GOOD, BUT THEY WERE A LITTLE TOO CONFIDENT.
THE GREATER THE ARTIST, THE GREATER THE DOUBT.
PERFECT CONFIDENCE IS GRANTED TO THE LESS TALENTED AS A CONSOLATION PRIZE.
GIVE ME SOME WEAKNESS.
OK.
...
EVERYONE IS TULIP.

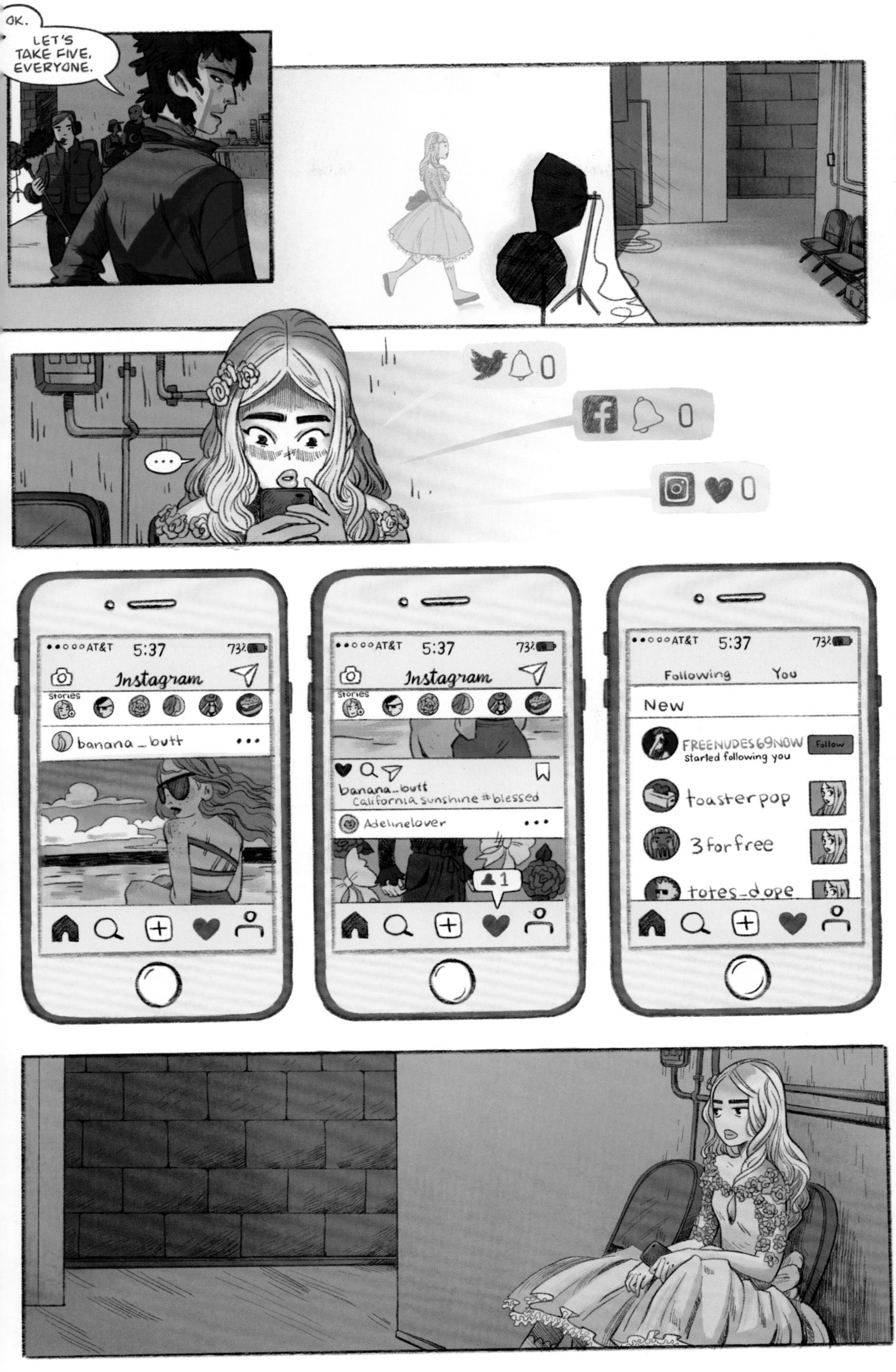
OK.
LET'S TAKE FIVE, EVERYONE.
...
0
0
0
AT&T 5:37 73%
Instagram
Stories
banana_butt
California sunshine #blessed
Adelinelover
1
Following You
New
FREENUDES69NOW started following you
Follow
toasterpop
3forfree
totes_dope

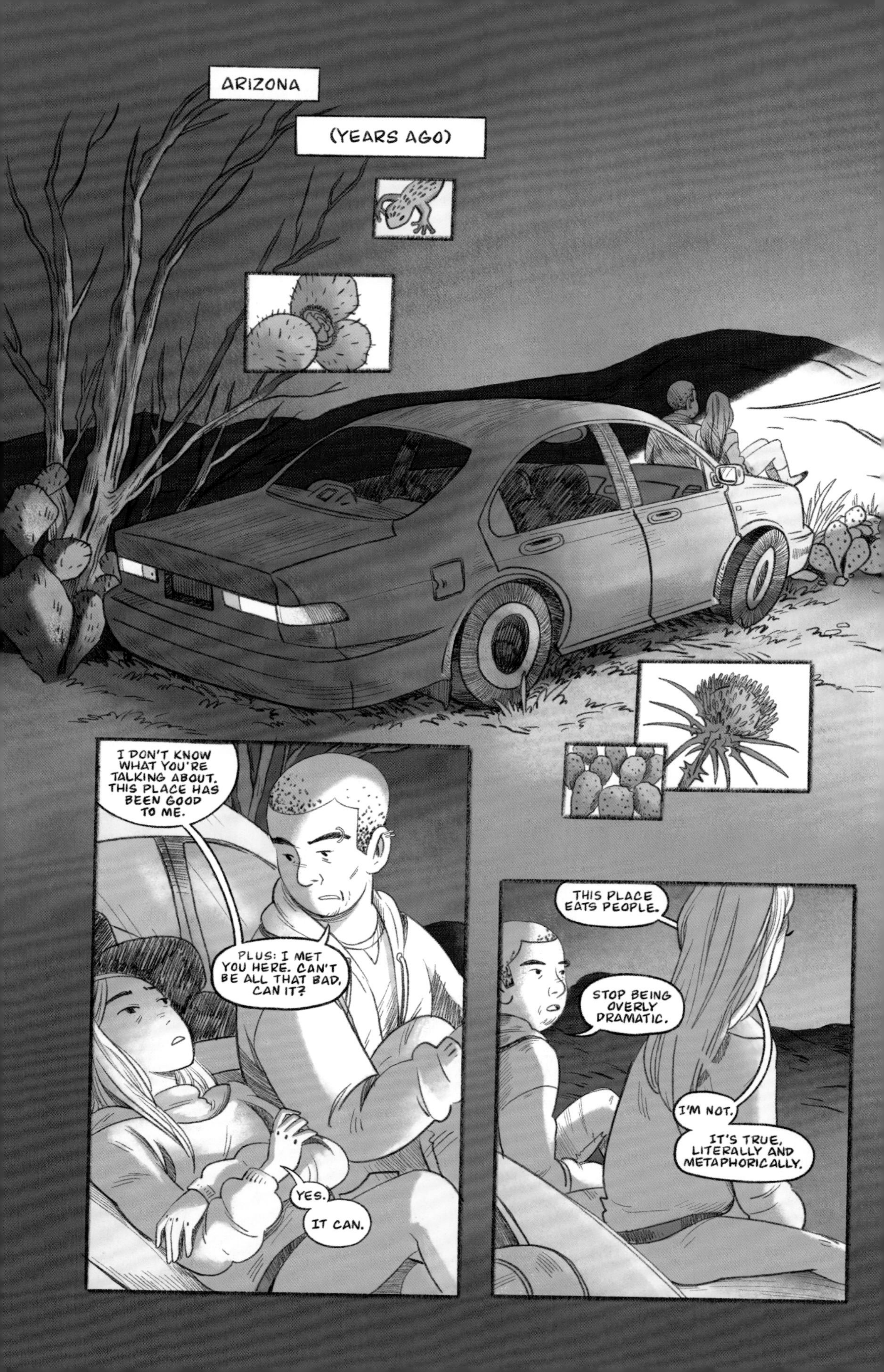
ARIZONA
(YEARS AGO)
I DON'T KNOW WHAT YOU'RE TALKING ABOUT. THIS PLACE HAS BEEN GOOD TO ME.
PLUS: I MET YOU HERE. CAN'T BE ALL THAT BAD, CAN IT?
YES.
IT CAN.
THIS PLACE EATS PEOPLE.
STOP BEING OVERLY DRAMATIC.
I'M NOT.
IT'S TRUE, LITERALLY AND METAPHORICALLY.

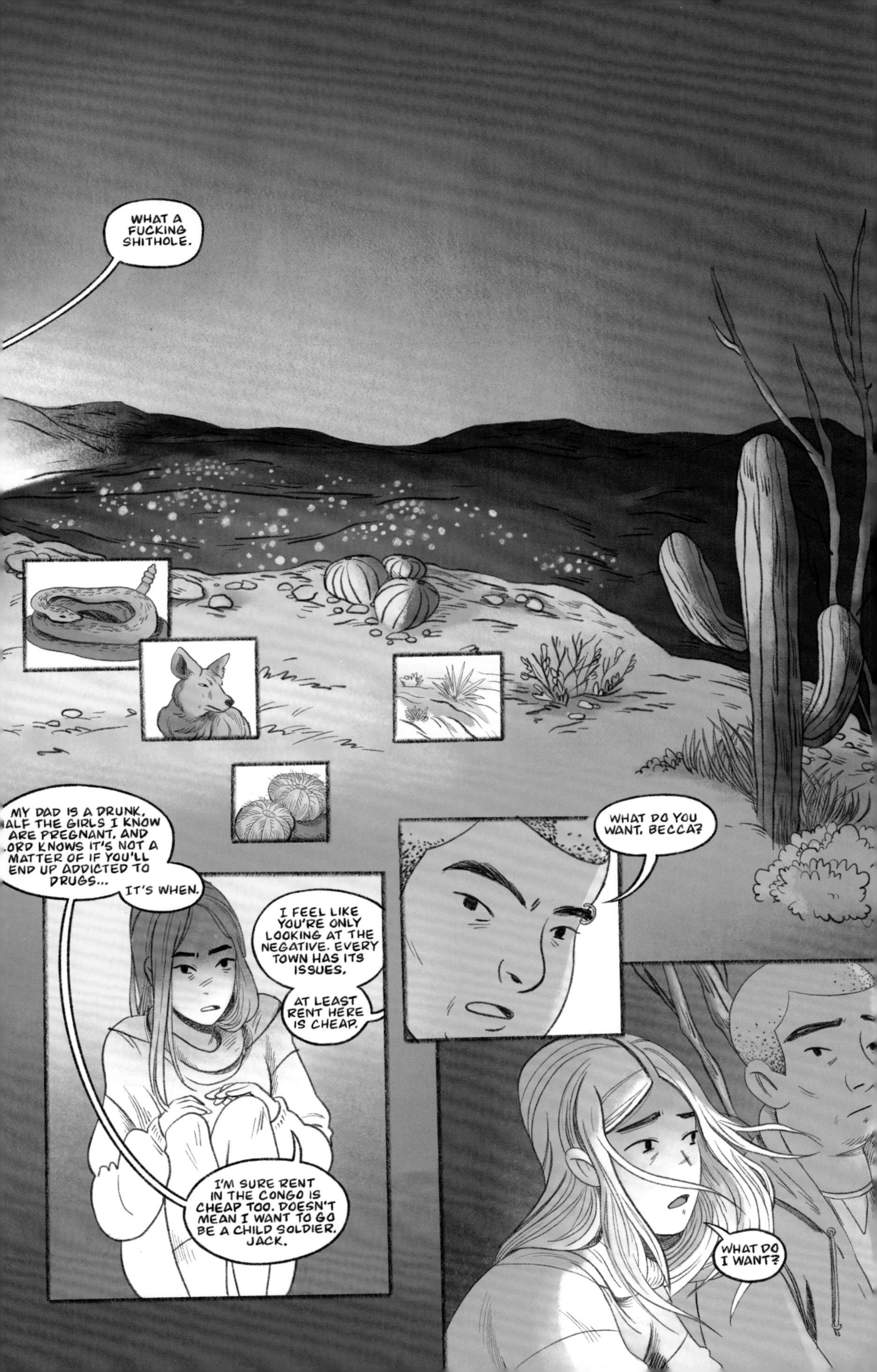
WHAT A FUCKING SHITHOLE.
MY DAD IS A DRUNK, ALF THE GIRLS I KNOW ARE PREGNANT, AND ORD KNOWS IT'S NOT A MATTER OF IF YOU'LL END UP ADDICTED TO DRUGS...
IT'S WHEN.
I FEEL LIKE YOU'RE ONLY LOOKING AT THE NEGATIVE. EVERY TOWN HAS ITS ISSUES.
AT LEAST RENT HERE IS CHEAP.
I'M SURE RENT IN THE CONGO IS CHEAP TOO. DOESN'T MEAN I WANT TO GO BE A CHILD SOLDIER, JACK.
WHAT DO YOU WANT, BECCA?
WHAT DO I WANT?

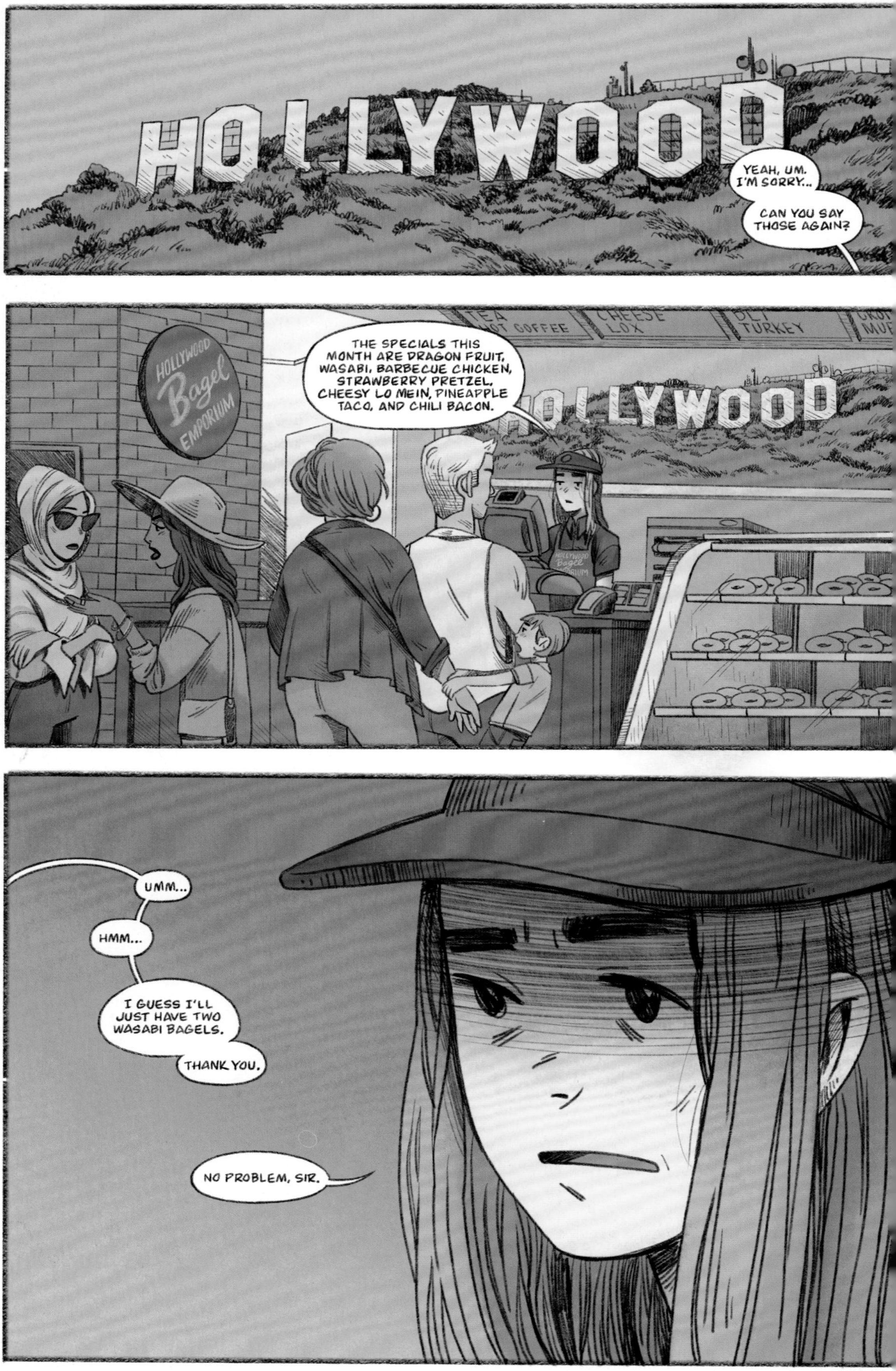
HOLLYWOOD
YEAH, UM. I'M SORRY...
CAN YOU SAY THOSE AGAIN?
HOLLYWOOD Bagel EMPORIUM
THE SPECIALS THIS MONTH ARE DRAGON FRUIT, WASABI, BARBECUE CHICKEN, STRAWBERRY PRETZEL, CHEESY LO MEIN, PINEAPPLE TACO, AND CHILI BACON.
UMM...
HMM...
I GUESS I'LL JUST HAVE TWO WASABI BAGELS.
THANK YOU.
NO PROBLEM, SIR.

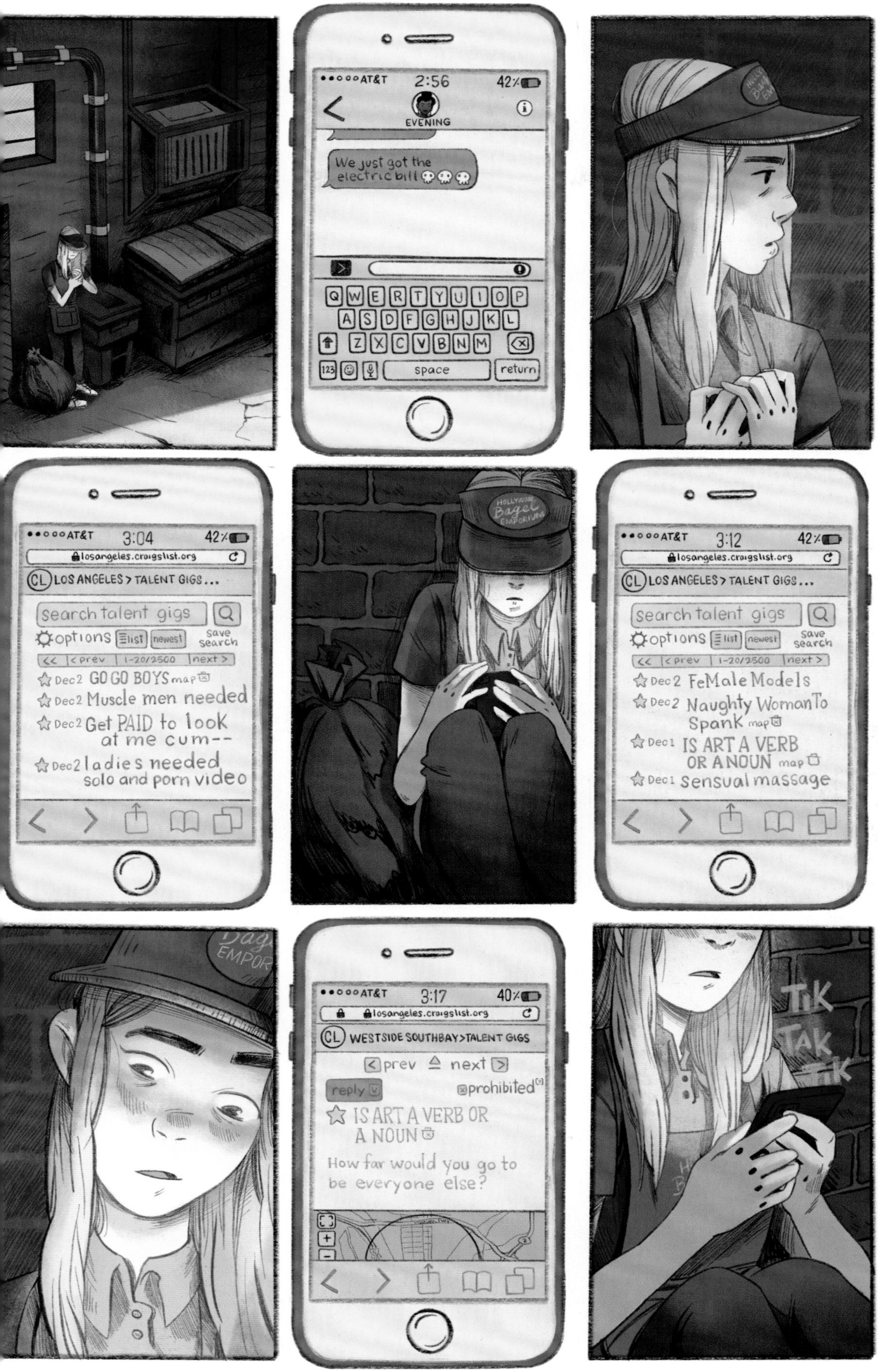

•••○○AT&T 2:56 42%
EVENING
We just got the electric bill 💀💀💀
space
return
•••○○AT&T 3:04 42%
losangeles.craigslist.org
CL LOS ANGELES > TALENT GIGS...
search talent gigs
options list newest save search
<< < prev 1-20/2500 next >
Dec2 GO GO BOYS map
Dec2 Muscle men needed
Dec2 Get PAID to look at me cum--
Dec2 ladies needed solo and porn video
HOLLYWOOD Bagel EMPORIUM
•••○○AT&T 3:12 42%
losangeles.craigslist.org
CL LOS ANGELES > TALENT GIGS...
search talent gigs
options list newest save search
<< < prev 1-20/2500 next >
Dec2 FeMale Models
Dec2 Naughty Woman To Spank map
Dec1 IS ART A VERB OR A NOUN map
Dec1 sensual massage
•••○○AT&T 3:17 40%
losangeles.craigslist.org
CL WESTSIDE SOUTHBAY > TALENT GIGS
< prev next >
reply
prohibited
IS ART A VERB OR A NOUN
How far would you go to be everyone else?
TIK
TAK

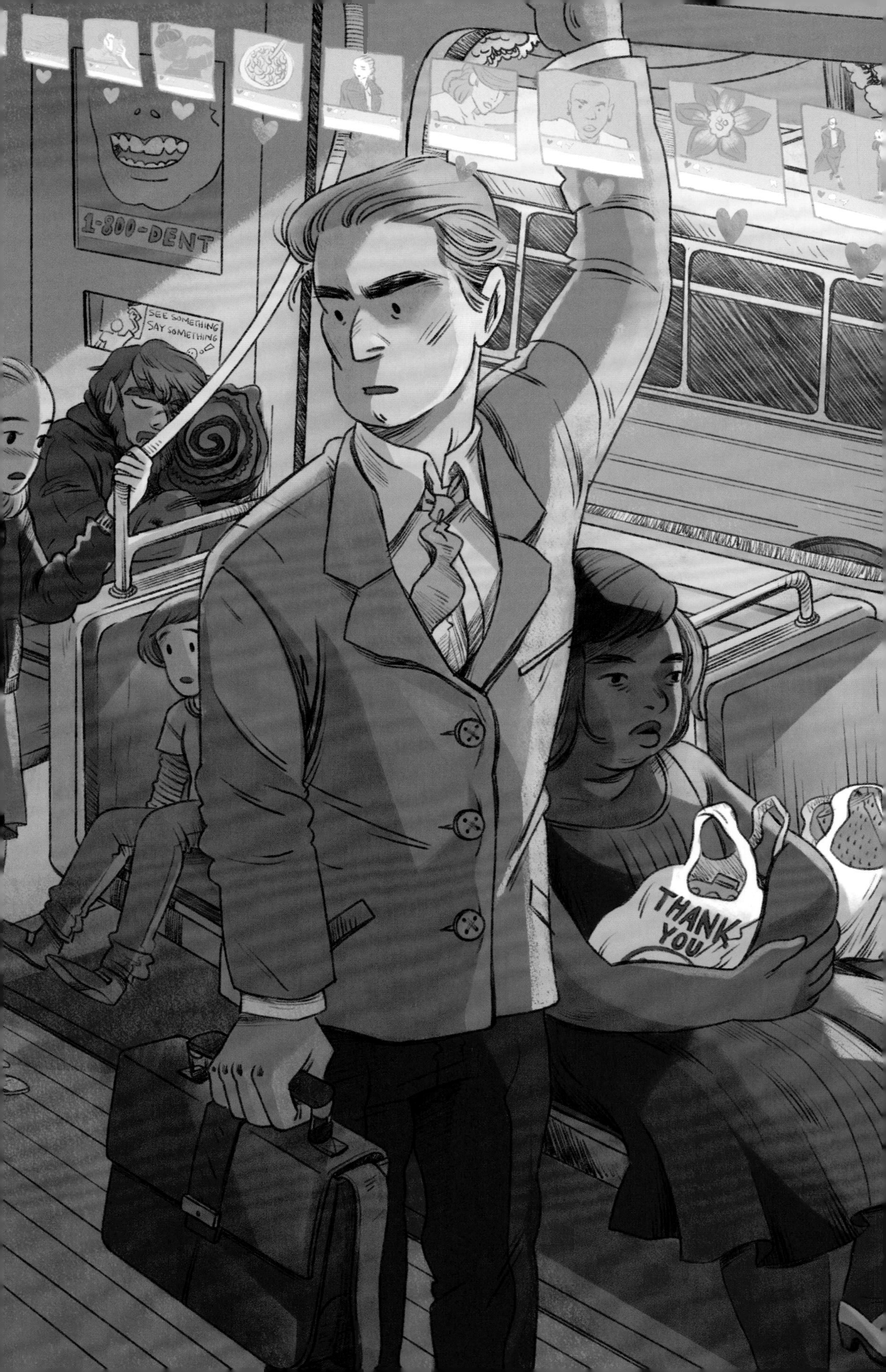
1-800-DENT
SEE SOMETHING
SAY SOMETHING
THANK YOU

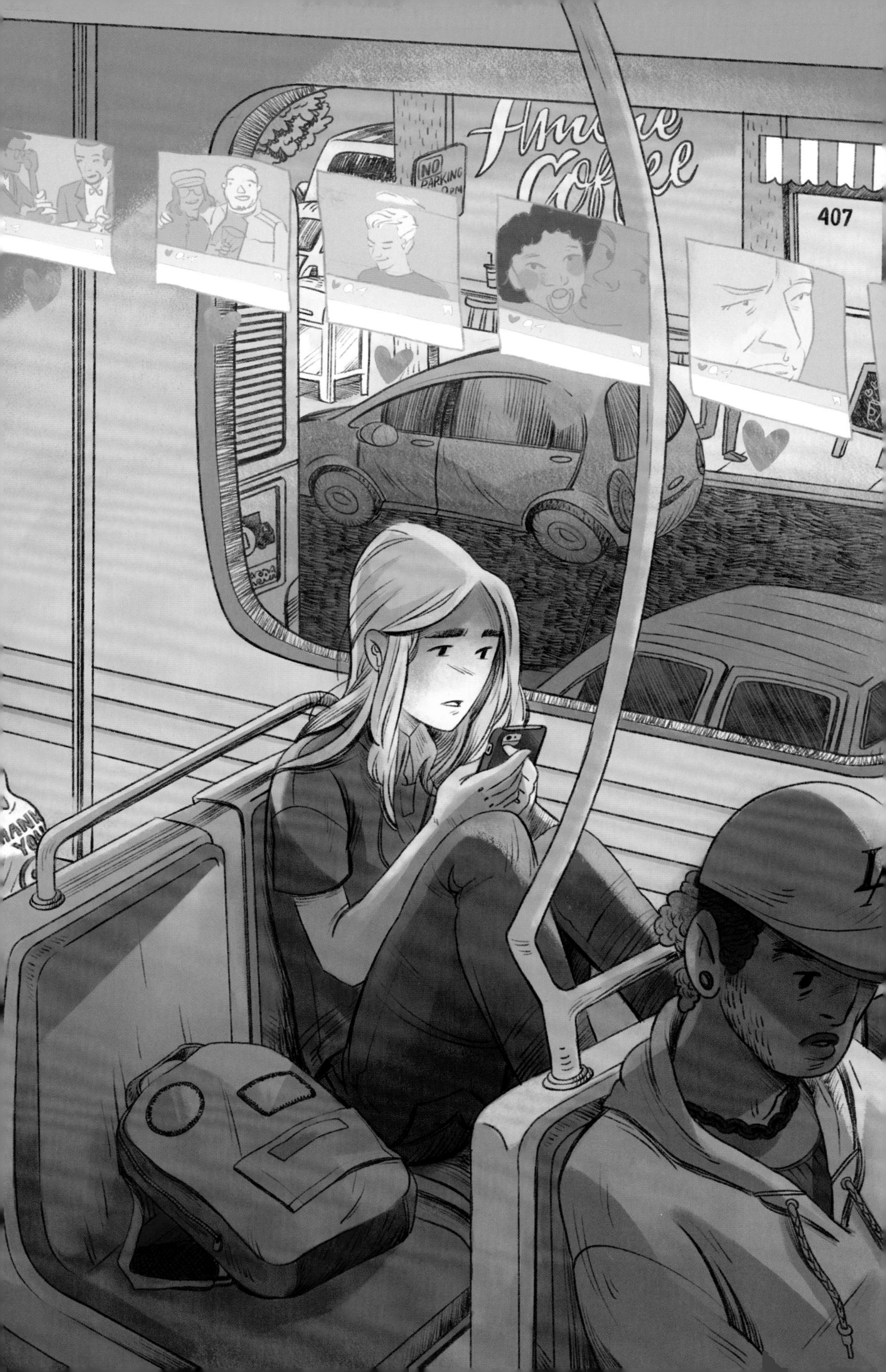
NO PARKING
407

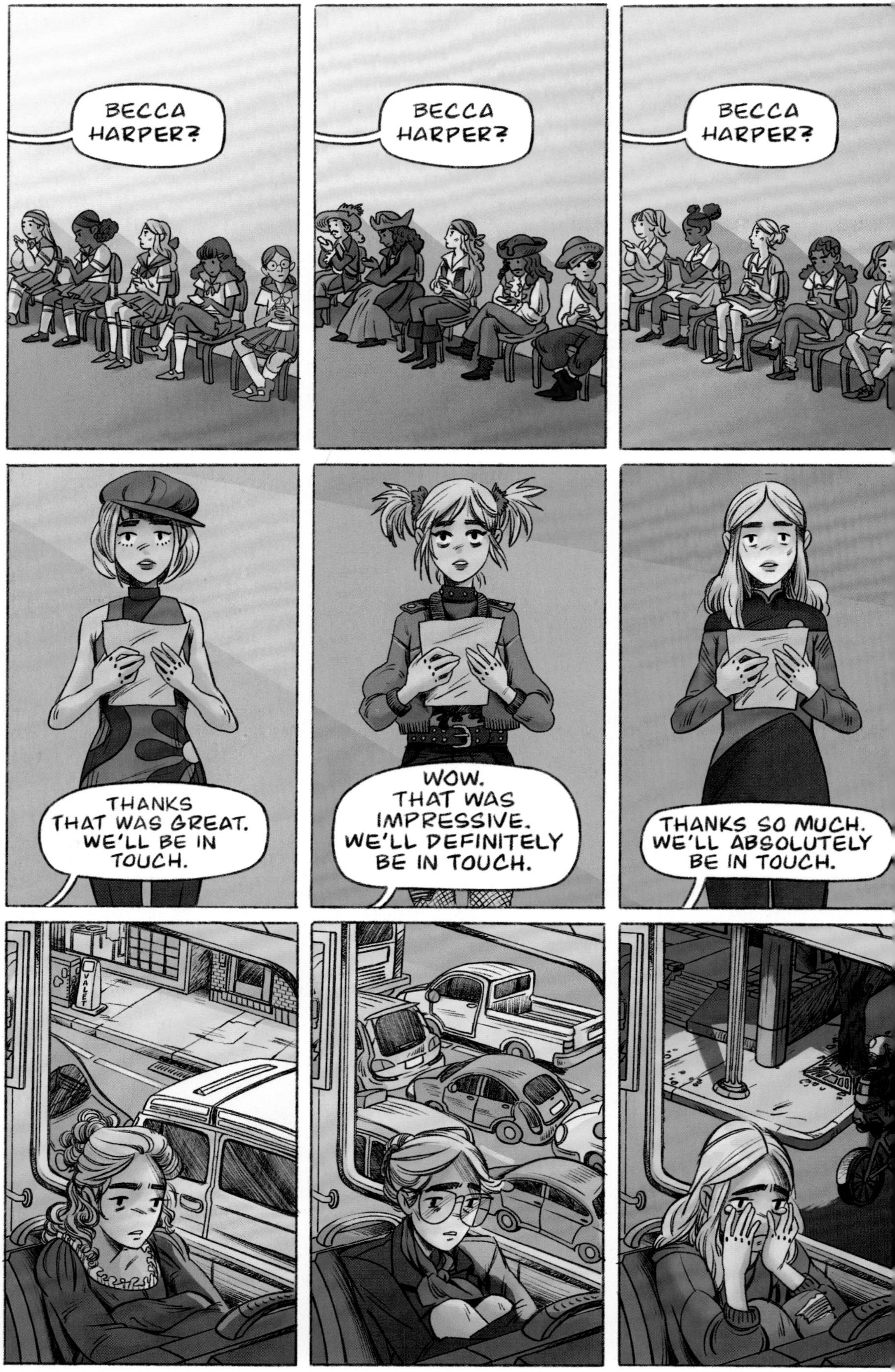
BECCA HARPER?
BECCA HARPER?
BECCA HARPER?
THANKS THAT WAS GREAT. WE'LL BE IN TOUCH.
WOW. THAT WAS IMPRESSIVE. WE'LL DEFINITELY BE IN TOUCH.
THANKS SO MUCH. WE'LL ABSOLUTELY BE IN TOUCH.
VALET

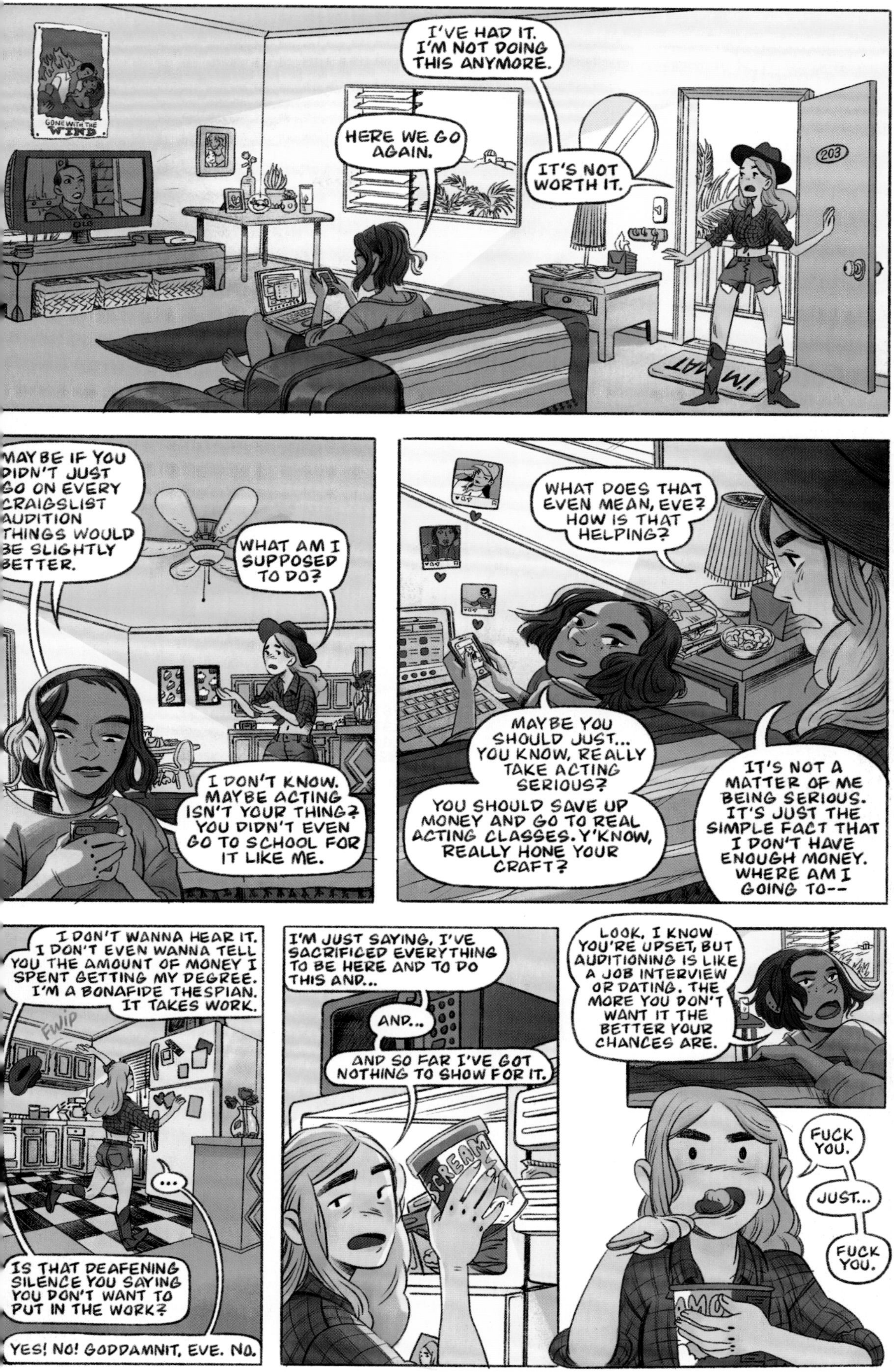
GONE WITH THE WIND
I'VE HAD IT. I'M NOT DOING THIS ANYMORE.
HERE WE GO AGAIN.
IT'S NOT WORTH IT.
203
I'M MAT
MAYBE IF YOU DIDN'T JUST GO ON EVERY CRAIGSLIST AUDITION THINGS WOULD BE SLIGHTLY BETTER.
WHAT AM I SUPPOSED TO DO?
I DON'T KNOW. MAYBE ACTING ISN'T YOUR THING? YOU DIDN'T EVEN GO TO SCHOOL FOR IT LIKE ME.
WHAT DOES THAT EVEN MEAN, EVE? HOW IS THAT HELPING?
MAYBE YOU SHOULD JUST... YOU KNOW, REALLY TAKE ACTING SERIOUS?
YOU SHOULD SAVE UP MONEY AND GO TO REAL ACTING CLASSES. Y'KNOW, REALLY HONE YOUR CRAFT?
IT'S NOT A MATTER OF ME BEING SERIOUS. IT'S JUST THE SIMPLE FACT THAT I DON'T HAVE ENOUGH MONEY. WHERE AM I GOING TO--
I DON'T WANNA HEAR IT. I DON'T EVEN WANNA TELL YOU THE AMOUNT OF MONEY I SPENT GETTING MY DEGREE. I'M A BONAFIDE THESPIAN. IT TAKES WORK.
FWIP
...
IS THAT DEAFENING SILENCE YOU SAYING YOU DON'T WANT TO PUT IN THE WORK?
YES! NO! GODDAMNIT, EVE. NO.
I'M JUST SAYING, I'VE SACRIFICED EVERYTHING TO BE HERE AND TO DO THIS AND...
AND...
AND SO FAR I'VE GOT NOTHING TO SHOW FOR IT.
SCREAM
LOOK, I KNOW YOU'RE UPSET, BUT AUDITIONING IS LIKE A JOB INTERVIEW OR DATING. THE MORE YOU DON'T WANT IT THE BETTER YOUR CHANCES ARE.
FUCK YOU.
JUST...
FUCK YOU.

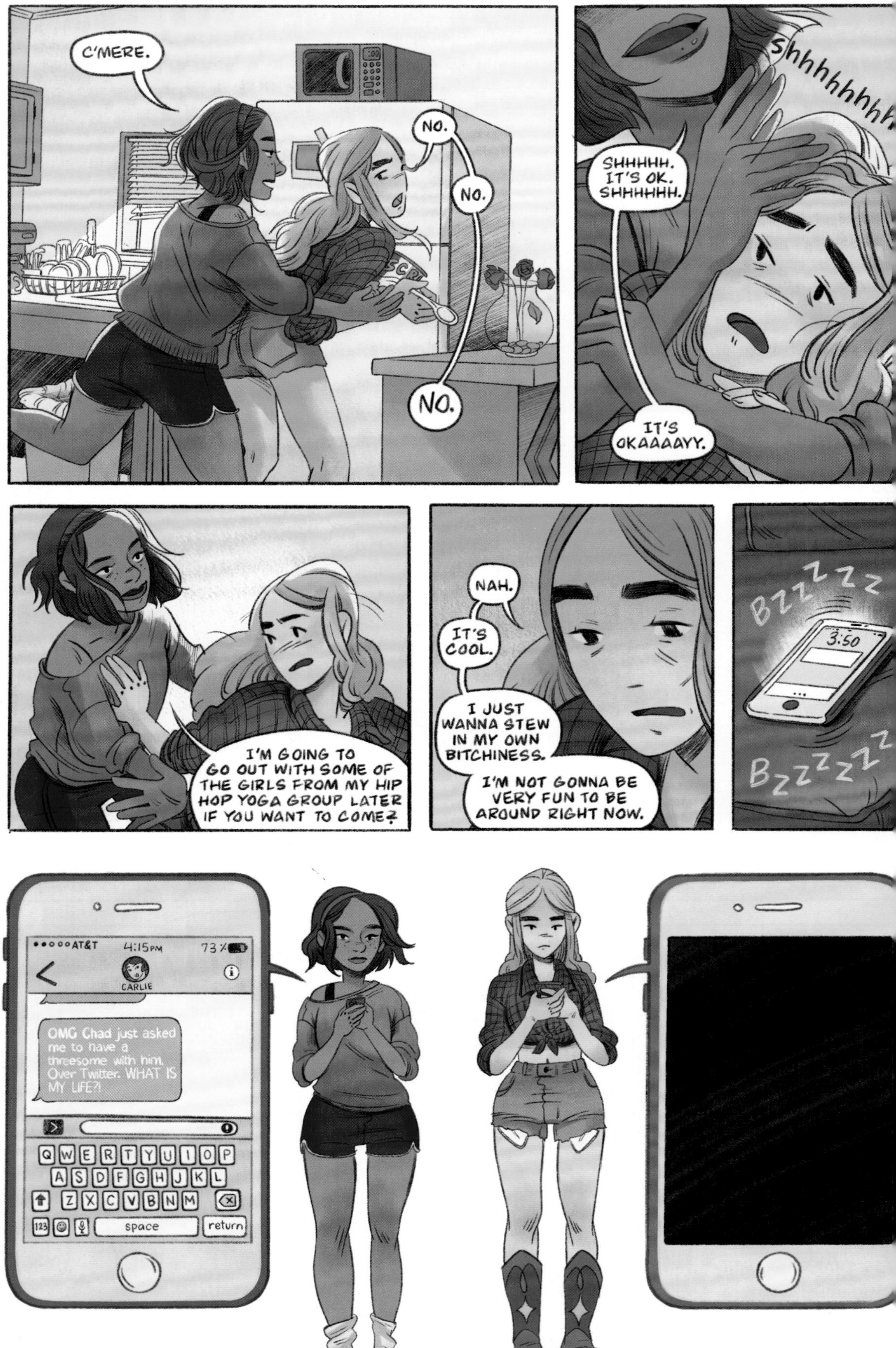
C'MERE.
NO.
NO.
NO.
Shhhhhhhh
SHHHHH. IT'S OK. SHHHHHH.
IT'S OKAAAAYY.
I'M GOING TO GO OUT WITH SOME OF THE GIRLS FROM MY HIP HOP YOGA GROUP LATER IF YOU WANT TO COME?
NAH.
IT'S COOL.
I JUST WANNA STEW IN MY OWN BITCHINESS.
I'M NOT GONNA BE VERY FUN TO BE AROUND RIGHT NOW.
BZZZZZ
3:50
BZZZZZZ
AT&T 4:15PM 73%
CARLIE
OMG Chad just asked me to have a threesome with him. Over Twitter. WHAT IS MY LIFE?!
space
return

From: Paradox XL
Hide XL

RE: IS ART A VERB
OR A NOUN?

Today at 11:40 PM

Is the medium
the message
or the
message the
medium?

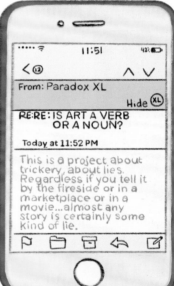
THE FUCK?

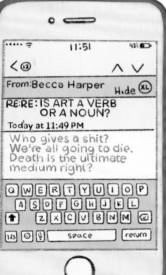
From: Becca Harper
Hide XL

RE:RE: IS ART A VERB
OR A NOUN?

Today at 11:49 PM

Who gives a shit?
We're all going to die.
Death is the ultimate
medium right?

QWERTYUIOP
ASDFGHJKL
ZXCVBNM
123   space   return

HEH.

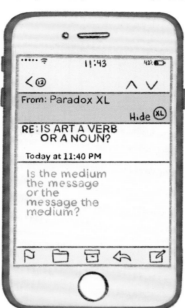
From: Paradox XL
Hide XL

RE:RE: IS ART A VERB
OR A NOUN?

Today at 11:52 PM

This is a project about
trickery, about lies.
Regardless if you tell it
by the fireside or in a
marketplace or in a
movie...almost any
story is certainly some
kind of lie.

WHAT
THE HELL?

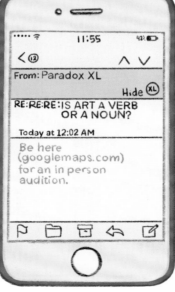
From: Paradox XL
Hide XL

RE:RE:RE: IS ART A VERB
OR A NOUN?

Today at 12:02 AM

Be here
(googlemaps.com)
for an in person
audition.

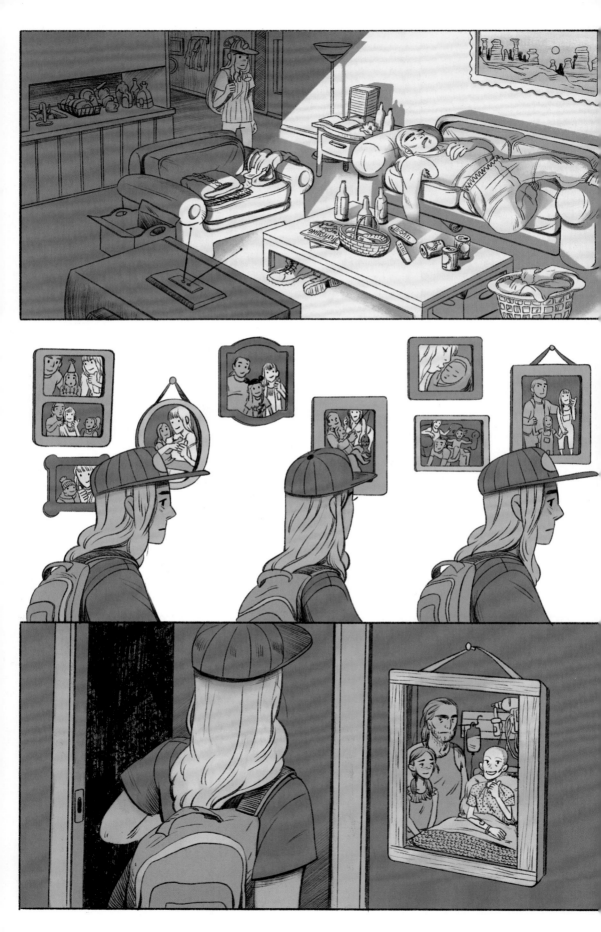

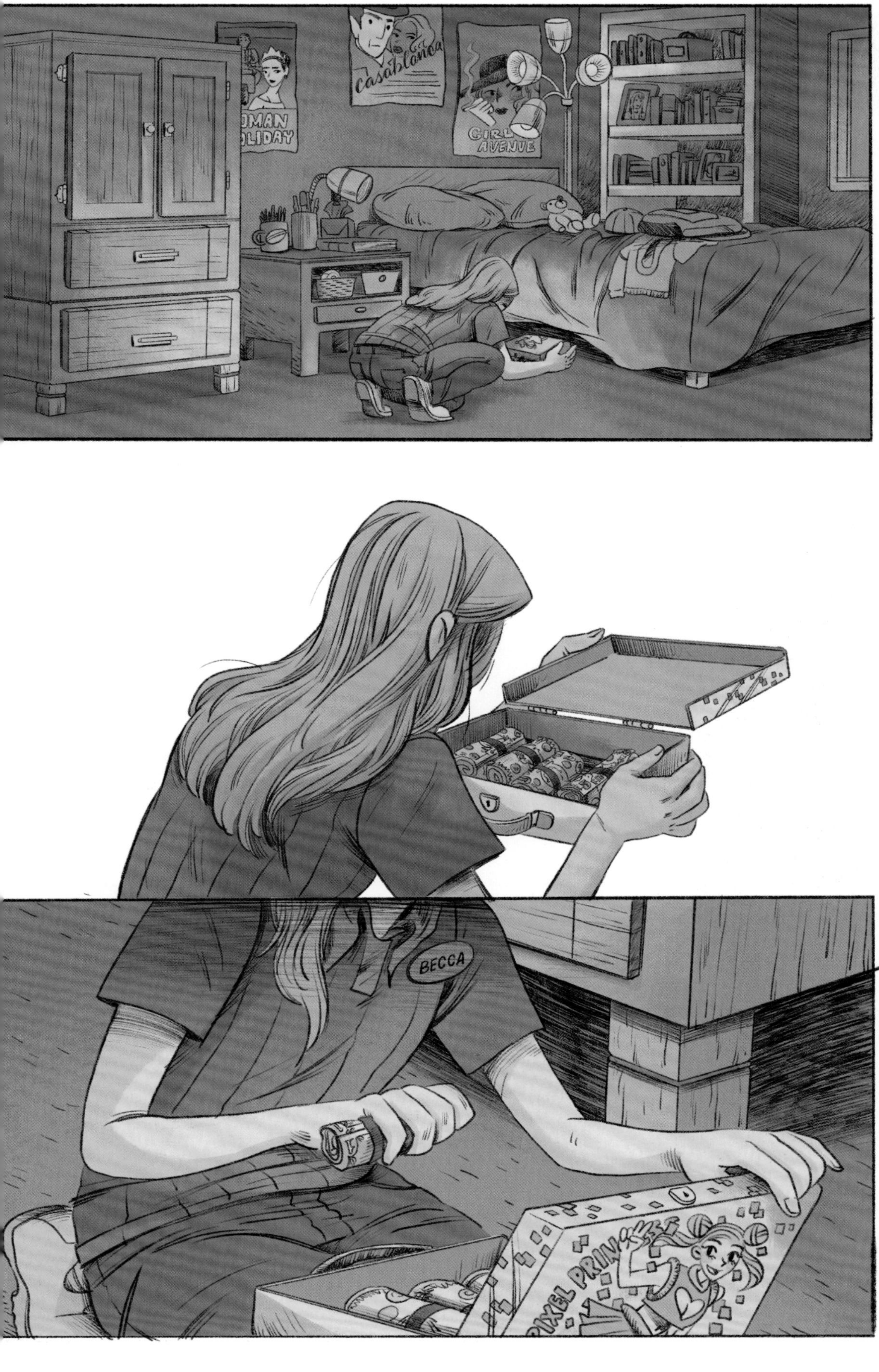
casablanca
GIRL AVENUE
BECCA

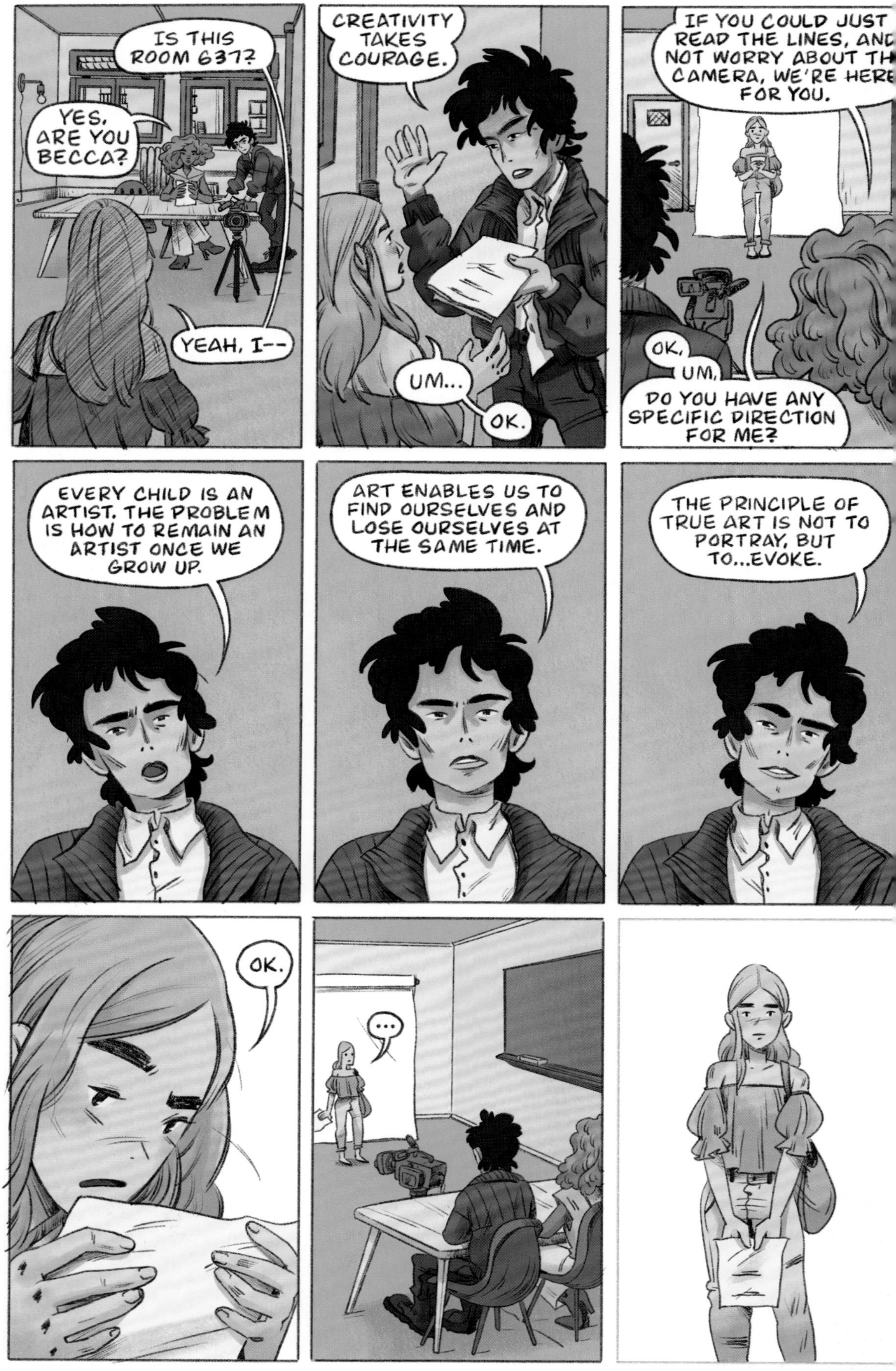
IS THIS ROOM 637?
YES, ARE YOU BECCA?
YEAH, I--
CREATIVITY TAKES COURAGE.
UM...
OK.
IF YOU COULD JUST READ THE LINES, AND NOT WORRY ABOUT THE CAMERA, WE'RE HERE FOR YOU.
OK,
UM,
DO YOU HAVE ANY SPECIFIC DIRECTION FOR ME?
EVERY CHILD IS AN ARTIST. THE PROBLEM IS HOW TO REMAIN AN ARTIST ONCE WE GROW UP.
ART ENABLES US TO FIND OURSELVES AND LOSE OURSELVES AT THE SAME TIME.
THE PRINCIPLE OF TRUE ART IS NOT TO PORTRAY, BUT TO...EVOKE.
OK.
...

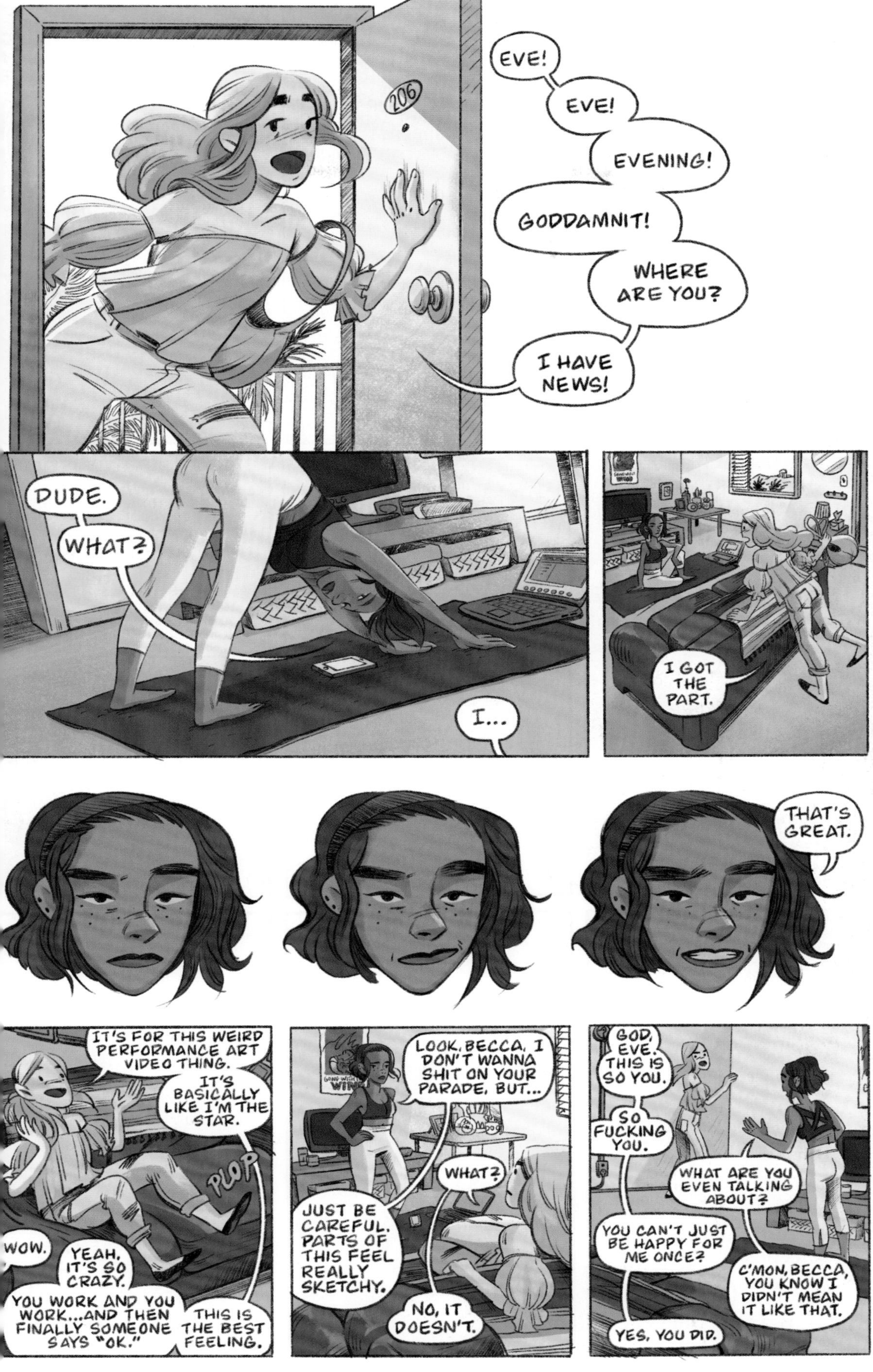

EVE!
EVE!
EVENING!
GODDAMNIT!
WHERE ARE YOU?
I HAVE NEWS!
DUDE.
WHAT?
I...
I GOT THE PART.
THAT'S GREAT.
IT'S FOR THIS WEIRD PERFORMANCE ART VIDEO THING.
IT'S BASICALLY LIKE I'M THE STAR.
PLOP
WOW.
YEAH, IT'S SO CRAZY.
YOU WORK AND YOU WORK...AND THEN FINALLY SOMEONE SAYS "OK."
THIS IS THE BEST FEELING.
LOOK, BECCA, I DON'T WANNA SHIT ON YOUR PARADE, BUT...
WHAT?
JUST BE CAREFUL. PARTS OF THIS FEEL REALLY SKETCHY.
NO, IT DOESN'T.
GOD, EVE. THIS IS SO YOU.
SO FUCKING YOU.
WHAT ARE YOU EVEN TALKING ABOUT?
YOU CAN'T JUST BE HAPPY FOR ME ONCE?
C'MON, BECCA, YOU KNOW I DIDN'T MEAN IT LIKE THAT.
YES, YOU DID.

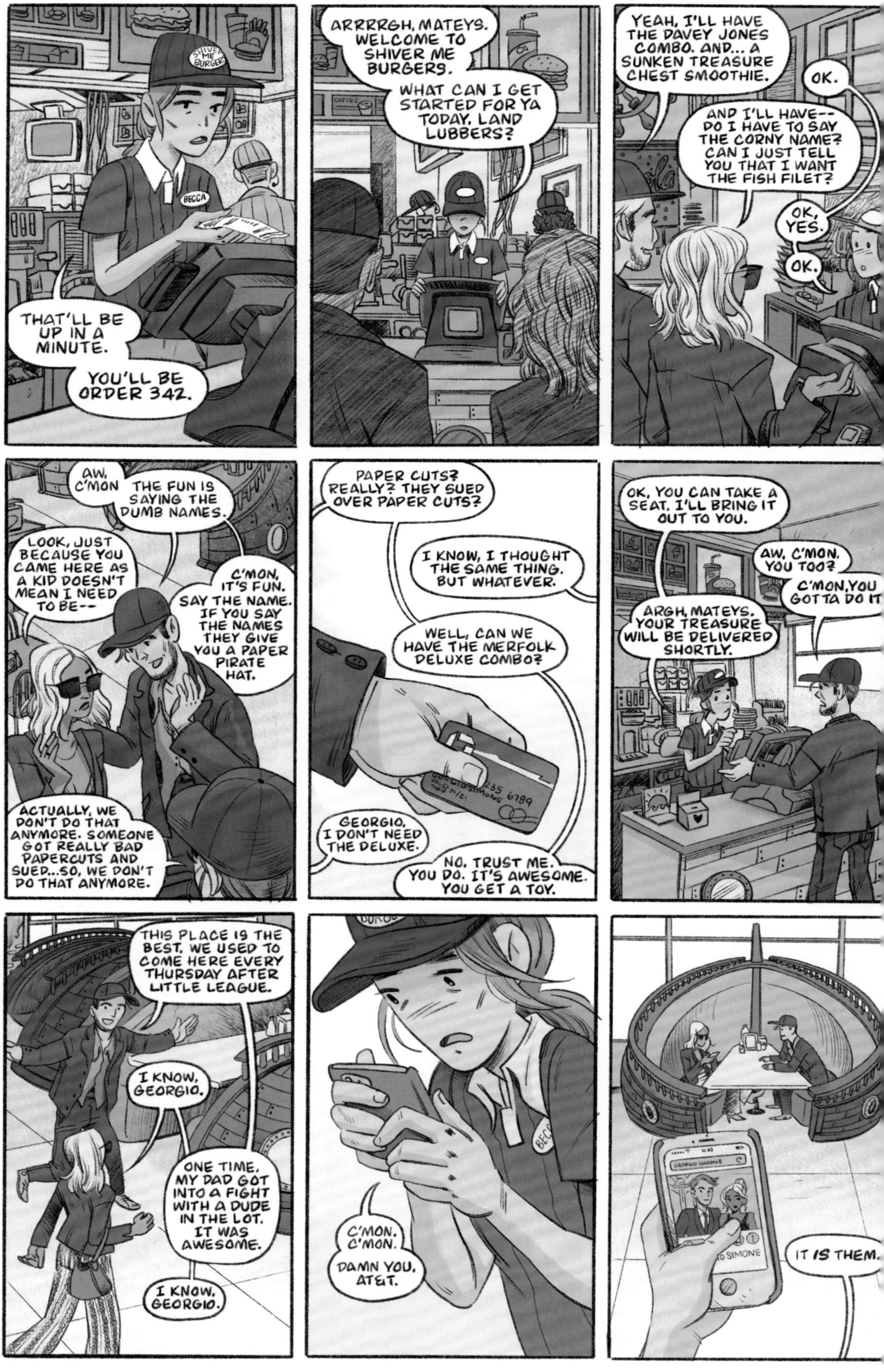
SHIVER ME BURGERS
BECCA
THAT'LL BE UP IN A MINUTE.
YOU'LL BE ORDER 342.
ARRRRGH, MATEYS. WELCOME TO SHIVER ME BURGERS.
WHAT CAN I GET STARTED FOR YA TODAY, LAND LUBBERS?
YEAH, I'LL HAVE THE DAVEY JONES COMBO. AND... A SUNKEN TREASURE CHEST SMOOTHIE.
OK.
AND I'LL HAVE-- DO I HAVE TO SAY THE CORNY NAME? CAN I JUST TELL YOU THAT I WANT THE FISH FILET?
OK, YES.
OK.
AW, C'MON
THE FUN IS SAYING THE DUMB NAMES.
LOOK, JUST BECAUSE YOU CAME HERE AS A KID DOESN'T MEAN I NEED TO BE--
C'MON, IT'S FUN. SAY THE NAME. IF YOU SAY THE NAMES THEY GIVE YOU A PAPER PIRATE HAT.
ACTUALLY, WE DON'T DO THAT ANYMORE. SOMEONE GOT REALLY BAD PAPERCUTS AND SUED...SO, WE DON'T DO THAT ANYMORE.
PAPER CUTS? REALLY? THEY SUED OVER PAPER CUTS?
I KNOW, I THOUGHT THE SAME THING. BUT WHATEVER.
WELL, CAN WE HAVE THE MERFOLK DELUXE COMBO?
GEORGIO, I DON'T NEED THE DELUXE.
NO. TRUST ME. YOU DO. IT'S AWESOME. YOU GET A TOY.
OK, YOU CAN TAKE A SEAT. I'LL BRING IT OUT TO YOU.
AW, C'MON. YOU TOO?
C'MON,YOU GOTTA DO IT
ARGH, MATEYS. YOUR TREASURE WILL BE DELIVERED SHORTLY.
THIS PLACE IS THE BEST. WE USED TO COME HERE EVERY THURSDAY AFTER LITTLE LEAGUE.
I KNOW, GEORGIO.
ONE TIME, MY DAD GOT INTO A FIGHT WITH A DUDE IN THE LOT. IT WAS AWESOME.
I KNOW, GEORGIO.
C'MON, C'MON.
DAMN YOU, AT&T.
GEORGIO SIMONE
IT *IS* THEM.

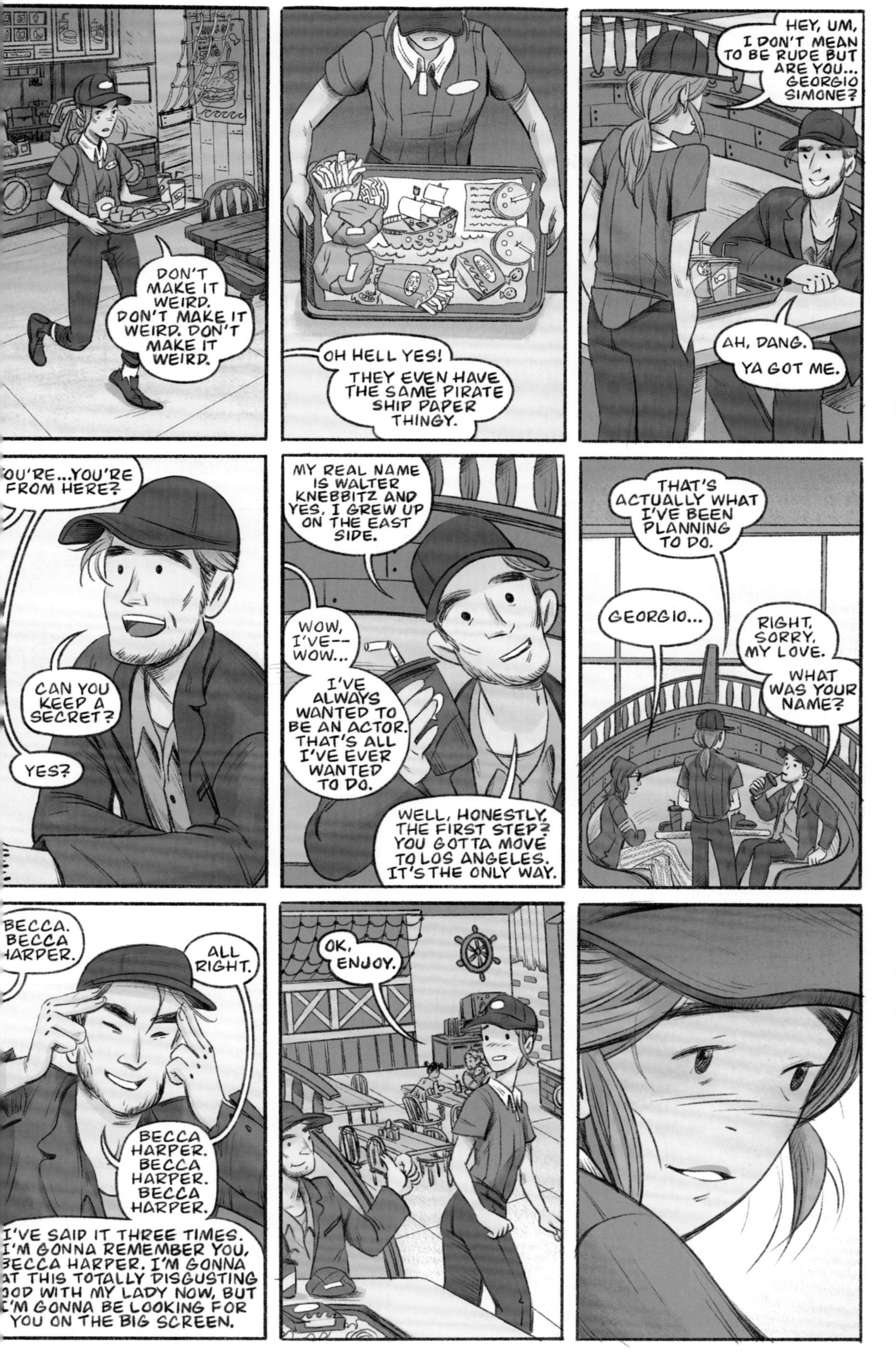
DON'T MAKE IT WEIRD. DON'T MAKE IT WEIRD. DON'T MAKE IT WEIRD.
OH HELL YES!
THEY EVEN HAVE THE SAME PIRATE SHIP PAPER THINGY.
HEY, UM, I DON'T MEAN TO BE RUDE BUT ARE YOU... GEORGIO SIMONE?
AH, DANG.
YA GOT ME.
OU'RE...YOU'RE FROM HERE?
CAN YOU KEEP A SECRET?
YES?
MY REAL NAME IS WALTER KNEBBITZ AND YES, I GREW UP ON THE EAST SIDE.
WOW, I'VE-- WOW...
I'VE ALWAYS WANTED TO BE AN ACTOR. THAT'S ALL I'VE EVER WANTED TO DO.
WELL, HONESTLY, THE FIRST STEP? YOU GOTTA MOVE TO LOS ANGELES. IT'S THE ONLY WAY.
THAT'S ACTUALLY WHAT I'VE BEEN PLANNING TO DO.
GEORGIO...
RIGHT, SORRY, MY LOVE.
WHAT WAS YOUR NAME?
BECCA. BECCA HARPER.
ALL RIGHT.
BECCA HARPER. BECCA HARPER. BECCA HARPER.
I'VE SAID IT THREE TIMES. I'M GONNA REMEMBER YOU, BECCA HARPER. I'M GONNA AT THIS TOTALLY DISGUSTING OOD WITH MY LADY NOW, BUT I'M GONNA BE LOOKING FOR YOU ON THE BIG SCREEN.
OK, ENJOY.

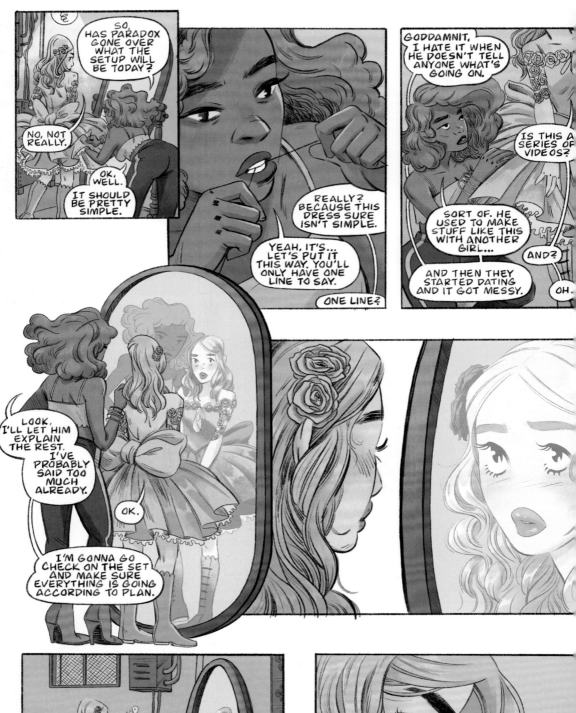

SO HAS PARADOX GONE OVER WHAT THE SETUP WILL BE TODAY?

NO, NOT REALLY.

OK. WELL. IT SHOULD BE PRETTY SIMPLE.

REALLY? BECAUSE THIS DRESS SURE ISN'T SIMPLE.

YEAH, IT'S... LET'S PUT IT THIS WAY. YOU'LL ONLY HAVE ONE LINE TO SAY.

ONE LINE?

GODDAMNIT, I HATE IT WHEN HE DOESN'T TELL ANYONE WHAT'S GOING ON.

IS THIS A SERIES OF VIDEOS?

SORT OF. HE USED TO MAKE STUFF LIKE THIS WITH ANOTHER GIRL...

AND?

AND THEN THEY STARTED DATING AND IT GOT MESSY.

OH.

LOOK, I'LL LET HIM EXPLAIN THE REST. I'VE PROBABLY SAID TOO MUCH ALREADY.

OK.

I'M GONNA GO CHECK ON THE SET AND MAKE SURE EVERYTHING IS GOING ACCORDING TO PLAN.

SNAP

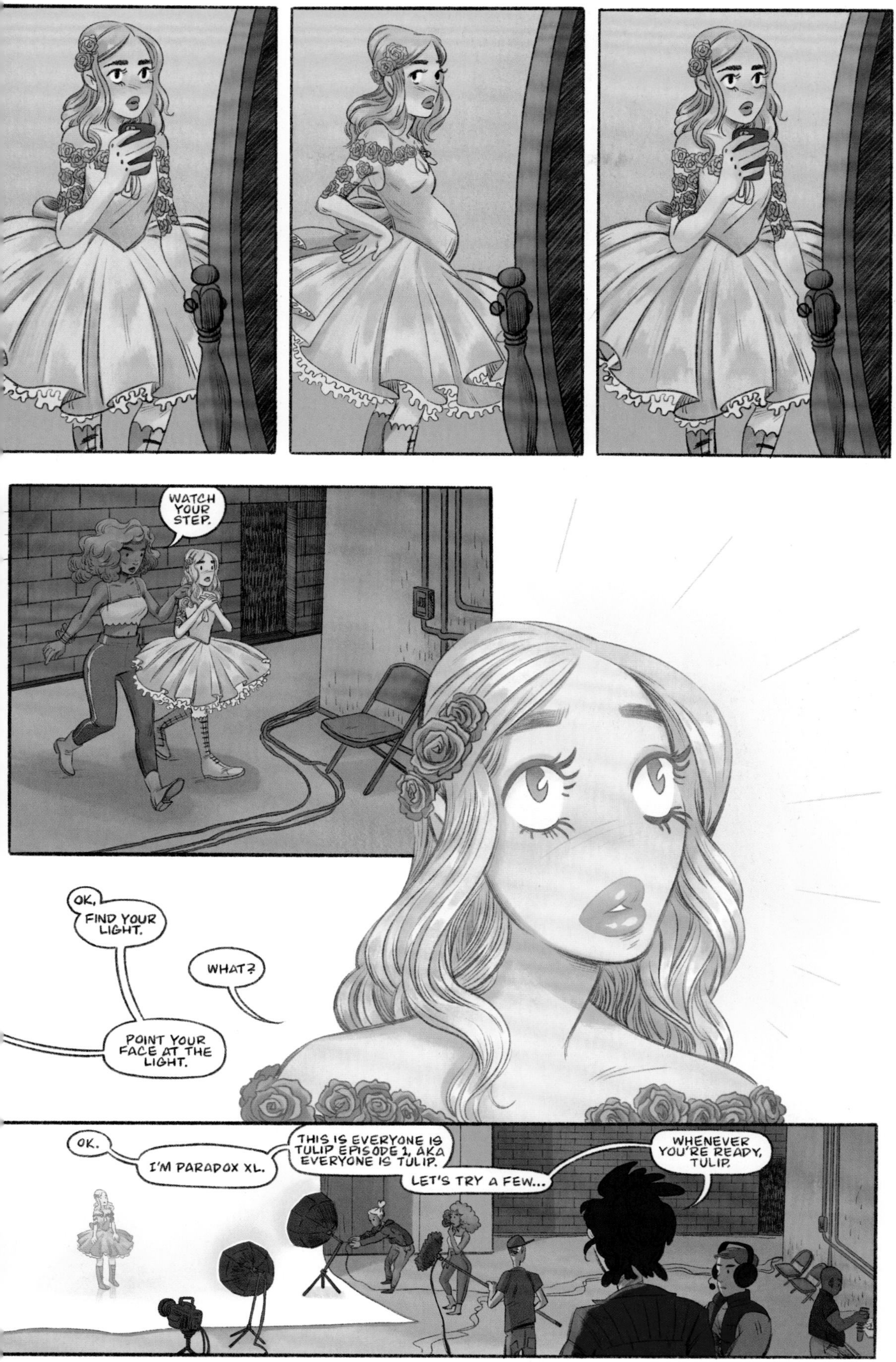
WATCH YOUR STEP.
OK,
FIND YOUR LIGHT.
WHAT?
POINT YOUR FACE AT THE LIGHT.
OK.
I'M PARADOX XL.
THIS IS EVERYONE IS TULIP EPISODE 1, AKA EVERYONE IS TULIP.
LET'S TRY A FEW...
WHENEVER YOU'RE READY, TULIP.

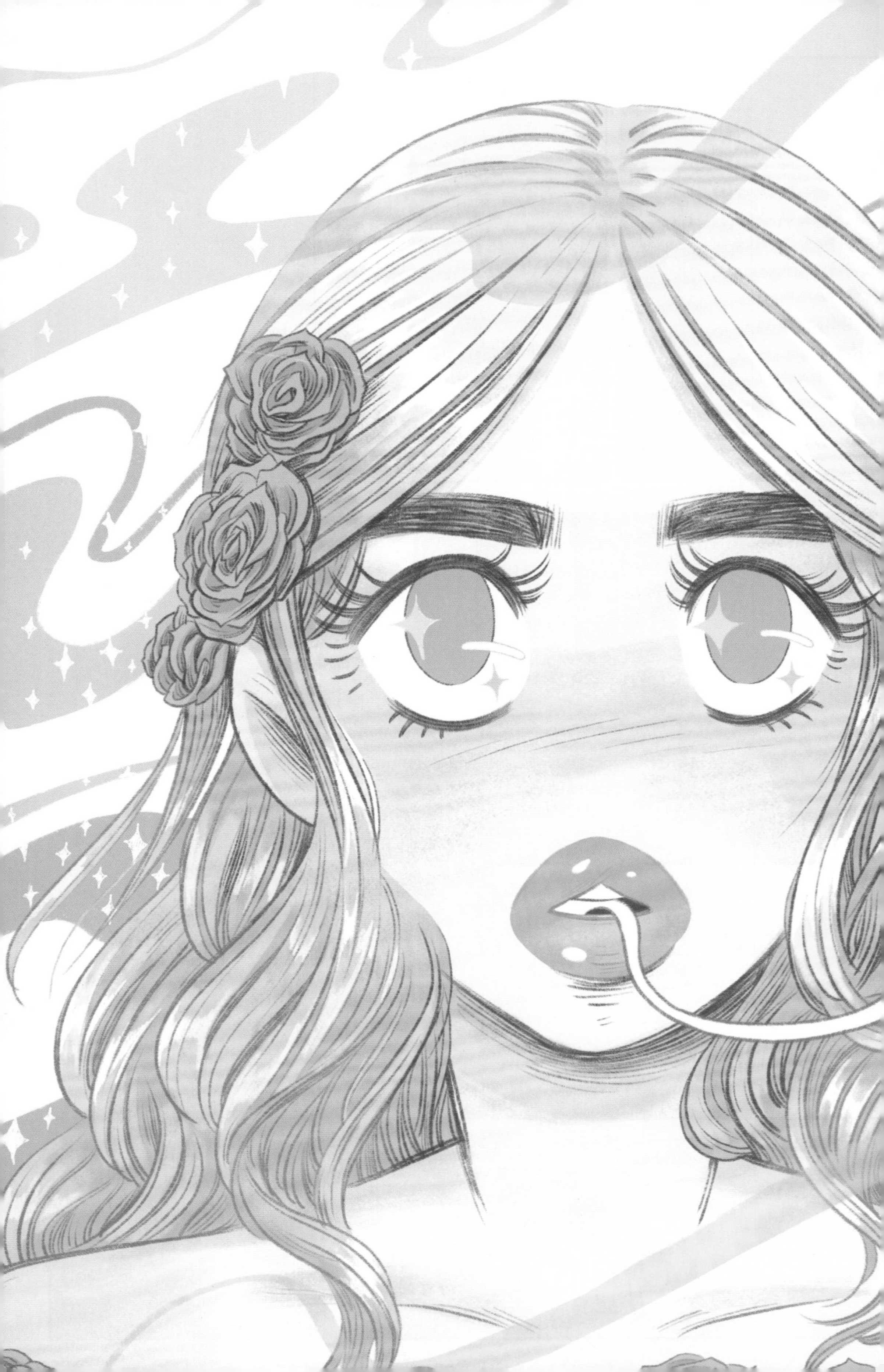

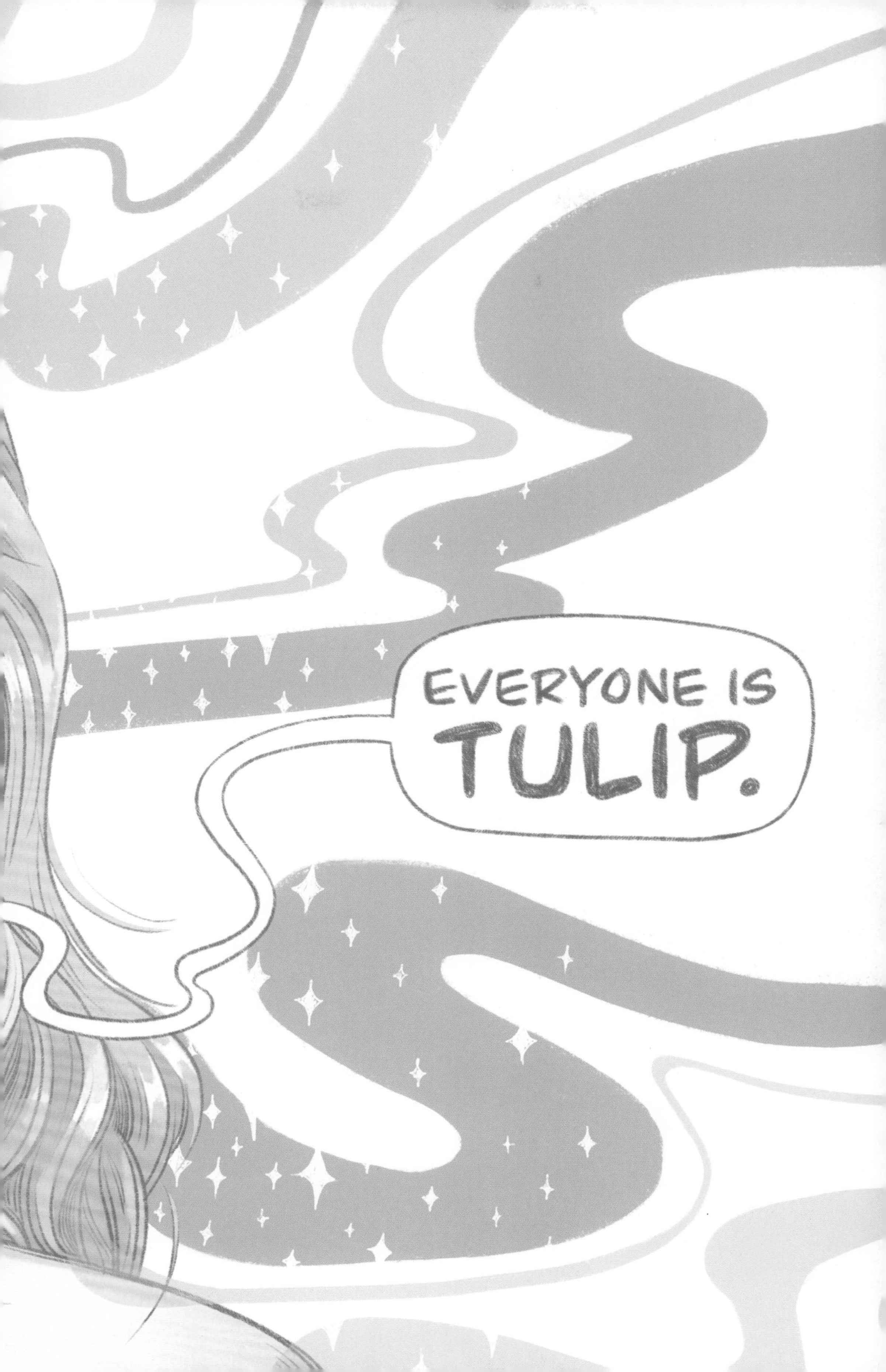
EVERYONE IS
TULIP.

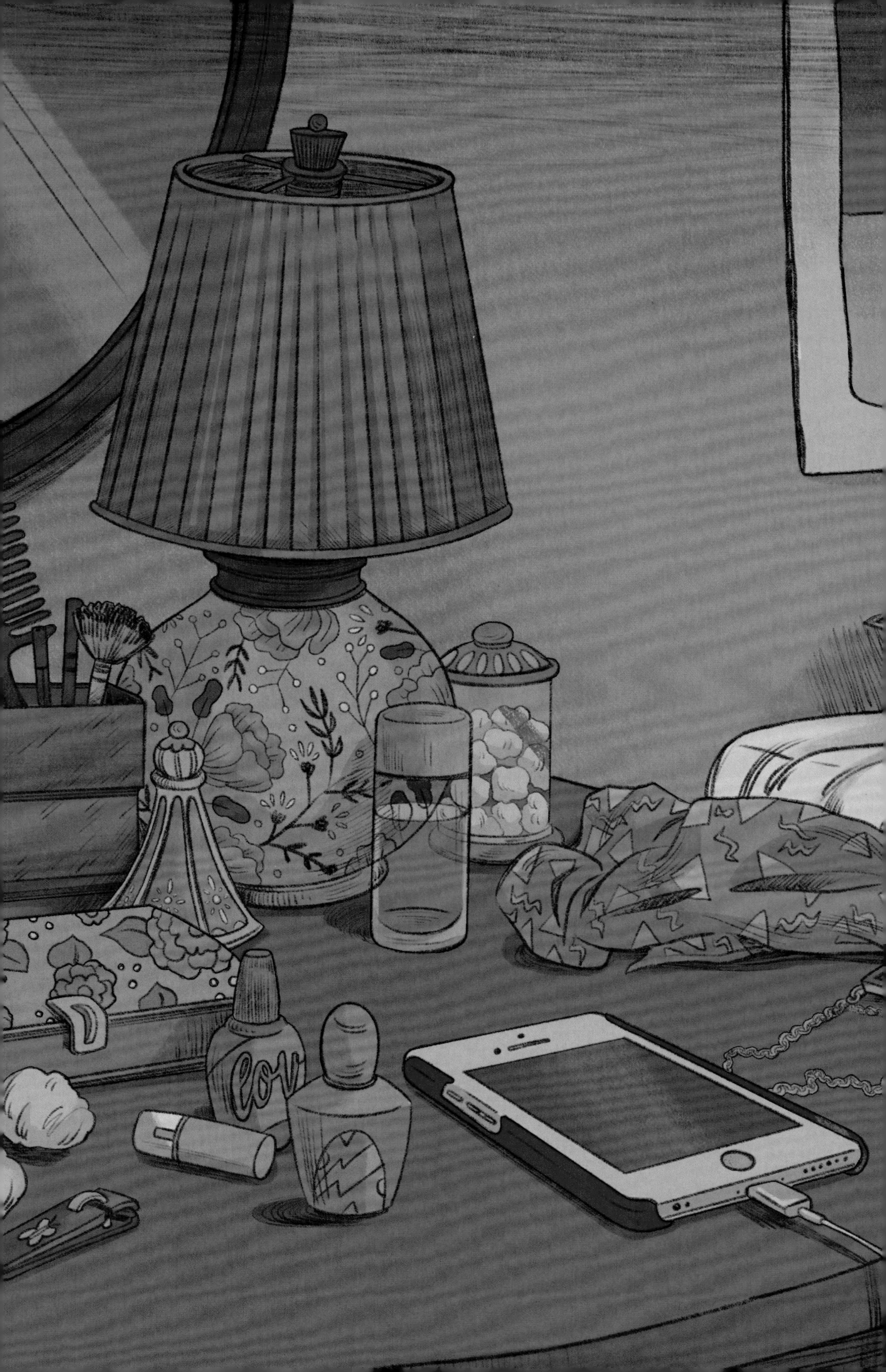
lov

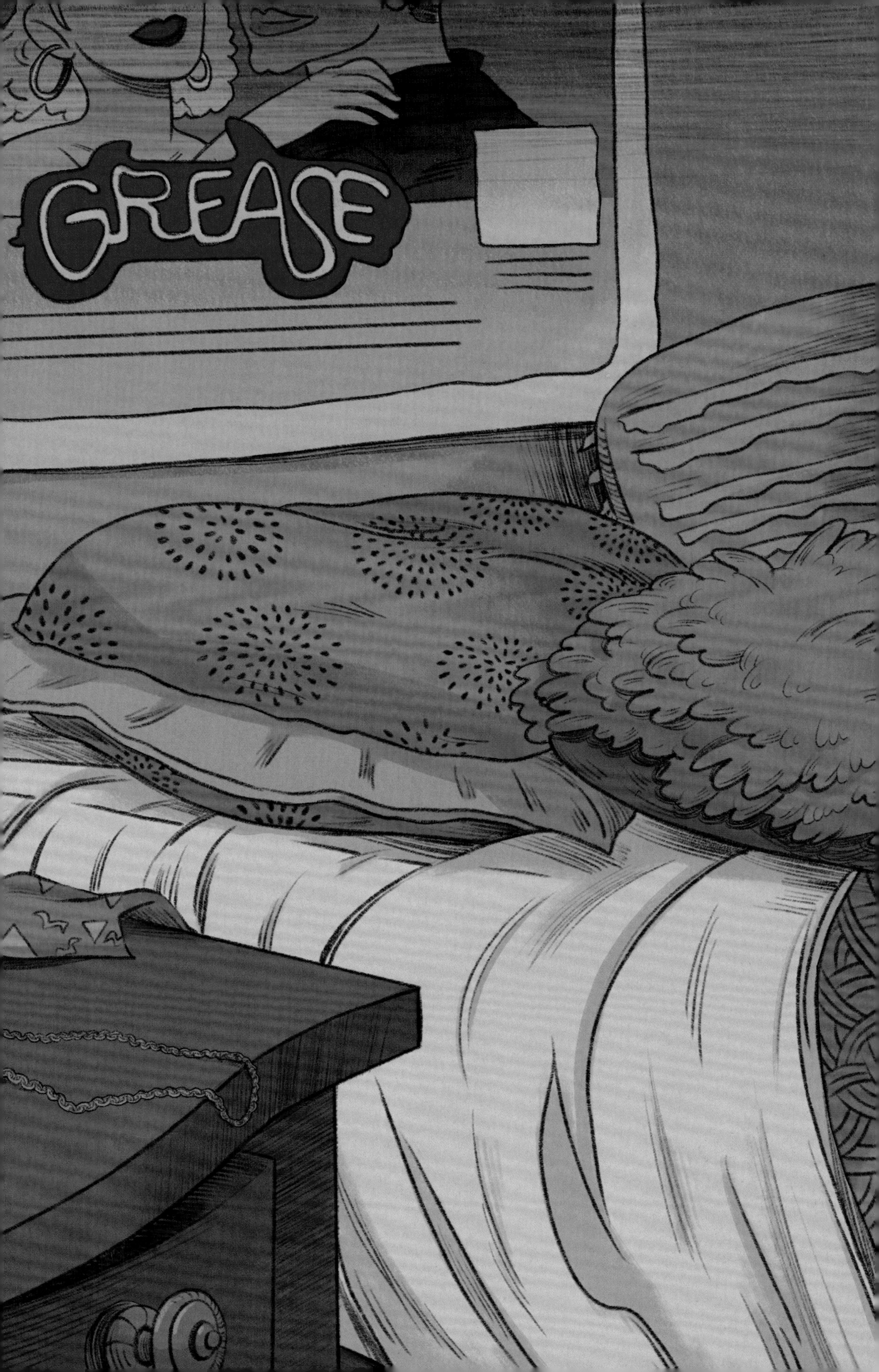
GREASE

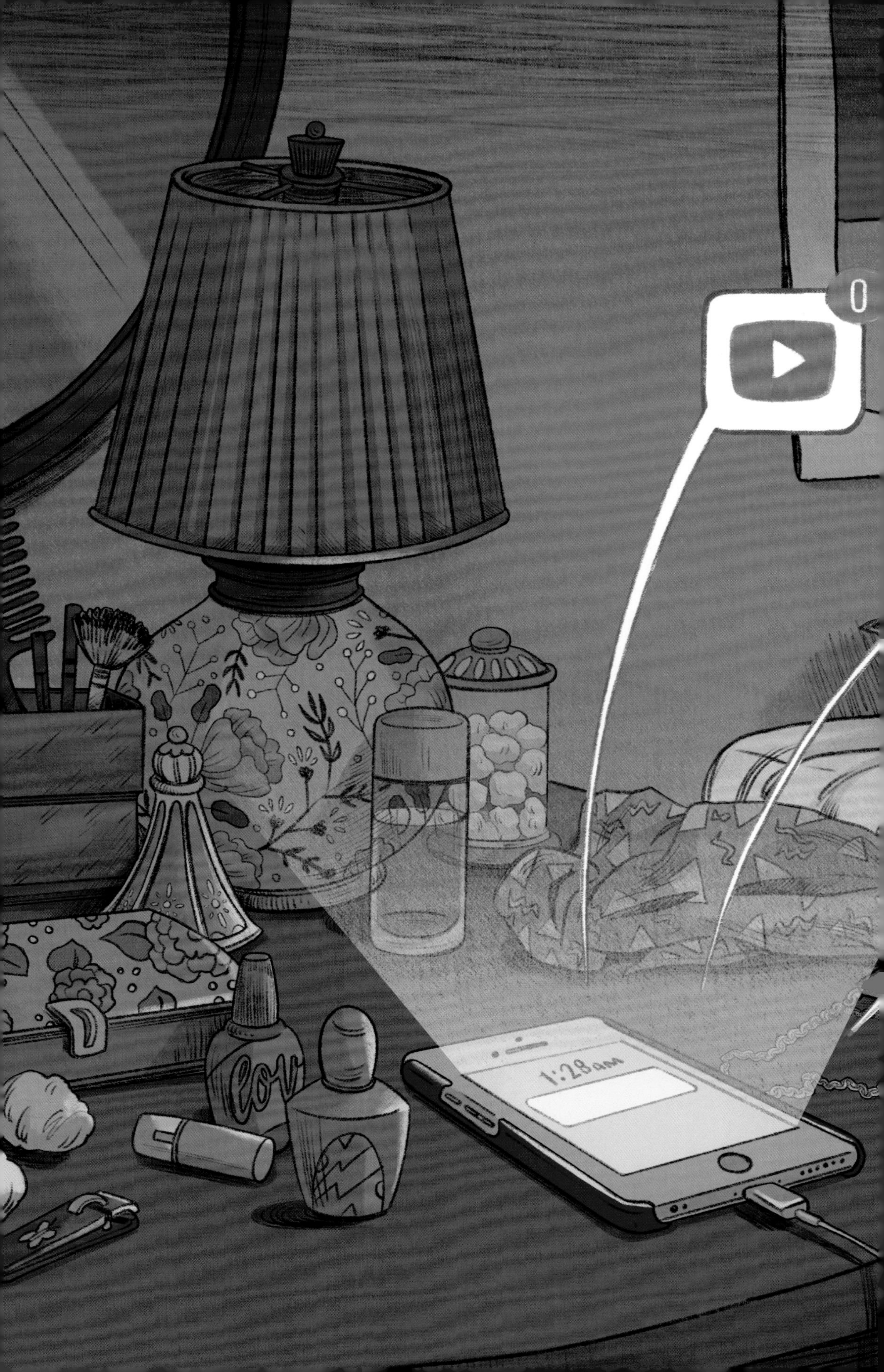
0
1:28am
lov

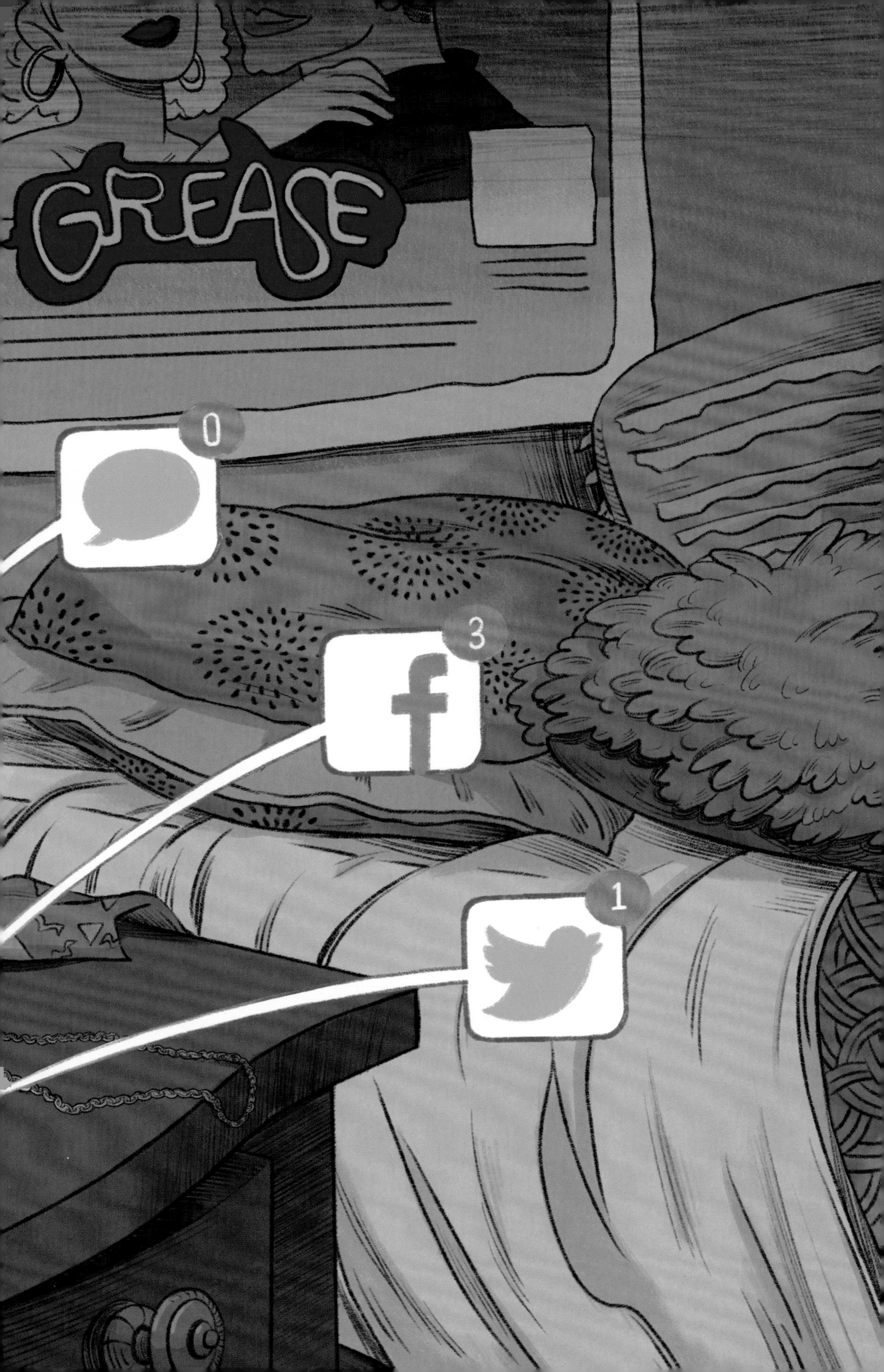
GREASE
0
3
1

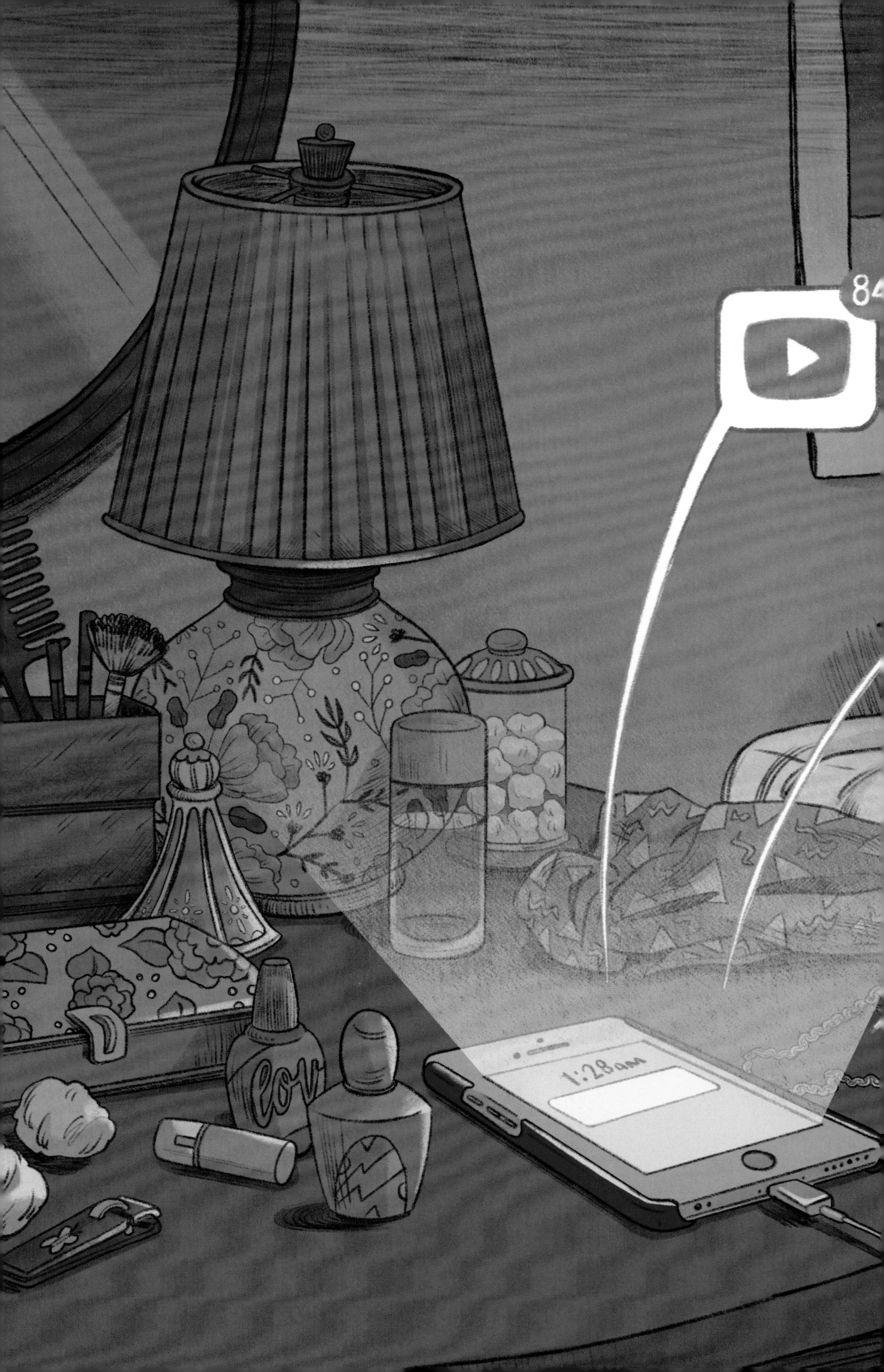
84
lov
1:28am

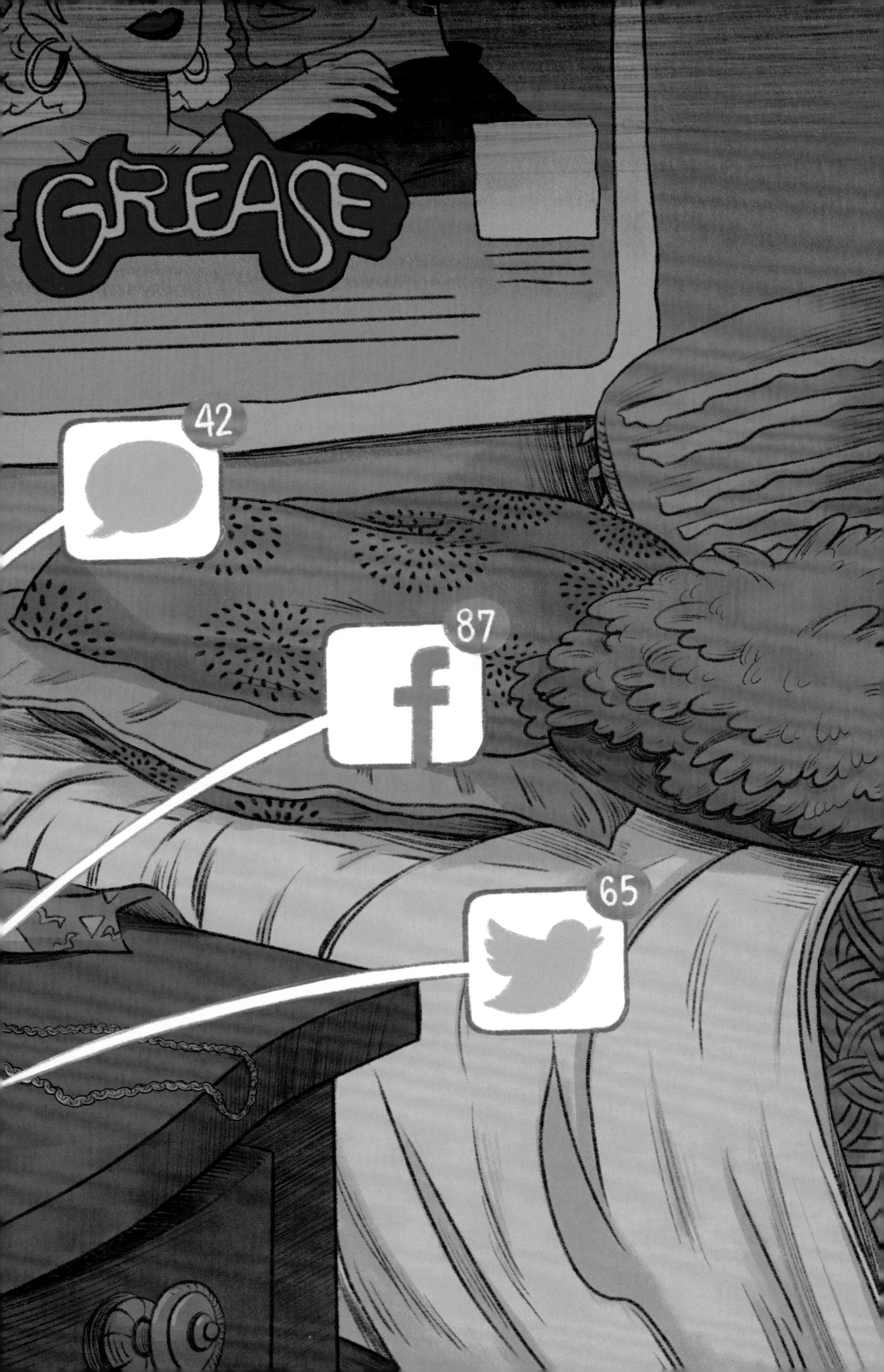
GREASE
42
87
65

CHAPTER 2

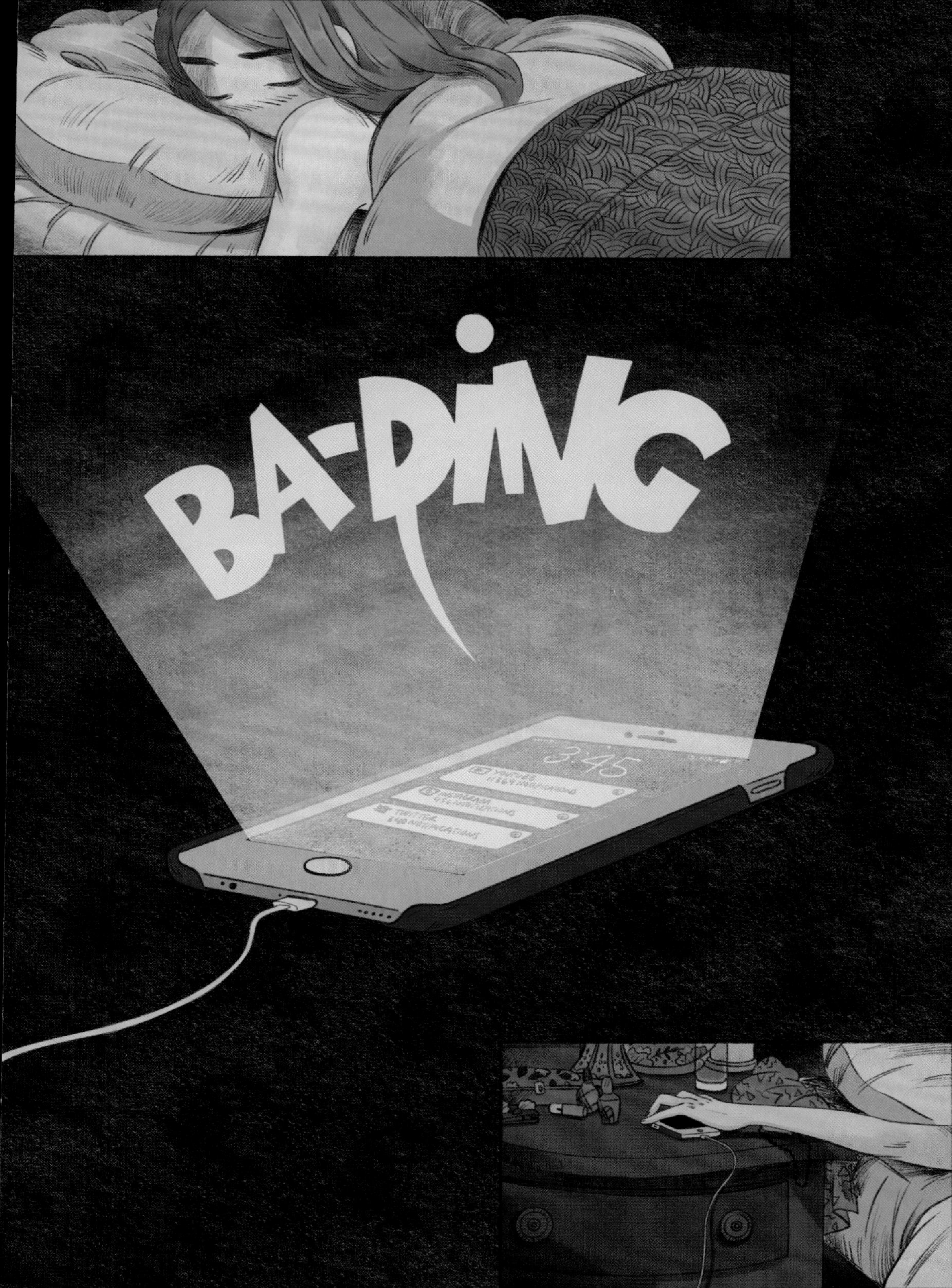
BA-DING
3:45

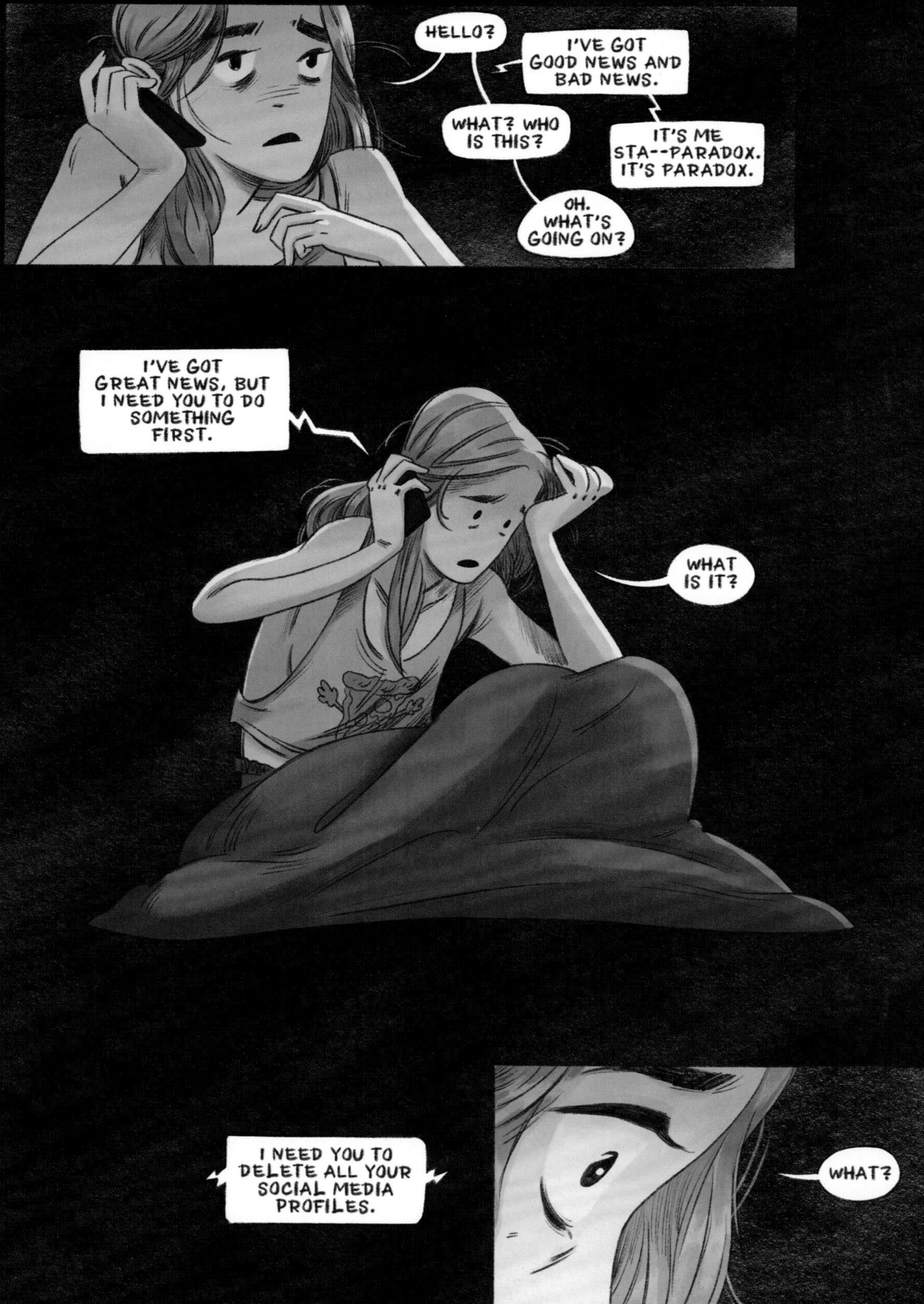
HELLO?
I'VE GOT GOOD NEWS AND BAD NEWS.
WHAT? WHO IS THIS?
IT'S ME STA--PARADOX. IT'S PARADOX.
OH. WHAT'S GOING ON?
I'VE GOT GREAT NEWS, BUT I NEED YOU TO DO SOMETHING FIRST.
WHAT IS IT?
I NEED YOU TO DELETE ALL YOUR SOCIAL MEDIA PROFILES.
WHAT?

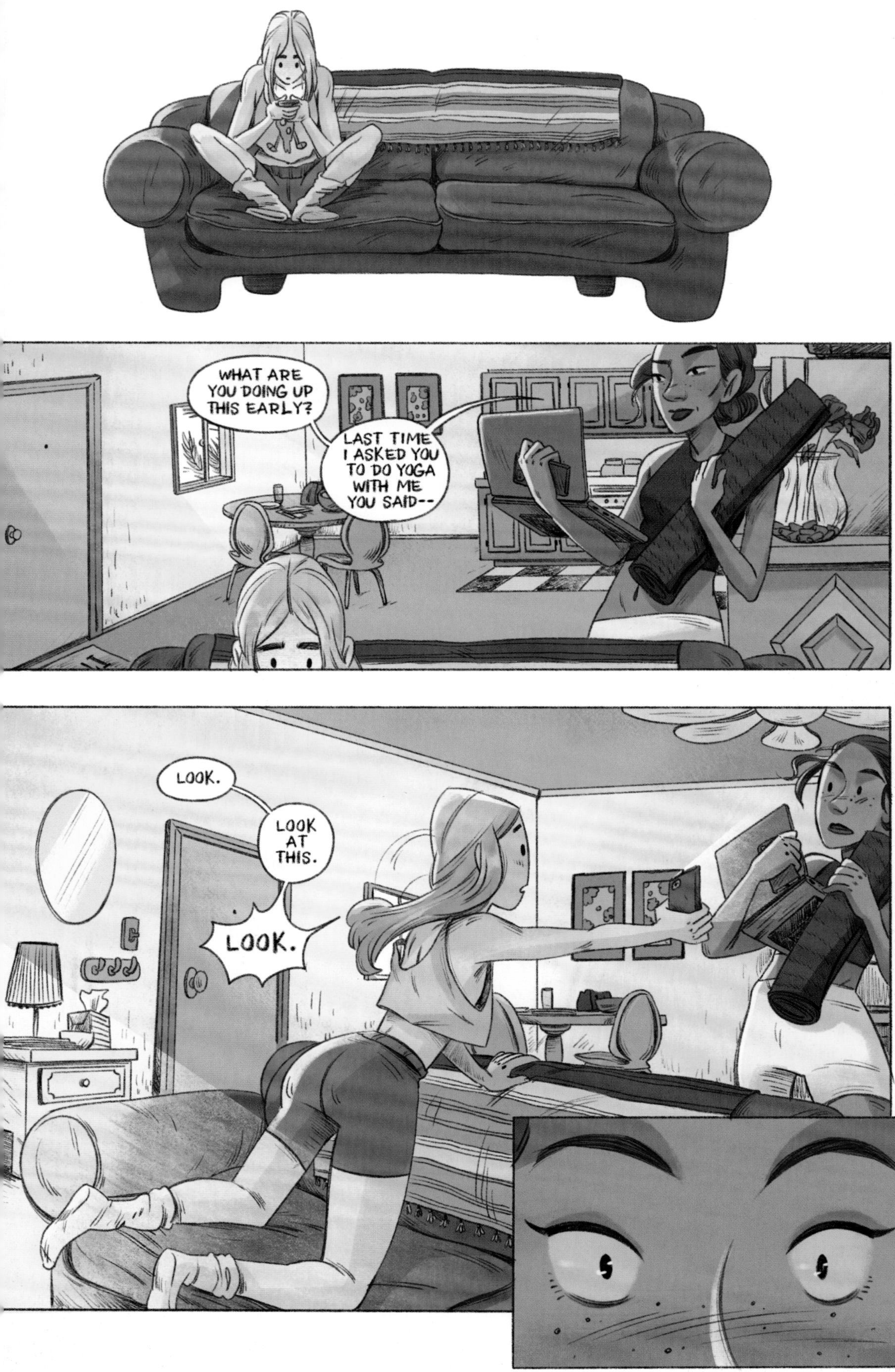

WHAT ARE YOU DOING UP THIS EARLY?
LAST TIME I ASKED YOU TO DO YOGA WITH ME YOU SAID--
LOOK.
LOOK AT THIS.
LOOK.

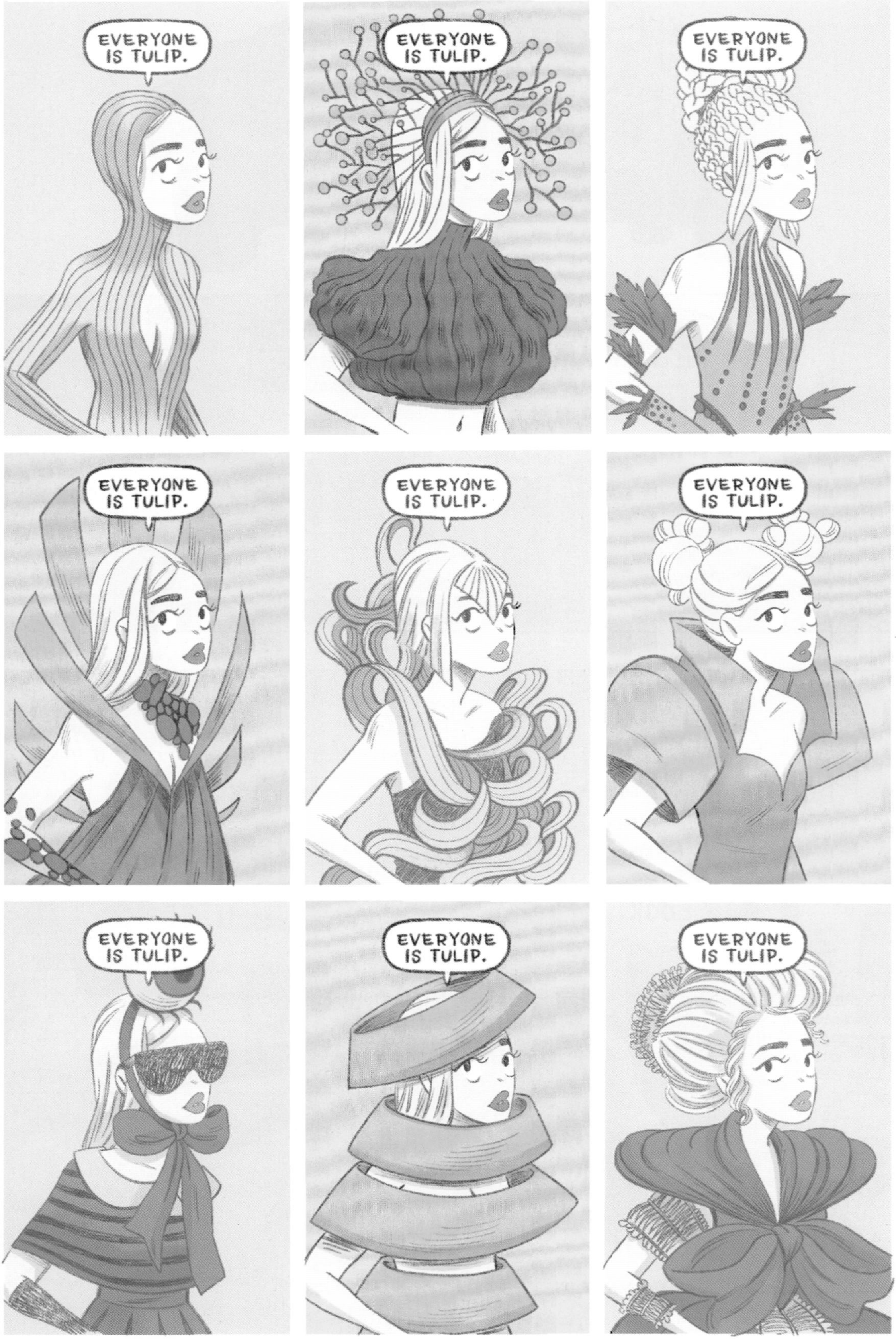
EVERYONE IS TULIP.
EVERYONE IS TULIP.
EVERYONE IS TULIP.
EVERYONE IS TULIP.
EVERYONE IS TULIP.
EVERYONE IS TULIP.
EVERYONE IS TULIP.
EVERYONE IS TULIP.
EVERYONE IS TULIP.

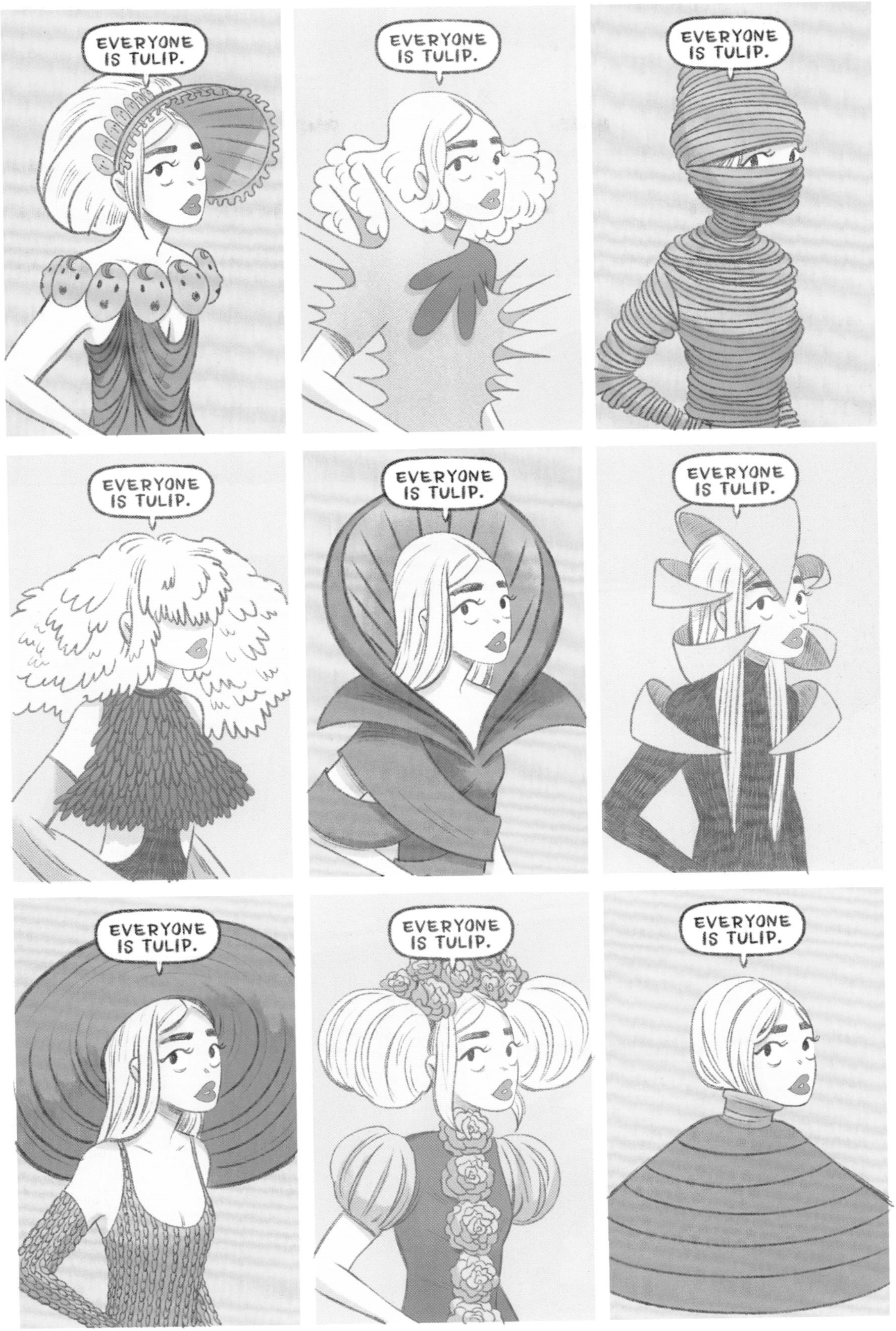
EVERYONE IS TULIP.
EVERYONE IS TULIP.
EVERYONE IS TULIP.
EVERYONE IS TULIP.
EVERYONE IS TULIP.
EVERYONE IS TULIP.
EVERYONE IS TULIP.
EVERYONE IS TULIP.
EVERYONE IS TULIP.

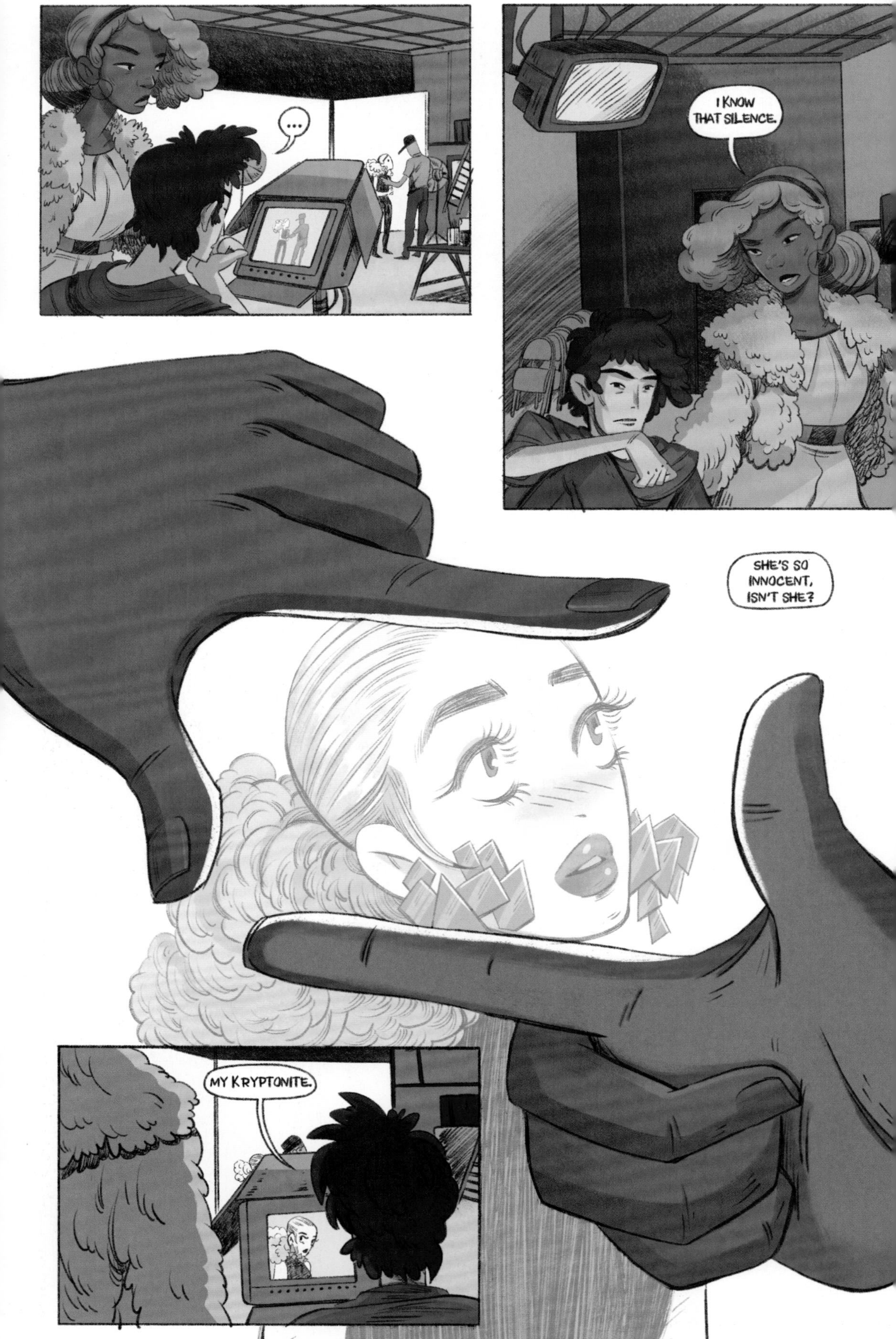
...
I KNOW THAT SILENCE.
SHE'S SO INNOCENT, ISN'T SHE?
MY KRYPTONITE.

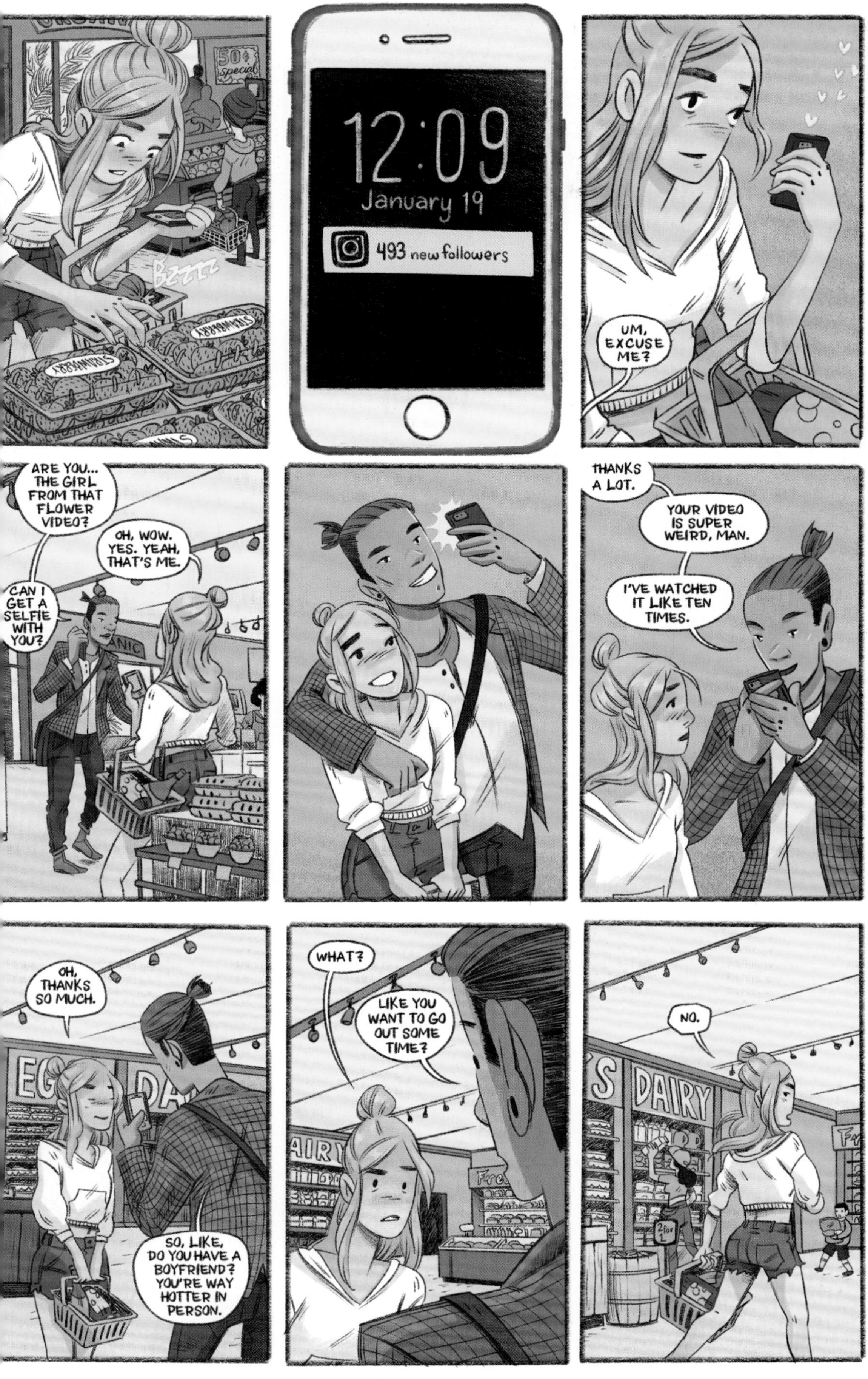

50¢ special
STRAWBERRY
STRAWBERRY
BZZZZ
12:09
January 19
493 new followers
UM, EXCUSE ME?
ARE YOU... THE GIRL FROM THAT FLOWER VIDEO?
OH, WOW. YES. YEAH, THAT'S ME.
CAN I GET A SELFIE WITH YOU?
THANKS A LOT.
YOUR VIDEO IS SUPER WEIRD, MAN.
I'VE WATCHED IT LIKE TEN TIMES.
OH, THANKS SO MUCH.
SO, LIKE, DO YOU HAVE A BOYFRIEND? YOU'RE WAY HOTTER IN PERSON.
WHAT?
LIKE YOU WANT TO GO OUT SOME TIME?
NO.
DAIRY

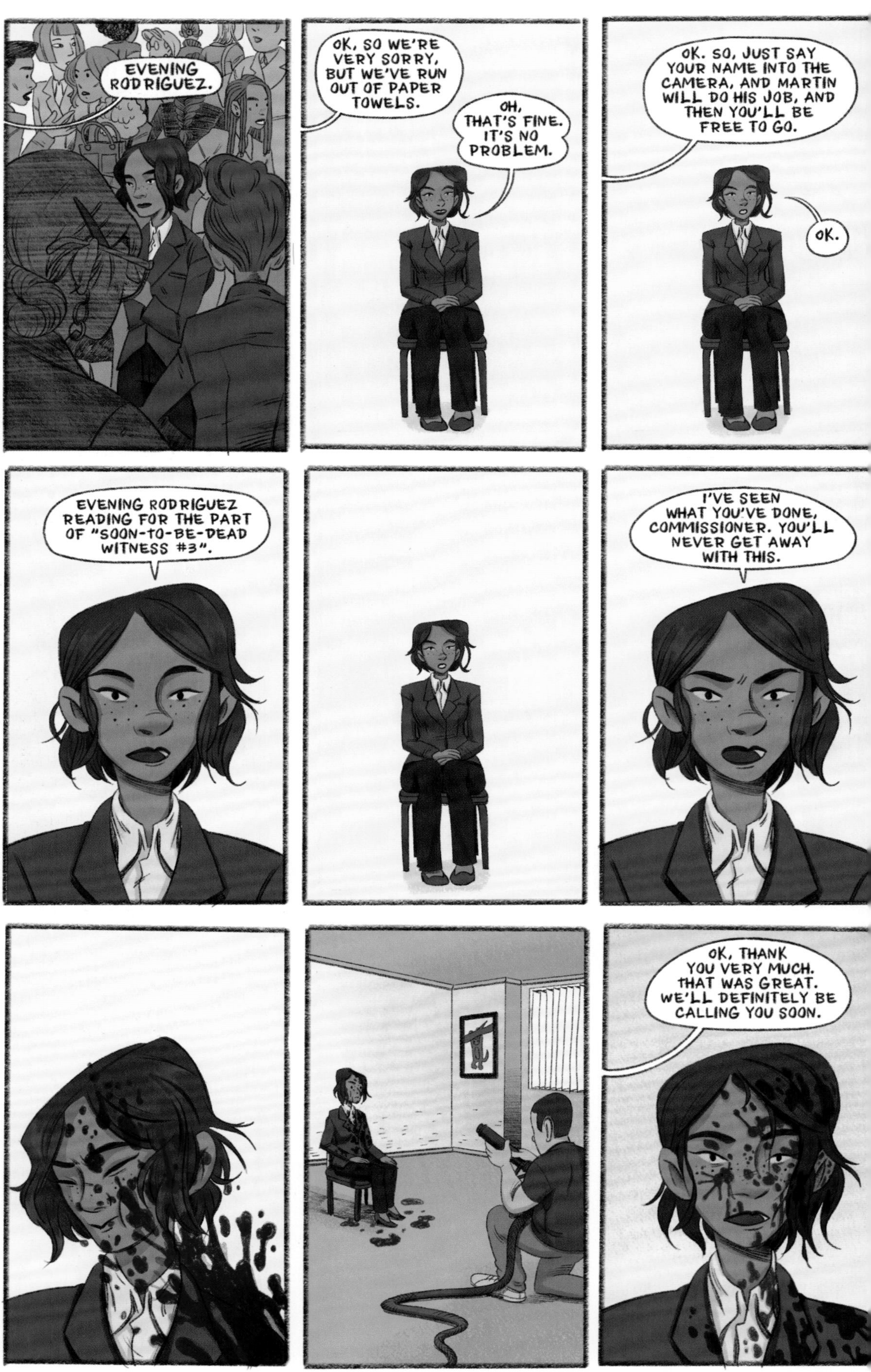
EVENING RODRIGUEZ.
OK, SO WE'RE VERY SORRY, BUT WE'VE RUN OUT OF PAPER TOWELS.
OH, THAT'S FINE. IT'S NO PROBLEM.
OK. SO, JUST SAY YOUR NAME INTO THE CAMERA, AND MARTIN WILL DO HIS JOB, AND THEN YOU'LL BE FREE TO GO.
OK.
EVENING RODRIGUEZ READING FOR THE PART OF "SOON-TO-BE-DEAD WITNESS #3".
I'VE SEEN WHAT YOU'VE DONE, COMMISSIONER. YOU'LL NEVER GET AWAY WITH THIS.
OK, THANK YOU VERY MUCH. THAT WAS GREAT. WE'LL DEFINITELY BE CALLING YOU SOON.

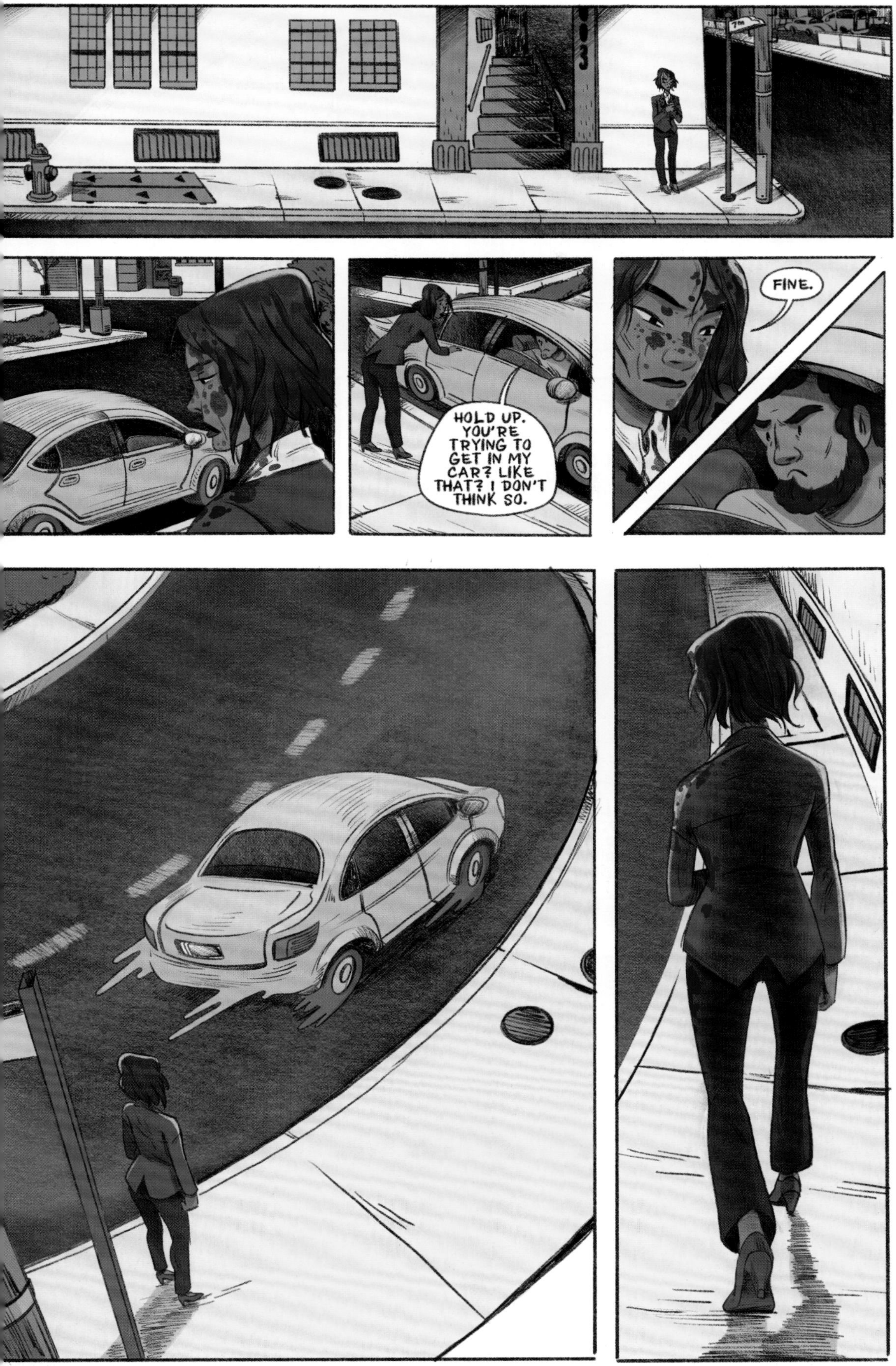
HOLD UP. YOU'RE TRYING TO GET IN MY CAR? LIKE THAT? I DON'T THINK SO.
FINE.

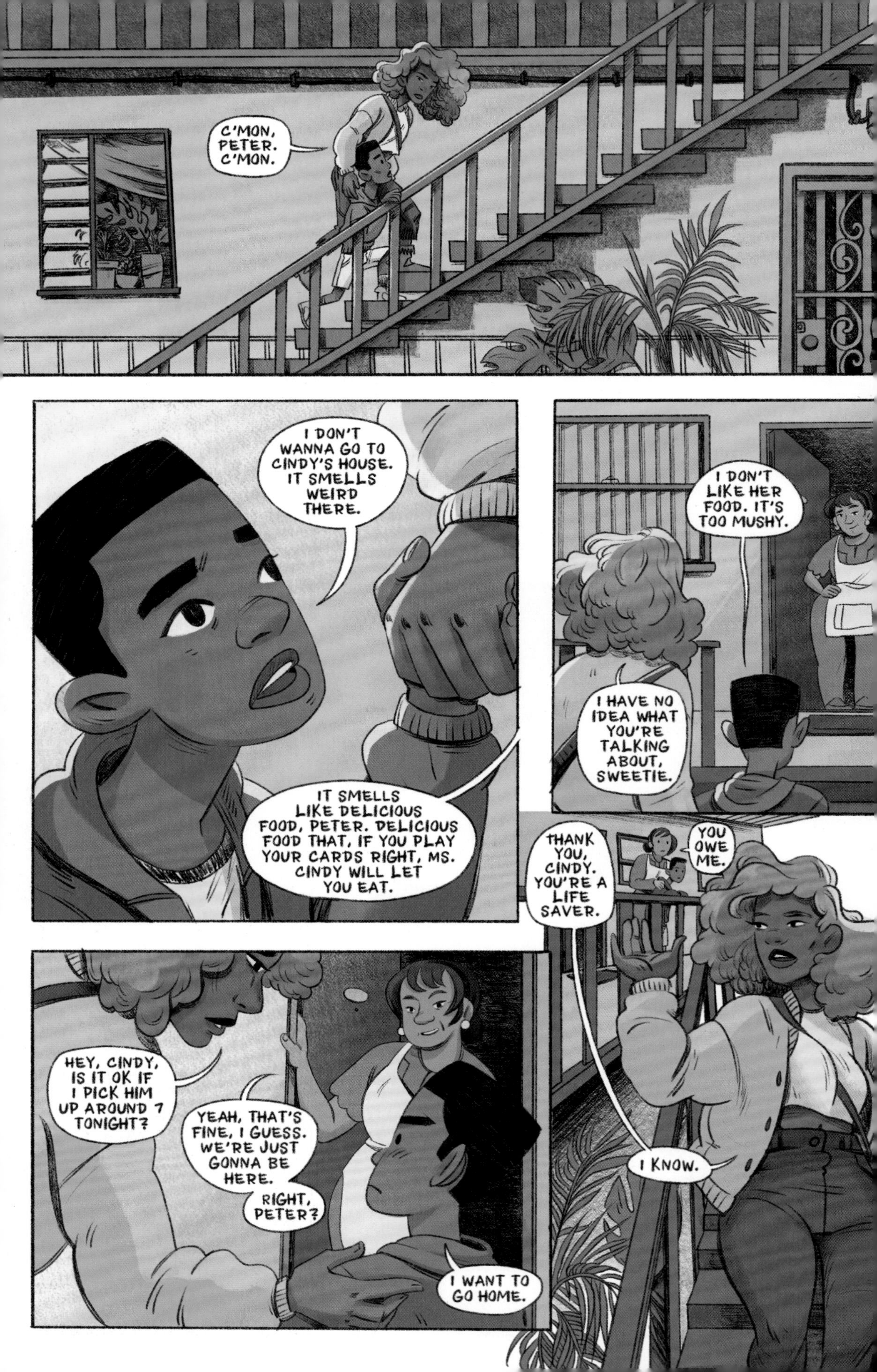
C'MON, PETER. C'MON.
I DON'T WANNA GO TO CINDY'S HOUSE. IT SMELLS WEIRD THERE.
IT SMELLS LIKE DELICIOUS FOOD, PETER. DELICIOUS FOOD THAT, IF YOU PLAY YOUR CARDS RIGHT, MS. CINDY WILL LET YOU EAT.
I DON'T LIKE HER FOOD. IT'S TOO MUSHY.
I HAVE NO IDEA WHAT YOU'RE TALKING ABOUT, SWEETIE.
HEY, CINDY, IS IT OK IF I PICK HIM UP AROUND 7 TONIGHT?
YEAH, THAT'S FINE, I GUESS. WE'RE JUST GONNA BE HERE.
RIGHT, PETER?
I WANT TO GO HOME.
THANK YOU, CINDY. YOU'RE A LIFE SAVER.
YOU OWE ME.
I KNOW.

GIMME DEM $ DOLLA$

IT JUST DON'T MAKE NO SENSE TO ME. WHY DON'T YOU POST MORE PHOTOS OF THAT LITTLE BOY OF YOURS?

●●○○○ AT&T   4:13   79%

STANLEY

We're shooting tomorrow night. Can you make it?

QWERTYUIOP
ASDFGHJKL
ZXCVBNM
123   space   return

I JUST DON'T LIKE POSTING THEM. IT CAN GET IN THE WAY OF WORK SOME TIMES.

●●○○○ AT&T   4:16   79%

STANLEY

night. Can you make it?

I'm on set right now. Booked tomorrow.

delivered

QWERTYUIOP
ASDFGHJKL
ZXCVBNM
123   space   return

WHAT ARE YOU TALKING ABOUT? PEOPLE LOVE BABIES. THEY LOVE 'EM. I'D THINK THAT WOULD HELP YOU GET MORE WORK.

●●○○○ AT&T   4:21   75%

STANLEY

I'm on set right now. Booked tomorrow.

delivered

Blow off the other production. I'll pay double.

QWERTYUIOP
ASDFGHJKL
ZXCVBNM
123   space   return

NO, IT'S MORE LIKE IF DUDES MY AGE KNOW I HAVE A KID, THEY'RE LESS LIKELY TO WANT TO FUCK ME AND THEREFORE LESS LIKELY TO HIRE ME.

●●○○○ AT&T   4:32   71%

STANLEY

Blow off the other production. I'll pay double.

delivered

QWERTYUIOP
ASDFGHJKL
ZXCVBNM
123   space   return

GIMME DEM $ DOLLA$

WELL, THAT'S JUST AWFUL.

IT IS WHAT IT IS.

JUST AWFUL.

I NEED YOU TO COVER MY SHIFT TOMORROW.

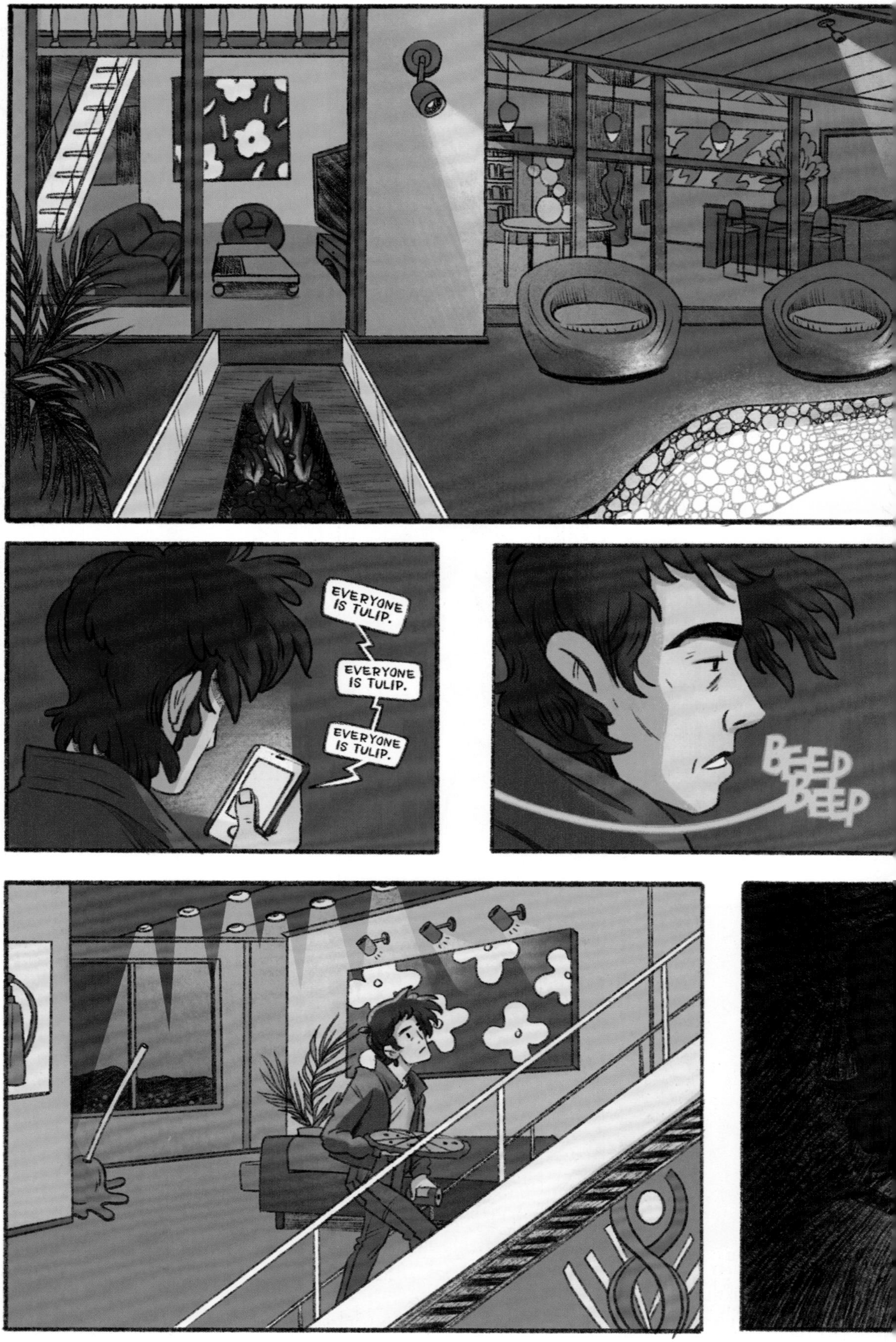
EVERYONE IS TULIP.
EVERYONE IS TULIP.
EVERYONE IS TULIP.
BEEP BEEP

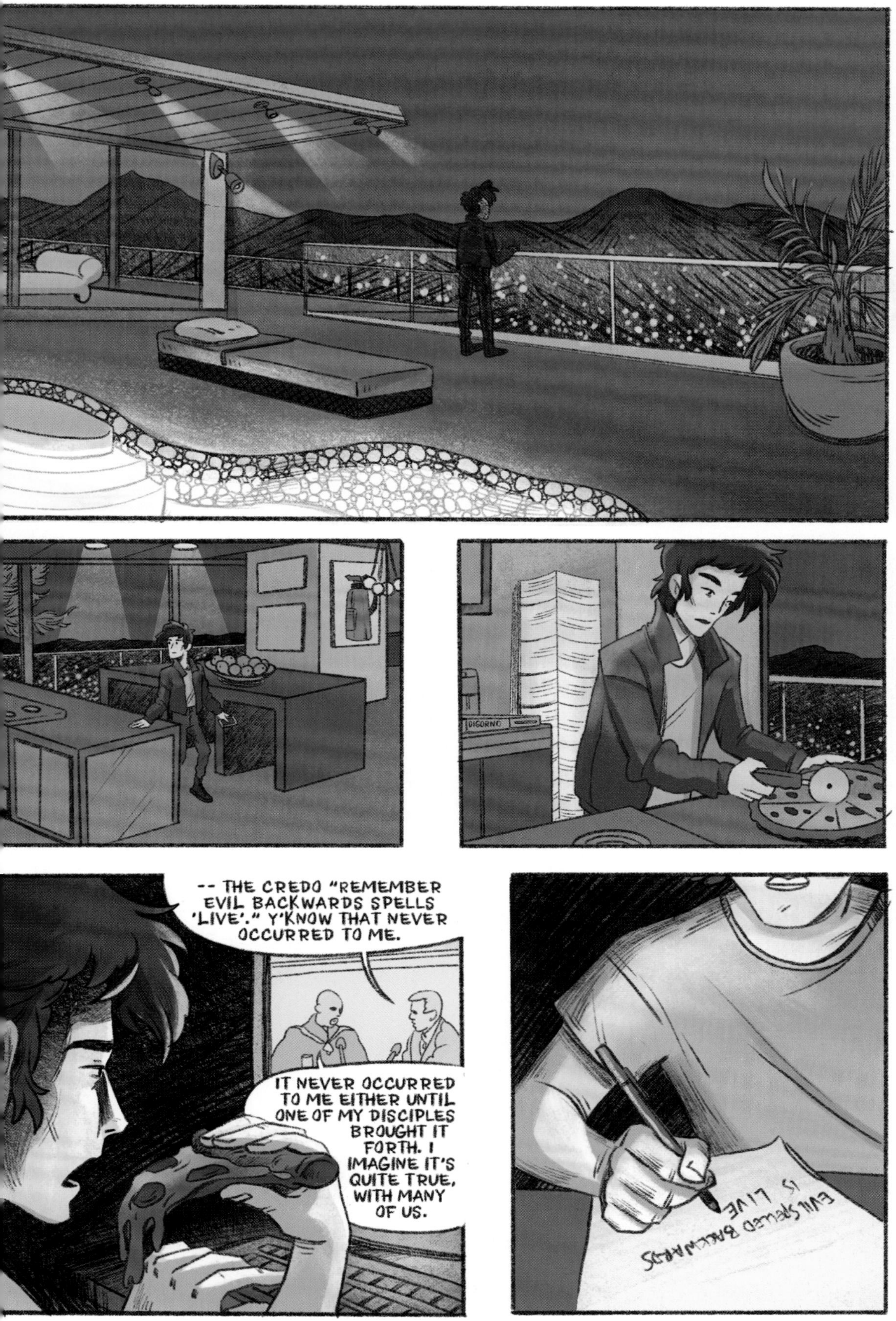
DIGORNO
-- THE CREDO "REMEMBER EVIL BACKWARDS SPELLS 'LIVE'." Y'KNOW THAT NEVER OCCURRED TO ME.
IT NEVER OCCURRED TO ME EITHER UNTIL ONE OF MY DISCIPLES BROUGHT IT FORTH. I IMAGINE IT'S QUITE TRUE, WITH MANY OF US.
EVIL SPELLED BACKWARDS IS LIVE

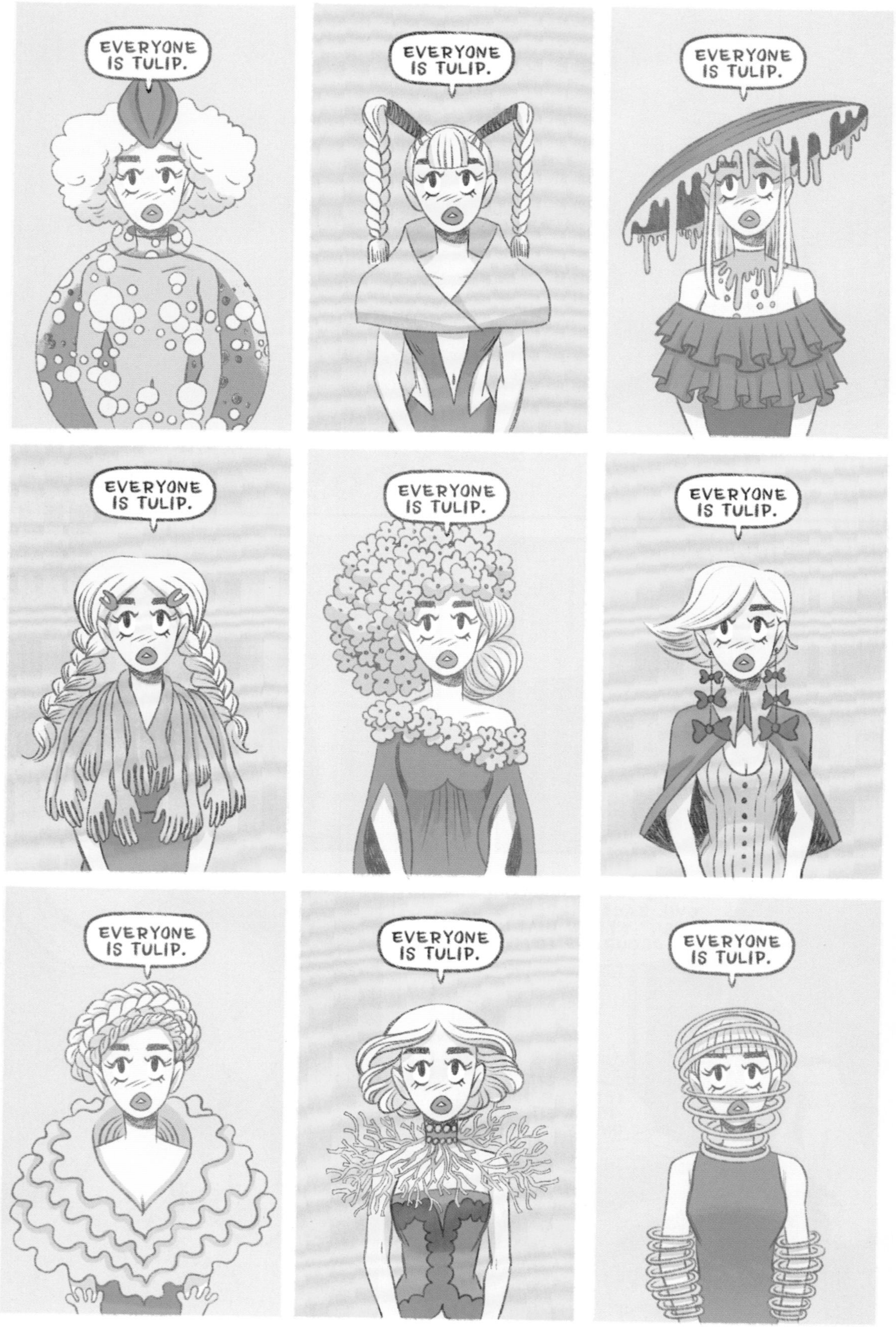
EVERYONE IS TULIP.
EVERYONE IS TULIP.
EVERYONE IS TULIP.
EVERYONE IS TULIP.
EVERYONE IS TULIP.
EVERYONE IS TULIP.
EVERYONE IS TULIP.
EVERYONE IS TULIP.
EVERYONE IS TULIP.

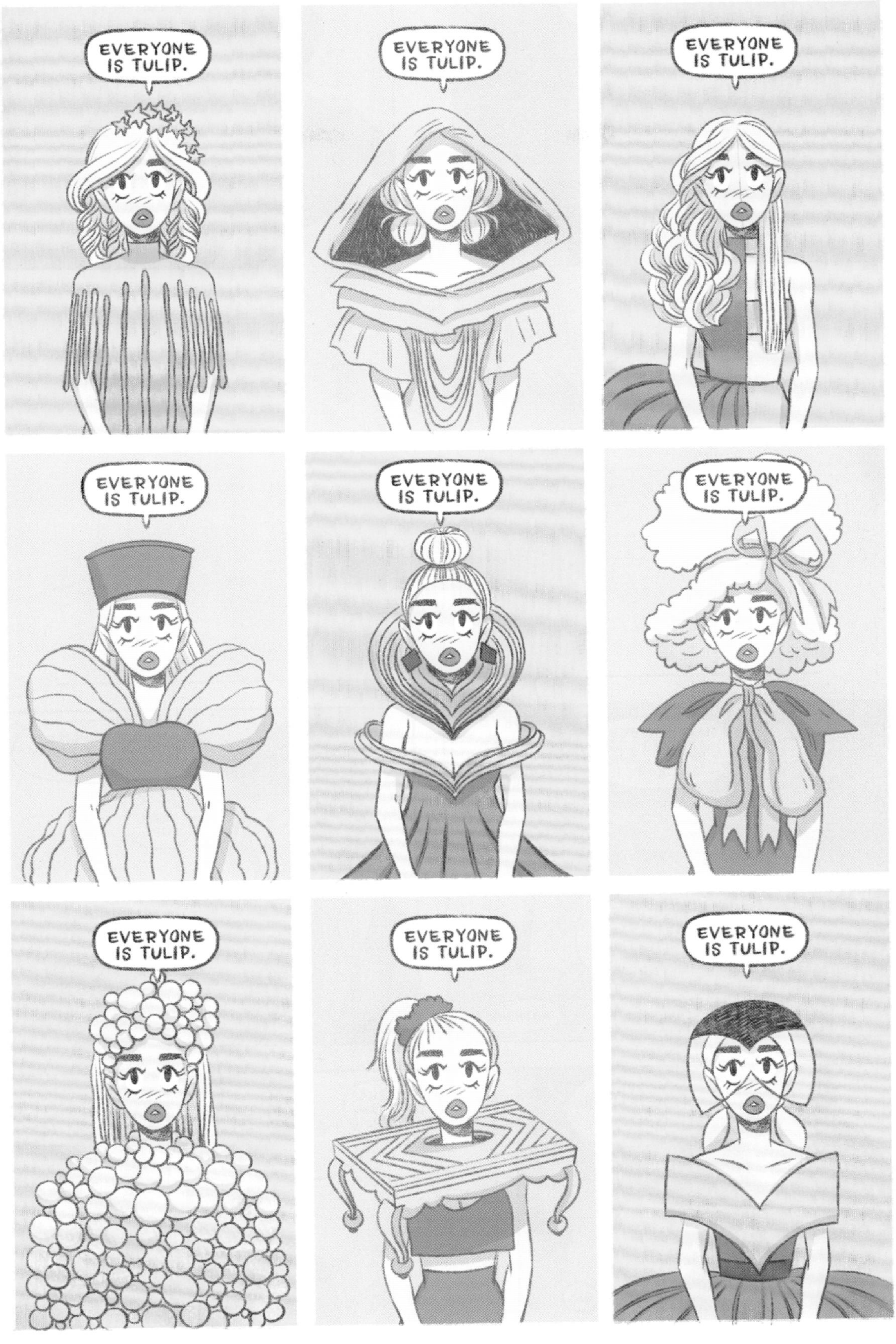
EVERYONE IS TULIP.
EVERYONE IS TULIP.
EVERYONE IS TULIP.
EVERYONE IS TULIP.
EVERYONE IS TULIP.
EVERYONE IS TULIP.
EVERYONE IS TULIP.
EVERYONE IS TULIP.
EVERYONE IS TULIP.

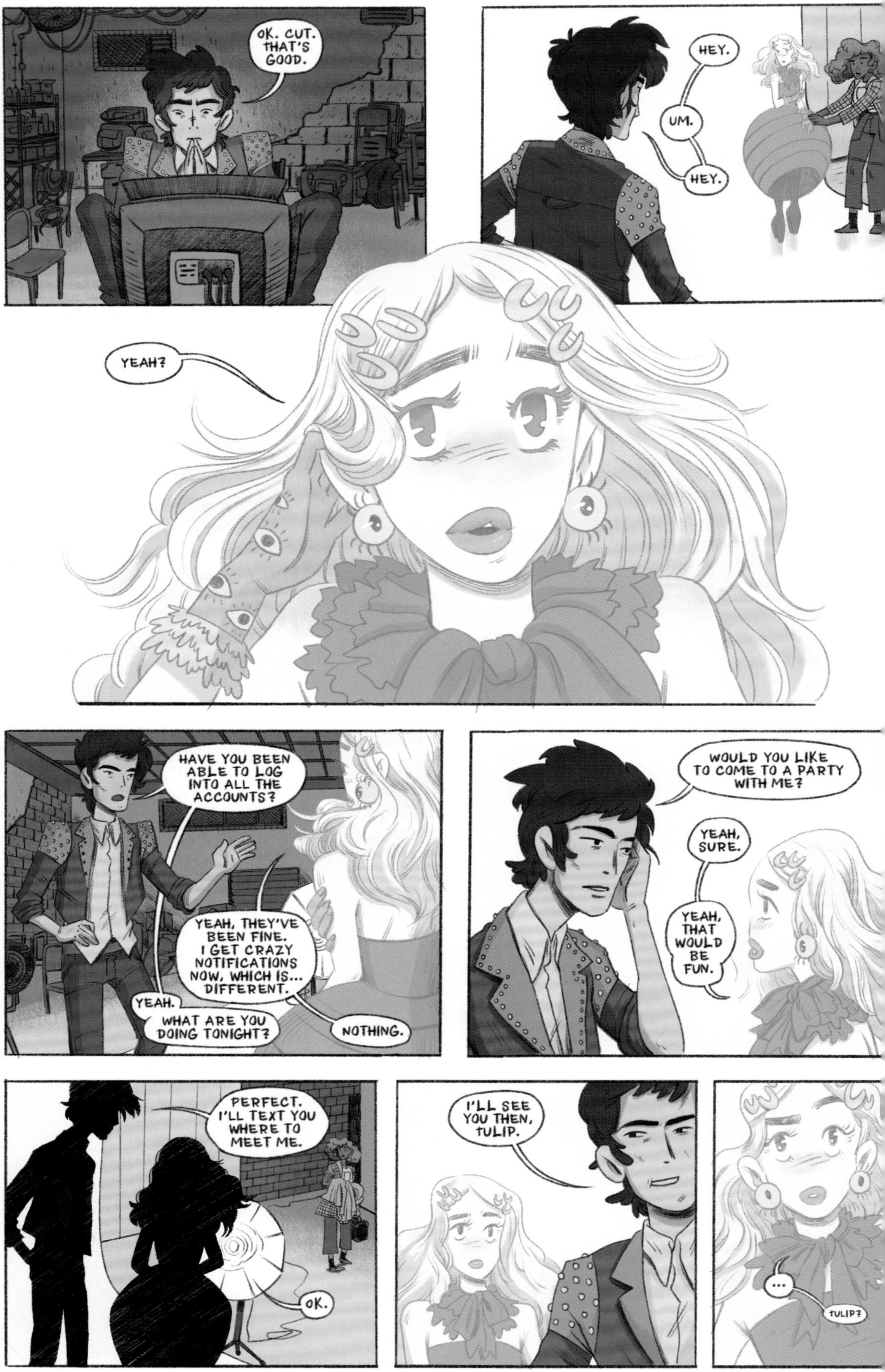
OK. CUT. THAT'S GOOD.
HEY.
UM.
HEY.
YEAH?
HAVE YOU BEEN ABLE TO LOG INTO ALL THE ACCOUNTS?
YEAH, THEY'VE BEEN FINE. I GET CRAZY NOTIFICATIONS NOW, WHICH IS... DIFFERENT.
YEAH.
WHAT ARE YOU DOING TONIGHT?
NOTHING.
WOULD YOU LIKE TO COME TO A PARTY WITH ME?
YEAH, SURE.
YEAH, THAT WOULD BE FUN.
PERFECT. I'LL TEXT YOU WHERE TO MEET ME.
OK.
I'LL SEE YOU THEN, TULIP.
...
TULIP?

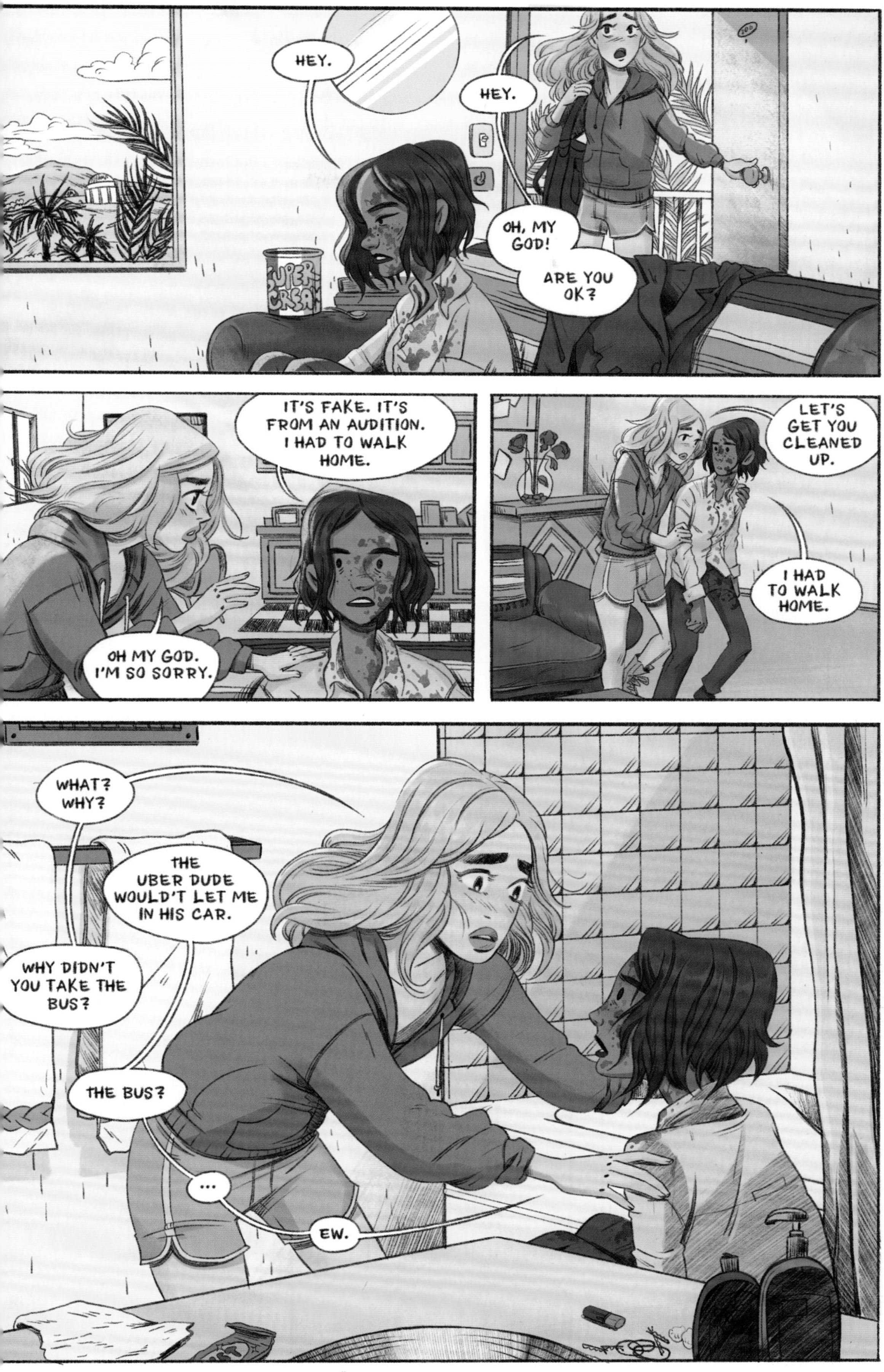
HEY.
HEY.
OH, MY GOD!
ARE YOU OK?
IT'S FAKE. IT'S FROM AN AUDITION. I HAD TO WALK HOME.
OH MY GOD. I'M SO SORRY.
LET'S GET YOU CLEANED UP.
I HAD TO WALK HOME.
WHAT? WHY?
THE UBER DUDE WOULD'T LET ME IN HIS CAR.
WHY DIDN'T YOU TAKE THE BUS?
THE BUS?
...
EW.

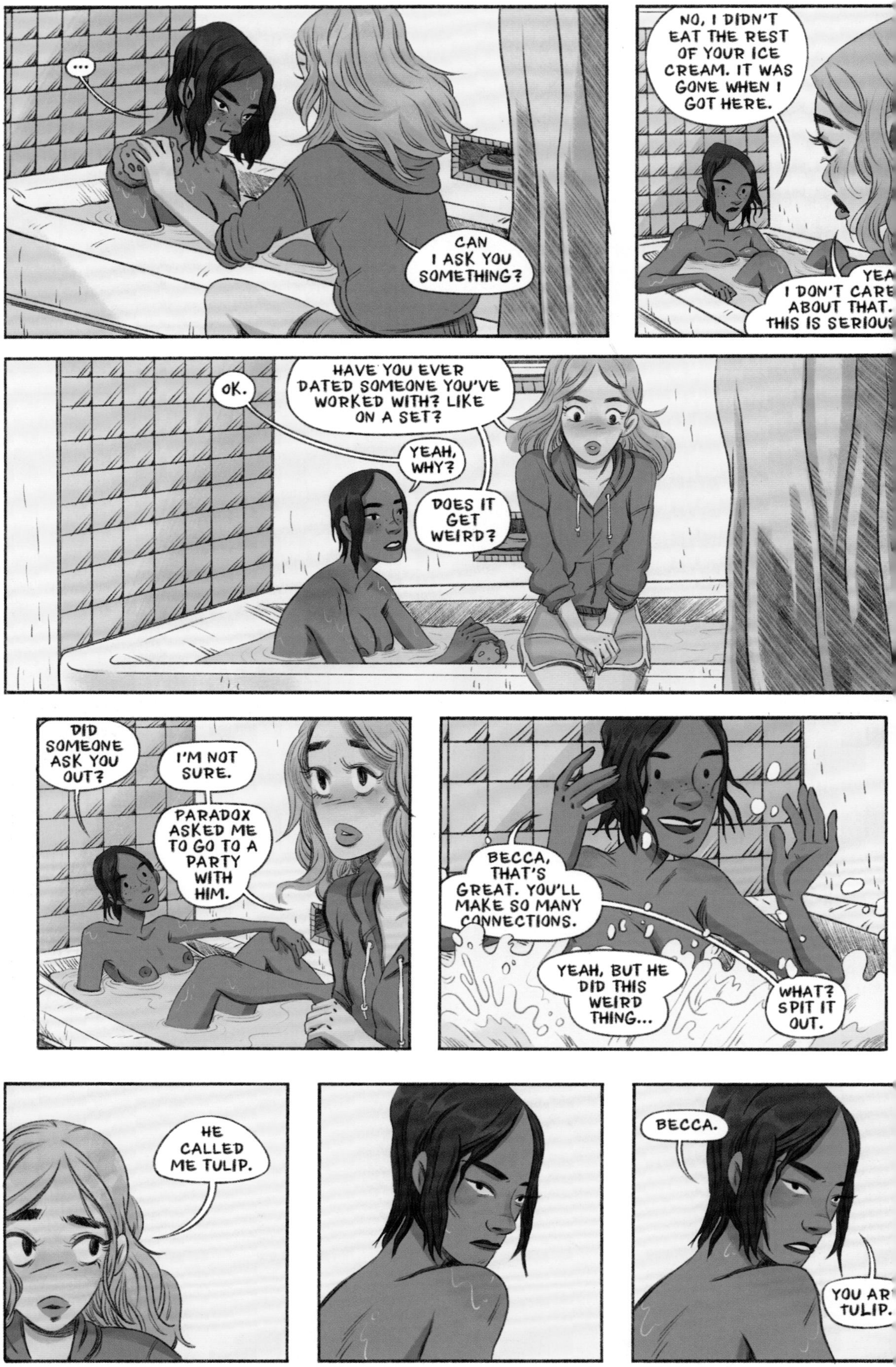
...
CAN I ASK YOU SOMETHING?
NO, I DIDN'T EAT THE REST OF YOUR ICE CREAM. IT WAS GONE WHEN I GOT HERE.
YEA I DON'T CARE ABOUT THAT. THIS IS SERIOUS
OK.
HAVE YOU EVER DATED SOMEONE YOU'VE WORKED WITH? LIKE ON A SET?
YEAH, WHY?
DOES IT GET WEIRD?
DID SOMEONE ASK YOU OUT?
I'M NOT SURE.
PARADOX ASKED ME TO GO TO A PARTY WITH HIM.
BECCA, THAT'S GREAT. YOU'LL MAKE SO MANY CONNECTIONS.
YEAH, BUT HE DID THIS WEIRD THING...
WHAT? SPIT IT OUT.
HE CALLED ME TULIP.
BECCA.
YOU AR TULIP.

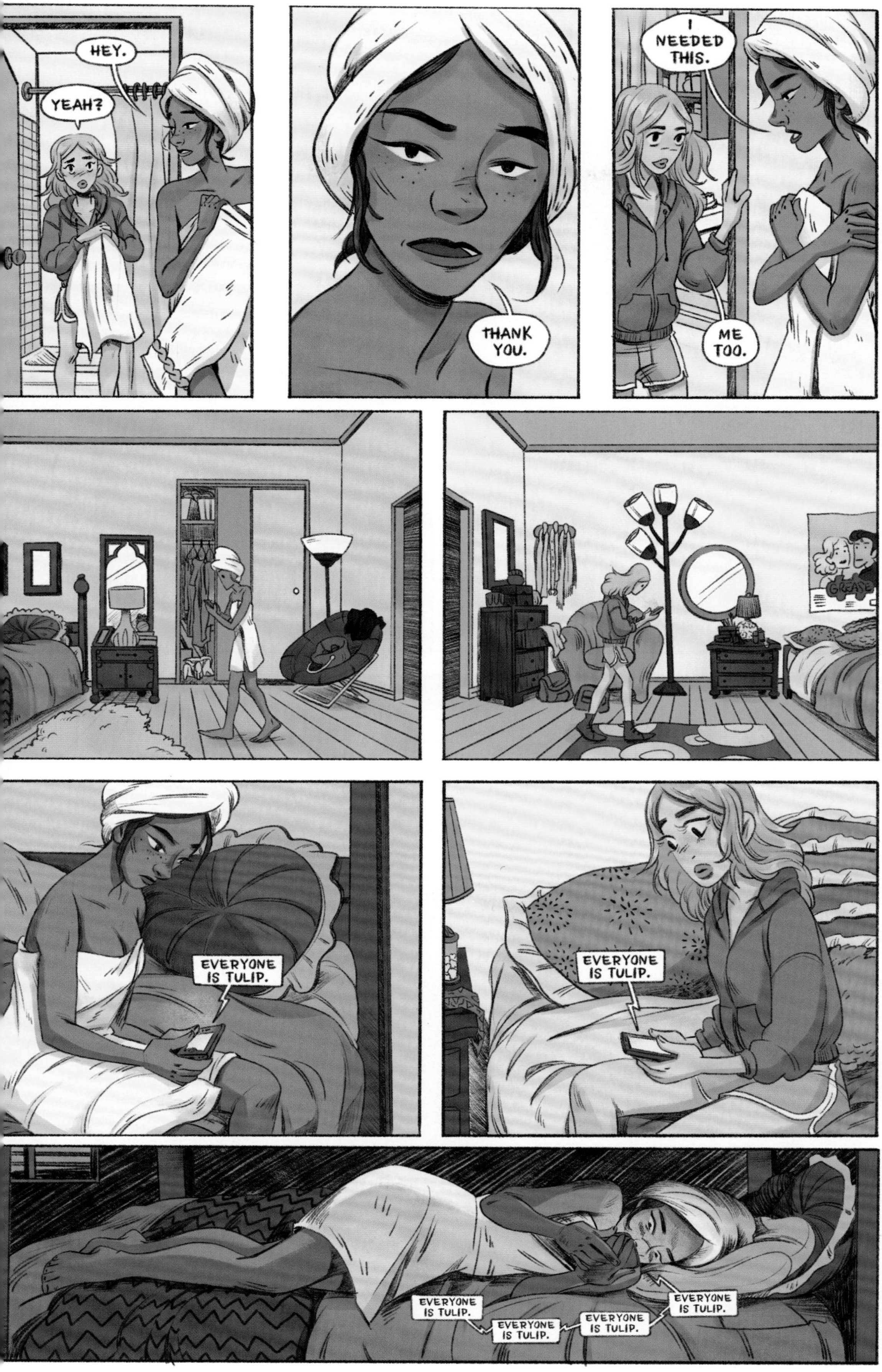
HEY.
YEAH?
THANK YOU.
I NEEDED THIS.
ME TOO.
GREASE
EVERYONE IS TULIP.
EVERYONE IS TULIP.
EVERYONE IS TULIP.
EVERYONE IS TULIP.
EVERYONE IS TULIP.
EVERYONE IS TULIP.

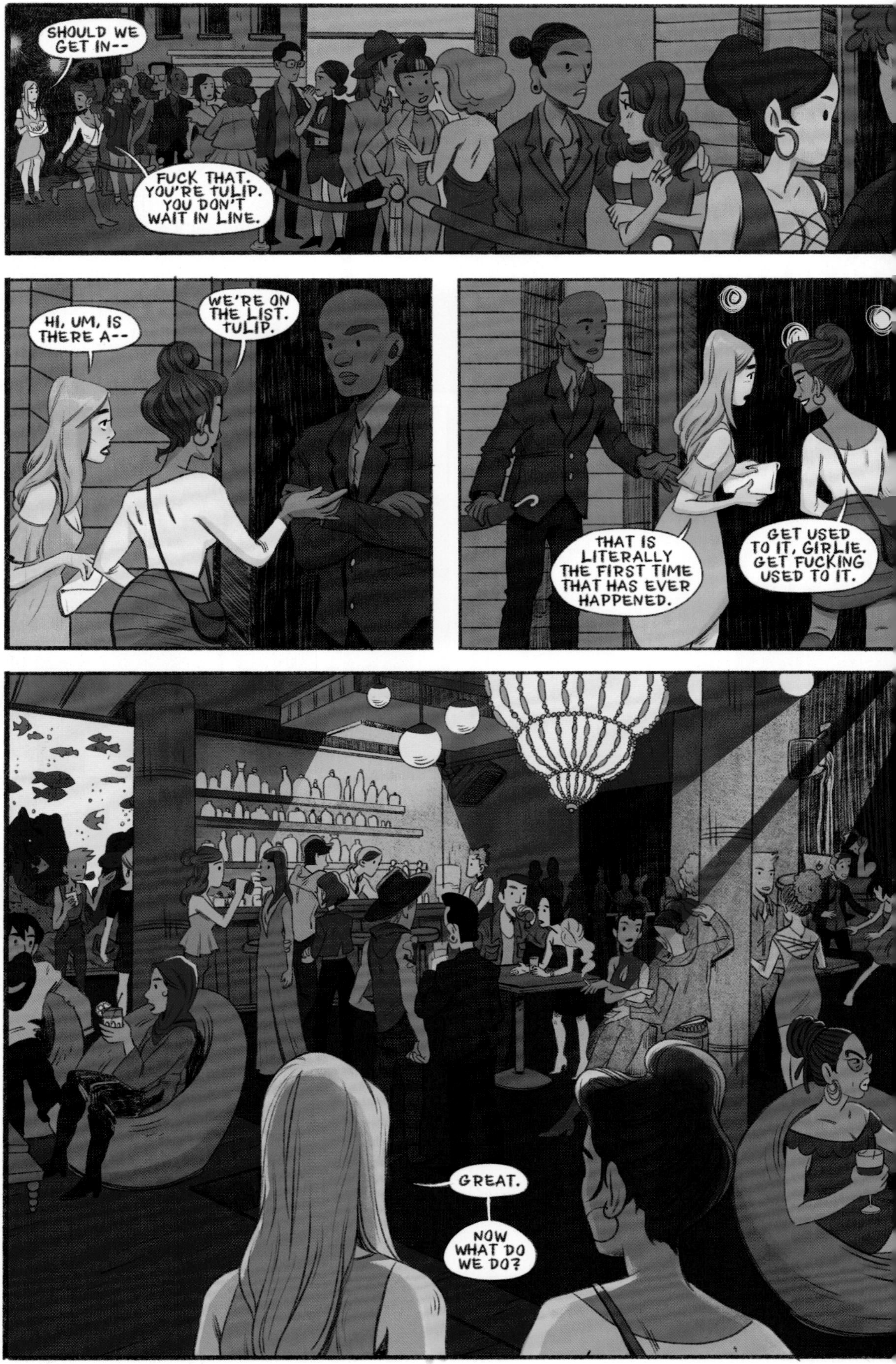
SHOULD WE GET IN--
FUCK THAT. YOU'RE TULIP. YOU DON'T WAIT IN LINE.
HI, UM, IS THERE A--
WE'RE ON THE LIST. TULIP.
THAT IS LITERALLY THE FIRST TIME THAT HAS EVER HAPPENED.
GET USED TO IT, GIRLIE. GET FUCKING USED TO IT.
GREAT.
NOW WHAT DO WE DO?

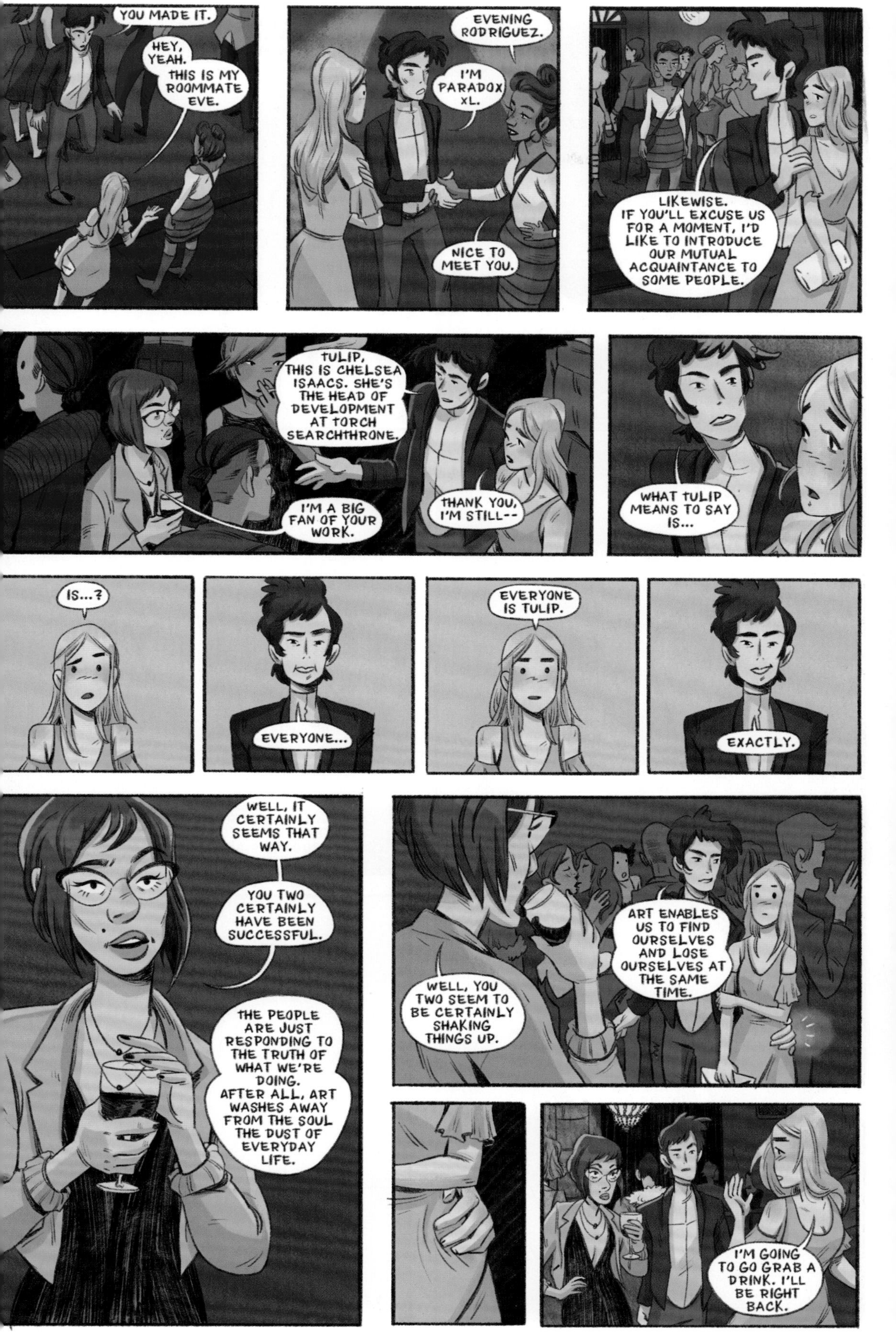
YOU MADE IT.
HEY, YEAH.
THIS IS MY ROOMMATE EVE.
EVENING RODRIGUEZ.
I'M PARADOX XL.
NICE TO MEET YOU.
LIKEWISE. IF YOU'LL EXCUSE US FOR A MOMENT, I'D LIKE TO INTRODUCE OUR MUTUAL ACQUAINTANCE TO SOME PEOPLE.
TULIP, THIS IS CHELSEA ISAACS. SHE'S THE HEAD OF DEVELOPMENT AT TORCH SEARCHTHRONE.
I'M A BIG FAN OF YOUR WORK.
THANK YOU, I'M STILL--
WHAT TULIP MEANS TO SAY IS...
IS...?
EVERYONE...
EVERYONE IS TULIP.
EXACTLY.
WELL, IT CERTAINLY SEEMS THAT WAY.
YOU TWO CERTAINLY HAVE BEEN SUCCESSFUL.
THE PEOPLE ARE JUST RESPONDING TO THE TRUTH OF WHAT WE'RE DOING. AFTER ALL, ART WASHES AWAY FROM THE SOUL THE DUST OF EVERYDAY LIFE.
WELL, YOU TWO SEEM TO BE CERTAINLY SHAKING THINGS UP.
ART ENABLES US TO FIND OURSELVES AND LOSE OURSELVES AT THE SAME TIME.
I'M GOING TO GO GRAB A DRINK. I'LL BE RIGHT BACK.

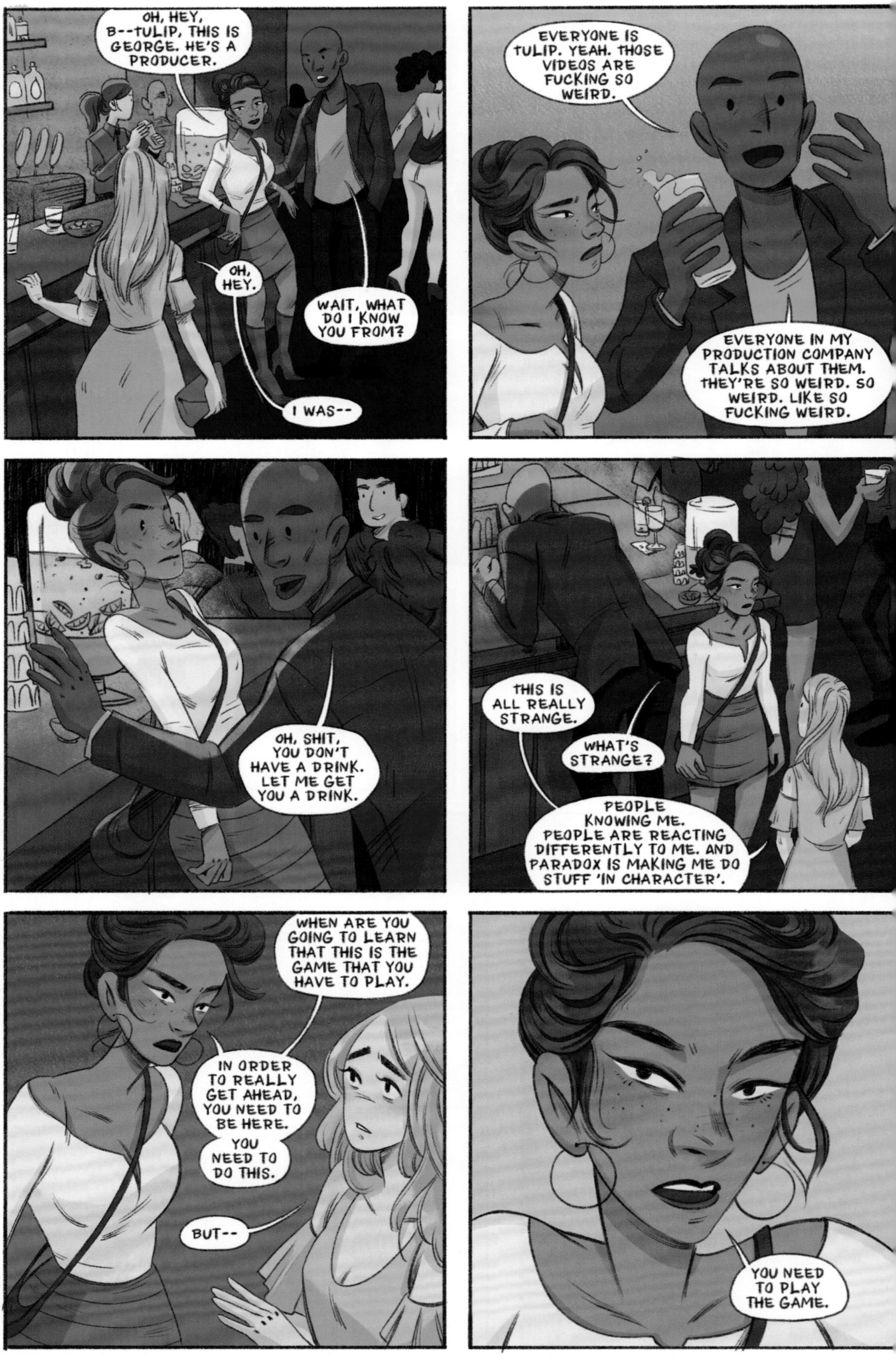
OH, HEY, B--TULIP, THIS IS GEORGE. HE'S A PRODUCER.
OH, HEY.
WAIT, WHAT DO I KNOW YOU FROM?
I WAS--
EVERYONE IS TULIP. YEAH. THOSE VIDEOS ARE FUCKING SO WEIRD.
EVERYONE IN MY PRODUCTION COMPANY TALKS ABOUT THEM. THEY'RE SO WEIRD. SO WEIRD. LIKE SO FUCKING WEIRD.
OH, SHIT, YOU DON'T HAVE A DRINK. LET ME GET YOU A DRINK.
THIS IS ALL REALLY STRANGE.
WHAT'S STRANGE?
PEOPLE KNOWING ME. PEOPLE ARE REACTING DIFFERENTLY TO ME. AND PARADOX IS MAKING ME DO STUFF 'IN CHARACTER'.
WHEN ARE YOU GOING TO LEARN THAT THIS IS THE GAME THAT YOU HAVE TO PLAY.
IN ORDER TO REALLY GET AHEAD, YOU NEED TO BE HERE.
YOU NEED TO DO THIS.
BUT--
YOU NEED TO PLAY THE GAME.

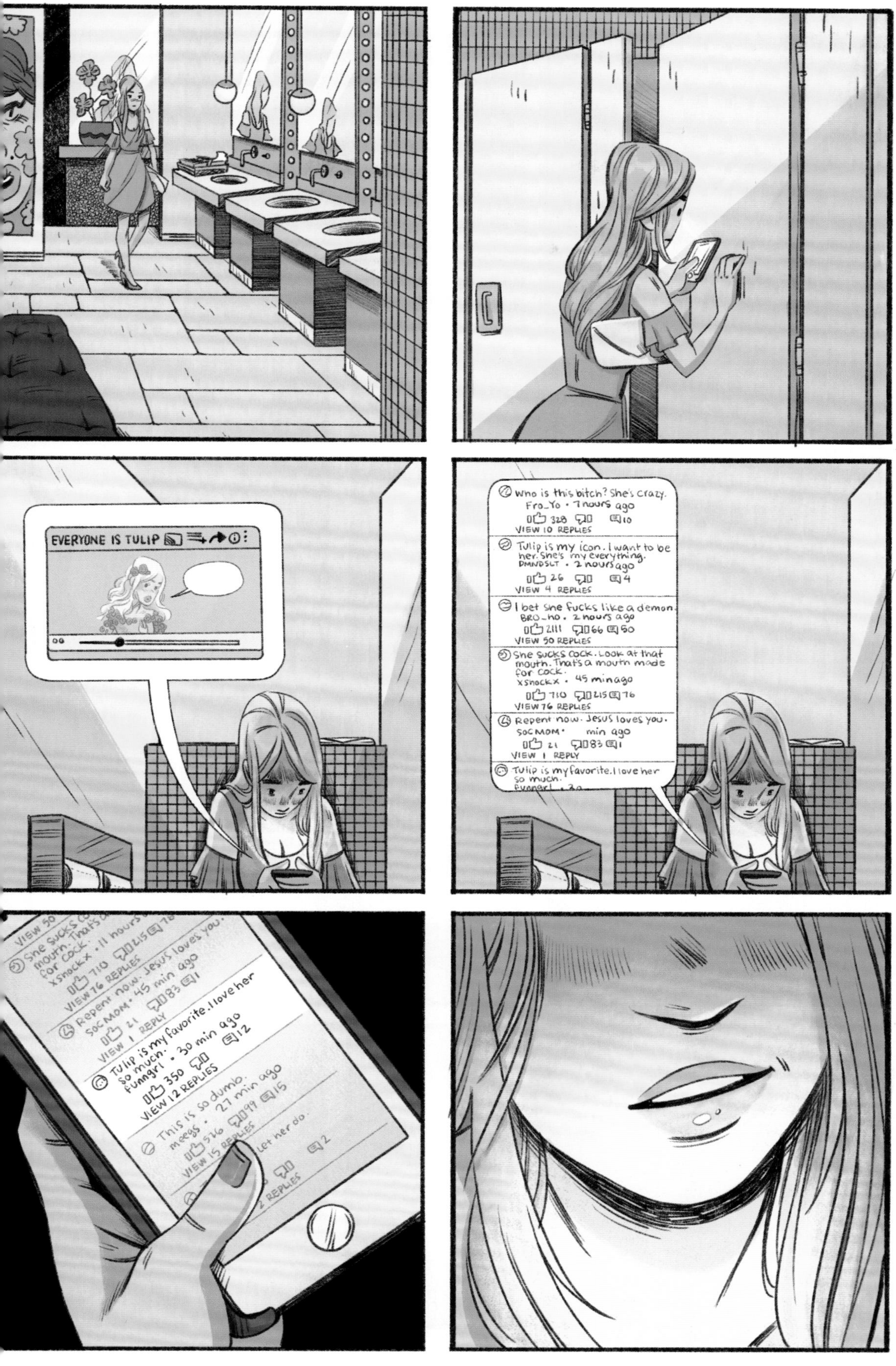

EVERYONE IS TULIP
Who is this bitch? She's crazy.
Fro_Yo • 7 hours ago
328 0 10
VIEW 10 REPLIES
Tulip is my icon. I want to be her. She's my everything.
DMNDSLT • 2 hours ago
26 0 4
VIEW 4 REPLIES
I bet she fucks like a demon.
BRO_ho • 2 hours ago
2111 66 50
VIEW 50 REPLIES
She sucks cock. Look at that mouth. That's a mouth made for cock.
xShockx • 45 min ago
710 215 76
VIEW 76 REPLIES
Repent now. Jesus loves you.
SOCMOM • min ago
21 83 1
VIEW 1 REPLY
Tulip is my favorite. I love her so much.
Repent now. Jesus loves you.
SOCMOM • 45 min ago
21 83 1
VIEW 1 REPLY
Tulip is my favorite. I love her so much.
funngrl • 30 min ago
350 0 12
VIEW 12 REPLIES
This is so dumb.
meegs • 27 min ago
576 99 15
VIEW 15 REPLIES

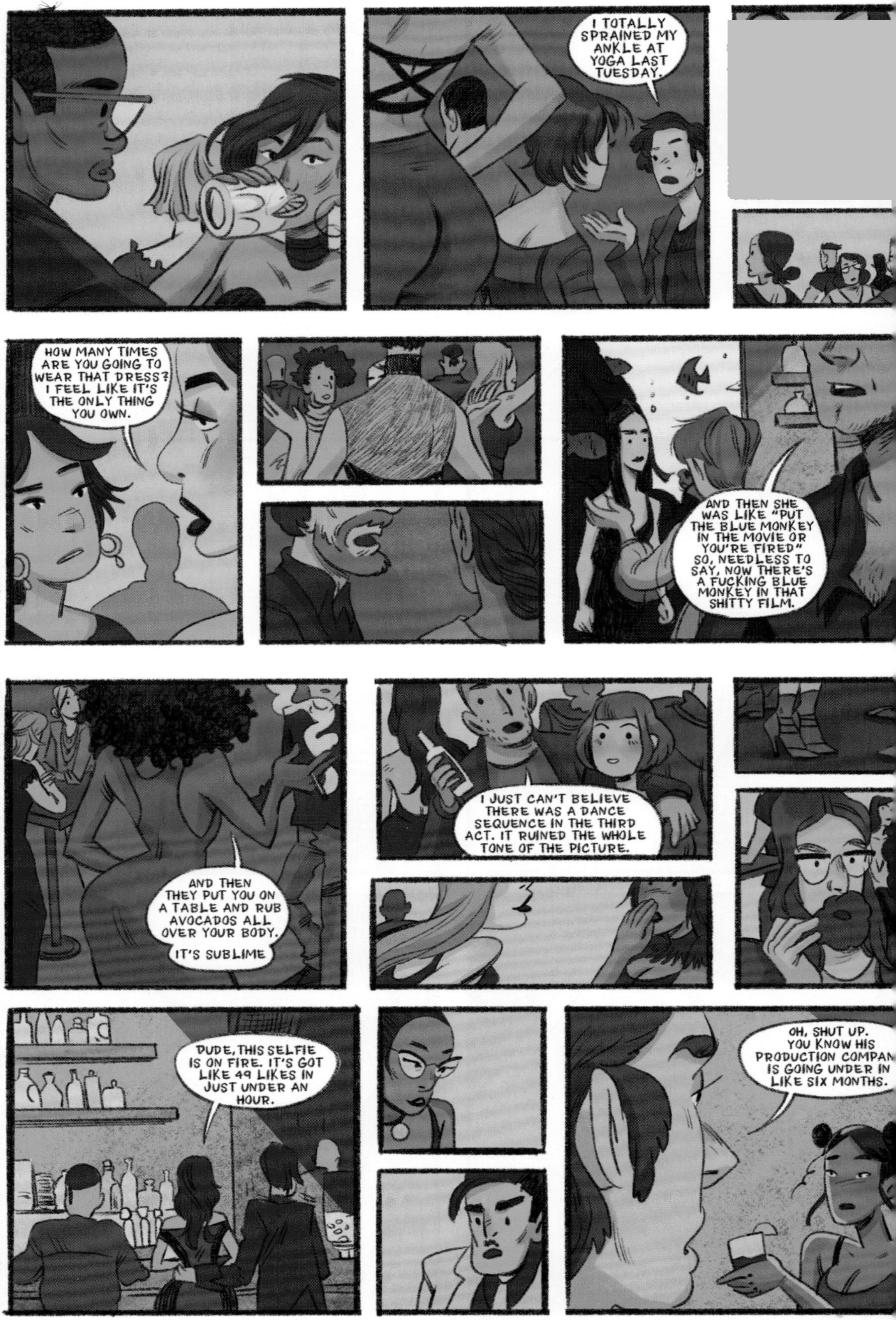
I TOTALLY SPRAINED MY ANKLE AT YOGA LAST TUESDAY.
HOW MANY TIMES ARE YOU GOING TO WEAR THAT DRESS? I FEEL LIKE IT'S THE ONLY THING YOU OWN.
AND THEN SHE WAS LIKE "PUT THE BLUE MONKEY IN THE MOVIE OR YOU'RE FIRED" SO, NEEDLESS TO SAY, NOW THERE'S A FUCKING BLUE MONKEY IN THAT SHITTY FILM.
AND THEN THEY PUT YOU ON A TABLE AND RUB AVOCADOS ALL OVER YOUR BODY.
IT'S SUBLIME
I JUST CAN'T BELIEVE THERE WAS A DANCE SEQUENCE IN THE THIRD ACT. IT RUINED THE WHOLE TONE OF THE PICTURE.
DUDE, THIS SELFIE IS ON FIRE. IT'S GOT LIKE 49 LIKES IN JUST UNDER AN HOUR.
OH, SHUT UP. YOU KNOW HIS PRODUCTION COMPAN IS GOING UNDER IN LIKE SIX MONTHS.

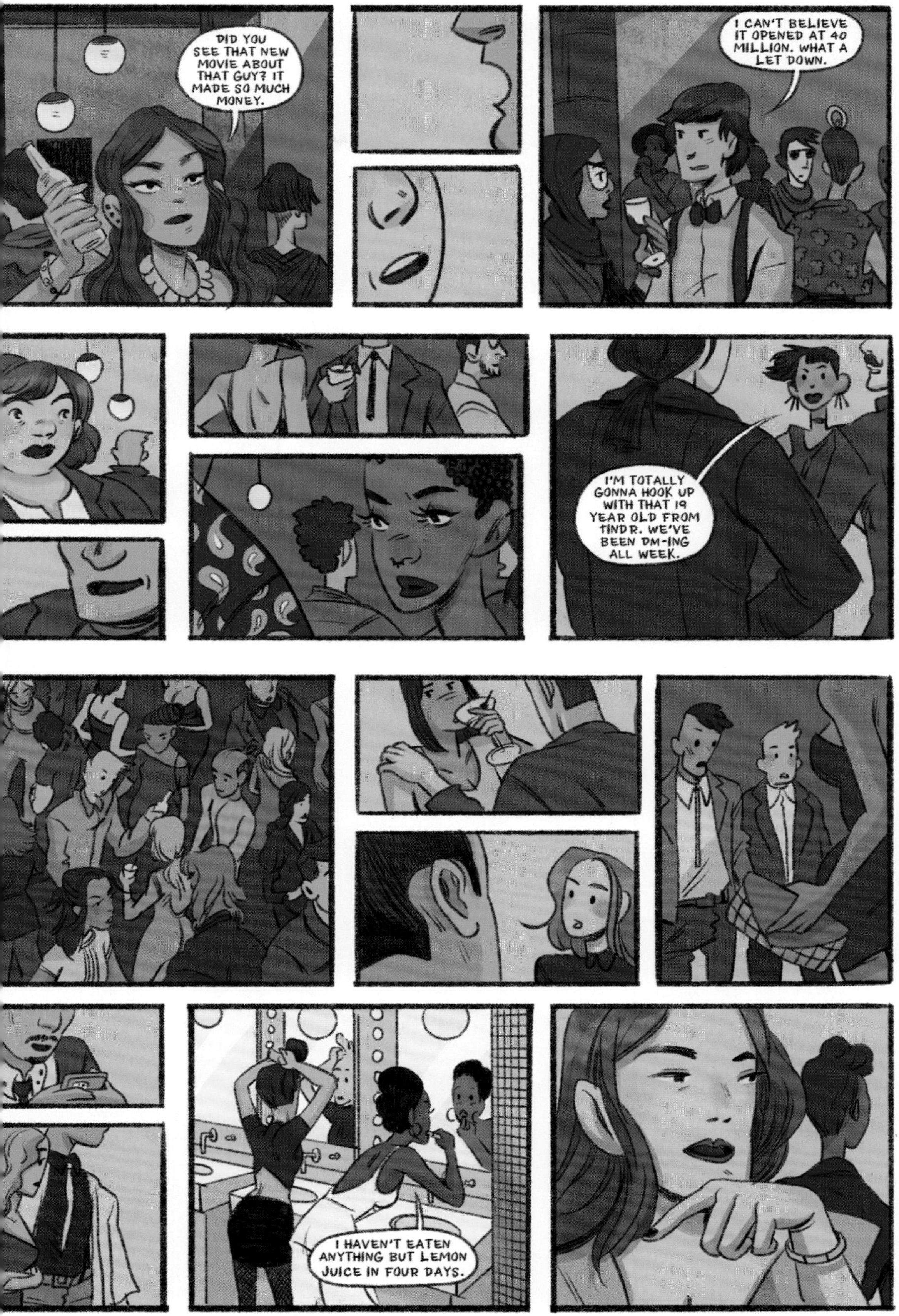

DID YOU SEE THAT NEW MOVIE ABOUT THAT GUY? IT MADE SO MUCH MONEY.
I CAN'T BELIEVE IT OPENED AT 40 MILLION. WHAT A LET DOWN.
I'M TOTALLY GONNA HOOK UP WITH THAT 19 YEAR OLD FROM TINDR. WE'VE BEEN DM-ING ALL WEEK.
I HAVEN'T EATEN ANYTHING BUT LEMON JUICE IN FOUR DAYS.

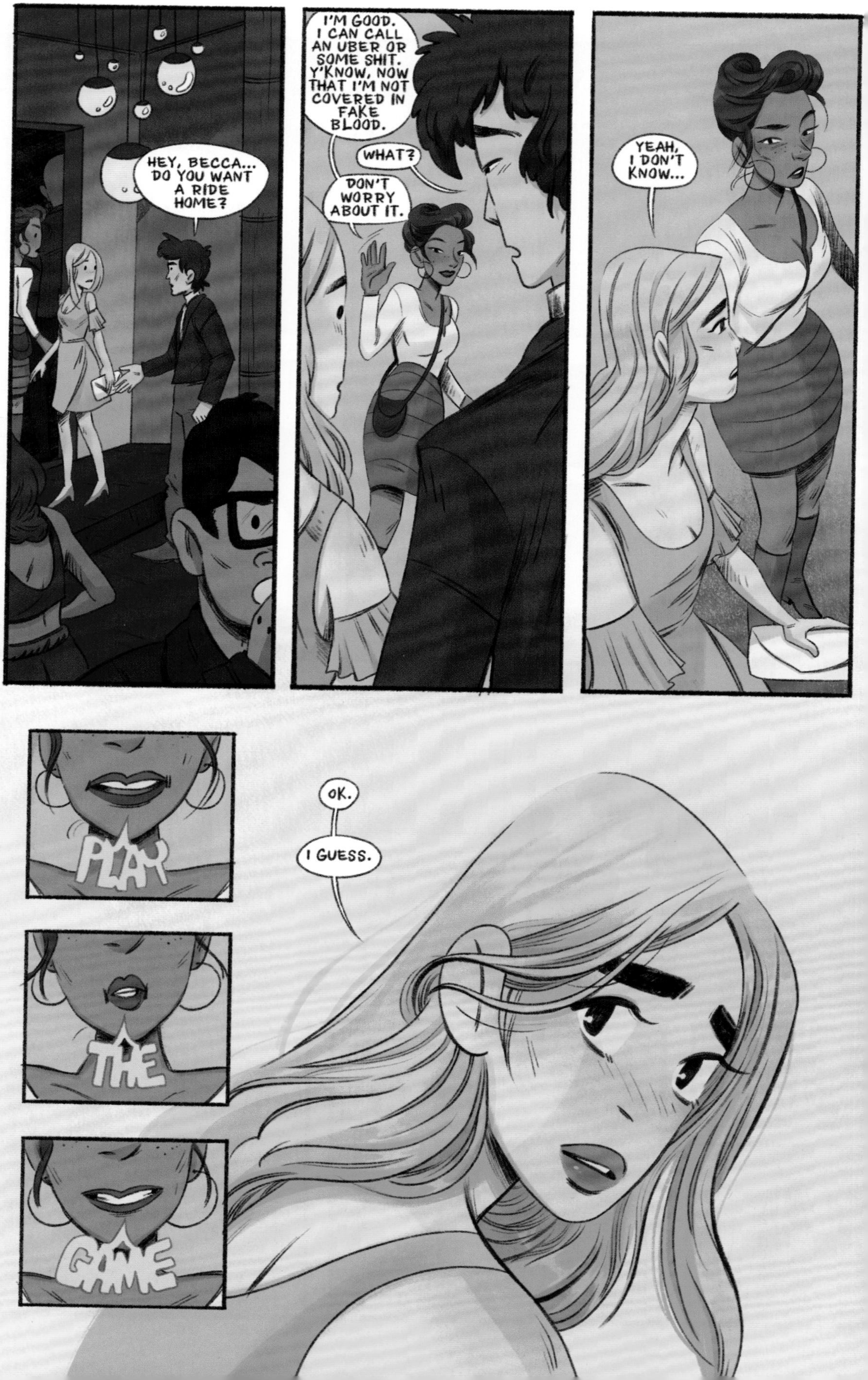
HEY, BECCA... DO YOU WANT A RIDE HOME?
I'M GOOD. I CAN CALL AN UBER OR SOME SHIT. Y'KNOW, NOW THAT I'M NOT COVERED IN FAKE BLOOD.
WHAT?
DON'T WORRY ABOUT IT.
YEAH, I DON'T KNOW...
PLAY
THE
GAME
OK.
I GUESS.

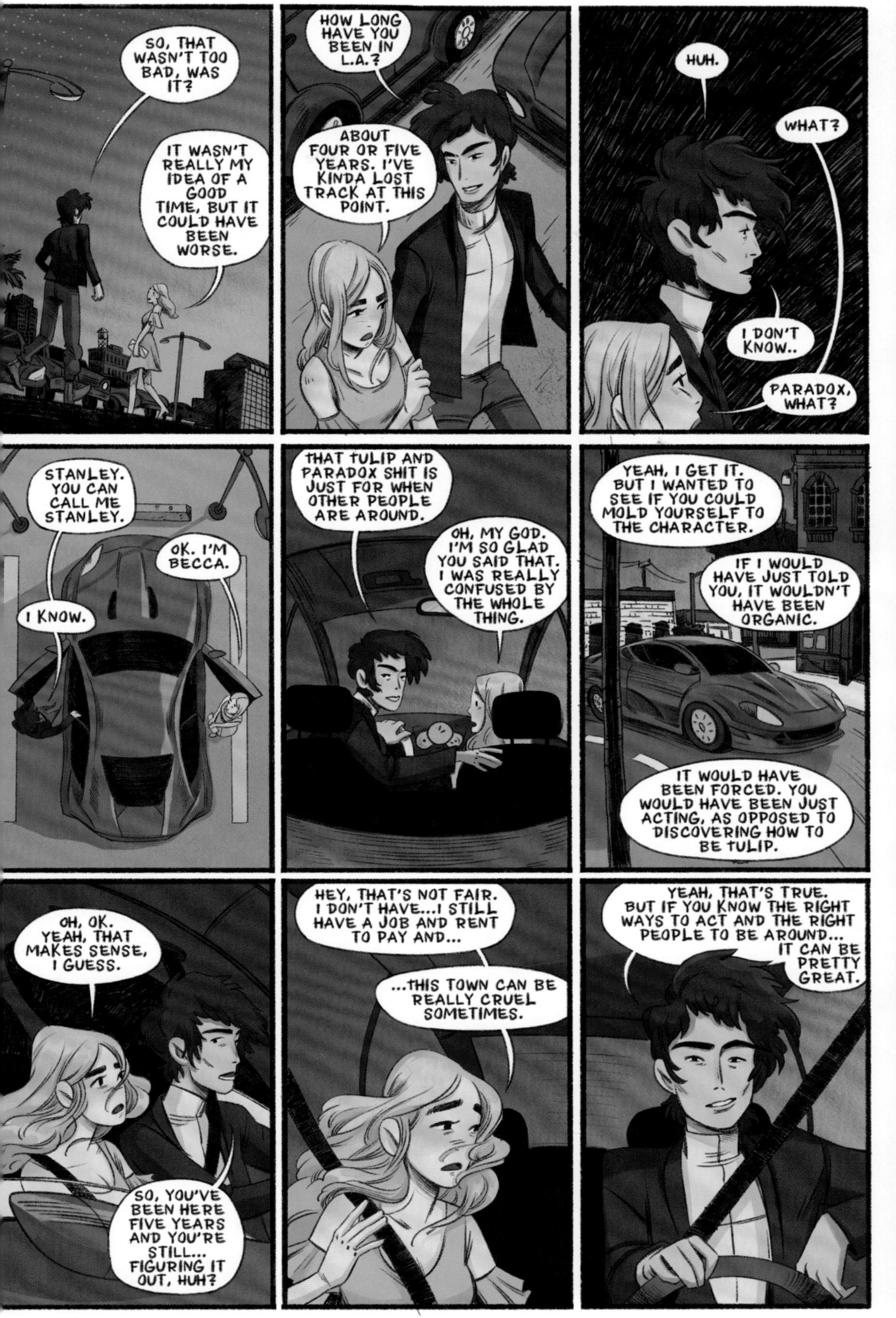
SO, THAT WASN'T TOO BAD, WAS IT?
IT WASN'T REALLY MY IDEA OF A GOOD TIME, BUT IT COULD HAVE BEEN WORSE.
HOW LONG HAVE YOU BEEN IN L.A.?
ABOUT FOUR OR FIVE YEARS. I'VE KINDA LOST TRACK AT THIS POINT.
HUH.
WHAT?
I DON'T KNOW..
PARADOX, WHAT?
STANLEY. YOU CAN CALL ME STANLEY.
OK. I'M BECCA.
I KNOW.
THAT TULIP AND PARADOX SHIT IS JUST FOR WHEN OTHER PEOPLE ARE AROUND.
OH, MY GOD. I'M SO GLAD YOU SAID THAT. I WAS REALLY CONFUSED BY THE WHOLE THING.
YEAH, I GET IT. BUT I WANTED TO SEE IF YOU COULD MOLD YOURSELF TO THE CHARACTER.
IF I WOULD HAVE JUST TOLD YOU, IT WOULDN'T HAVE BEEN ORGANIC.
IT WOULD HAVE BEEN FORCED. YOU WOULD HAVE BEEN JUST ACTING, AS OPPOSED TO DISCOVERING HOW TO BE TULIP.
OH, OK. YEAH, THAT MAKES SENSE, I GUESS.
SO, YOU'VE BEEN HERE FIVE YEARS AND YOU'RE STILL... FIGURING IT OUT, HUH?
HEY, THAT'S NOT FAIR. I DON'T HAVE...I STILL HAVE A JOB AND RENT TO PAY AND...
...THIS TOWN CAN BE REALLY CRUEL SOMETIMES.
YEAH, THAT'S TRUE. BUT IF YOU KNOW THE RIGHT WAYS TO ACT AND THE RIGHT PEOPLE TO BE AROUND...
IT CAN BE PRETTY GREAT.

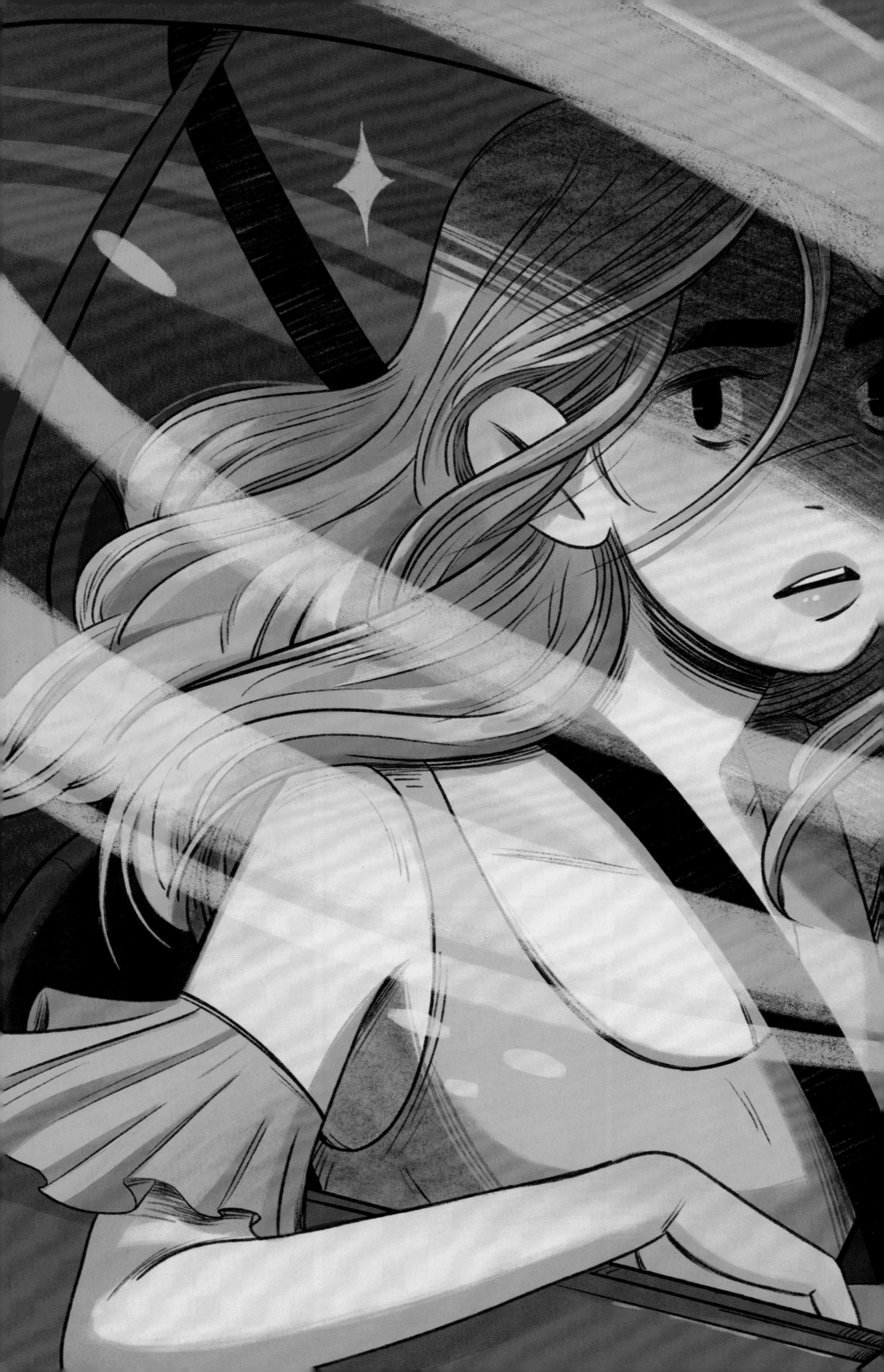

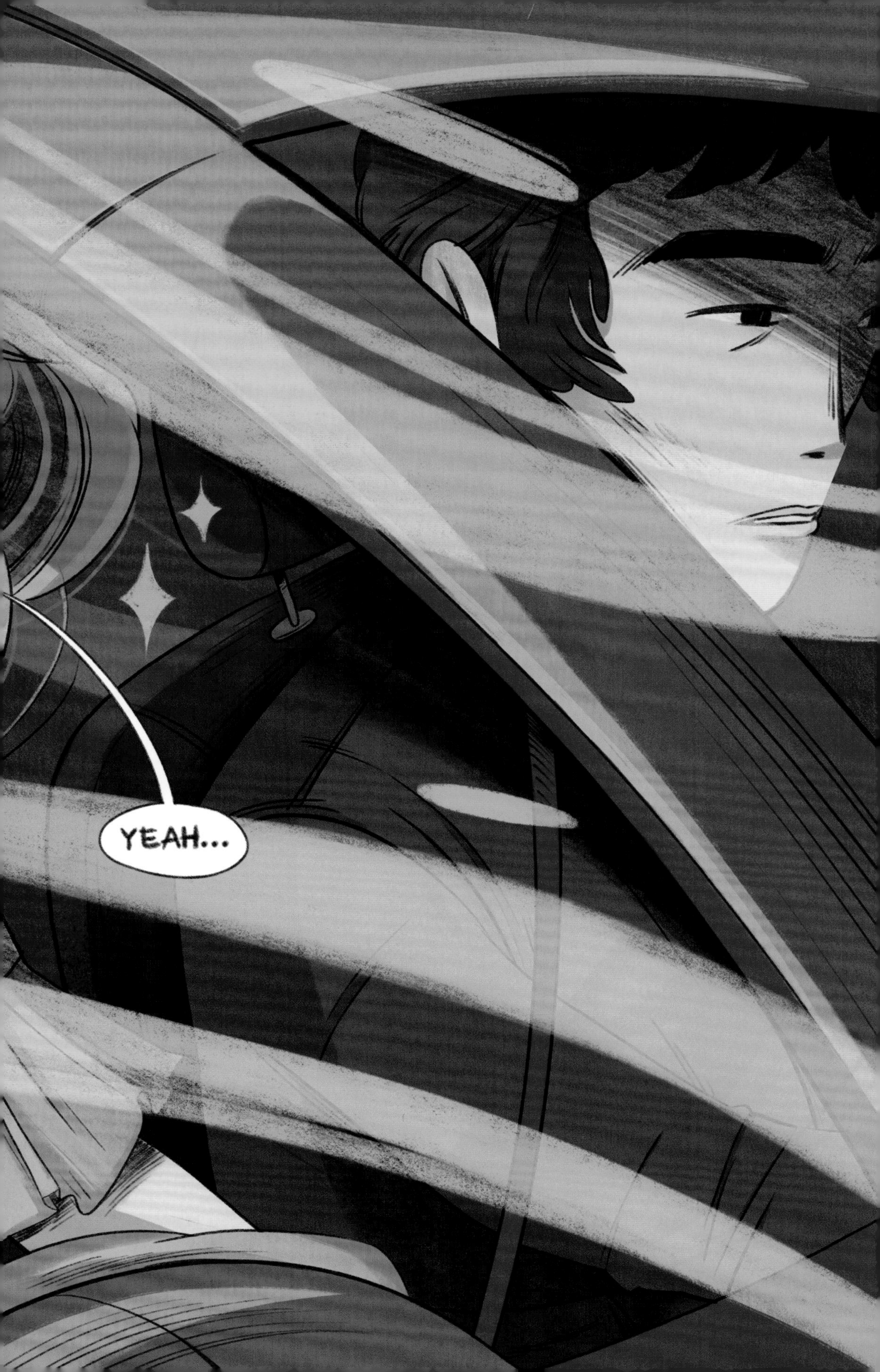
YEAH...

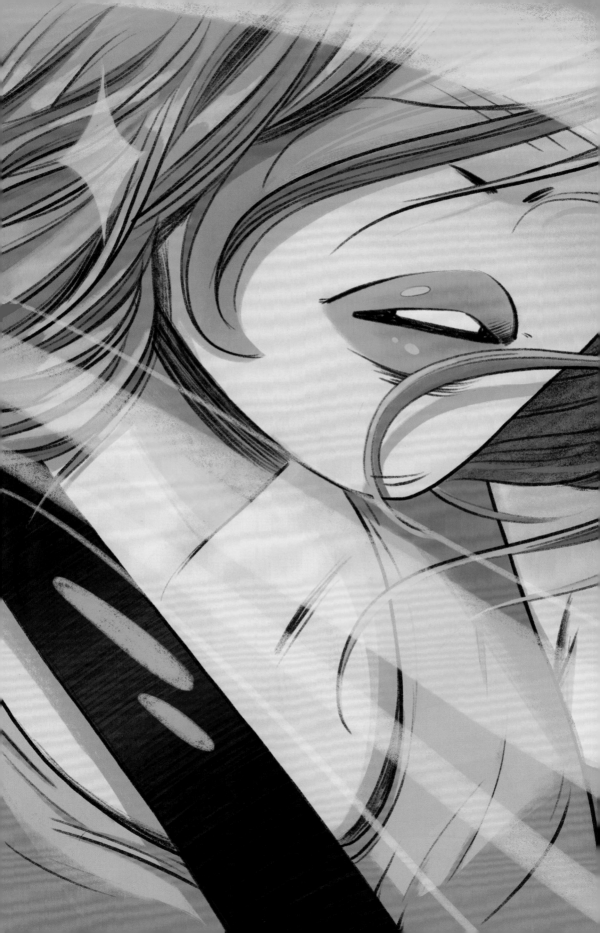

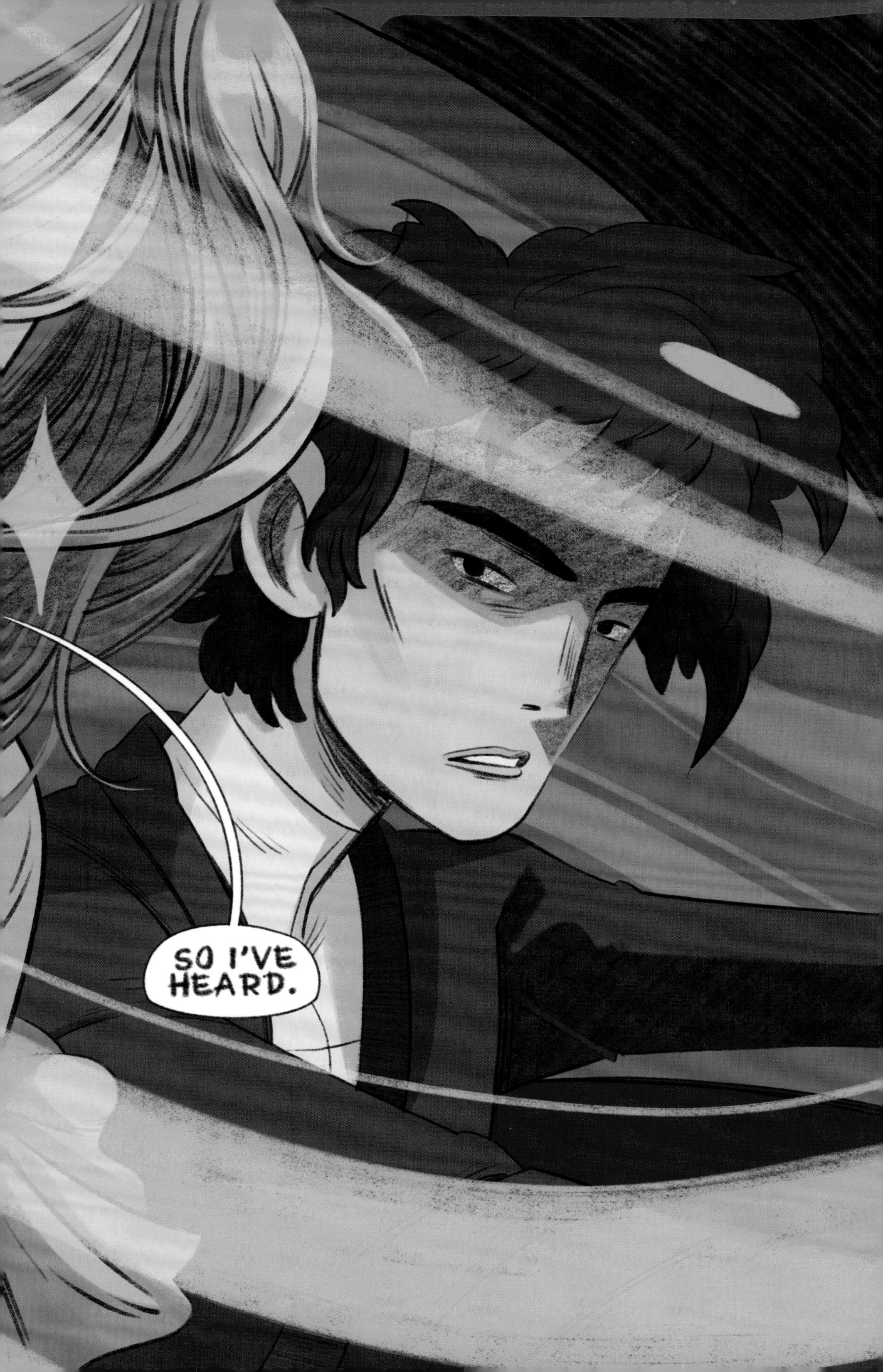
SO I'VE HEARD.

CHAPTER 3

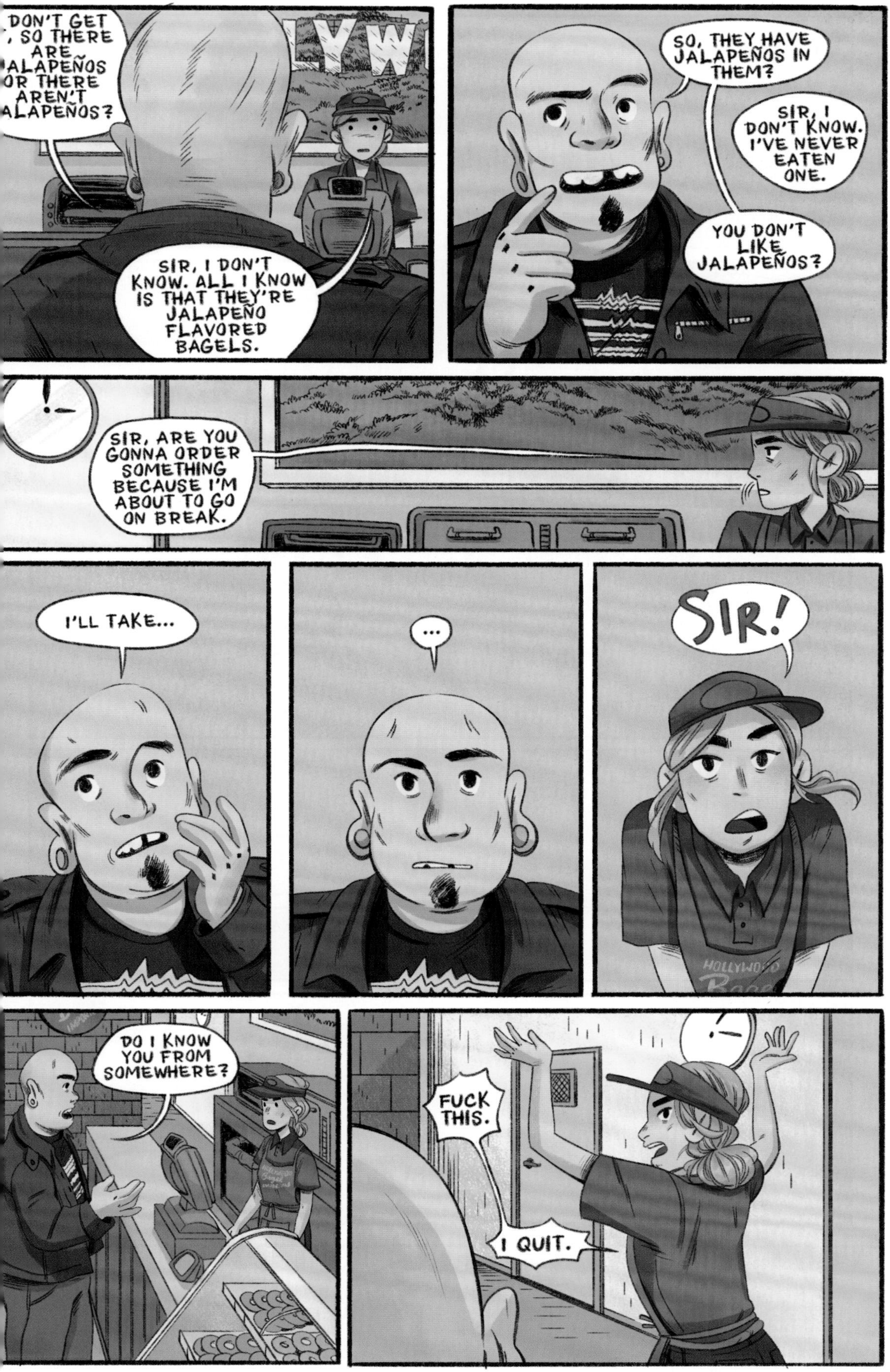
DON'T GET , SO THERE ARE ALAPEÑOS OR THERE AREN'T ALAPEÑOS?
SIR, I DON'T KNOW. ALL I KNOW IS THAT THEY'RE JALAPEÑO FLAVORED BAGELS.
SO, THEY HAVE JALAPEÑOS IN THEM?
SIR, I DON'T KNOW. I'VE NEVER EATEN ONE.
YOU DON'T LIKE JALAPEÑOS?
SIR, ARE YOU GONNA ORDER SOMETHING BECAUSE I'M ABOUT TO GO ON BREAK.
I'LL TAKE...
...
SIR!
DO I KNOW YOU FROM SOMEWHERE?
FUCK THIS.
I QUIT.

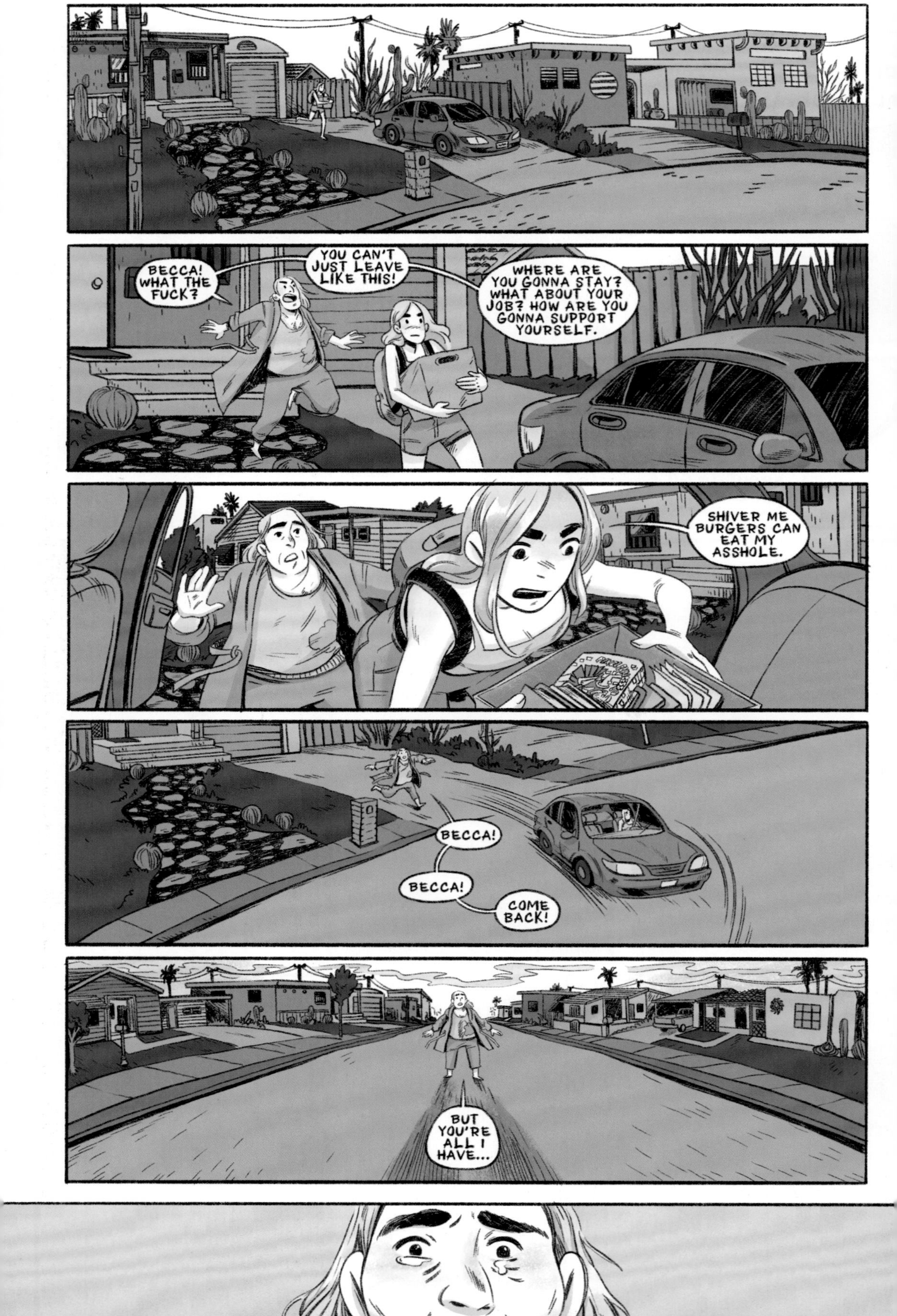

BECCA! WHAT THE FUCK?
YOU CAN'T JUST LEAVE LIKE THIS!
WHERE ARE YOU GONNA STAY? WHAT ABOUT YOUR JOB? HOW ARE YOU GONNA SUPPORT YOURSELF.
SHIVER ME BURGERS CAN EAT MY ASSHOLE.
BECCA!
BECCA!
COME BACK!
BUT YOU'RE ALL I HAVE...

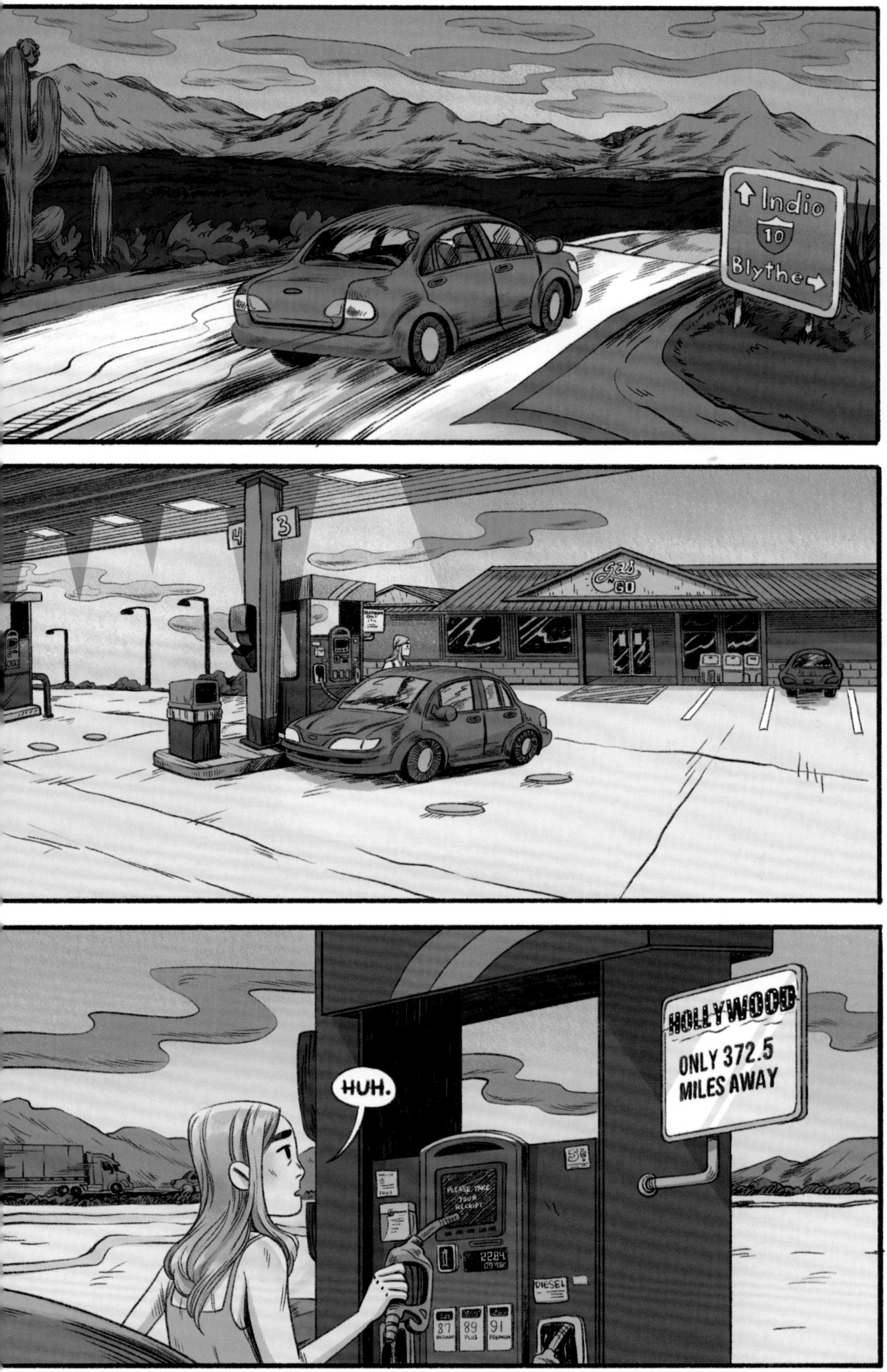
Indio
10
Blythe
4
3
GO
HUH.
HOLLYWOOD
ONLY 372.5
MILES AWAY
PLEASE TAKE YOUR RECEIPT
DIESEL
87
89
91

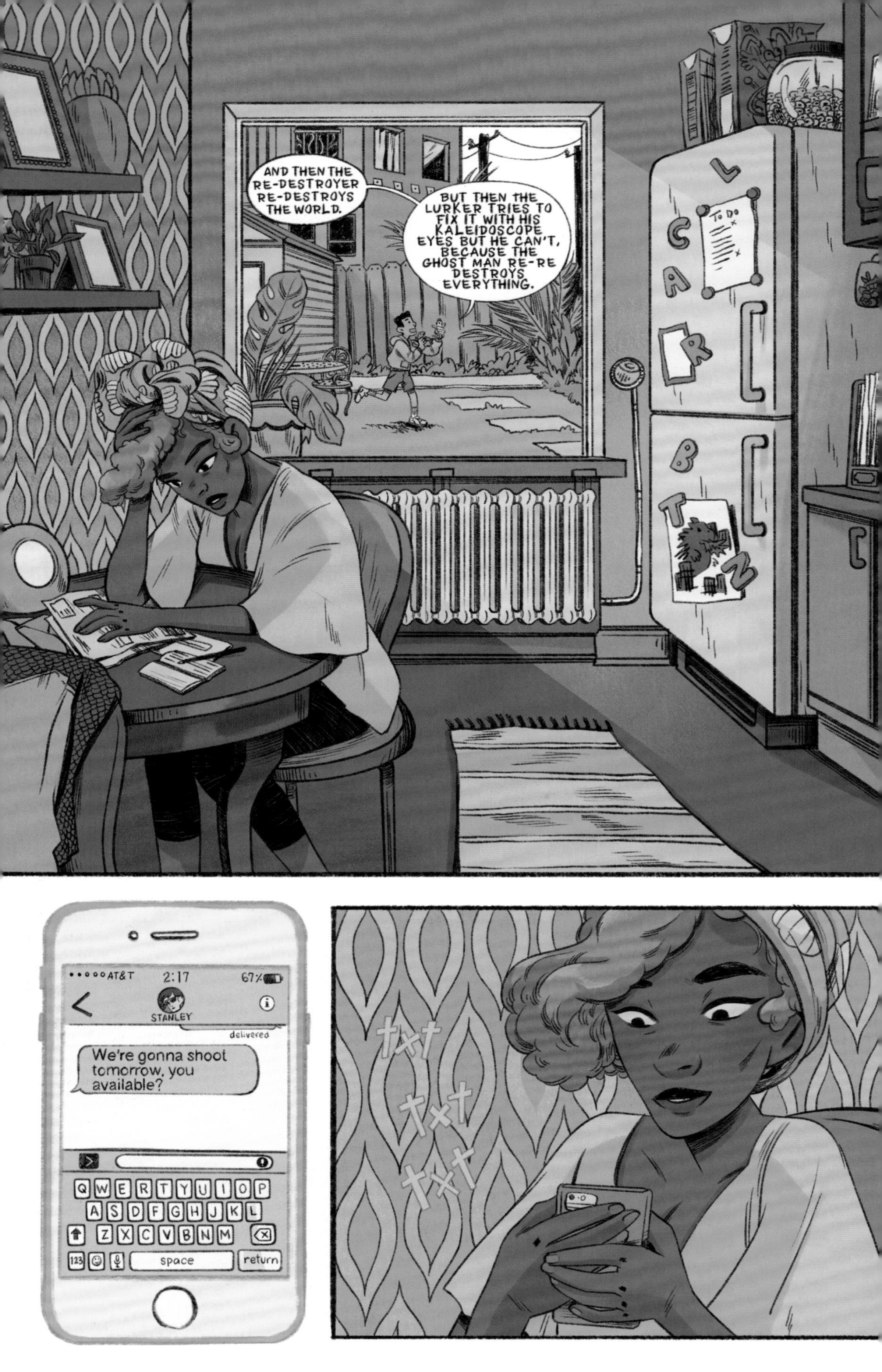
AND THEN THE RE-DESTROYER RE-DESTROYS THE WORLD.
BUT THEN THE LURKER TRIES TO FIX IT WITH HIS KALEIDOSCOPE EYES BUT HE CAN'T, BECAUSE THE GHOST MAN RE-RE DESTROYS EVERYTHING.
TO DO
•••••AT&T 2:17 67%
STANLEY
delivered
We're gonna shoot tomorrow, you available?
QWERTYUIOP
ASDFGHJKL
ZXCVBNM
123 space return
txt
txt
txt

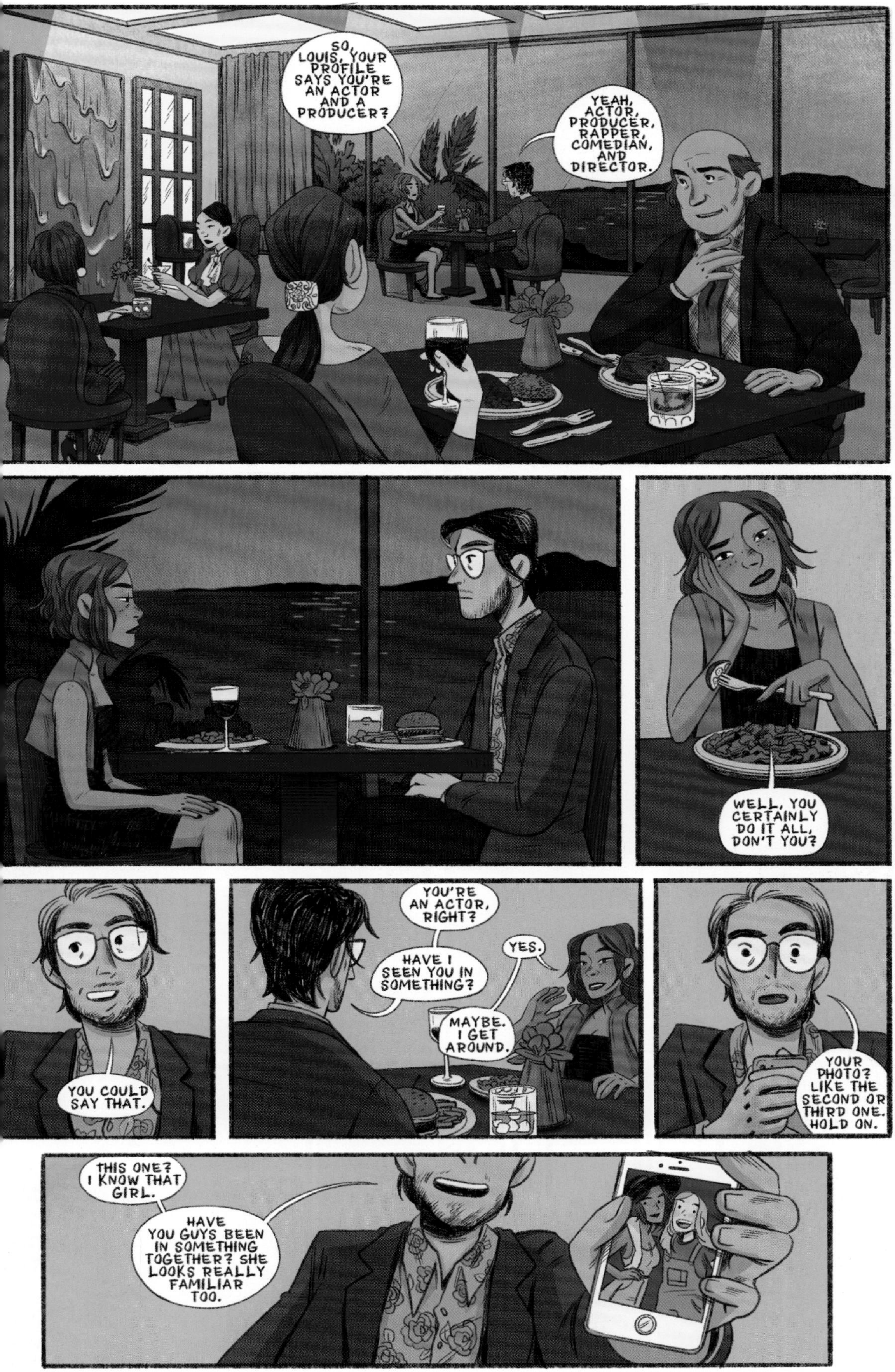
SO, LOUIS, YOUR PROFILE SAYS YOU'RE AN ACTOR AND A PRODUCER?
YEAH, ACTOR, PRODUCER, RAPPER, COMEDIAN, AND DIRECTOR.
WELL, YOU CERTAINLY DO IT ALL, DON'T YOU?
YOU COULD SAY THAT.
YOU'RE AN ACTOR, RIGHT?
HAVE I SEEN YOU IN SOMETHING?
YES.
MAYBE. I GET AROUND.
YOUR PHOTO? LIKE THE SECOND OR THIRD ONE. HOLD ON.
THIS ONE? I KNOW THAT GIRL.
HAVE YOU GUYS BEEN IN SOMETHING TOGETHER? SHE LOOKS REALLY FAMILIAR TOO.

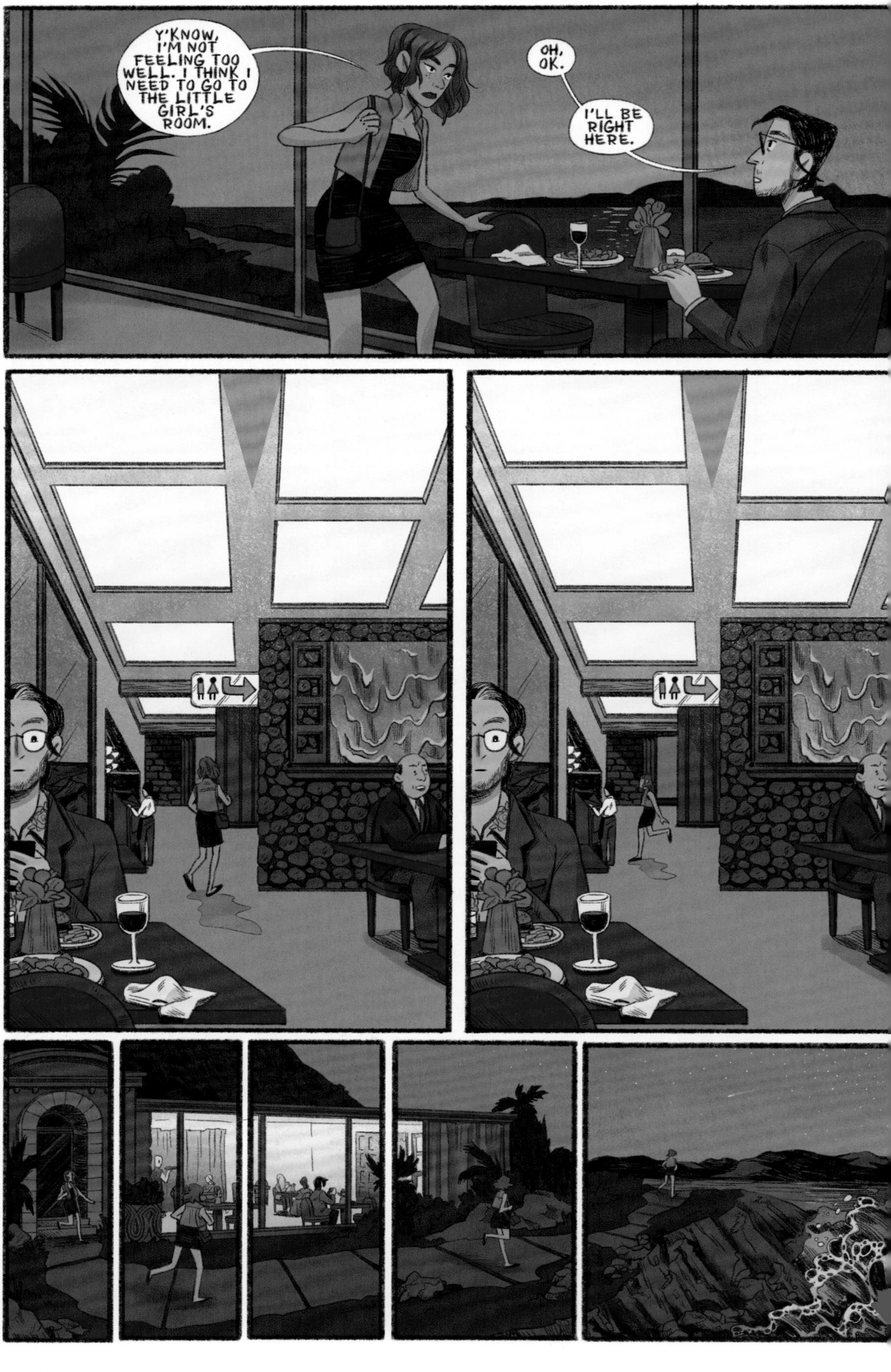
Y'KNOW, I'M NOT FEELING TOO WELL. I THINK I NEED TO GO TO THE LITTLE GIRL'S ROOM.
OH, OK.
I'LL BE RIGHT HERE.

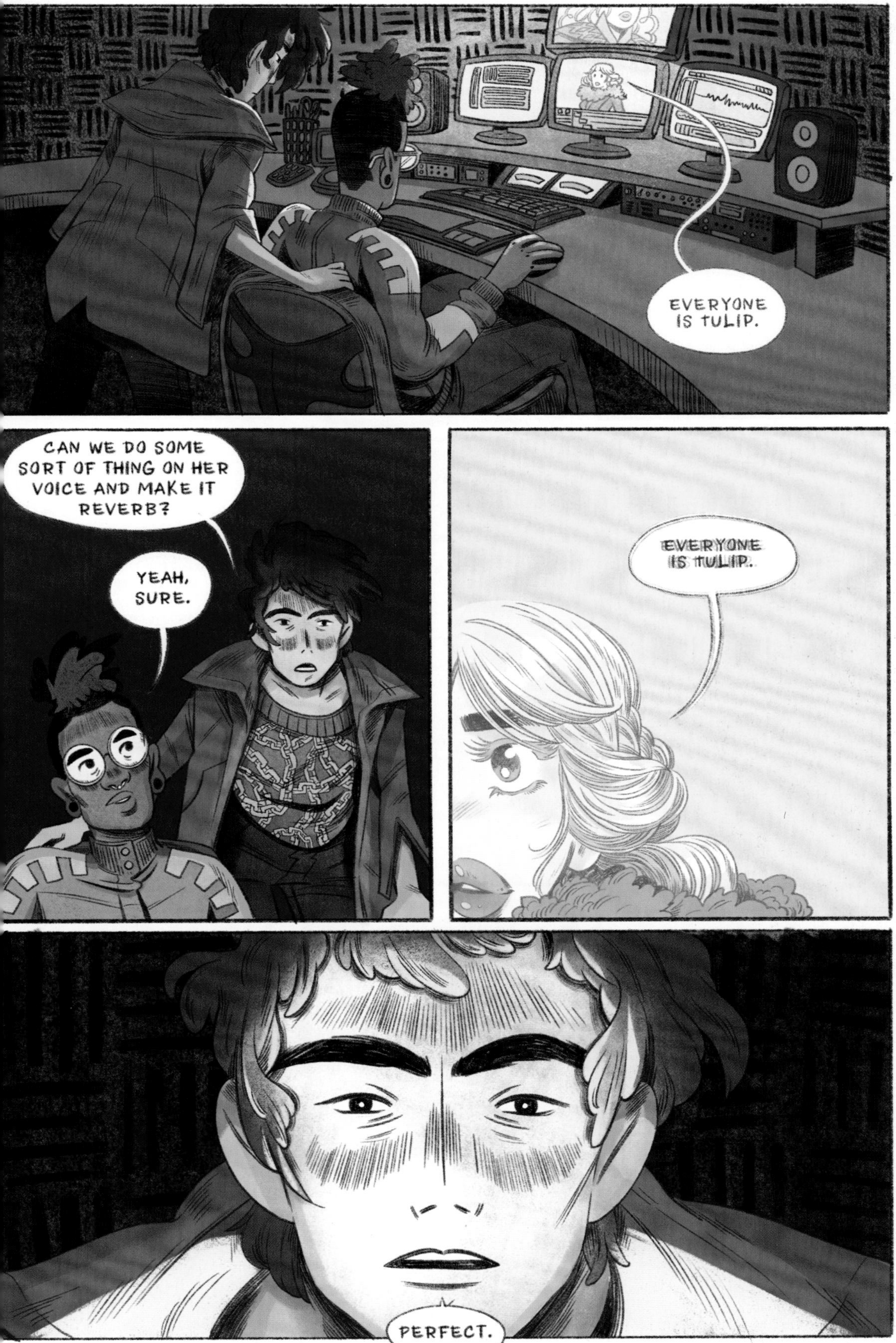
EVERYONE IS TULIP.
CAN WE DO SOME SORT OF THING ON HER VOICE AND MAKE IT REVERB?
YEAH, SURE.
EVERYONE IS TULIP.
PERFECT.

2:24 2:43
Add a public comment
Has anyone ever noticed that Tulip has like massive wrists? #wristfatty
Moonbeam • 4 days ago
Dude I would totally fuck her
Yolobrolo • 3 days ago
Tulip is a god
QT_king • 3 days ago
S_E_X_Y
Demondiaz • 2 days ago
2:24 2:43
S_E_X_Y
Demondiaz • 2 days ago
Haha #wristfatty I'll be your #wristdaddy
Stwabury • 2 days ago
Bruh her wrists are gross
Valazzy • 2 days ago
I wouldn't fuck her wrists, even if you paid me.
Beb segget • 3 days ago
2:24 2:43
Everyone hates #writsfatty.
KendoBox • 3 days ago
Has there ever been a person with wrists as fat as #EveryoneisWristfatty?
Lexxxi • 3 days ago
I hate people with fat wrists.
UrMom • 3 days ago
fuck fat wrists
Ihatemundayz • 3 days ago
2:24 2:43
fuck fat wrists
Ihatemundayz • 3 days ago
I think her wrists look normal.
Gmr_boiz • 4 days ago
2.4K
I just developed a wrist fetish.
LavaGuy • 4 days ago
#wristfatty

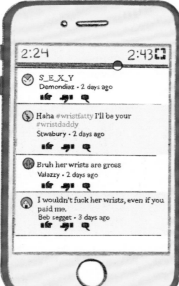

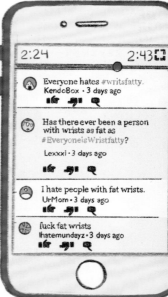

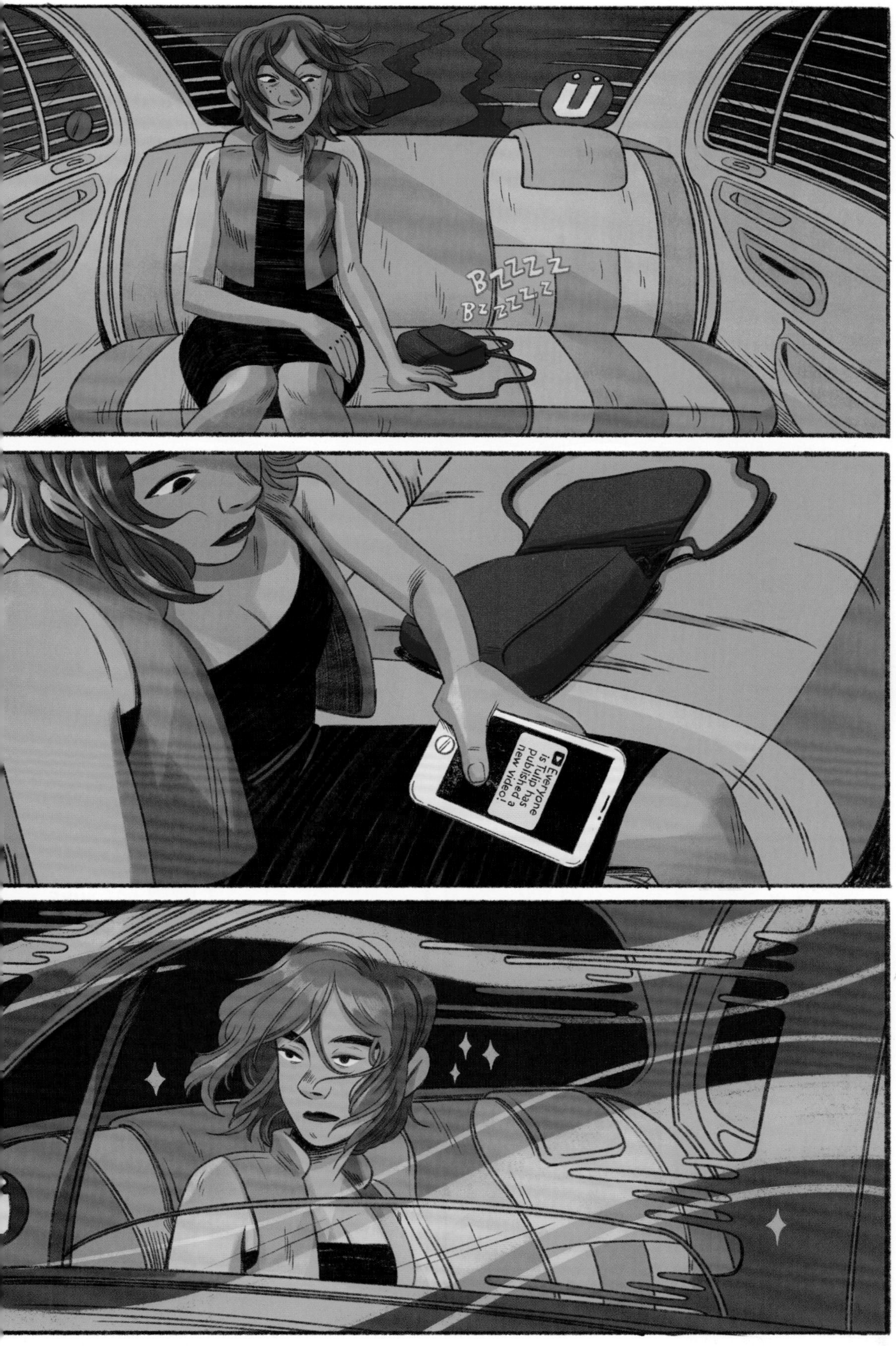
Bzzzz
Bzzzzz
Everyone is Tulip has published a new video!

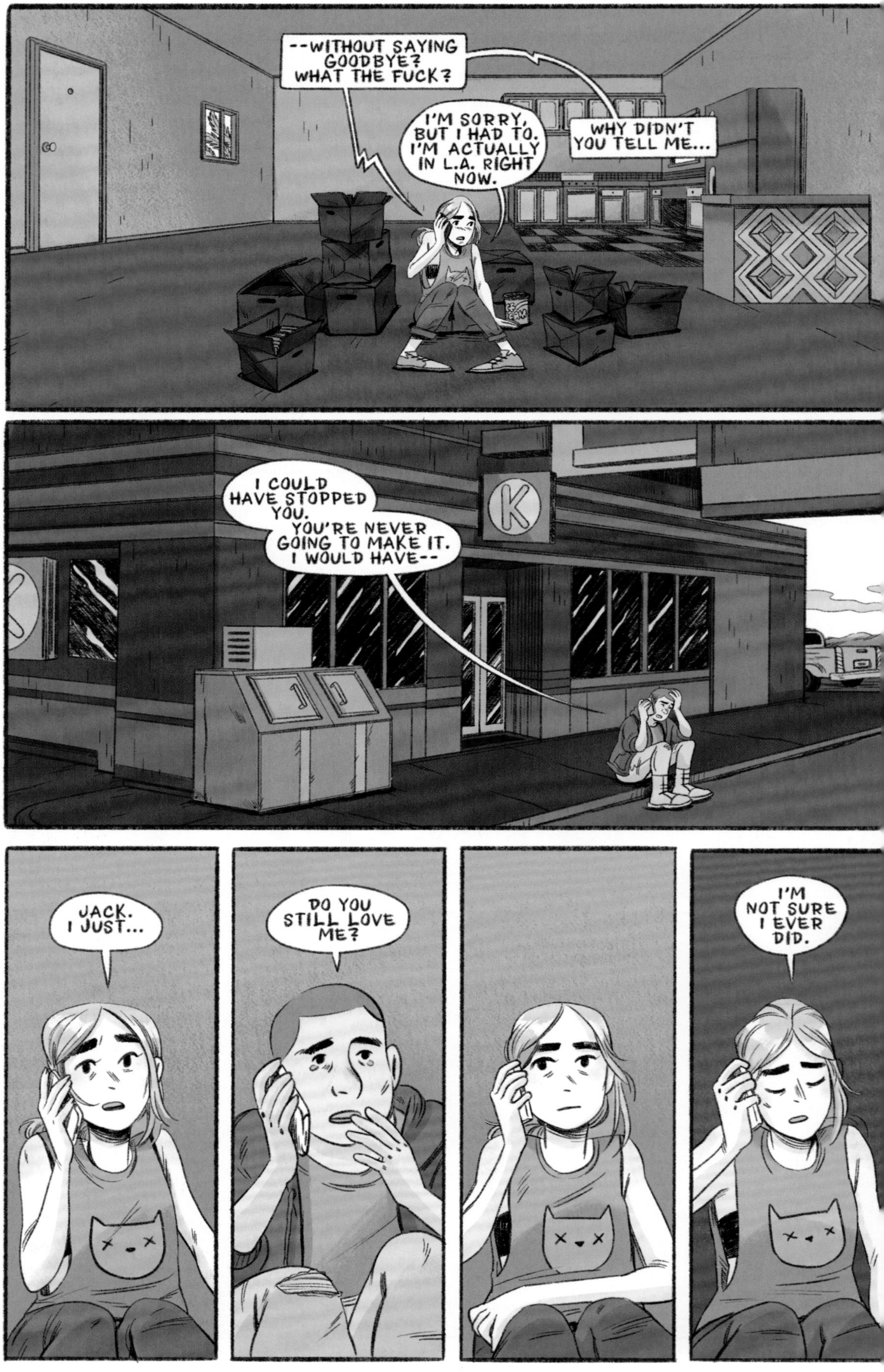
--WITHOUT SAYING GOODBYE? WHAT THE FUCK?
I'M SORRY, BUT I HAD TO. I'M ACTUALLY IN L.A. RIGHT NOW.
WHY DIDN'T YOU TELL ME...
I COULD HAVE STOPPED YOU.
YOU'RE NEVER GOING TO MAKE IT. I WOULD HAVE--
JACK. I JUST...
DO YOU STILL LOVE ME?
I'M NOT SURE I EVER DID.

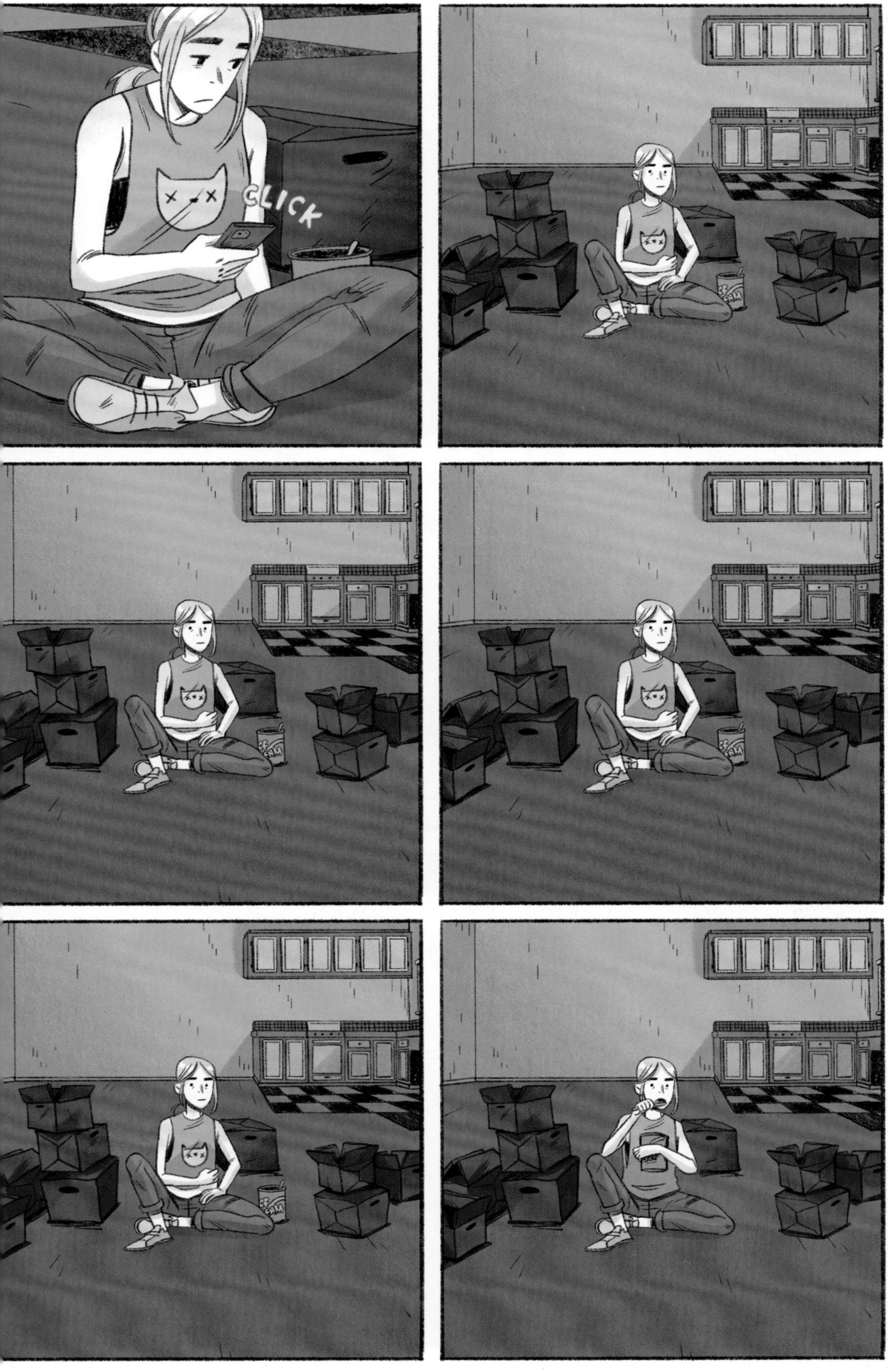
CLICK

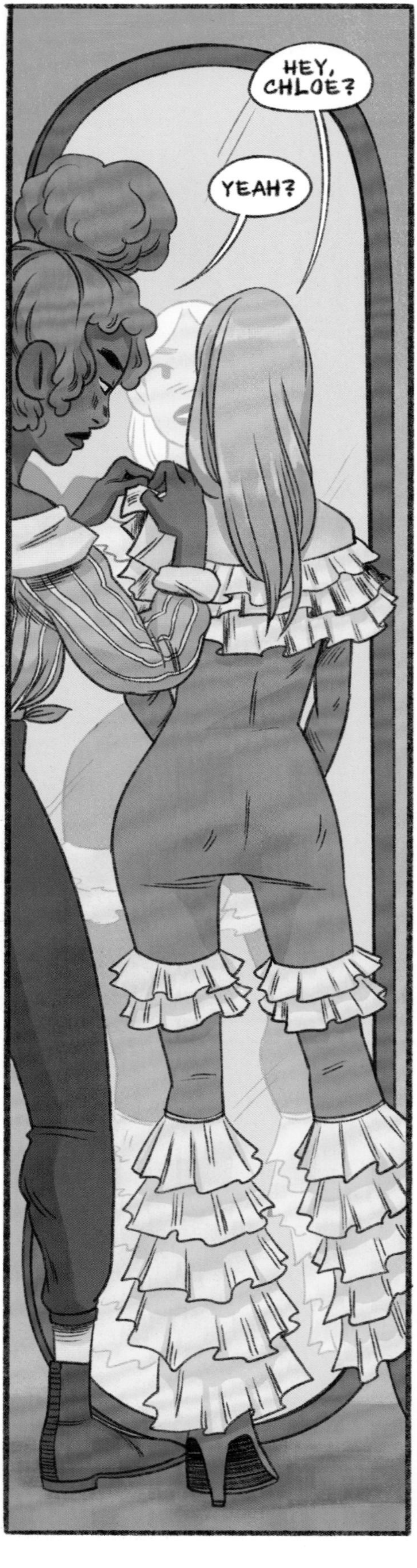
HEY, CHLOE?
YEAH?

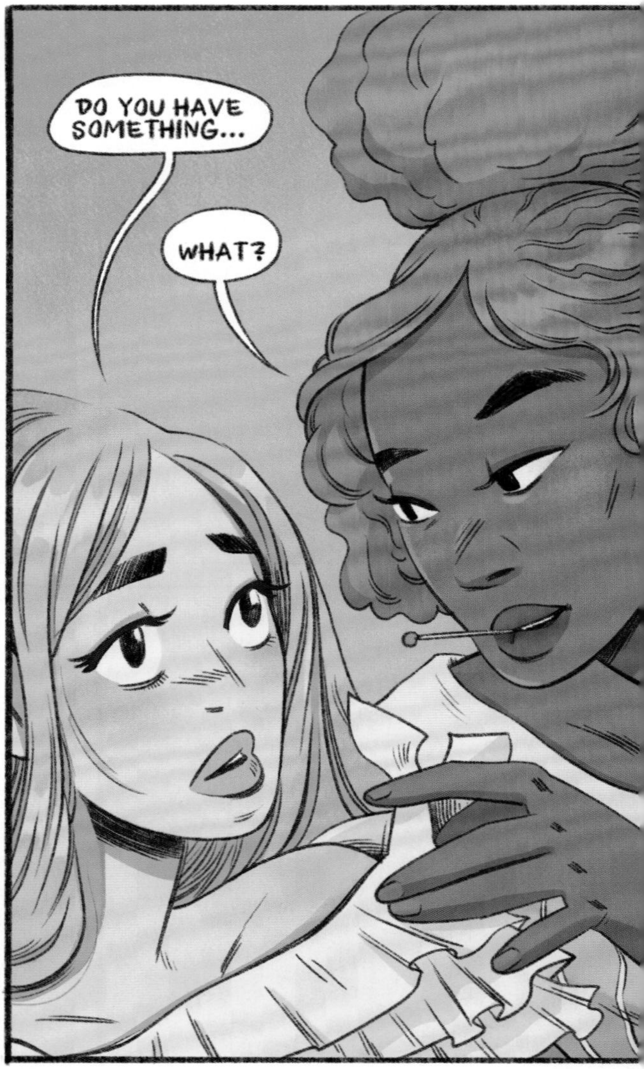
DO YOU HAVE SOMETHING...
WHAT?

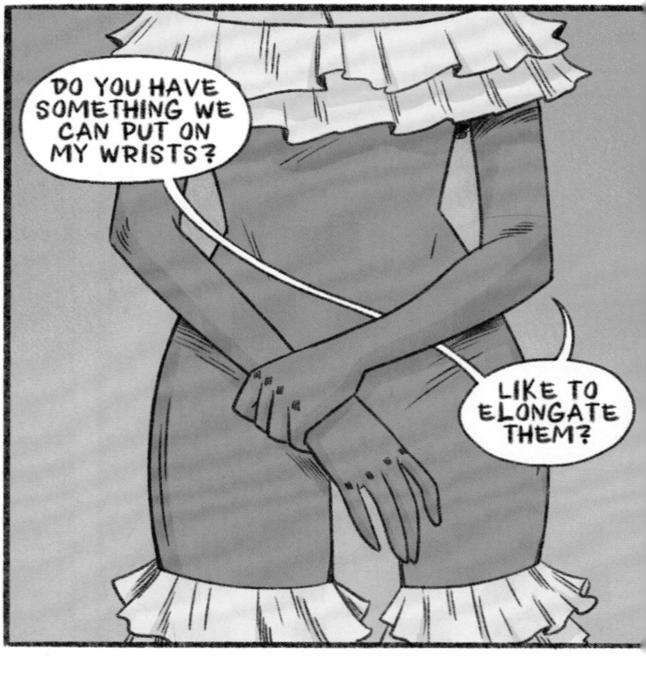
DO YOU HAVE SOMETHING WE CAN PUT ON MY WRISTS?
LIKE TO ELONGATE THEM?

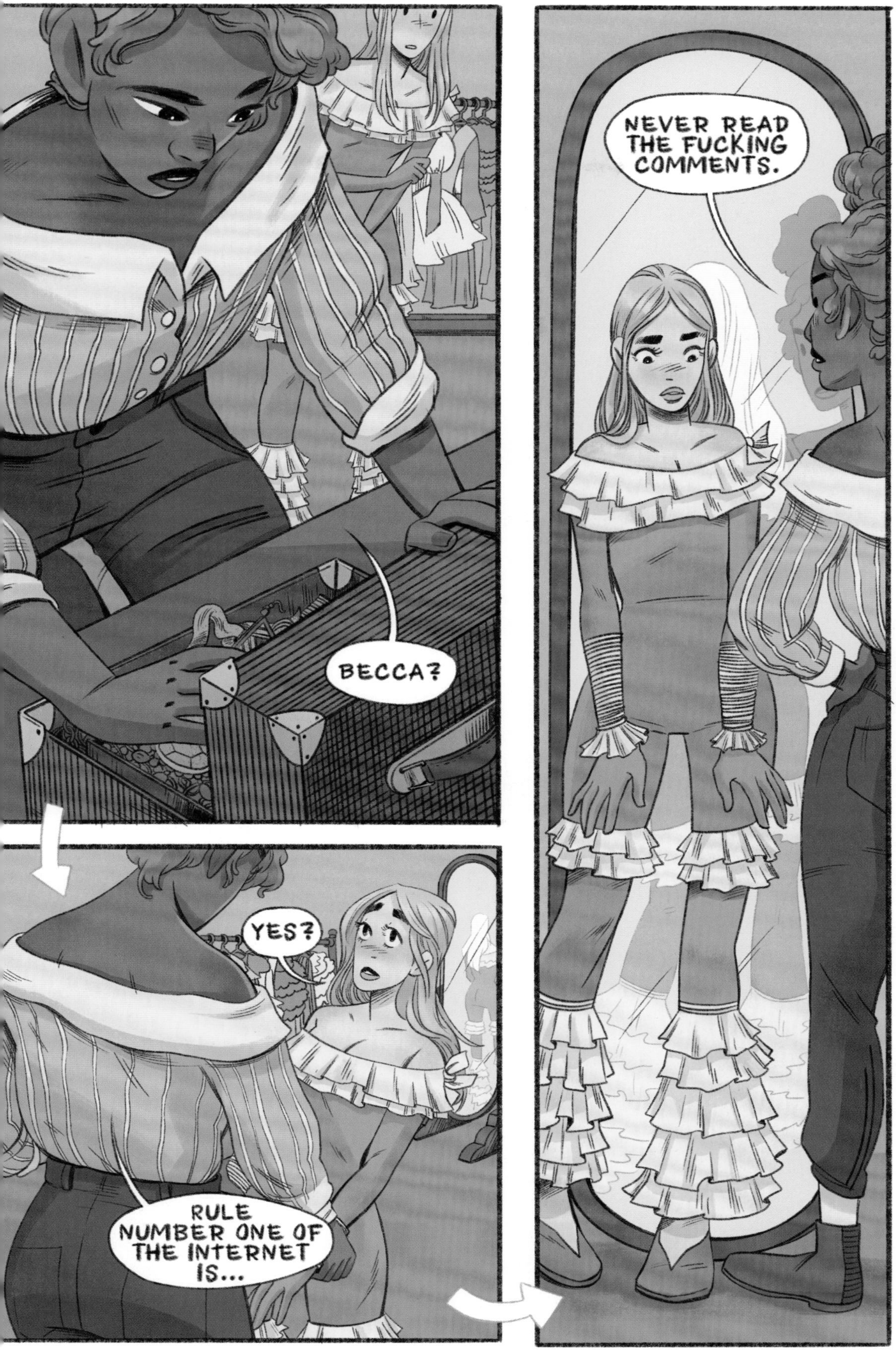
BECCA?
YES?
RULE NUMBER ONE OF THE INTERNET IS...
NEVER READ THE FUCKING COMMENTS.

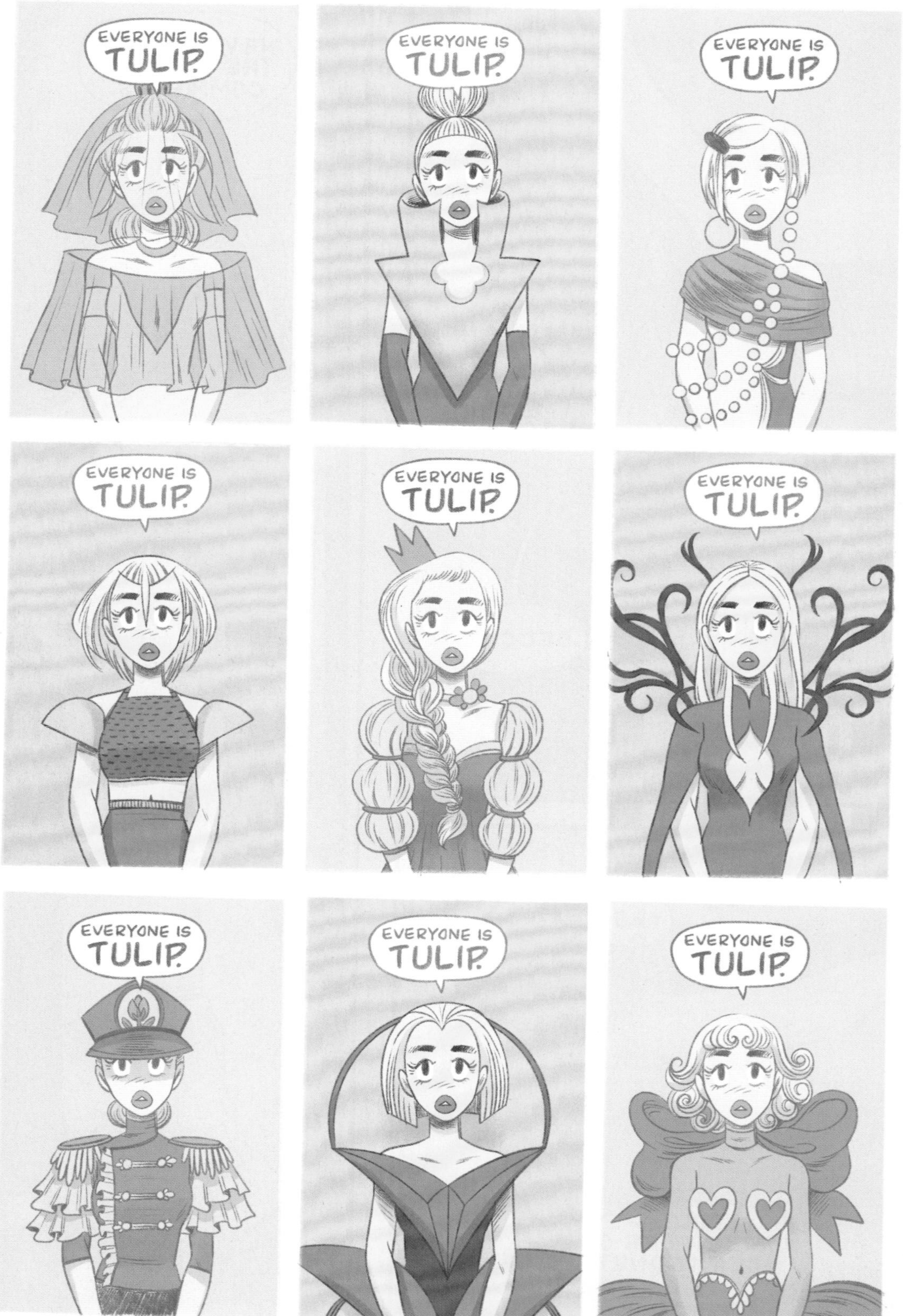
EVERYONE IS TULIP.
EVERYONE IS TULIP.
EVERYONE IS TULIP.
EVERYONE IS TULIP.
EVERYONE IS TULIP.
EVERYONE IS TULIP.
EVERYONE IS TULIP.
EVERYONE IS TULIP.
EVERYONE IS TULIP.

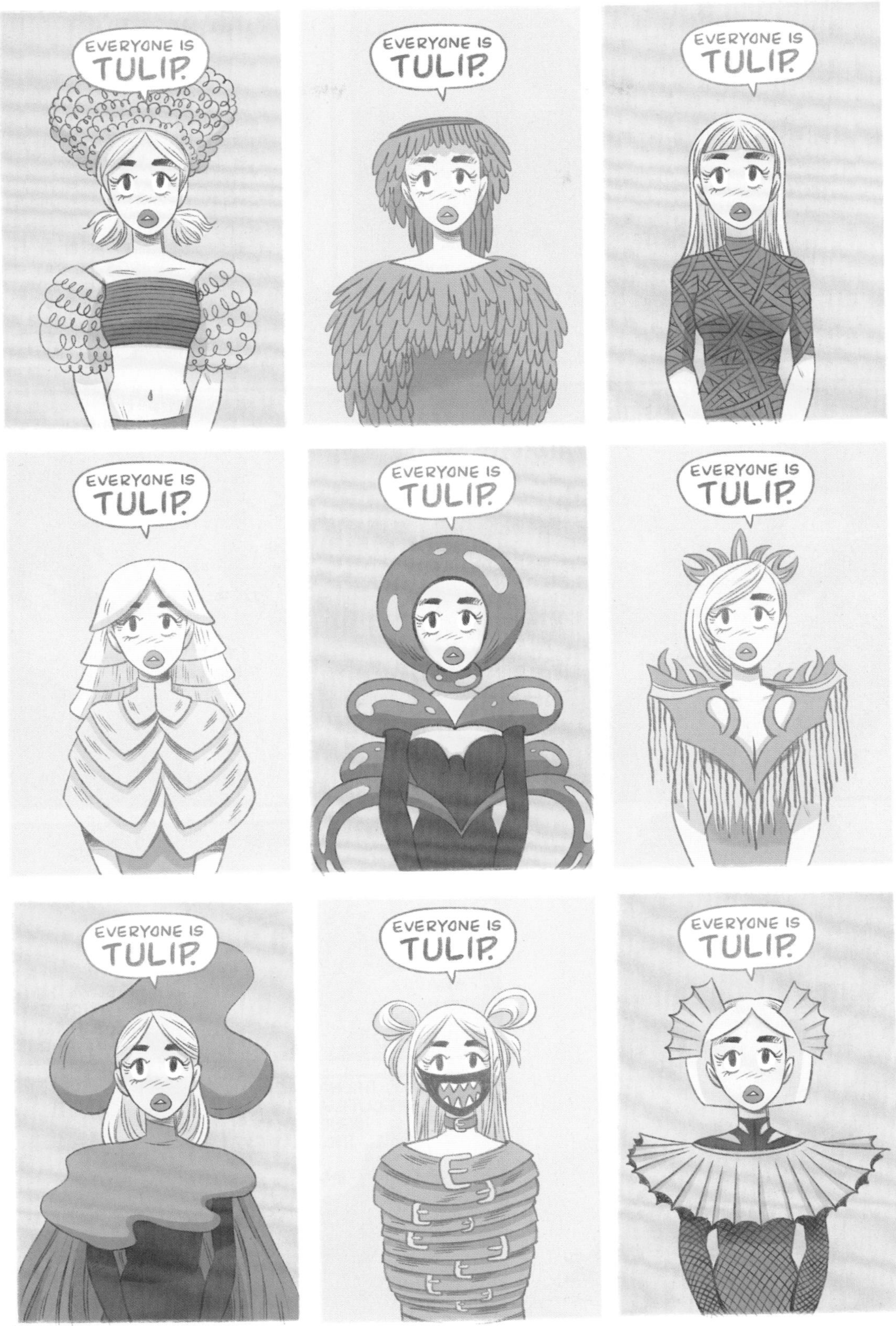
EVERYONE IS TULIP.
EVERYONE IS TULIP.
EVERYONE IS TULIP.
EVERYONE IS TULIP.
EVERYONE IS TULIP.
EVERYONE IS TULIP.
EVERYONE IS TULIP.
EVERYONE IS TULIP.
EVERYONE IS TULIP.

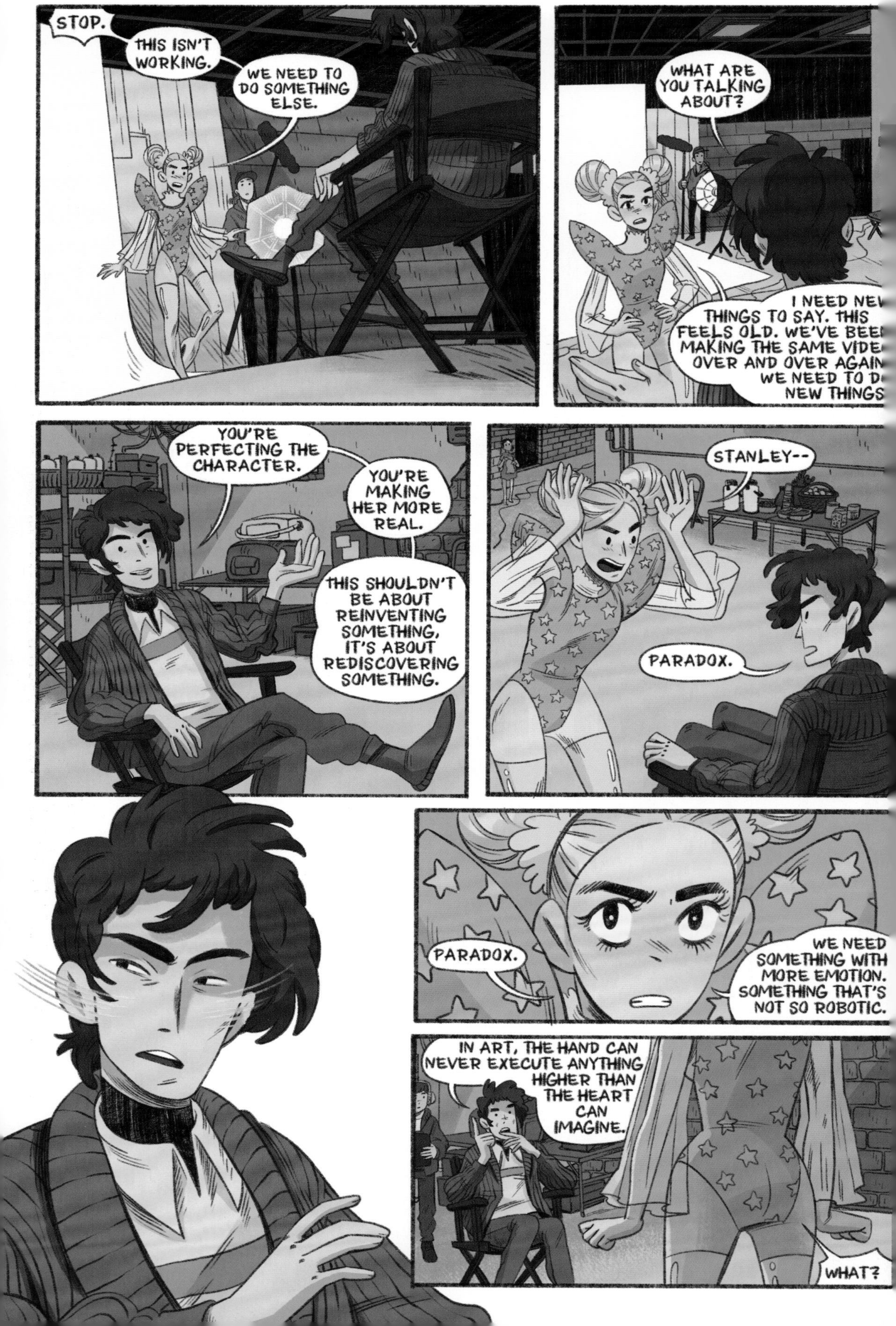
STOP.
THIS ISN'T WORKING.
WE NEED TO DO SOMETHING ELSE.
WHAT ARE YOU TALKING ABOUT?
I NEED NEW THINGS TO SAY. THIS FEELS OLD. WE'VE BEEN MAKING THE SAME VIDEO OVER AND OVER AGAIN. WE NEED TO DO NEW THINGS.
YOU'RE PERFECTING THE CHARACTER.
YOU'RE MAKING HER MORE REAL.
THIS SHOULDN'T BE ABOUT REINVENTING SOMETHING, IT'S ABOUT REDISCOVERING SOMETHING.
STANLEY--
PARADOX.
PARADOX.
WE NEED SOMETHING WITH MORE EMOTION. SOMETHING THAT'S NOT SO ROBOTIC.
IN ART, THE HAND CAN NEVER EXECUTE ANYTHING HIGHER THAN THE HEART CAN IMAGINE.
WHAT?

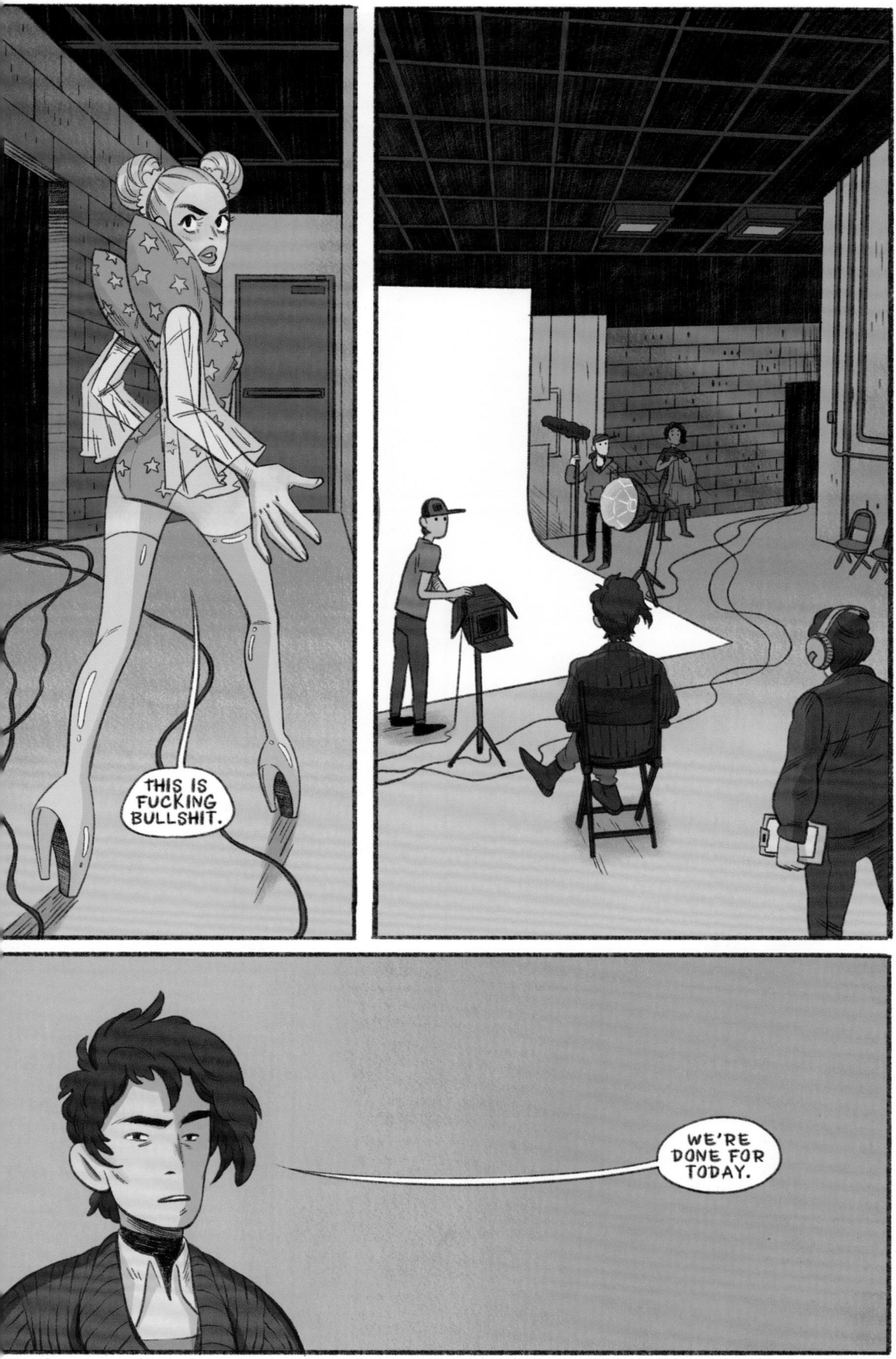
THIS IS FUCKING BULLSHIT.
WE'RE DONE FOR TODAY.

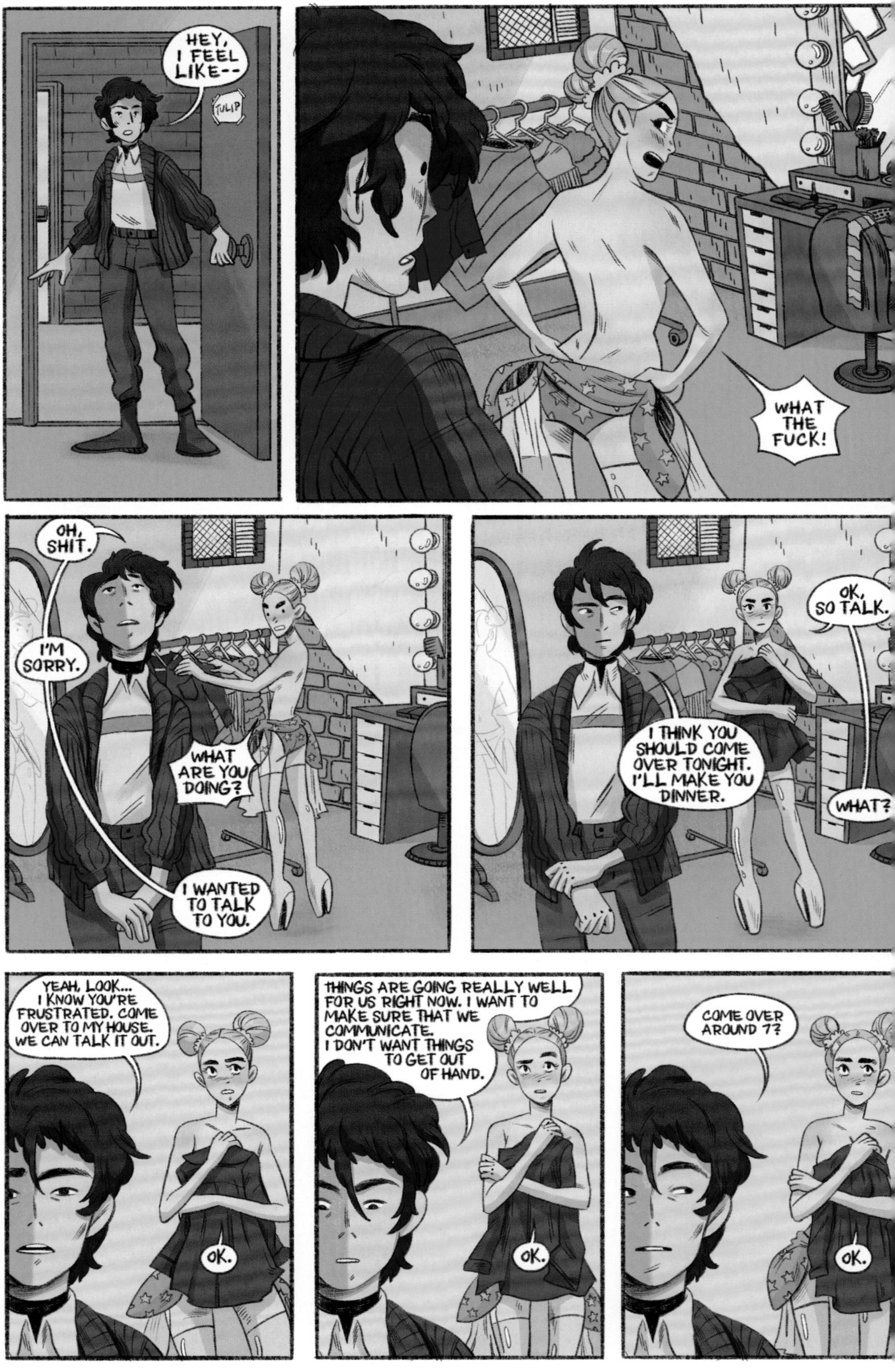
HEY, I FEEL LIKE--
TULIP?
WHAT THE FUCK!
OH, SHIT.
I'M SORRY.
WHAT ARE YOU DOING?
I WANTED TO TALK TO YOU.
OK, SO TALK.
I THINK YOU SHOULD COME OVER TONIGHT. I'LL MAKE YOU DINNER.
WHAT?
YEAH, LOOK... I KNOW YOU'RE FRUSTRATED. COME OVER TO MY HOUSE. WE CAN TALK IT OUT.
OK.
THINGS ARE GOING REALLY WELL FOR US RIGHT NOW. I WANT TO MAKE SURE THAT WE COMMUNICATE. I DON'T WANT THINGS TO GET OUT OF HAND.
OK.
COME OVER AROUND 7?
OK.

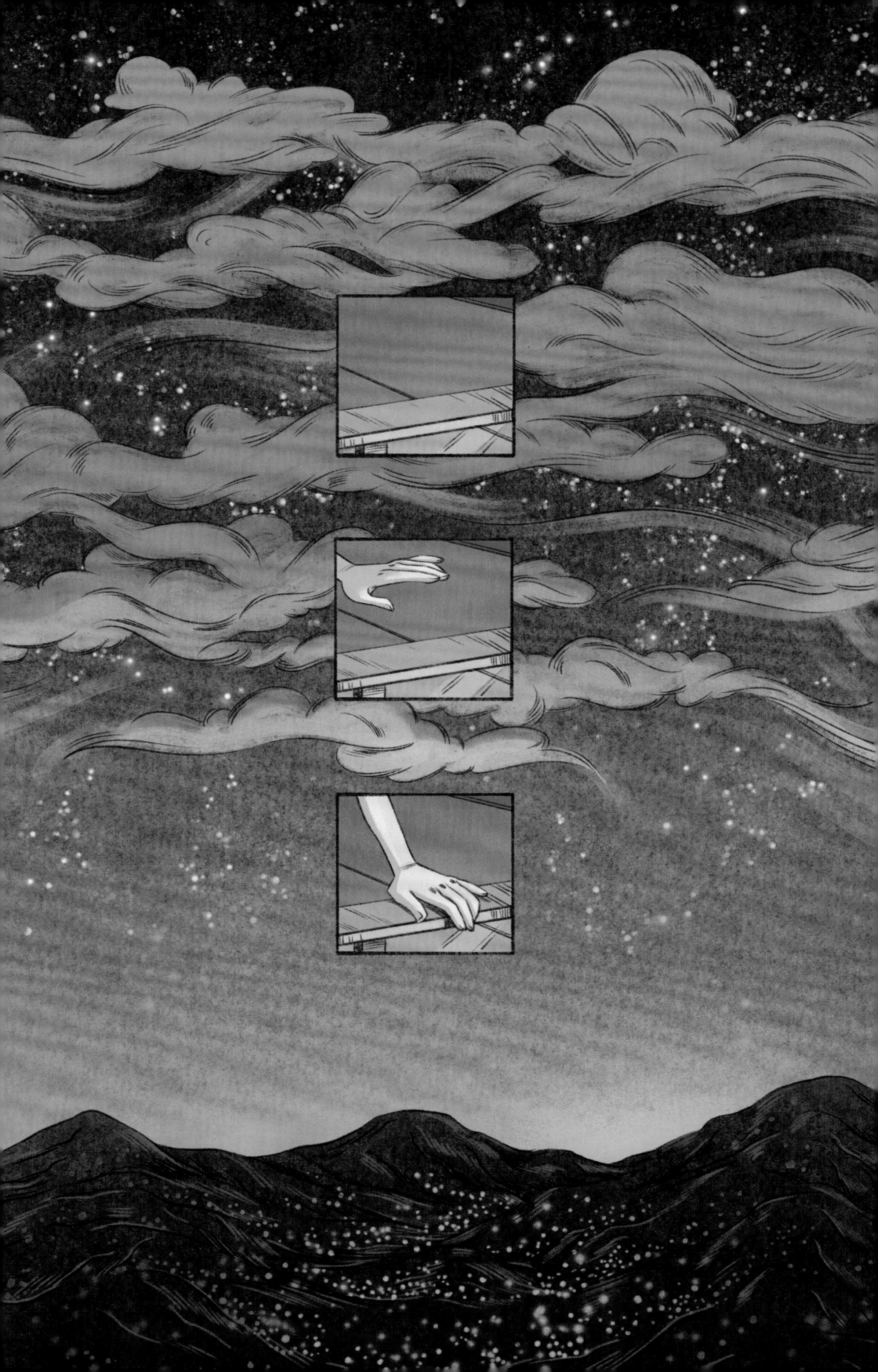

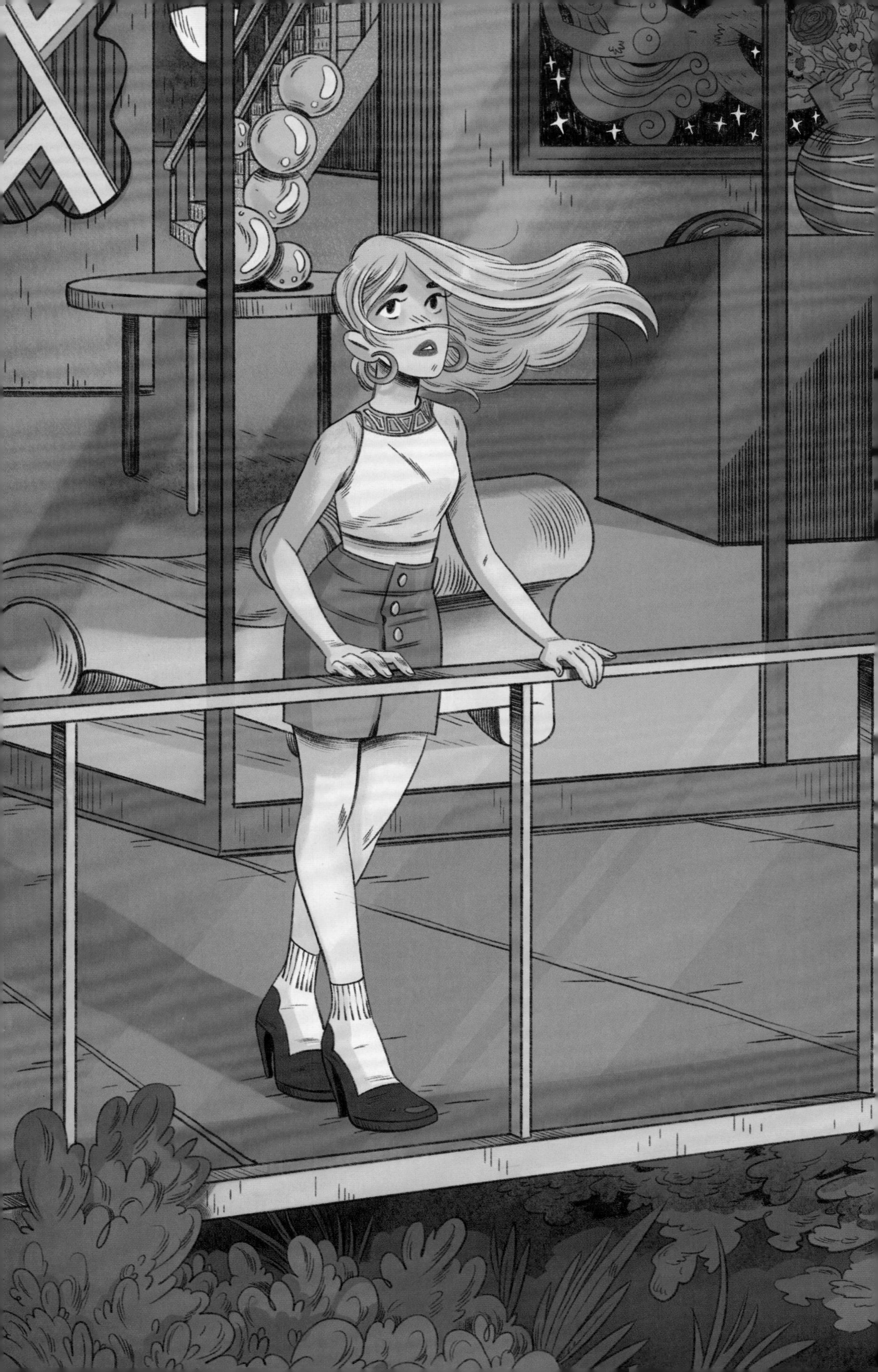

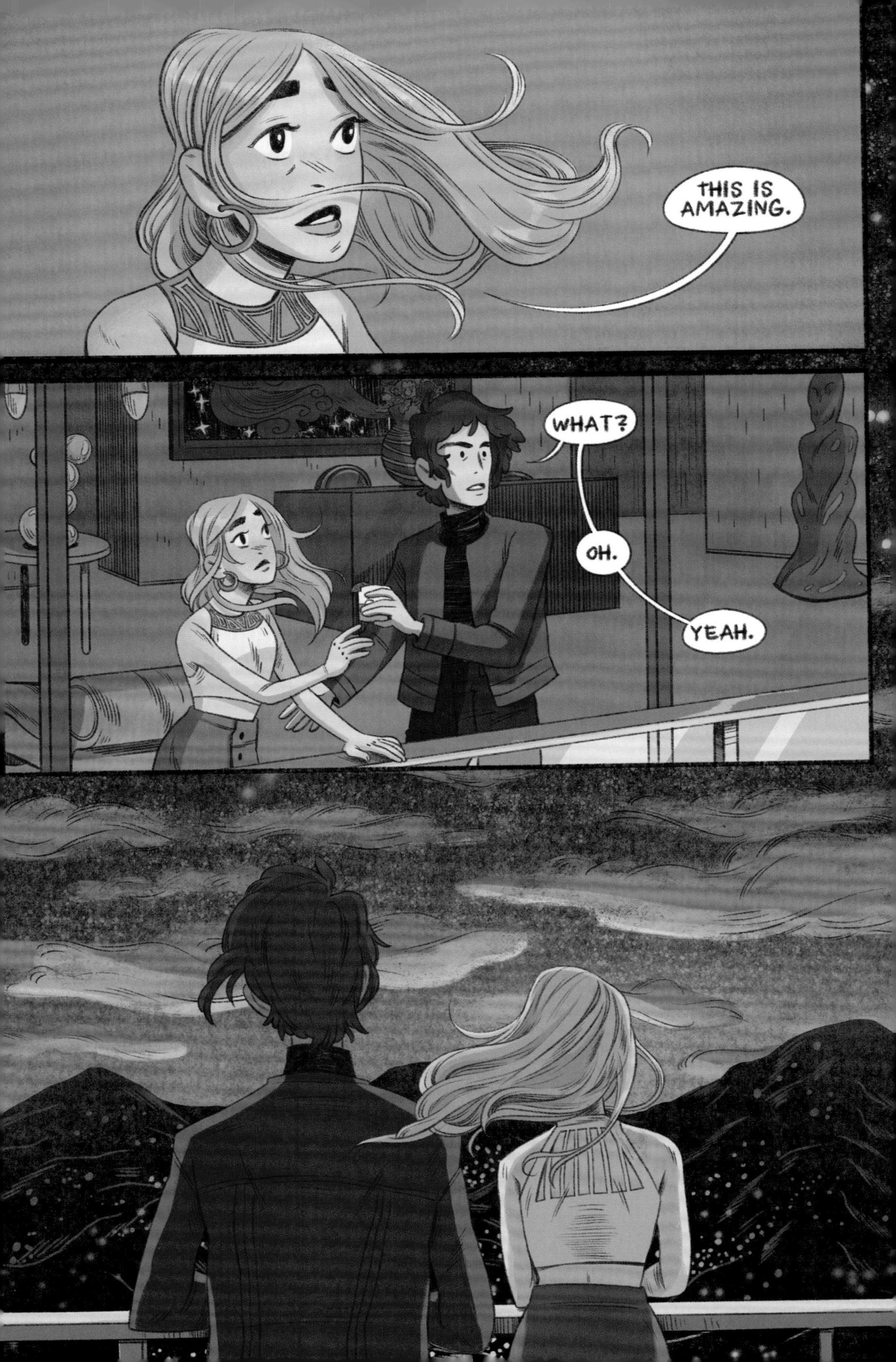
THIS IS AMAZING.
WHAT?
OH.
YEAH.

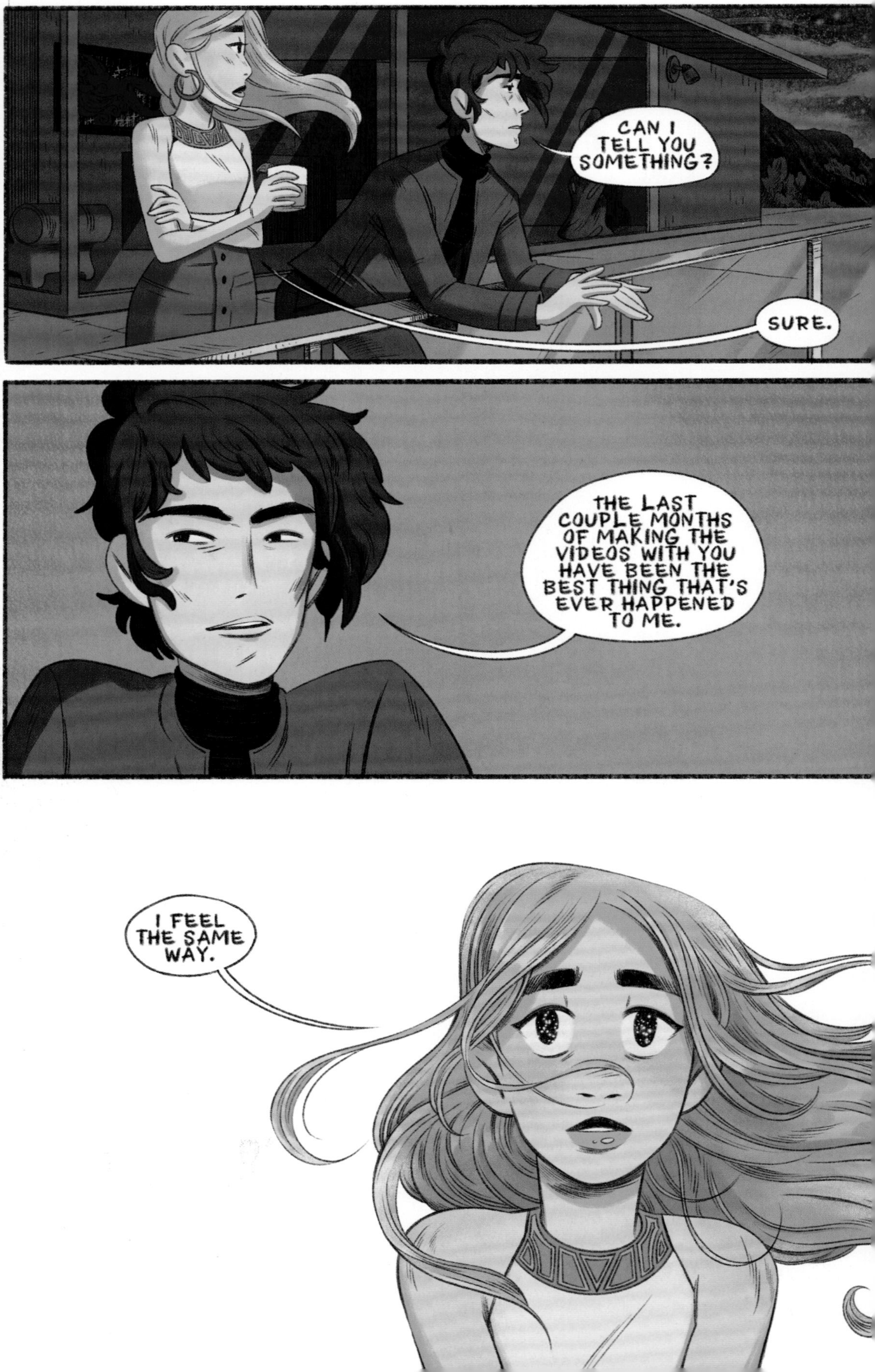

CAN I TELL YOU SOMETHING?
SURE.
THE LAST COUPLE MONTHS OF MAKING THE VIDEOS WITH YOU HAVE BEEN THE BEST THING THAT'S EVER HAPPENED TO ME.
I FEEL THE SAME WAY.

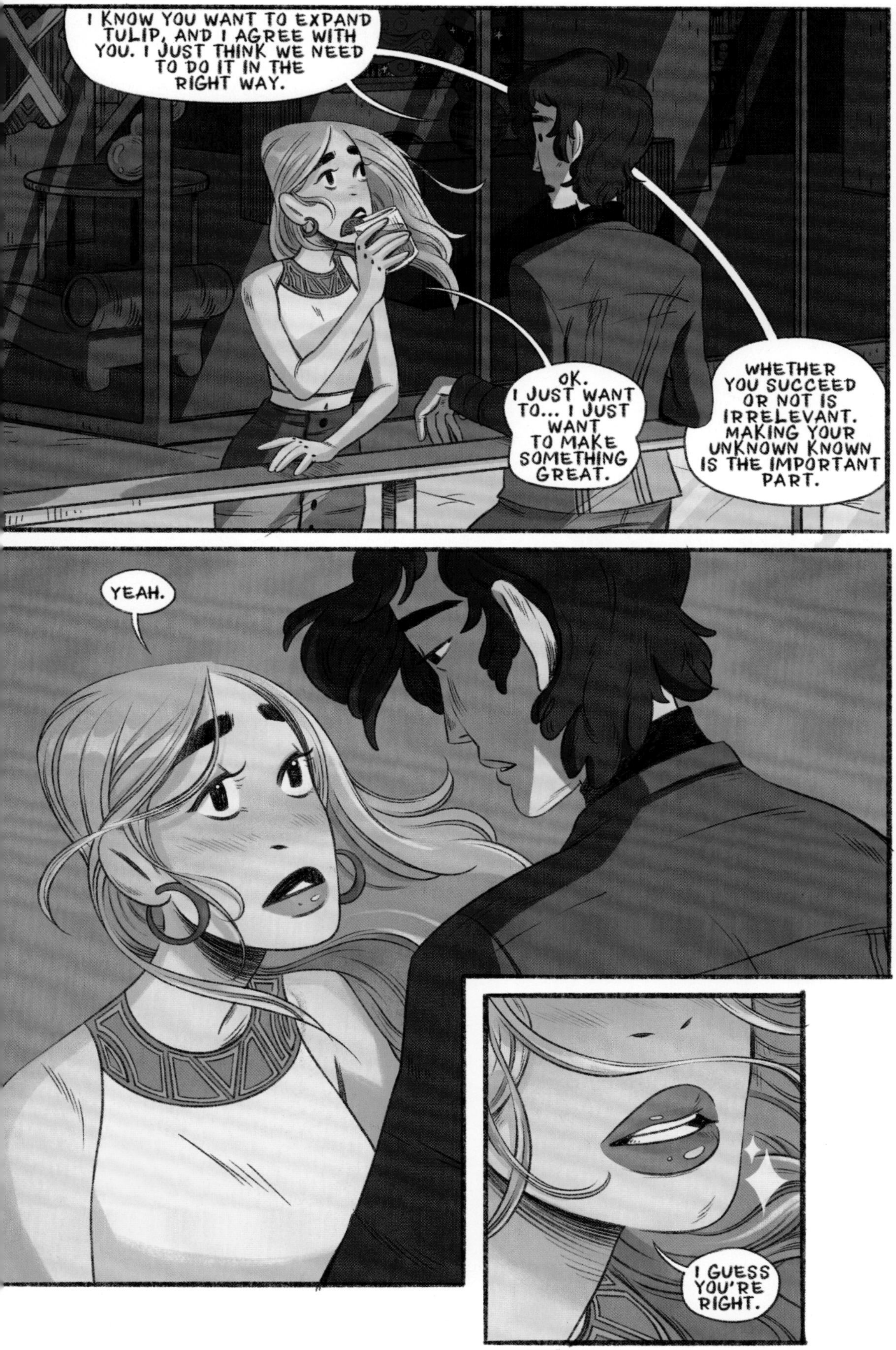
I KNOW YOU WANT TO EXPAND TULIP, AND I AGREE WITH YOU. I JUST THINK WE NEED TO DO IT IN THE RIGHT WAY.
OK. I JUST WANT TO... I JUST WANT TO MAKE SOMETHING GREAT.
WHETHER YOU SUCCEED OR NOT IS IRRELEVANT. MAKING YOUR UNKNOWN KNOWN IS THE IMPORTANT PART.
YEAH.
I GUESS YOU'RE RIGHT.

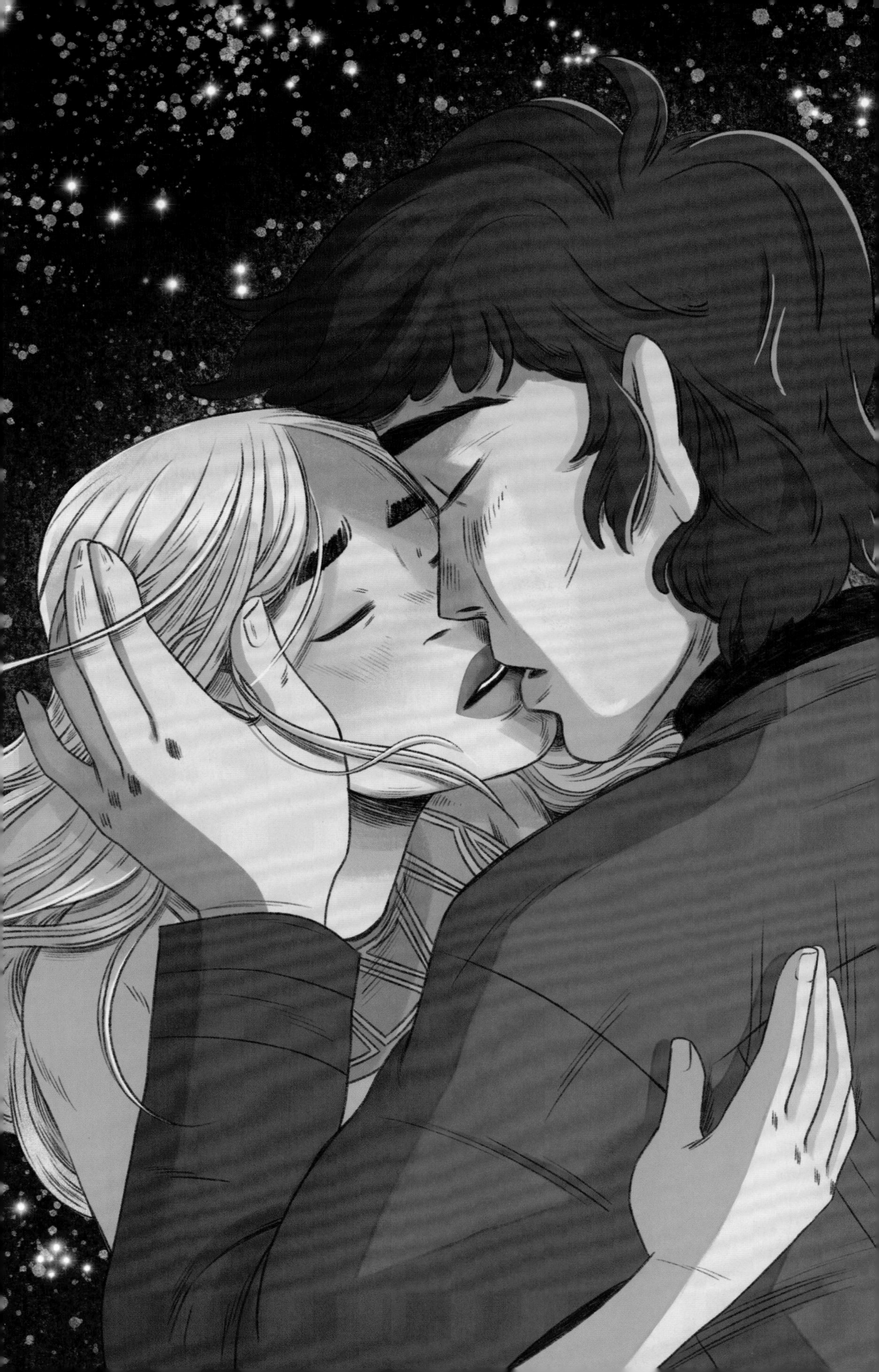

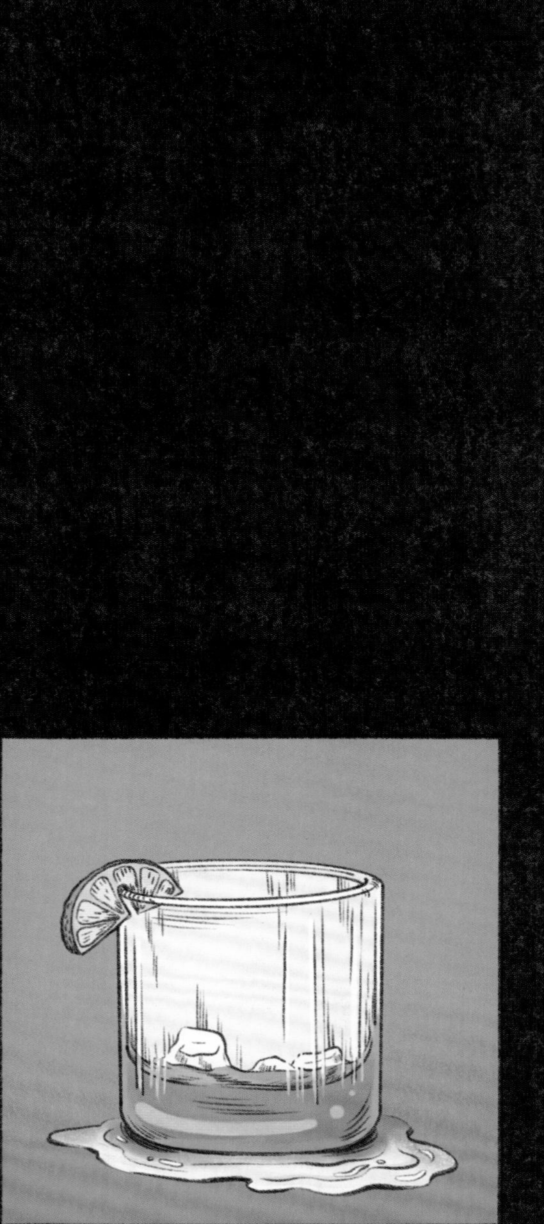

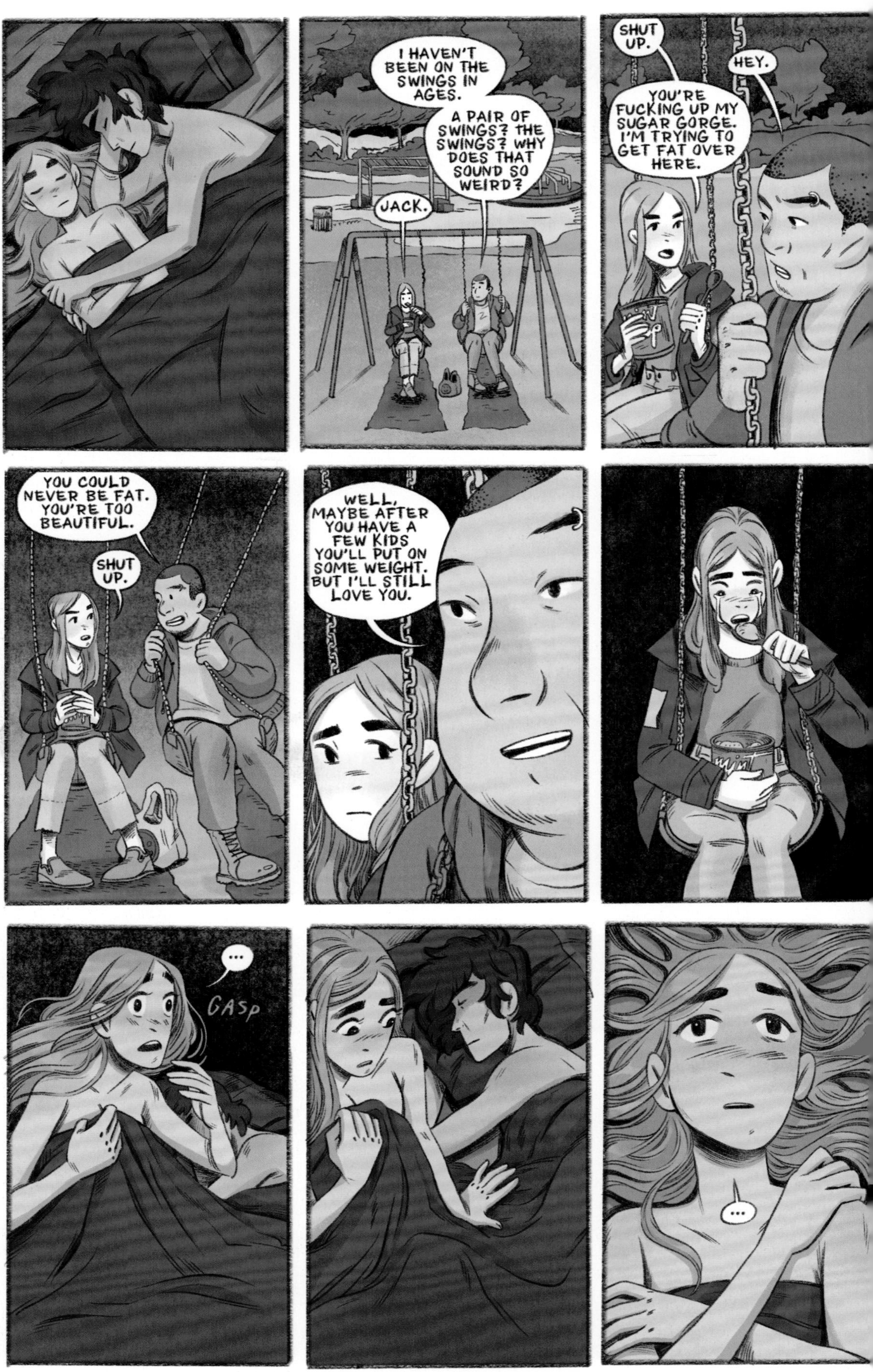
I HAVEN'T BEEN ON THE SWINGS IN AGES.
A PAIR OF SWINGS? THE SWINGS? WHY DOES THAT SOUND SO WEIRD?
JACK.
SHUT UP.
HEY.
YOU'RE FUCKING UP MY SUGAR GORGE. I'M TRYING TO GET FAT OVER HERE.
YOU COULD NEVER BE FAT. YOU'RE TOO BEAUTIFUL.
SHUT UP.
WELL, MAYBE AFTER YOU HAVE A FEW KIDS YOU'LL PUT ON SOME WEIGHT. BUT I'LL STILL LOVE YOU.
mint
...
GASP
...

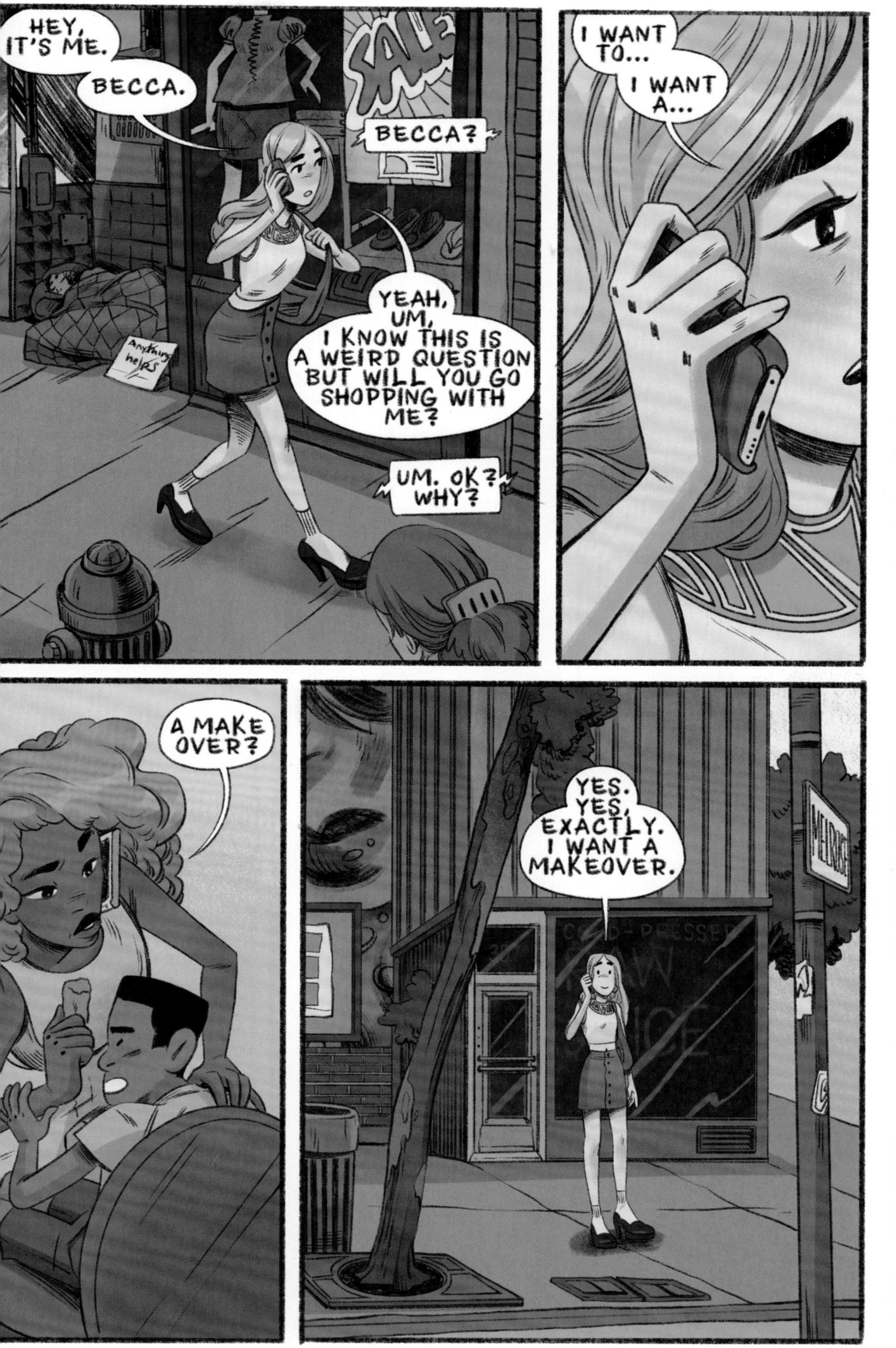
HEY, IT'S ME.
BECCA.
SALE
BECCA?
YEAH, UM, I KNOW THIS IS A WEIRD QUESTION BUT WILL YOU GO SHOPPING WITH ME?
Anything helps
UM. OK? WHY?
I WANT TO...
I WANT A...
A MAKE OVER?
YES. YES, EXACTLY. I WANT A MAKEOVER.
MELROSE

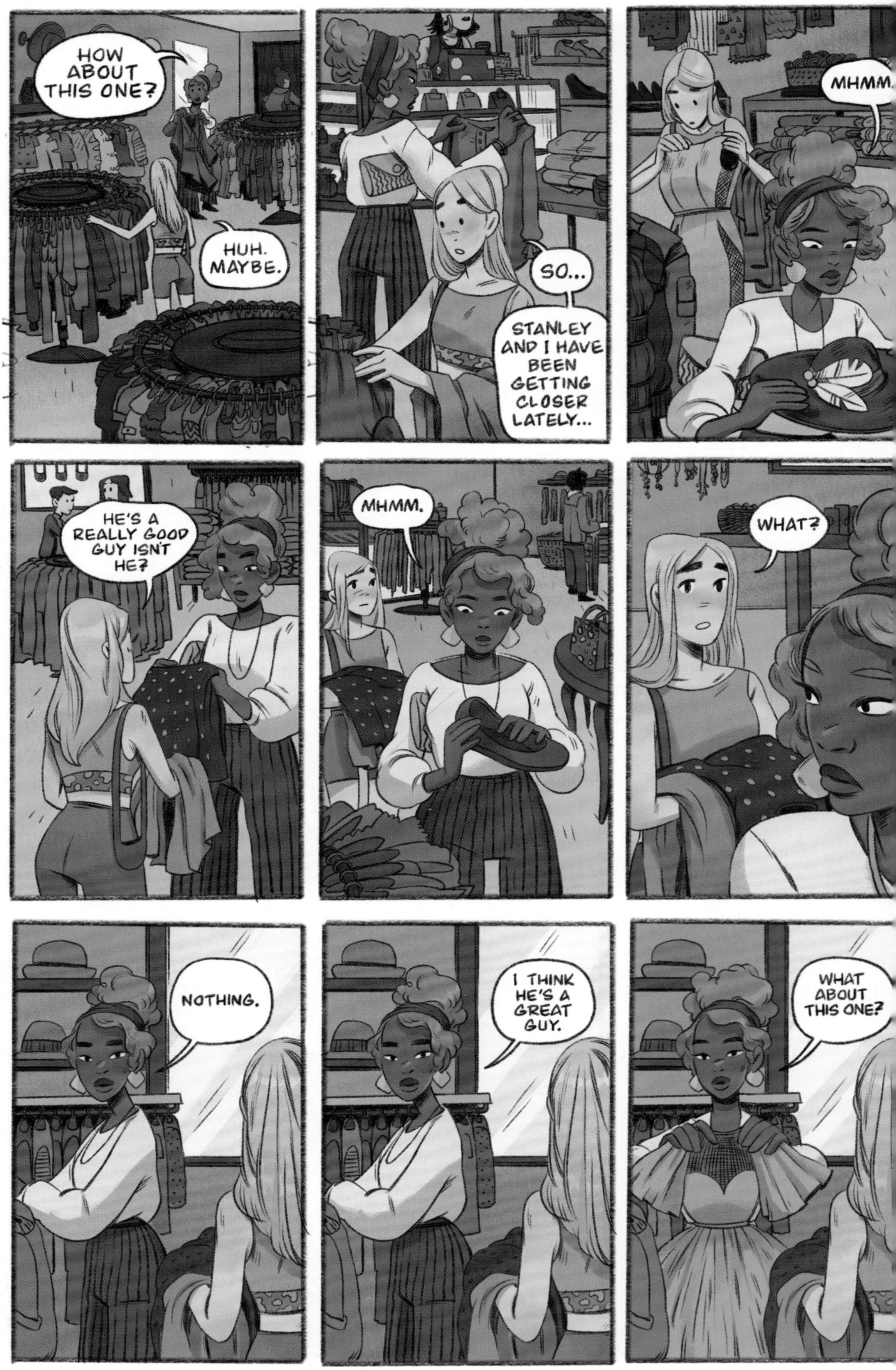
HOW ABOUT THIS ONE?
HUH. MAYBE.
SO...
STANLEY AND I HAVE BEEN GETTING CLOSER LATELY...
MHMM.
HE'S A REALLY GOOD GUY ISN'T HE?
MHMM.
WHAT?
NOTHING.
I THINK HE'S A GREAT GUY.
WHAT ABOUT THIS ONE?

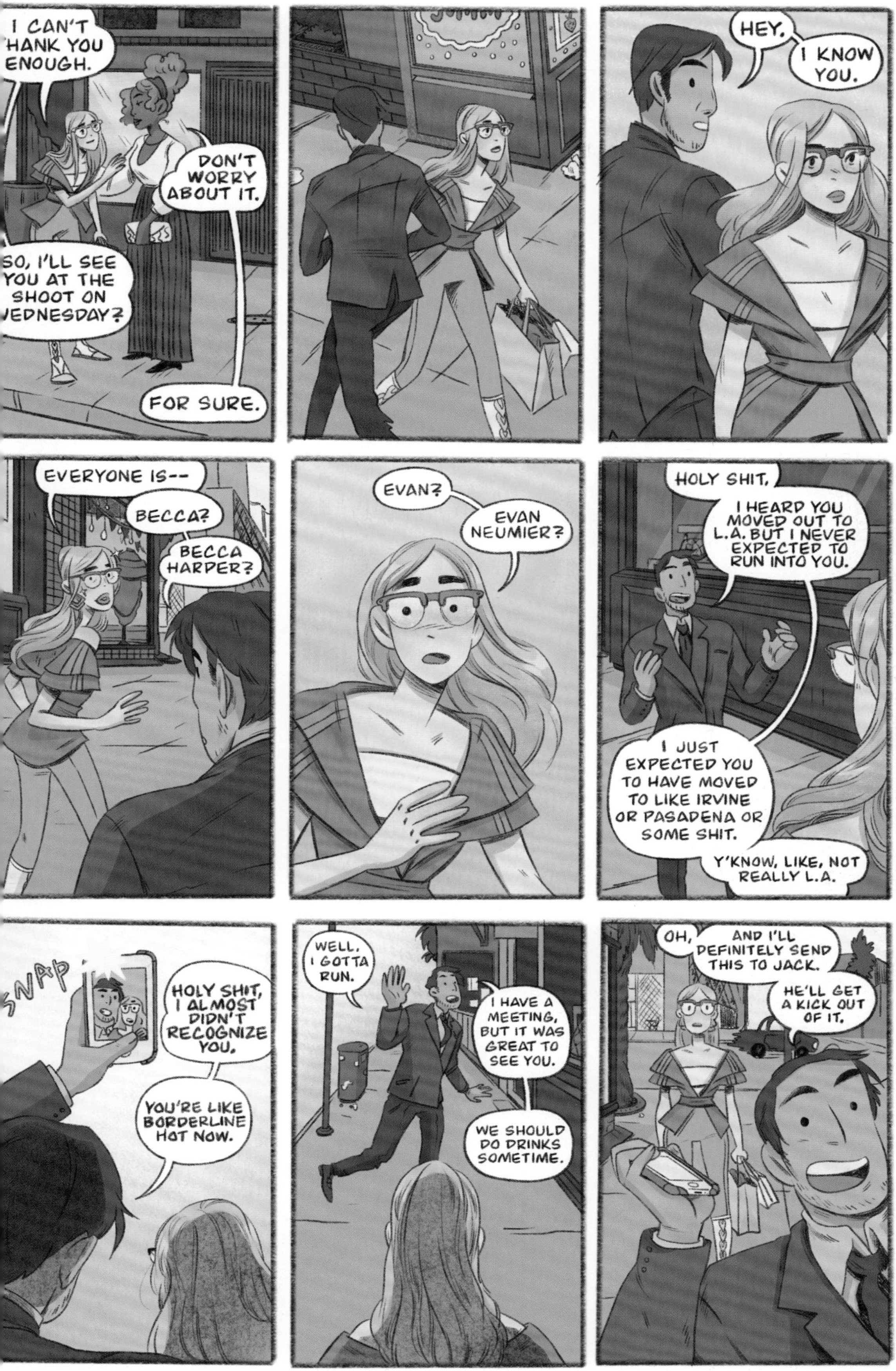

I CAN'T THANK YOU ENOUGH.
DON'T WORRY ABOUT IT.
SO, I'LL SEE YOU AT THE SHOOT ON WEDNESDAY?
FOR SURE.
HEY.
I KNOW YOU.
EVERYONE IS--
BECCA?
BECCA HARPER?
EVAN?
EVAN NEUMIER?
HOLY SHIT.
I HEARD YOU MOVED OUT TO L.A. BUT I NEVER EXPECTED TO RUN INTO YOU.
I JUST EXPECTED YOU TO HAVE MOVED TO LIKE IRVINE OR PASADENA OR SOME SHIT.
Y'KNOW, LIKE, NOT REALLY L.A.
SNAP
HOLY SHIT, I ALMOST DIDN'T RECOGNIZE YOU.
YOU'RE LIKE BORDERLINE HOT NOW.
WELL, I GOTTA RUN.
I HAVE A MEETING, BUT IT WAS GREAT TO SEE YOU.
WE SHOULD DO DRINKS SOMETIME.
OH,
AND I'LL DEFINITELY SEND THIS TO JACK.
HE'LL GET A KICK OUT OF IT.

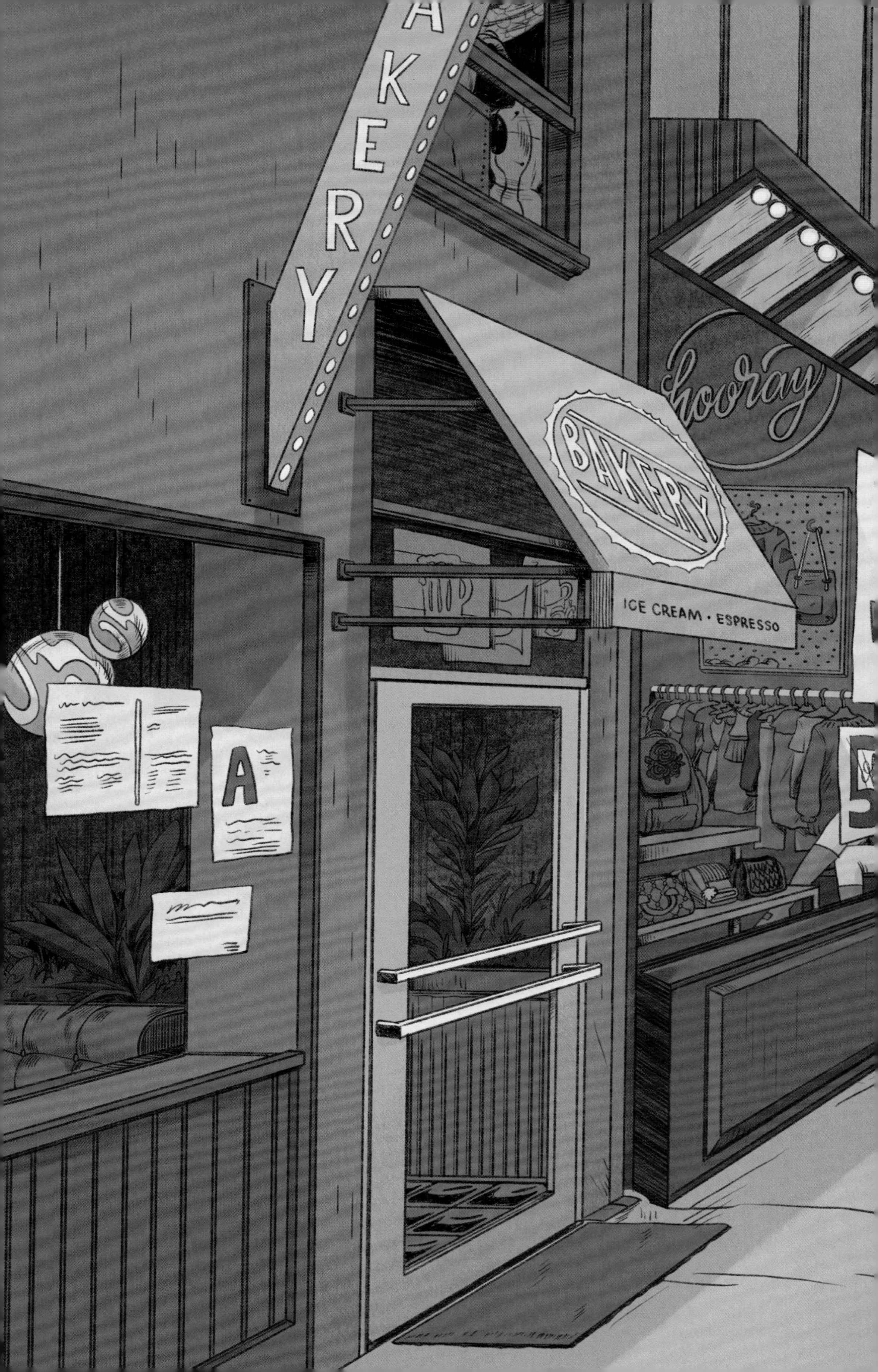
AKERY
BAKERY
ICE CREAM • ESPRESSO
hooray
A

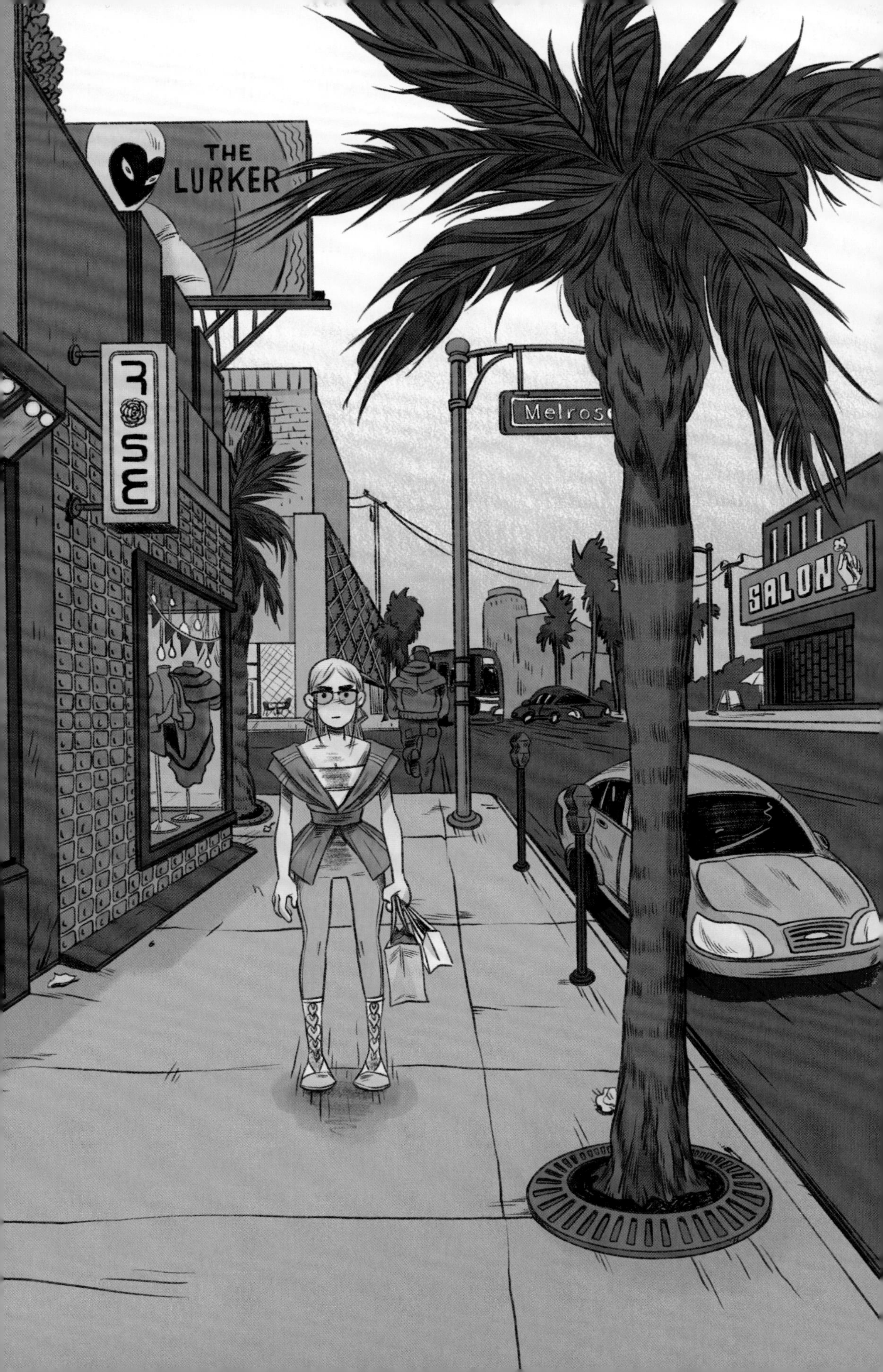
THE LURKER
ROSE
Melrose
SALON

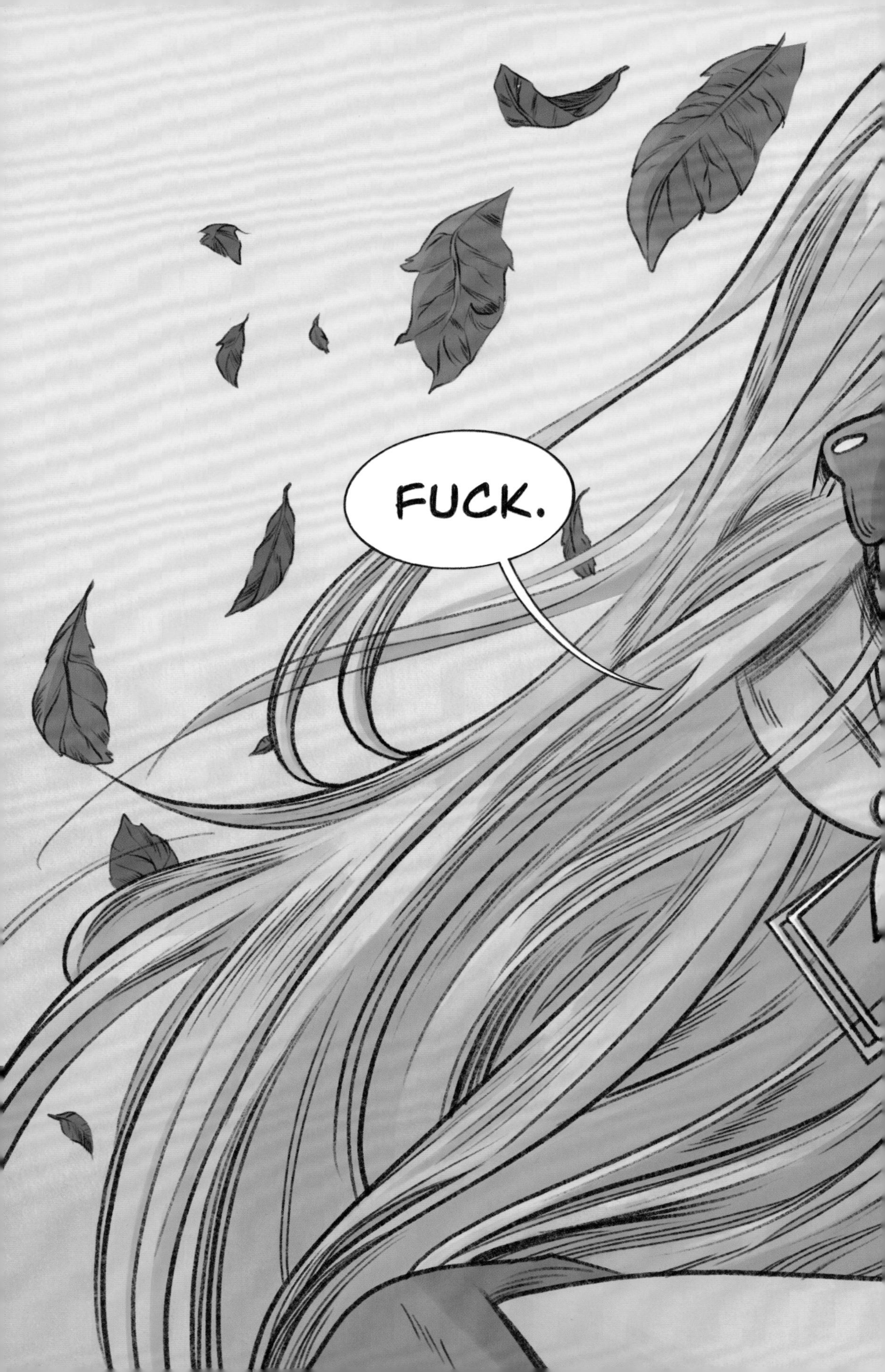
FUCK.

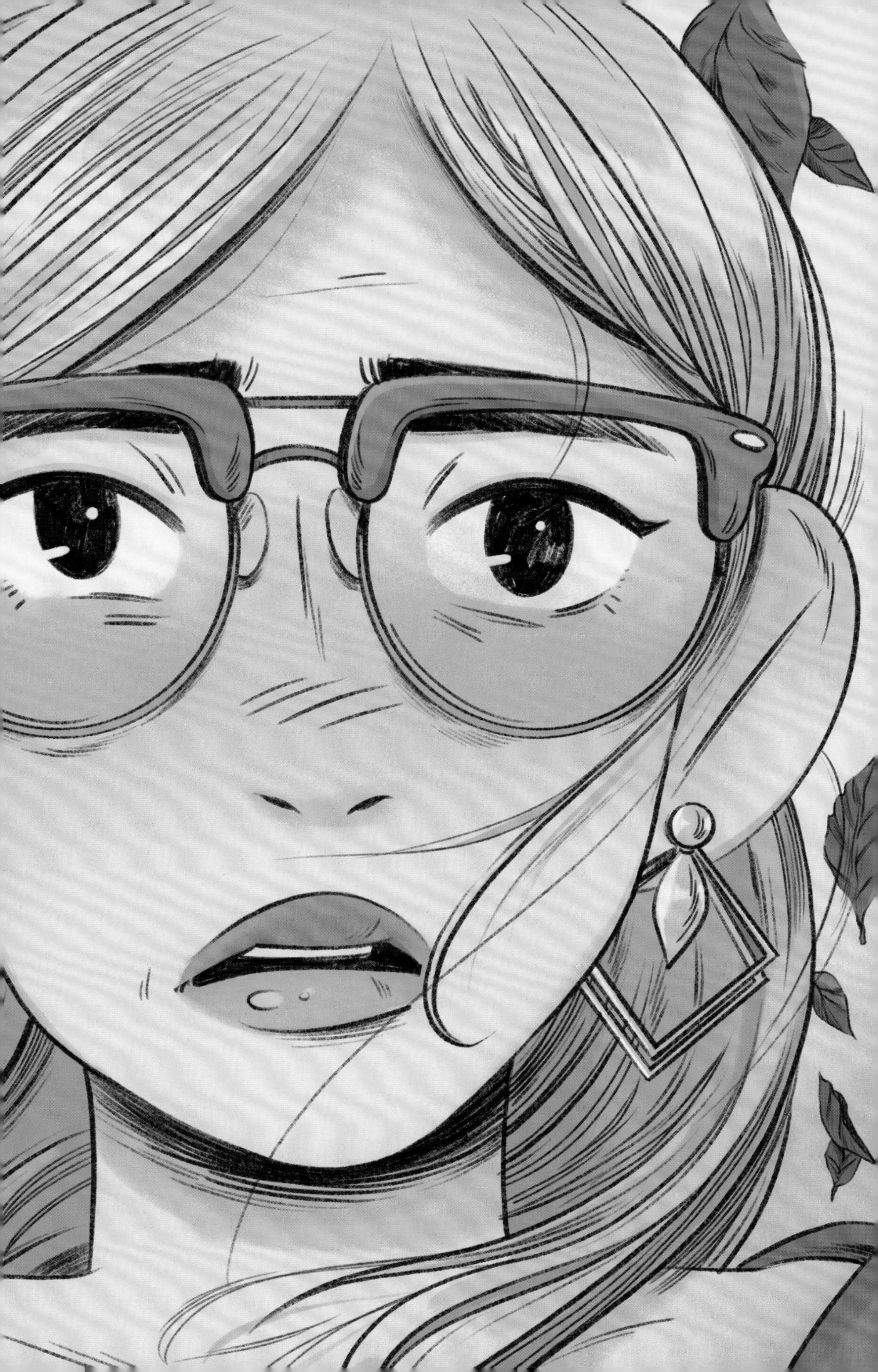

CHAPTER 4

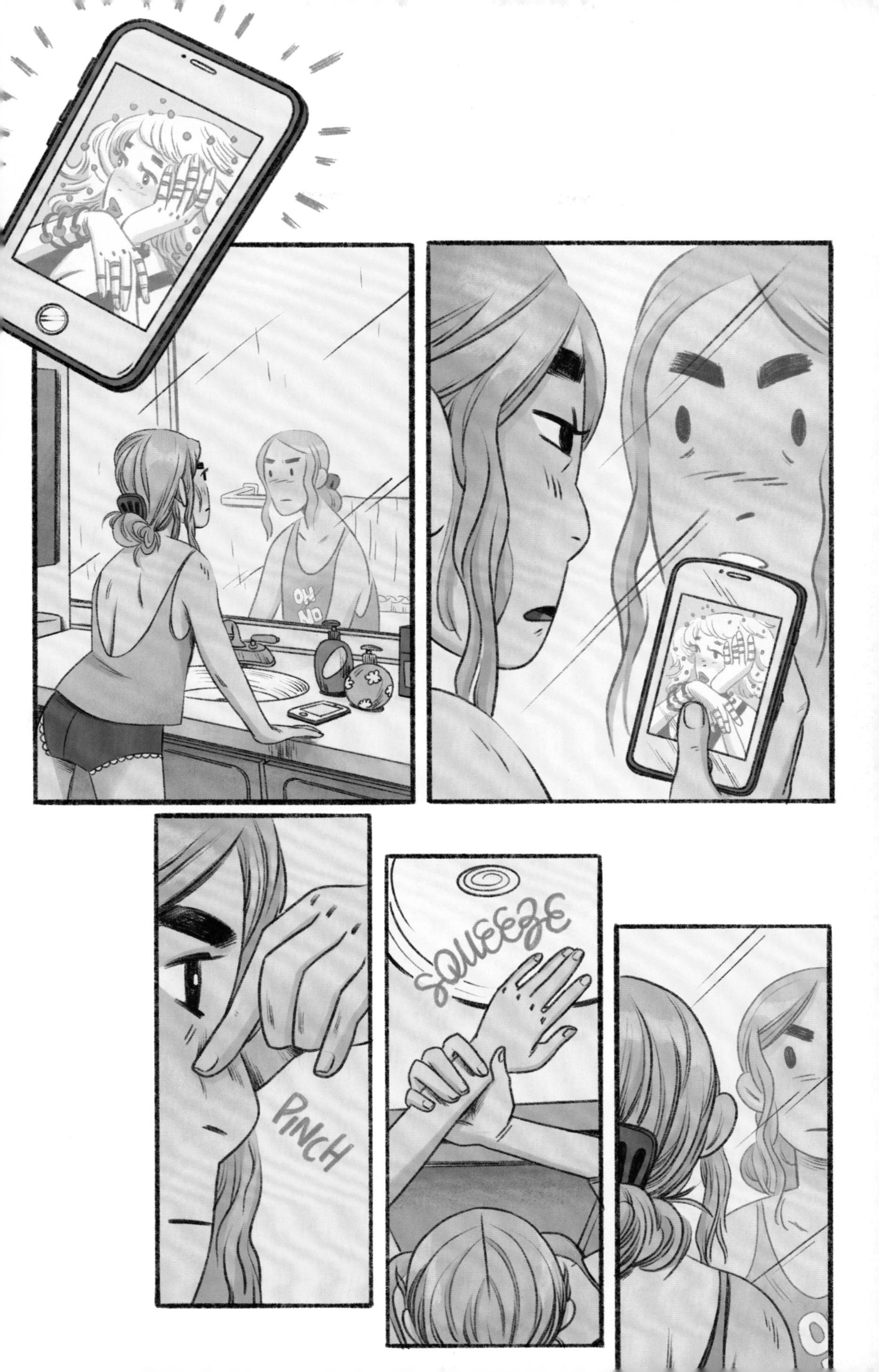
OH NO
PINCH
SQUEEZE

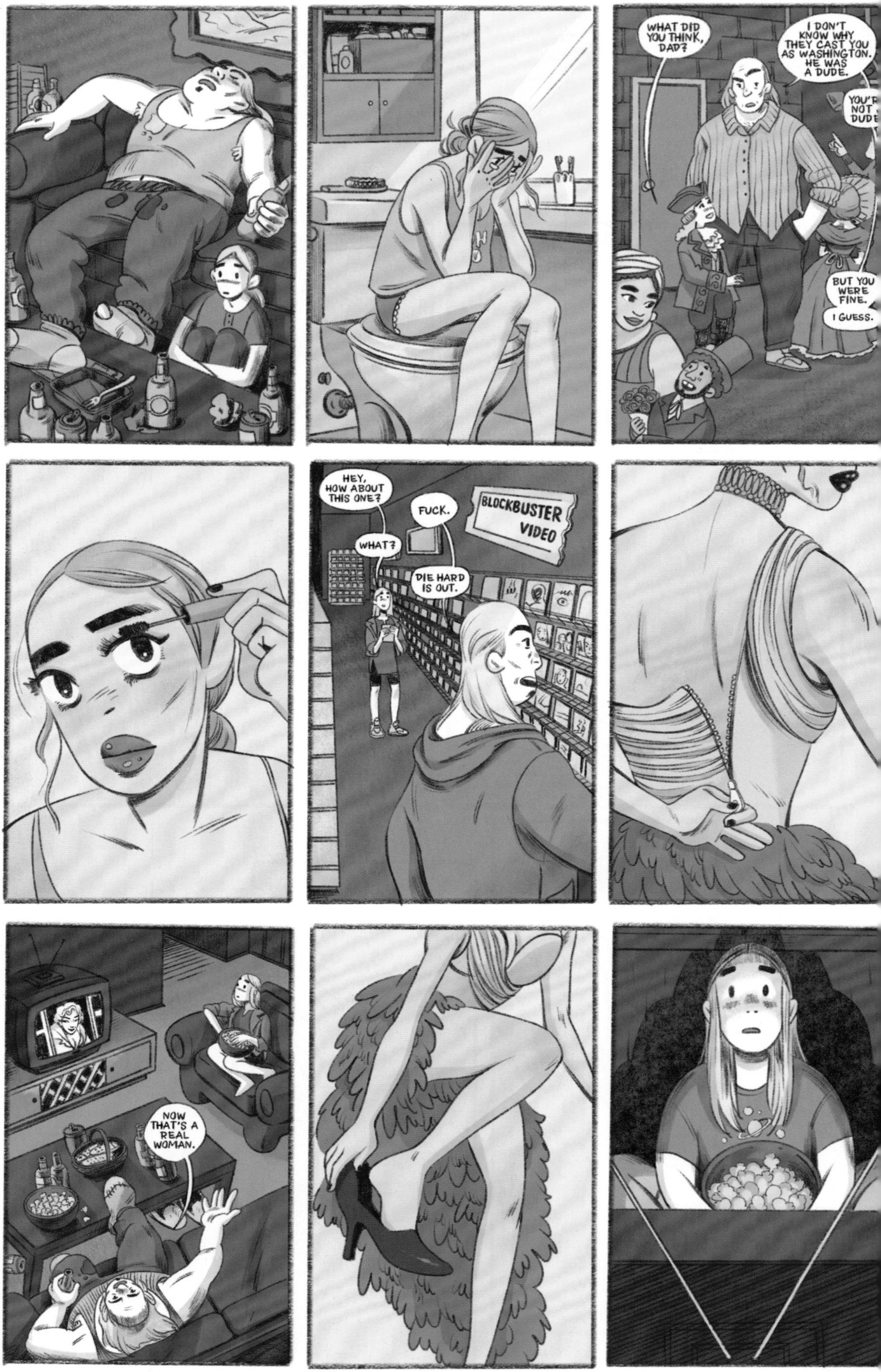
WHAT DID YOU THINK, DAD?
I DON'T KNOW WHY THEY CAST YOU AS WASHINGTON. HE WAS A DUDE.
YOU'R NOT DUDE
BUT YOU WERE FINE.
I GUESS.
HEY, HOW ABOUT THIS ONE?
WHAT?
FUCK.
DIE HARD IS OUT.
BLOCKBUSTER VIDEO
NOW THAT'S A REAL WOMAN.

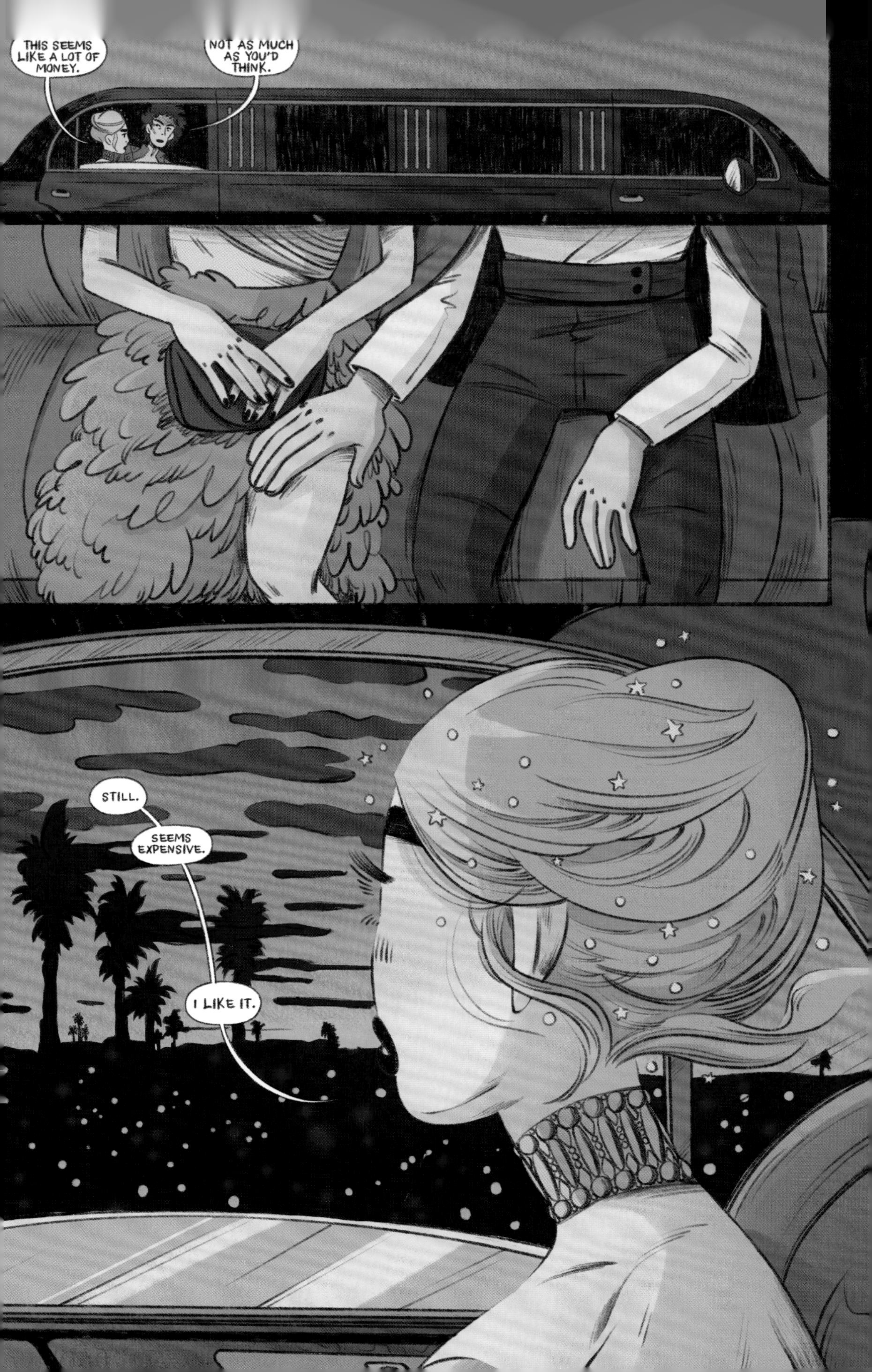
THIS SEEMS LIKE A LOT OF MONEY.
NOT AS MUCH AS YOU'D THINK.
STILL.
SEEMS EXPENSIVE.
I LIKE IT.

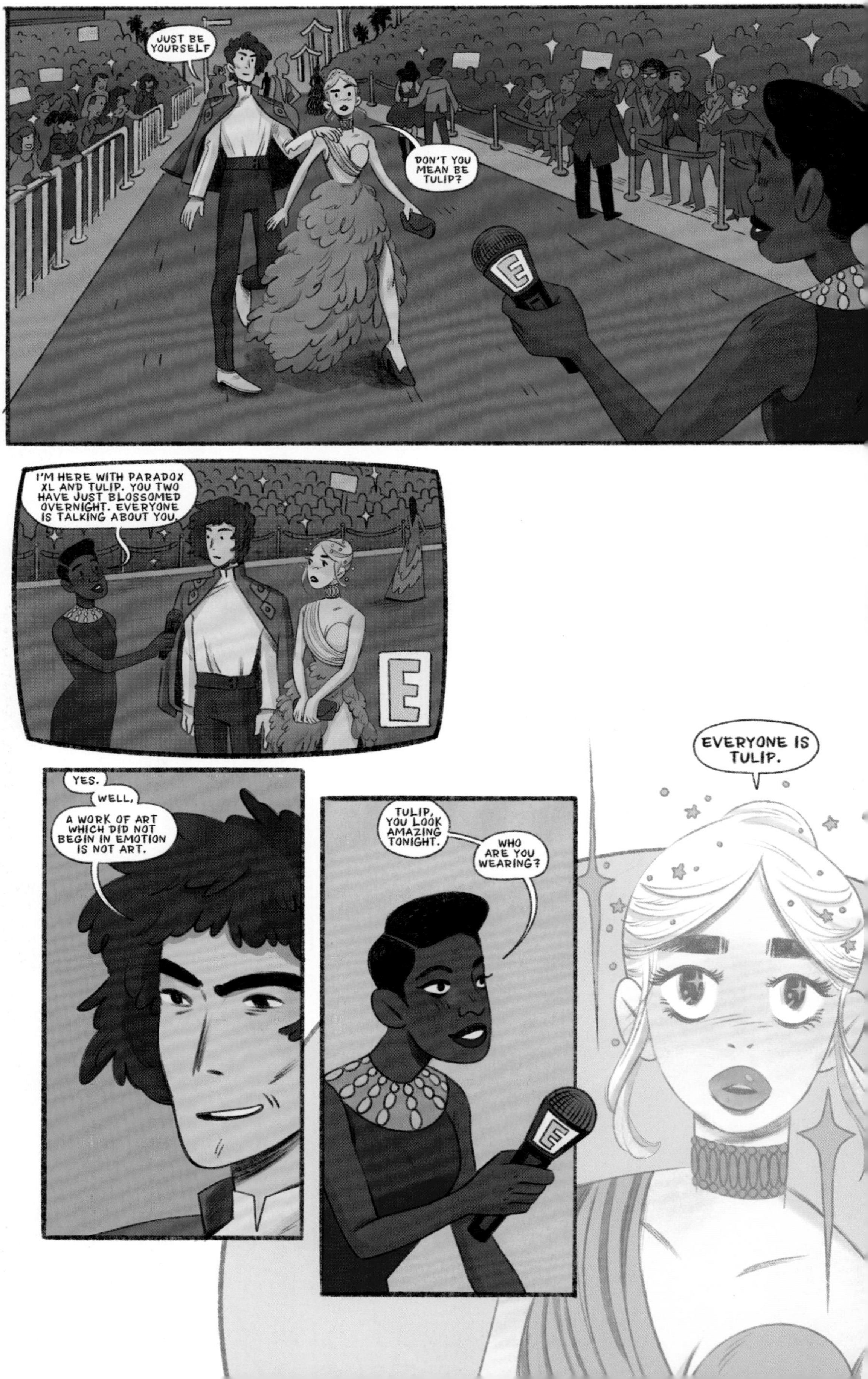
JUST BE YOURSELF
DON'T YOU MEAN BE TULIP?
I'M HERE WITH PARADOX XL AND TULIP. YOU TWO HAVE JUST BLOSSOMED OVERNIGHT. EVERYONE IS TALKING ABOUT YOU.
E
YES.
WELL,
A WORK OF ART WHICH DID NOT BEGIN IN EMOTION IS NOT ART.
TULIP, YOU LOOK AMAZING TONIGHT.
WHO ARE YOU WEARING?
EVERYONE IS TULIP.

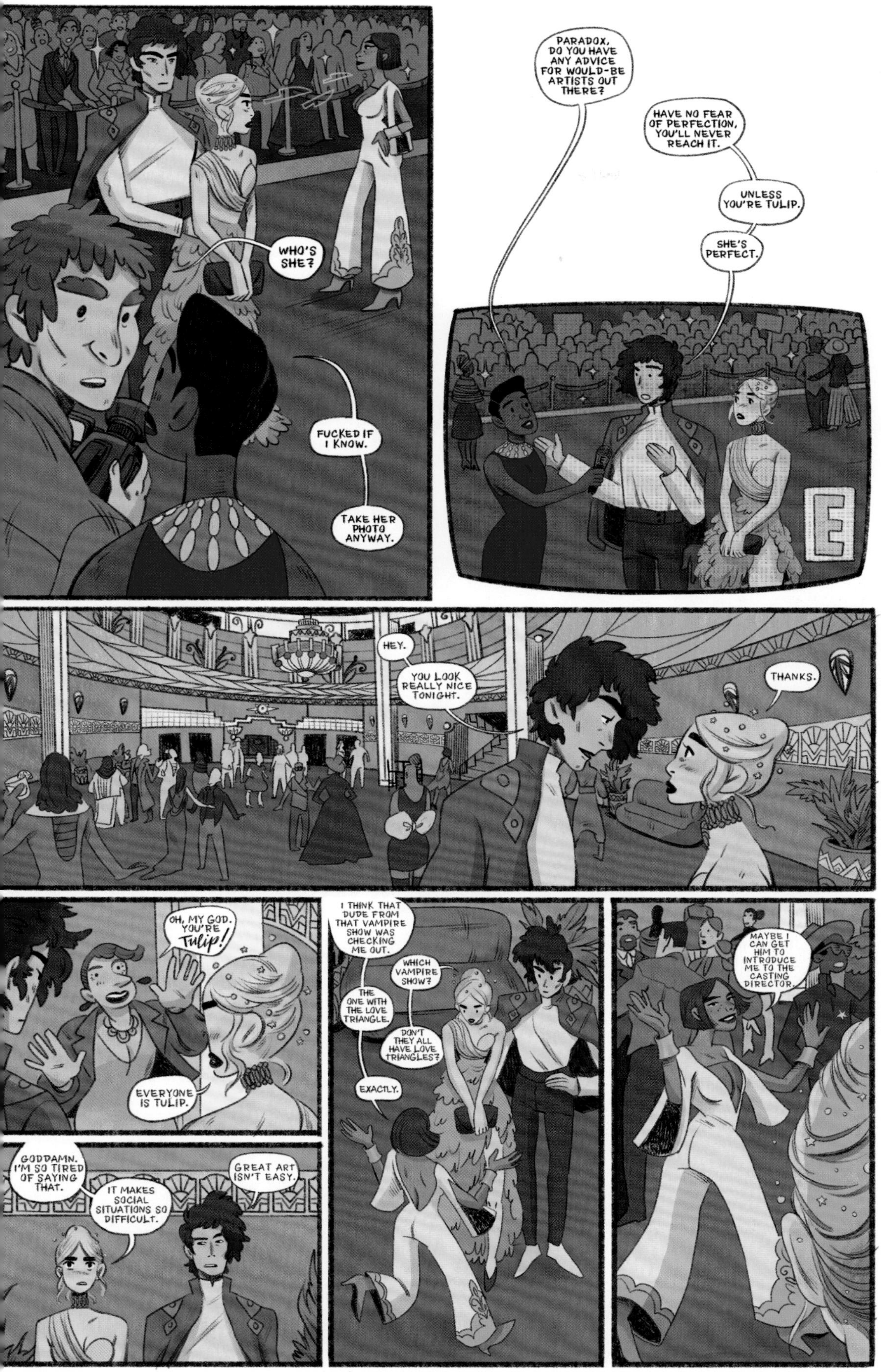
WHO'S SHE?
FUCKED IF I KNOW.
TAKE HER PHOTO ANYWAY.
PARADOX, DO YOU HAVE ANY ADVICE FOR WOULD-BE ARTISTS OUT THERE?
HAVE NO FEAR OF PERFECTION, YOU'LL NEVER REACH IT.
UNLESS YOU'RE TULIP.
SHE'S PERFECT.
E
HEY.
YOU LOOK REALLY NICE TONIGHT.
THANKS.
OH, MY GOD. YOU'RE Tulip!
EVERYONE IS TULIP.
GODDAMN. I'M SO TIRED OF SAYING THAT.
IT MAKES SOCIAL SITUATIONS SO DIFFICULT.
GREAT ART ISN'T EASY.
I THINK THAT DUDE FROM THAT VAMPIRE SHOW WAS CHECKING ME OUT.
WHICH VAMPIRE SHOW?
THE ONE WITH THE LOVE TRIANGLE.
DON'T THEY ALL HAVE LOVE TRIANGLES?
EXACTLY.
MAYBE I CAN GET HIM TO INTRODUCE ME TO THE CASTING DIRECTOR.

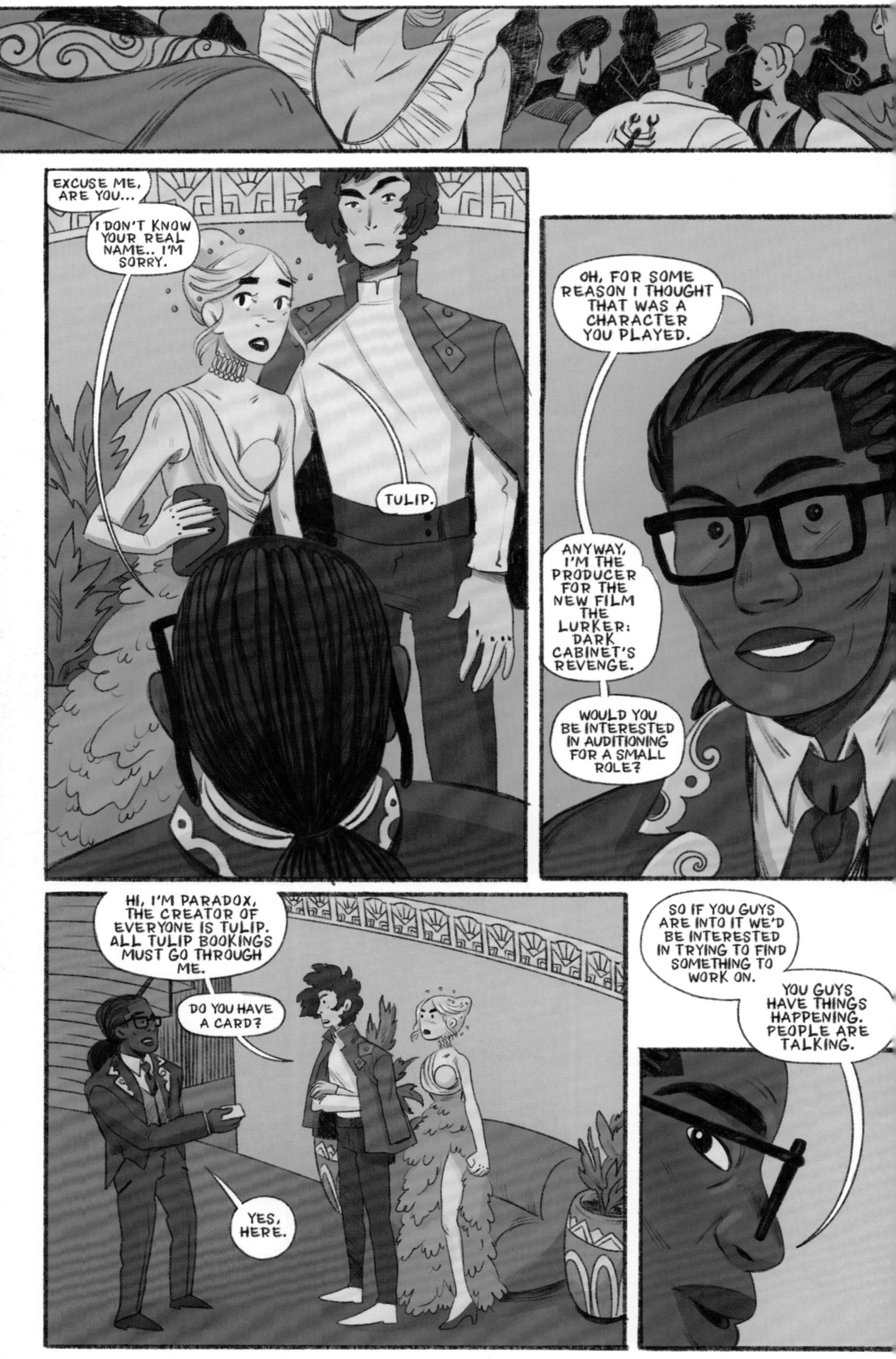
EXCUSE ME, ARE YOU...
I DON'T KNOW YOUR REAL NAME.. I'M SORRY.
TULIP.
OH, FOR SOME REASON I THOUGHT THAT WAS A CHARACTER YOU PLAYED.
ANYWAY, I'M THE PRODUCER FOR THE NEW FILM THE LURKER: DARK CABINET'S REVENGE.
WOULD YOU BE INTERESTED IN AUDITIONING FOR A SMALL ROLE?
HI, I'M PARADOX, THE CREATOR OF EVERYONE IS TULIP. ALL TULIP BOOKINGS MUST GO THROUGH ME.
DO YOU HAVE A CARD?
YES, HERE.
SO IF YOU GUYS ARE INTO IT WE'D BE INTERESTED IN TRYING TO FIND SOMETHING TO WORK ON.
YOU GUYS HAVE THINGS HAPPENING. PEOPLE ARE TALKING.

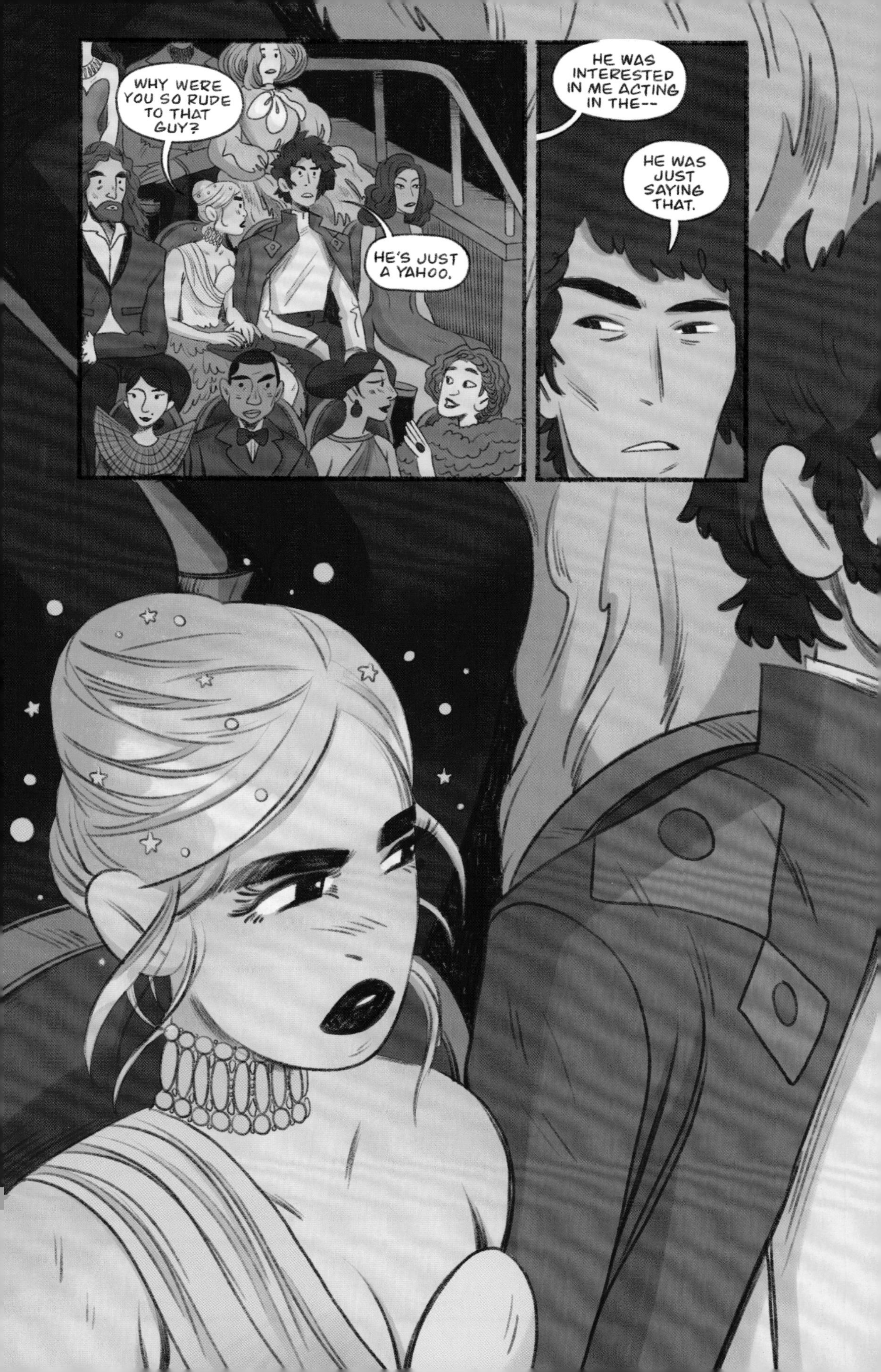
WHY WERE YOU SO RUDE TO THAT GUY?
HE'S JUST A YAHOO.
HE WAS INTERESTED IN ME ACTING IN THE--
HE WAS JUST SAYING THAT.

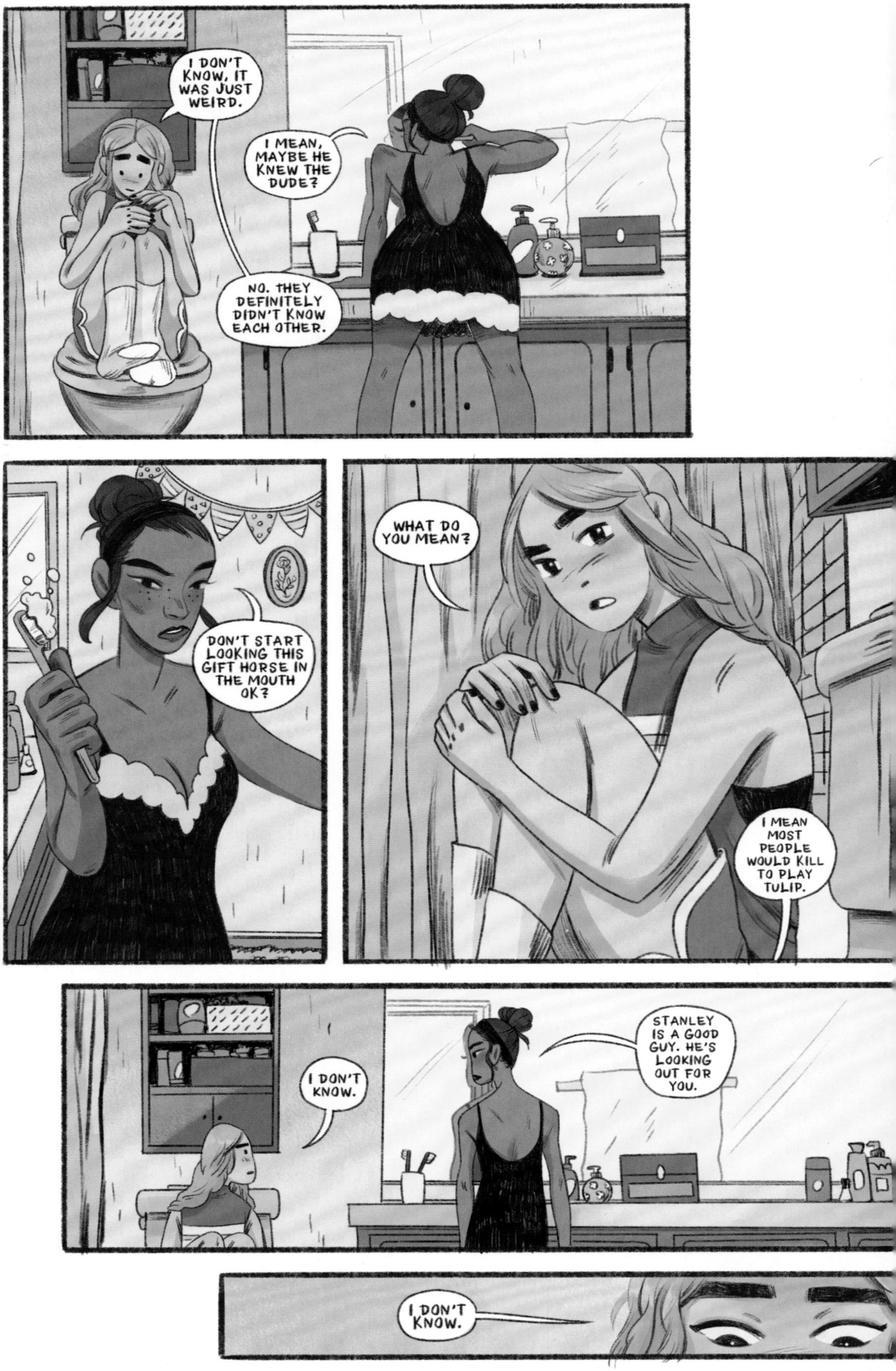
I DON'T KNOW, IT WAS JUST WEIRD.
I MEAN, MAYBE HE KNEW THE DUDE?
NO. THEY DEFINITELY DIDN'T KNOW EACH OTHER.
DON'T START LOOKING THIS GIFT HORSE IN THE MOUTH OK?
WHAT DO YOU MEAN?
I MEAN MOST PEOPLE WOULD KILL TO PLAY TULIP.
I DON'T KNOW.
STANLEY IS A GOOD GUY. HE'S LOOKING OUT FOR YOU.
I DON'T KNOW.

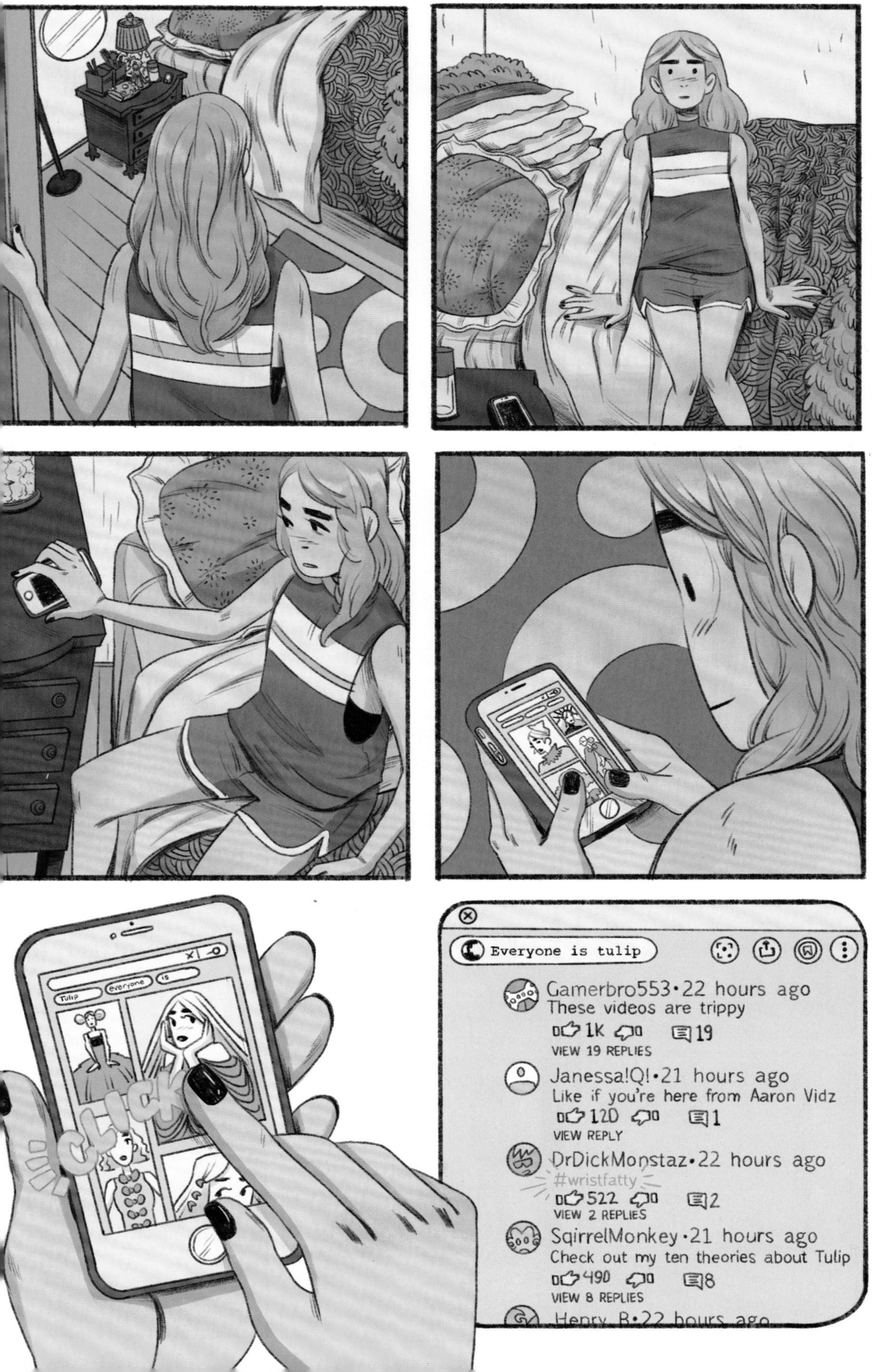
Tulip
everyone
is
CLICK
Everyone is tulip
Gamerbro553•22 hours ago
These videos are trippy
1K 0 19
VIEW 19 REPLIES
Janessa!Q!•21 hours ago
Like if you're here from Aaron Vidz
120 0 1
VIEW REPLY
DrDickMonstaz•22 hours ago
#wristfatty
522 0 2
VIEW 2 REPLIES
SqirrelMonkey•21 hours ago
Check out my ten theories about Tulip
490 0 8
VIEW 8 REPLIES
Henry B•22 hours ago

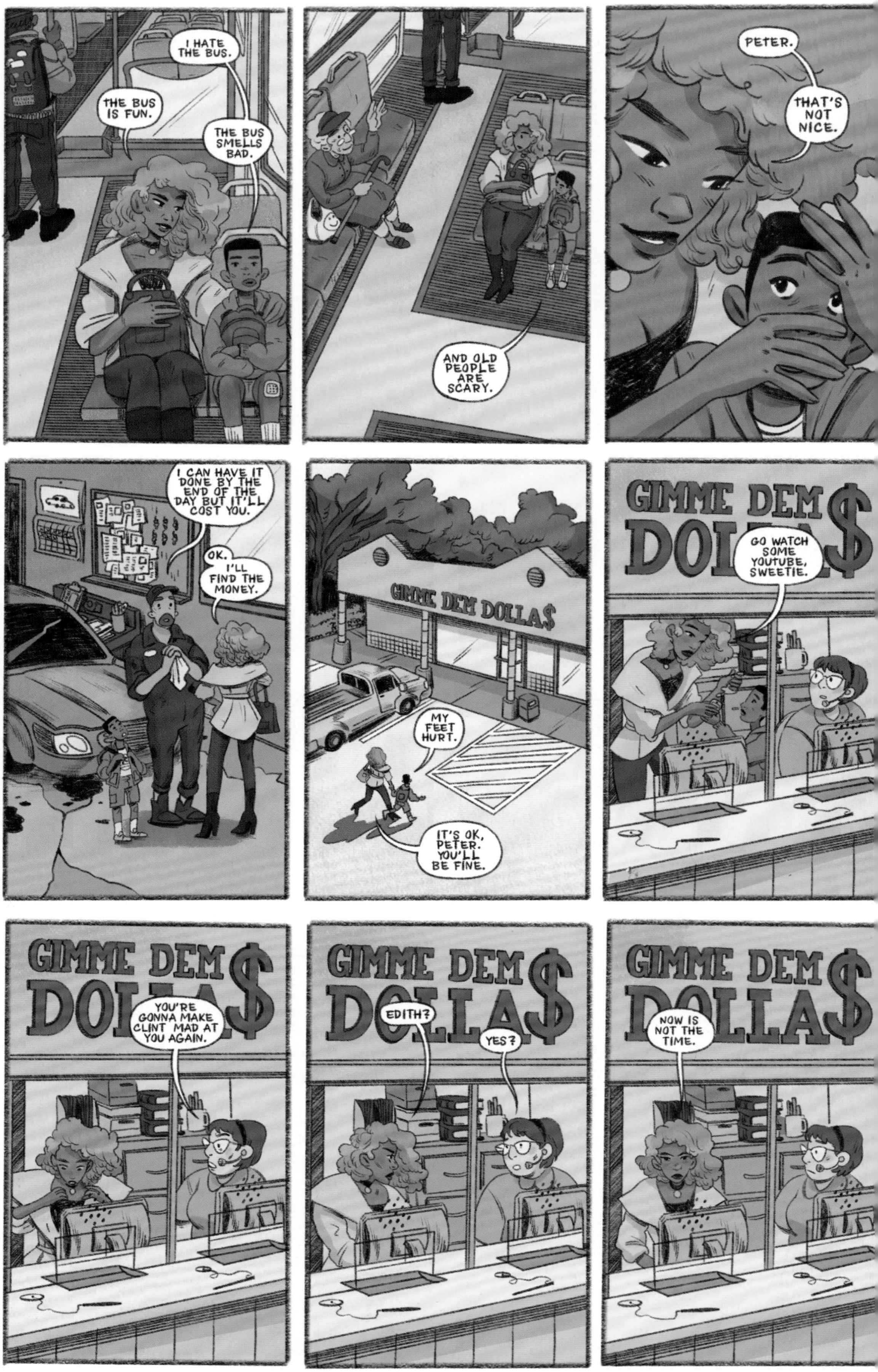
I HATE THE BUS.
THE BUS IS FUN.
THE BUS SMELLS BAD.
AND OLD PEOPLE ARE SCARY.
PETER.
THAT'S NOT NICE.
I CAN HAVE IT DONE BY THE END OF THE DAY BUT IT'LL COST YOU.
OK. I'LL FIND THE MONEY.
GIMME DEM DOLLA$
MY FEET HURT.
IT'S OK, PETER. YOU'LL BE FINE.
GIMME DEM DOLLA$
GO WATCH SOME YOUTUBE, SWEETIE.
GIMME DEM DOLLA$
YOU'RE GONNA MAKE CLINT MAD AT YOU AGAIN.
GIMME DEM DOLLA$
EDITH?
YES?
GIMME DEM DOLLA$
NOW IS NOT THE TIME.

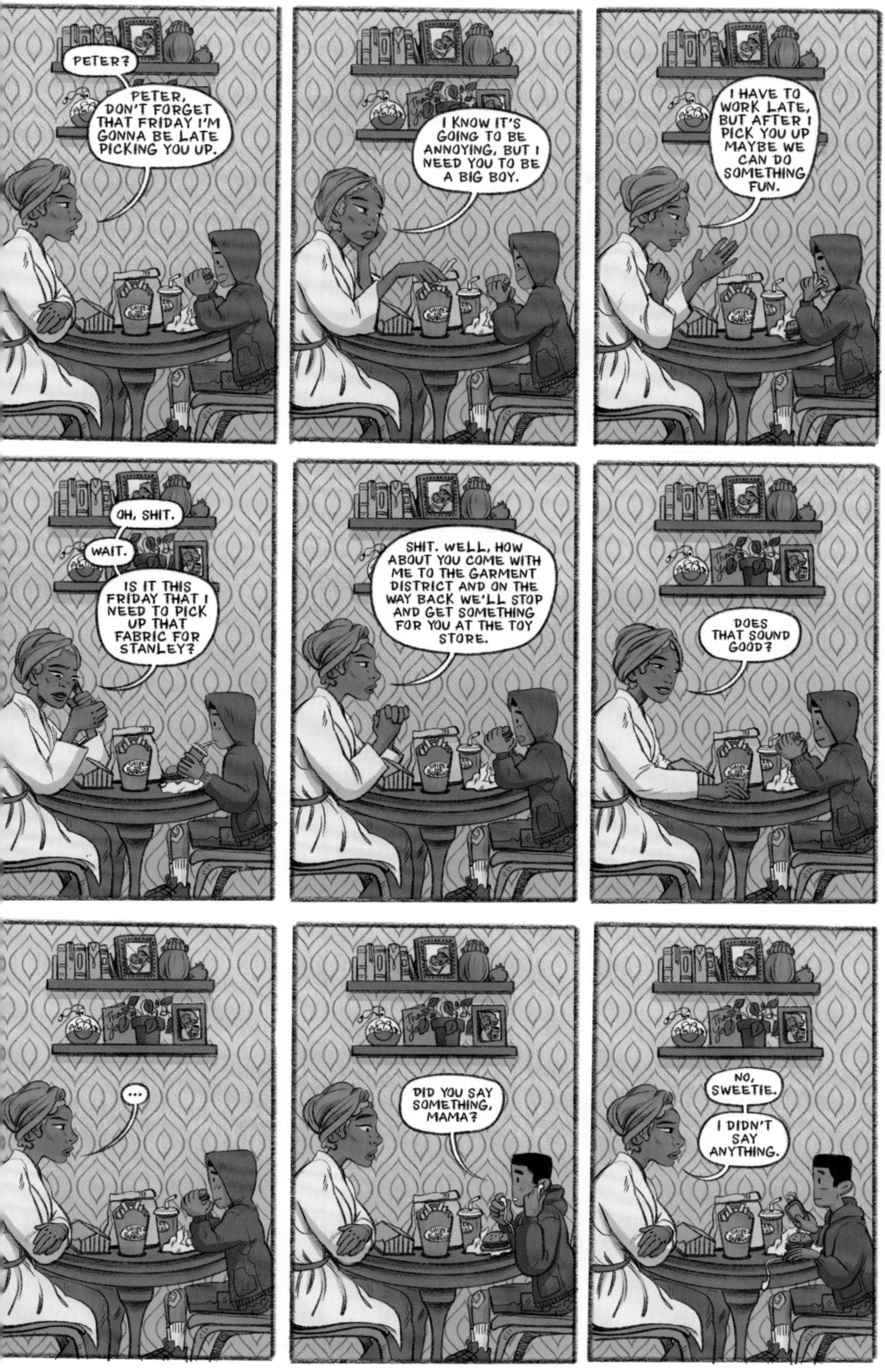
PETER?
PETER, DON'T FORGET THAT FRIDAY I'M GONNA BE LATE PICKING YOU UP.
I KNOW IT'S GOING TO BE ANNOYING, BUT I NEED YOU TO BE A BIG BOY.
I HAVE TO WORK LATE, BUT AFTER I PICK YOU UP MAYBE WE CAN DO SOMETHING FUN.
OH, SHIT.
WAIT.
IS IT THIS FRIDAY THAT I NEED TO PICK UP THAT FABRIC FOR STANLEY?
SHIT. WELL, HOW ABOUT YOU COME WITH ME TO THE GARMENT DISTRICT AND ON THE WAY BACK WE'LL STOP AND GET SOMETHING FOR YOU AT THE TOY STORE.
DOES THAT SOUND GOOD?
...
DID YOU SAY SOMETHING, MAMA?
NO, SWEETIE.
I DIDN'T SAY ANYTHING.

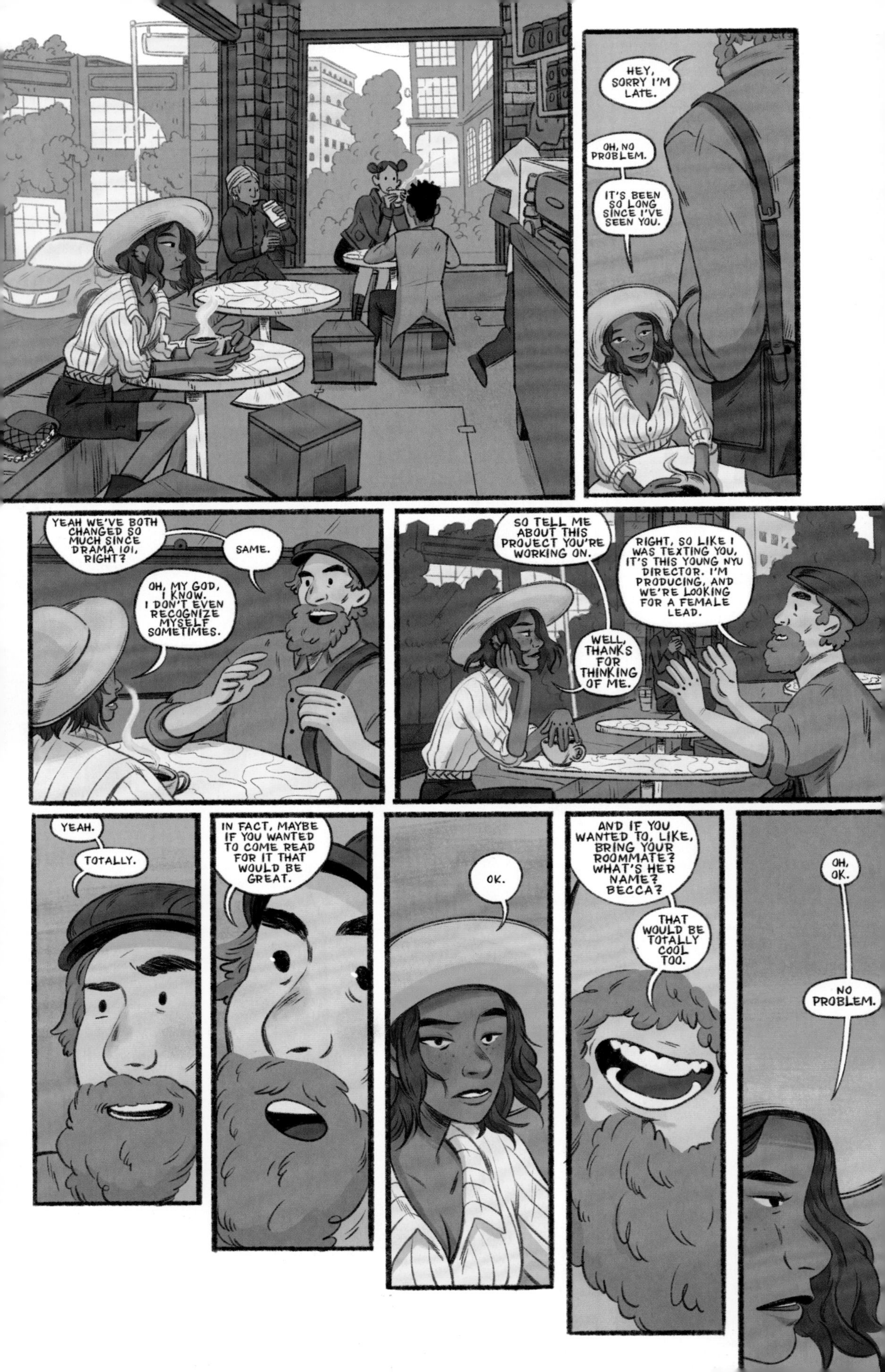
HEY, SORRY I'M LATE.
OH, NO PROBLEM.
IT'S BEEN SO LONG SINCE I'VE SEEN YOU.
YEAH WE'VE BOTH CHANGED SO MUCH SINCE DRAMA 101, RIGHT?
SAME.
OH, MY GOD, I KNOW. I DON'T EVEN RECOGNIZE MYSELF SOMETIMES.
SO TELL ME ABOUT THIS PROJECT YOU'RE WORKING ON.
RIGHT, SO LIKE I WAS TEXTING YOU, IT'S THIS YOUNG NYU DIRECTOR. I'M PRODUCING, AND WE'RE LOOKING FOR A FEMALE LEAD.
WELL, THANKS FOR THINKING OF ME.
YEAH.
TOTALLY.
IN FACT, MAYBE IF YOU WANTED TO COME READ FOR IT THAT WOULD BE GREAT.
OK.
AND IF YOU WANTED TO, LIKE, BRING YOUR ROOMMATE? WHAT'S HER NAME? BECCA?
THAT WOULD BE TOTALLY COOL TOO.
OH, OK.
NO PROBLEM.

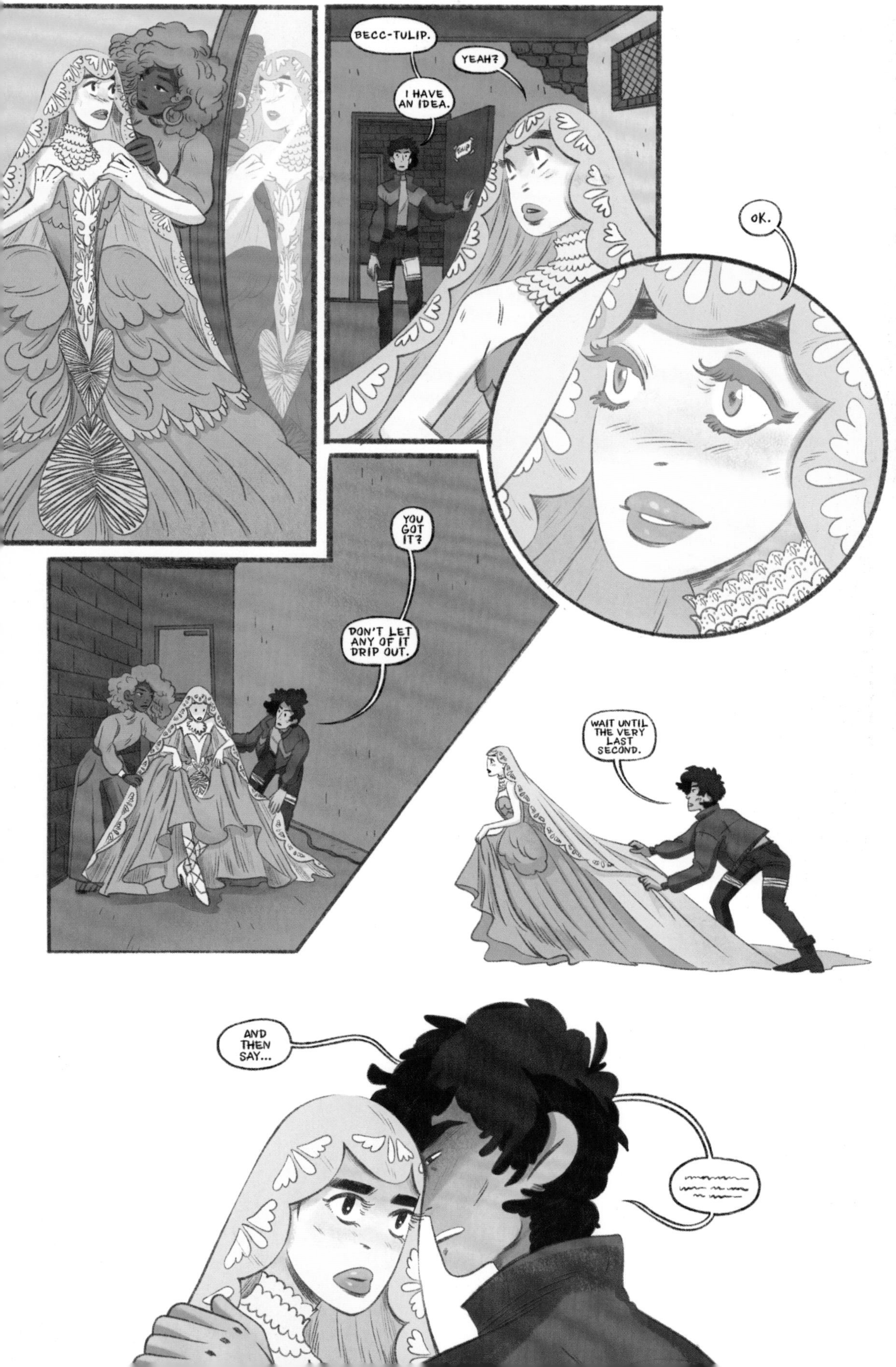
BECC-TULIP.
I HAVE AN IDEA.
YEAH?
OK.
YOU GOT IT?
DON'T LET ANY OF IT DRIP OUT.
WAIT UNTIL THE VERY LAST SECOND.
AND THEN SAY...

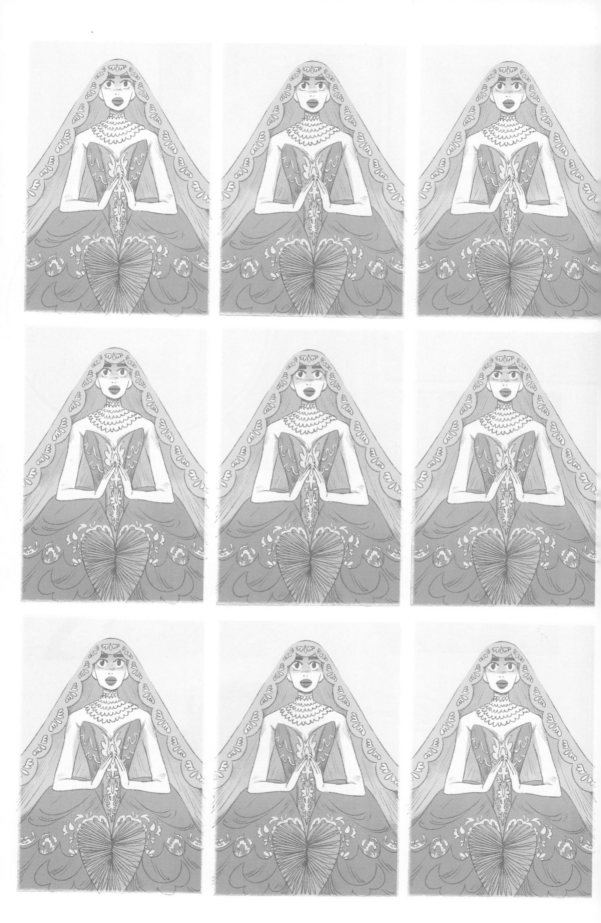

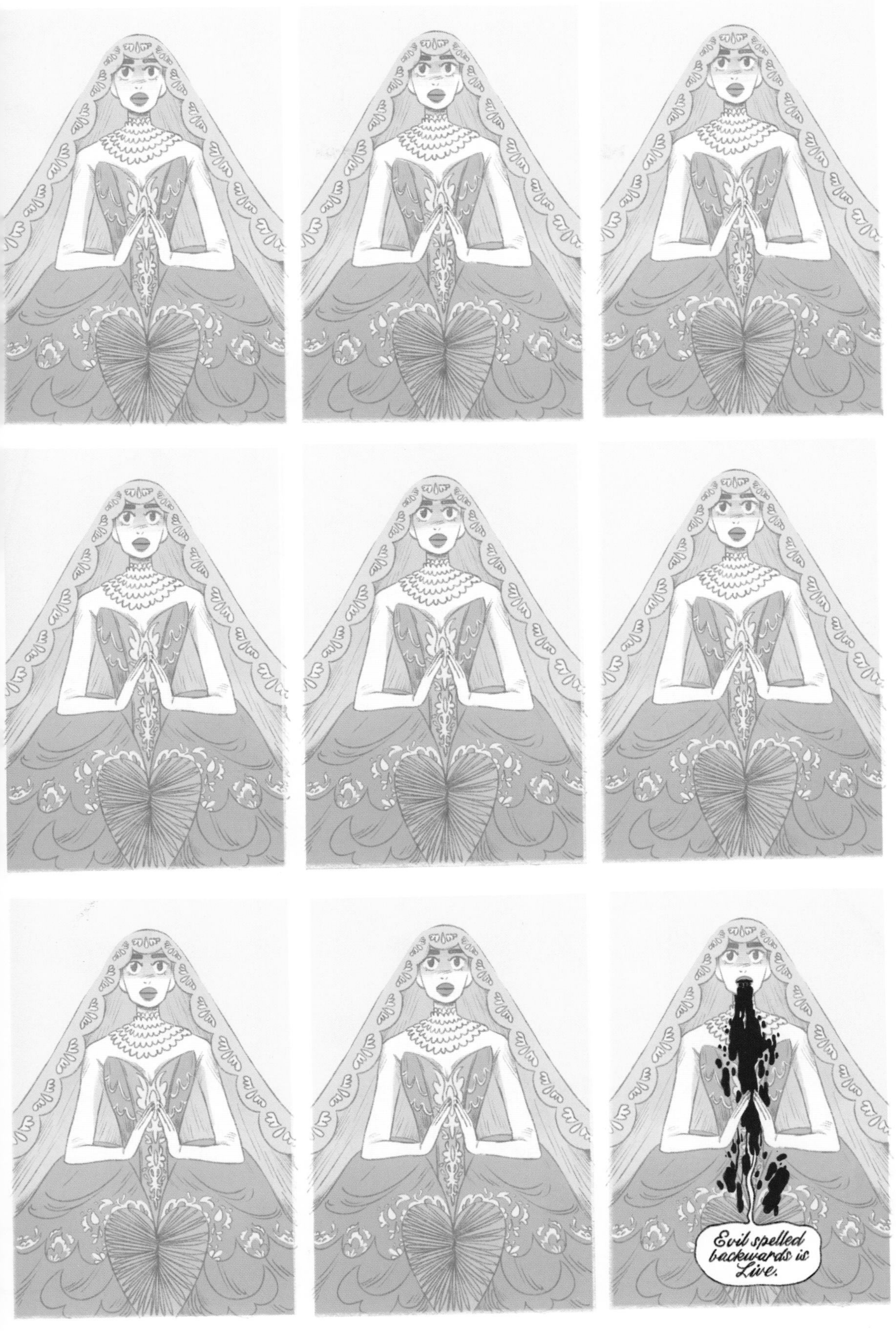
Evil spelled backwards is Live.

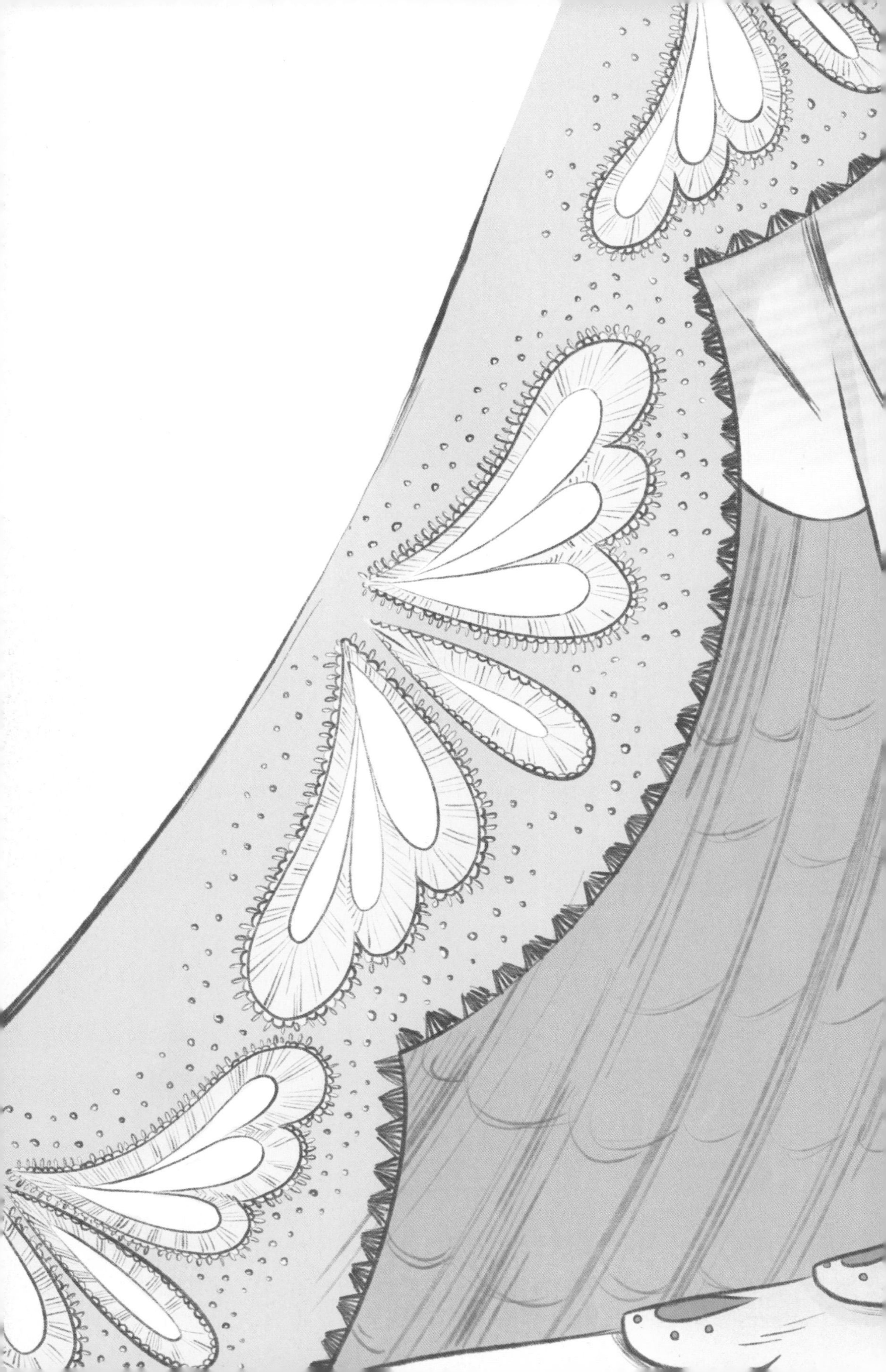

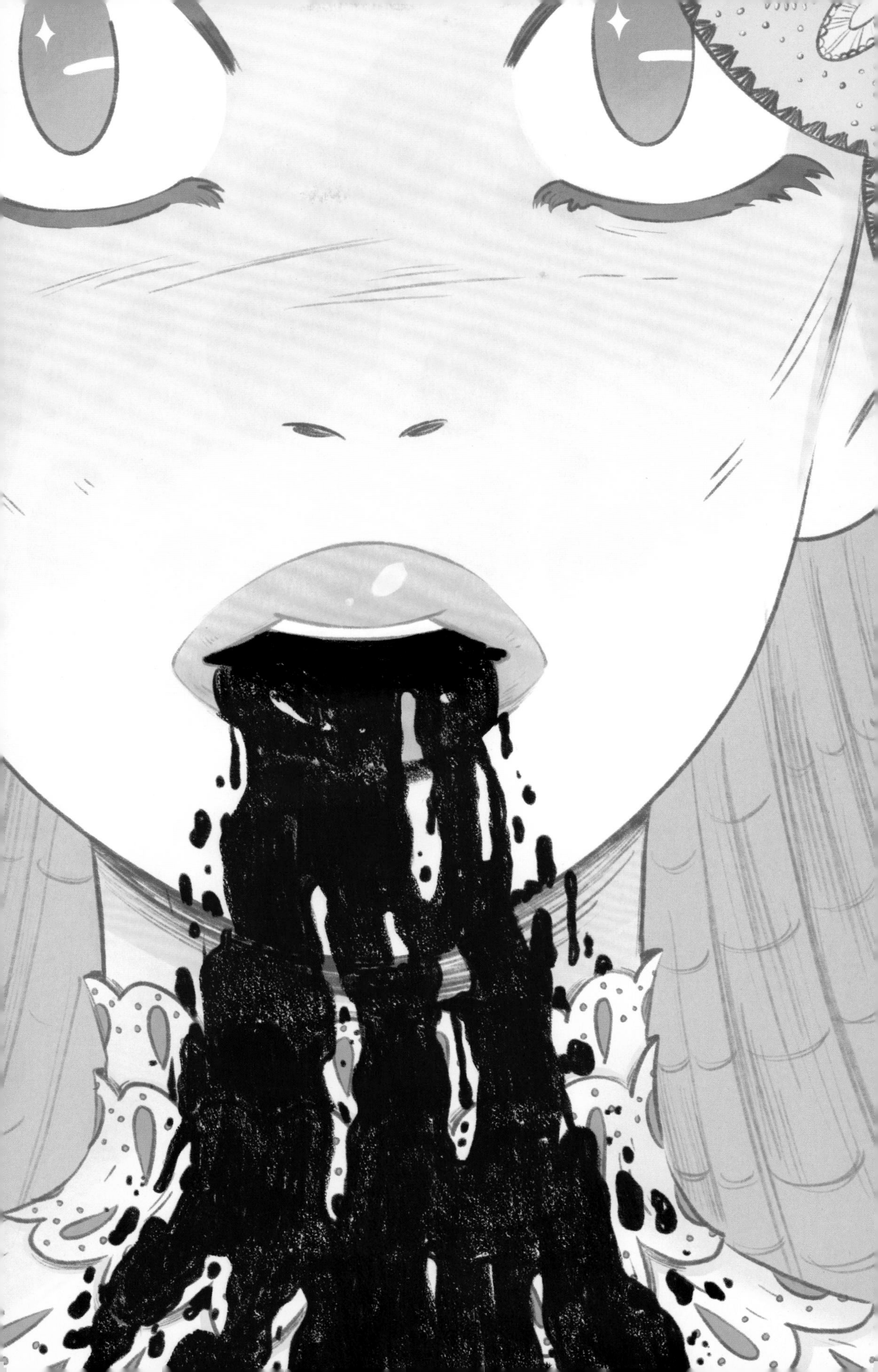

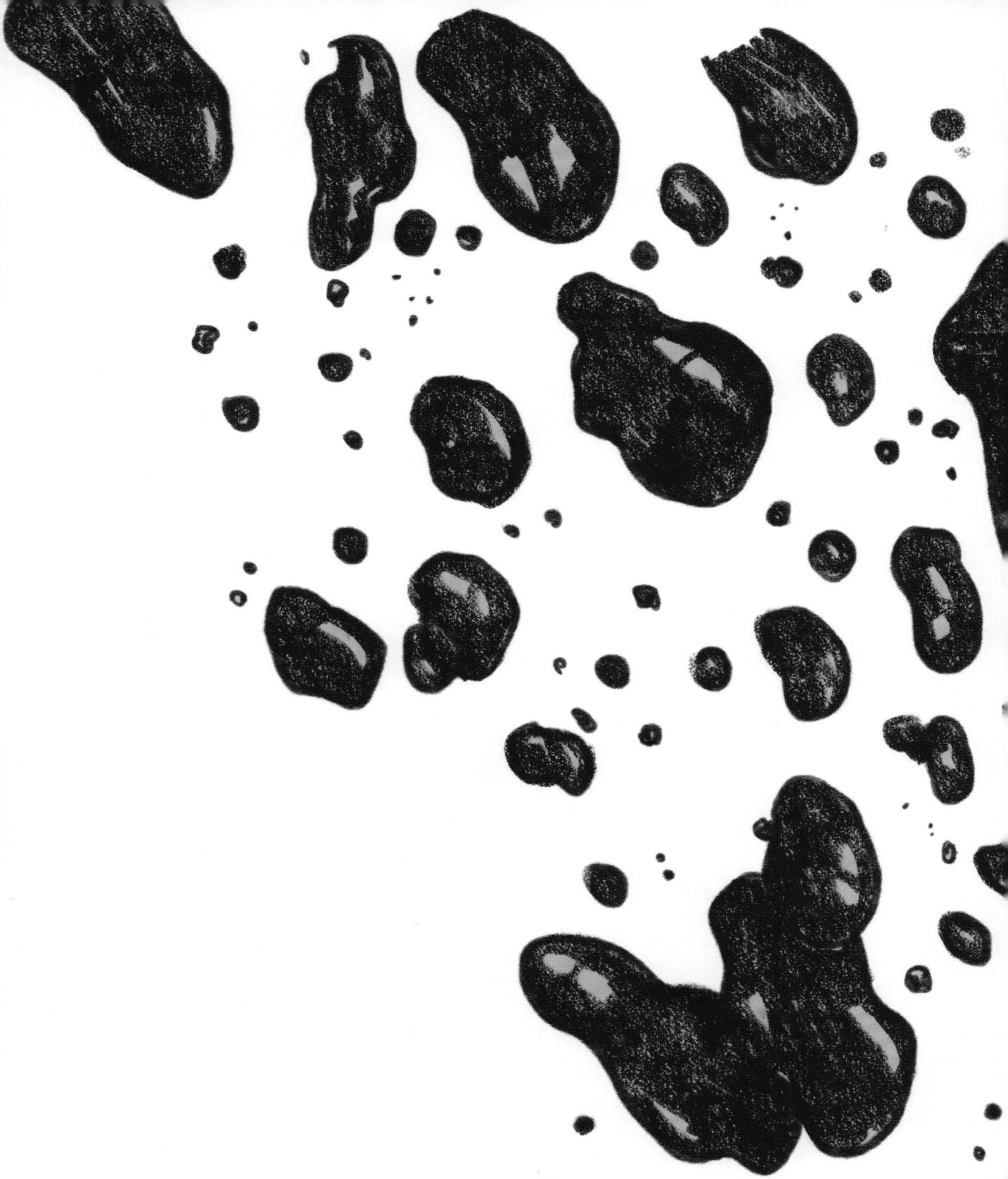

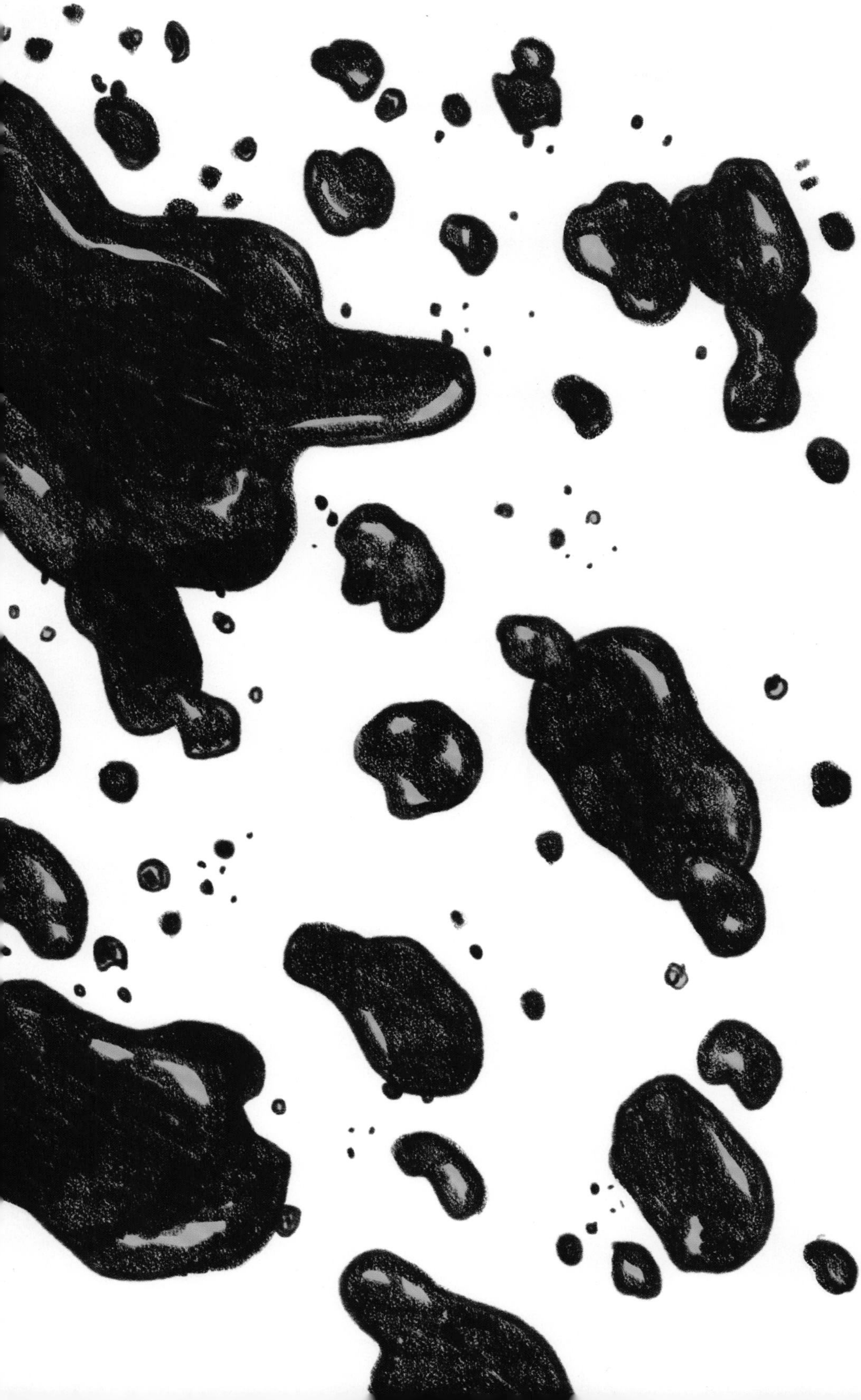

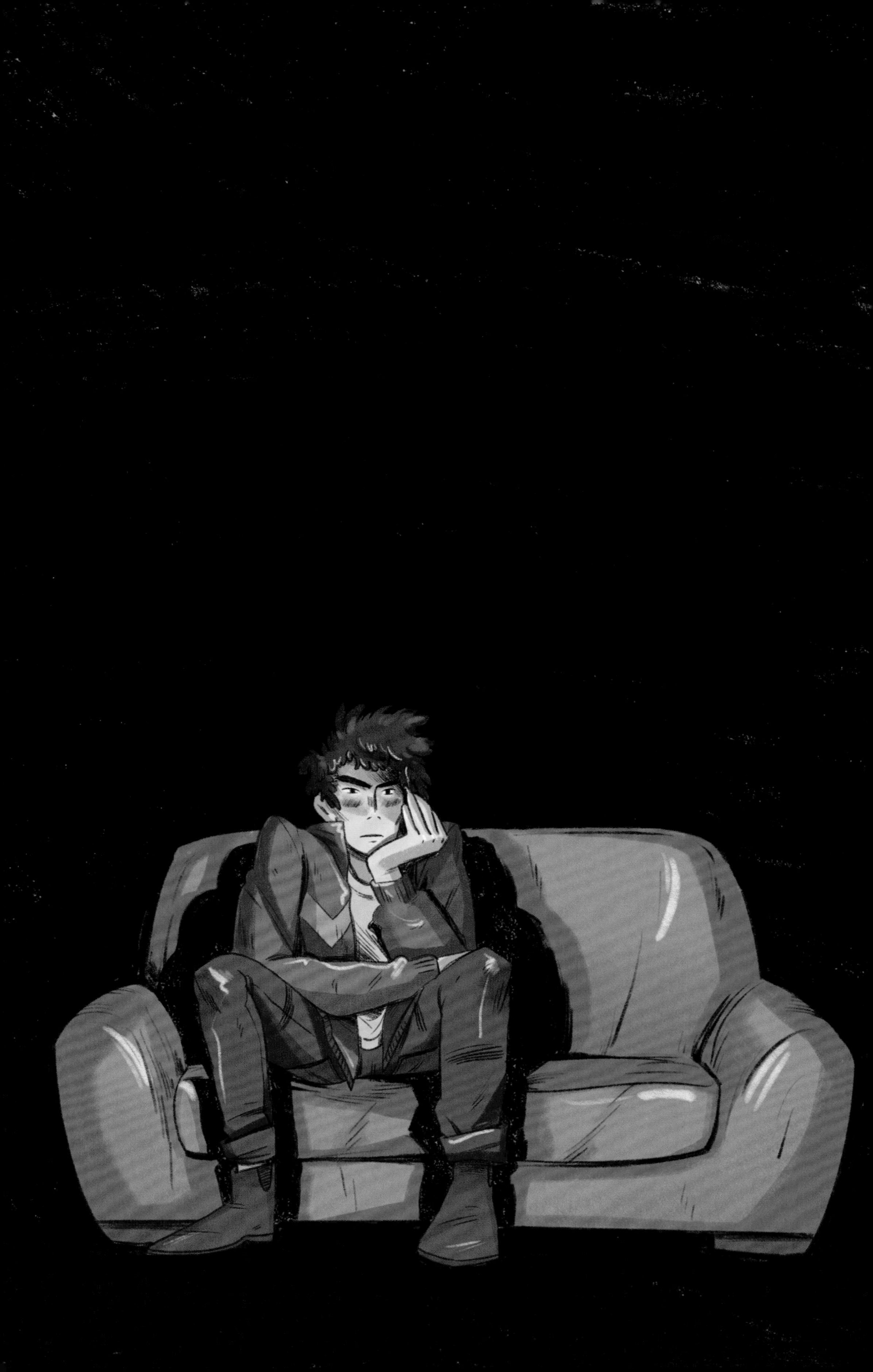

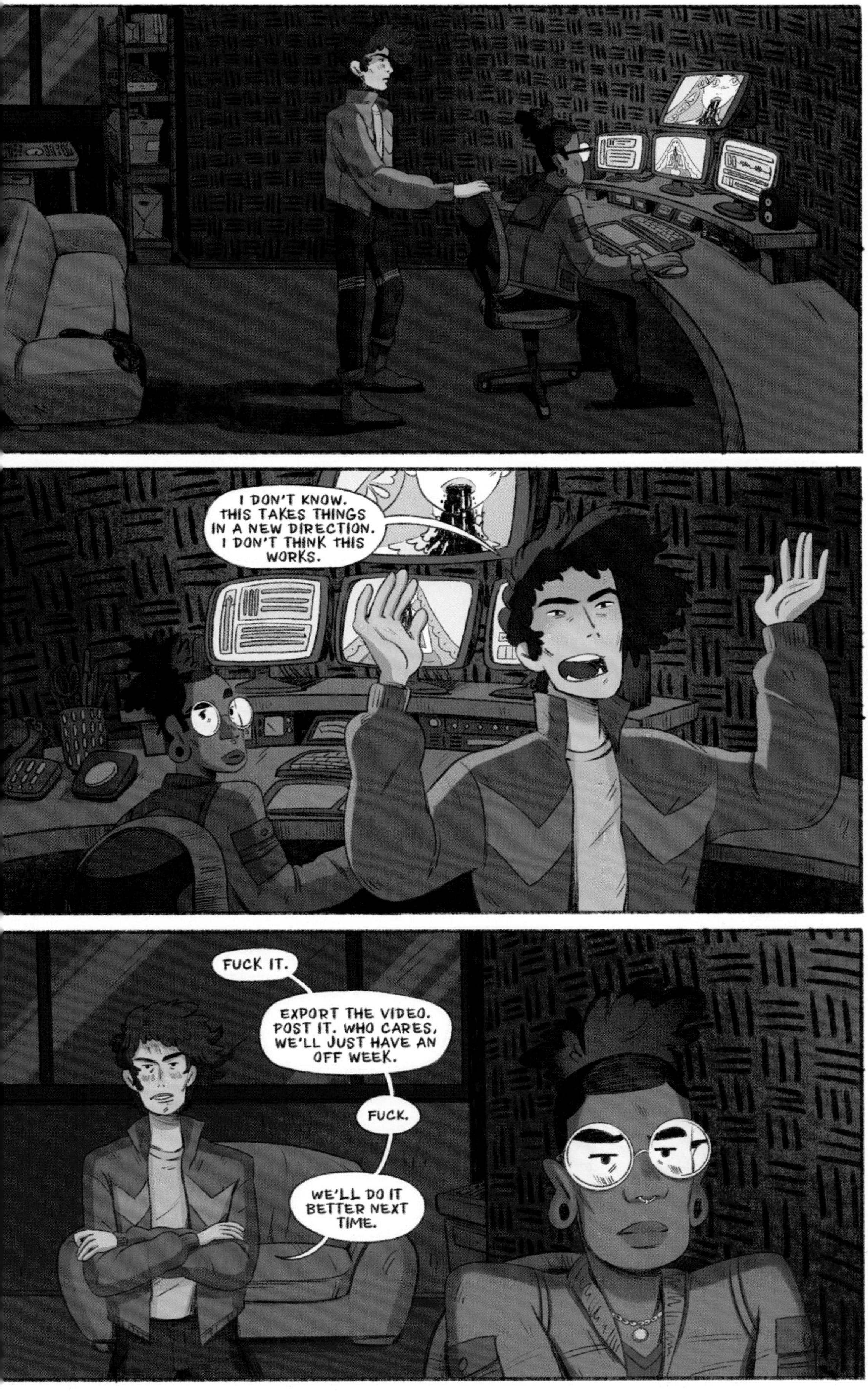
I DON'T KNOW. THIS TAKES THINGS IN A NEW DIRECTION. I DON'T THINK THIS WORKS.
FUCK IT.
EXPORT THE VIDEO. POST IT. WHO CARES, WE'LL JUST HAVE AN OFF WEEK.
FUCK.
WE'LL DO IT BETTER NEXT TIME.

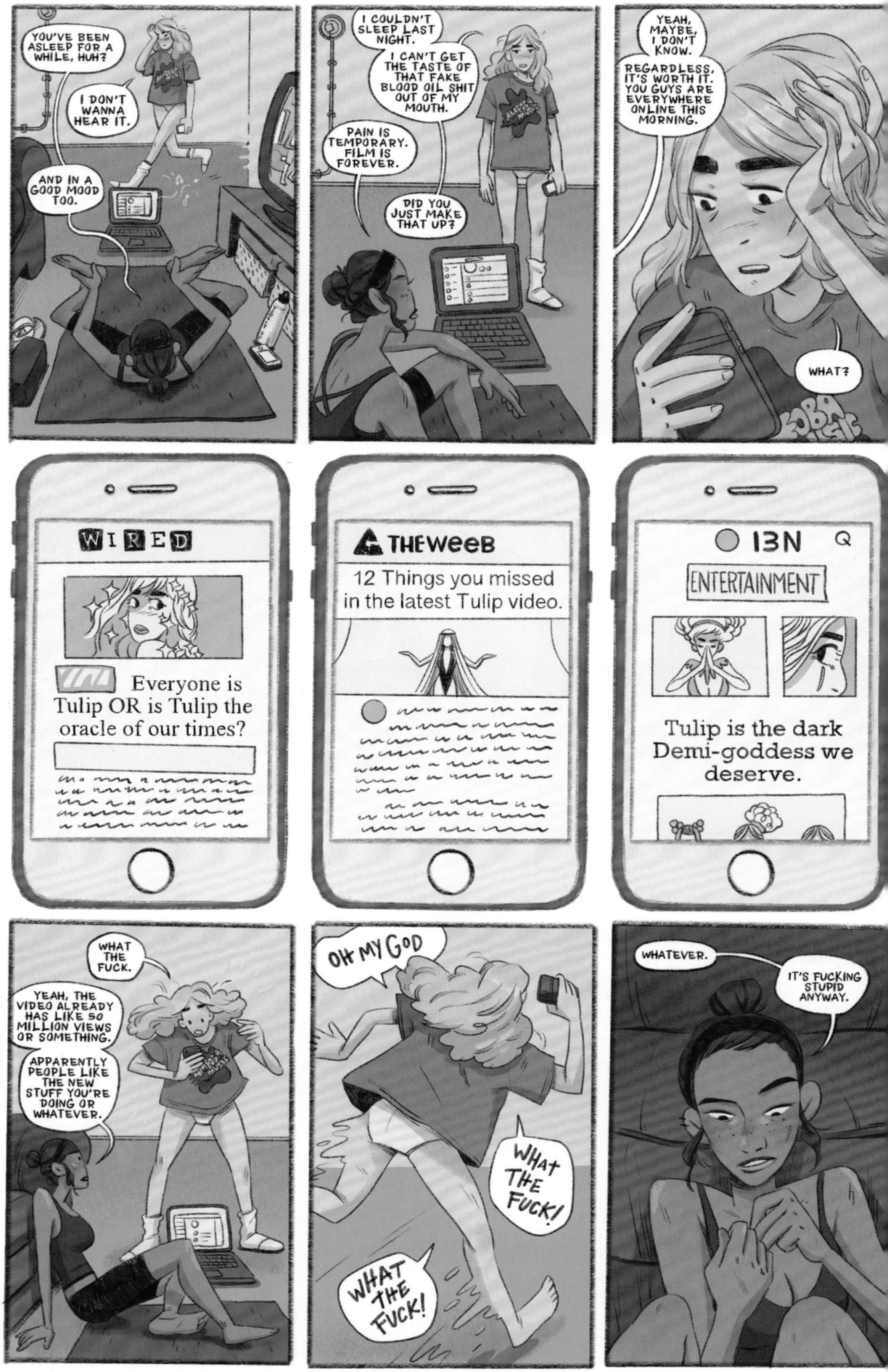
YOU'VE BEEN ASLEEP FOR A WHILE, HUH?
I DON'T WANNA HEAR IT.
AND IN A GOOD MOOD TOO.
I COULDN'T SLEEP LAST NIGHT.
I CAN'T GET THE TASTE OF THAT FAKE BLOOD OIL SHIT OUT OF MY MOUTH.
PAIN IS TEMPORARY. FILM IS FOREVER.
DID YOU JUST MAKE THAT UP?
YEAH, MAYBE, I DON'T KNOW.
REGARDLESS, IT'S WORTH IT. YOU GUYS ARE EVERYWHERE ONLINE THIS MORNING.
WHAT?
WIRED
Everyone is Tulip OR is Tulip the oracle of our times?
THEWEEB
12 Things you missed in the latest Tulip video.
I3N
ENTERTAINMENT
Tulip is the dark Demi-goddess we deserve.
WHAT THE FUCK.
YEAH, THE VIDEO ALREADY HAS LIKE 50 MILLION VIEWS OR SOMETHING.
APPARENTLY PEOPLE LIKE THE NEW STUFF YOU'RE DOING OR WHATEVER.
OH MY GOD
WHAT THE FUCK!
WHAT THE FUCK!
WHATEVER.
IT'S FUCKING STUPID ANYWAY.

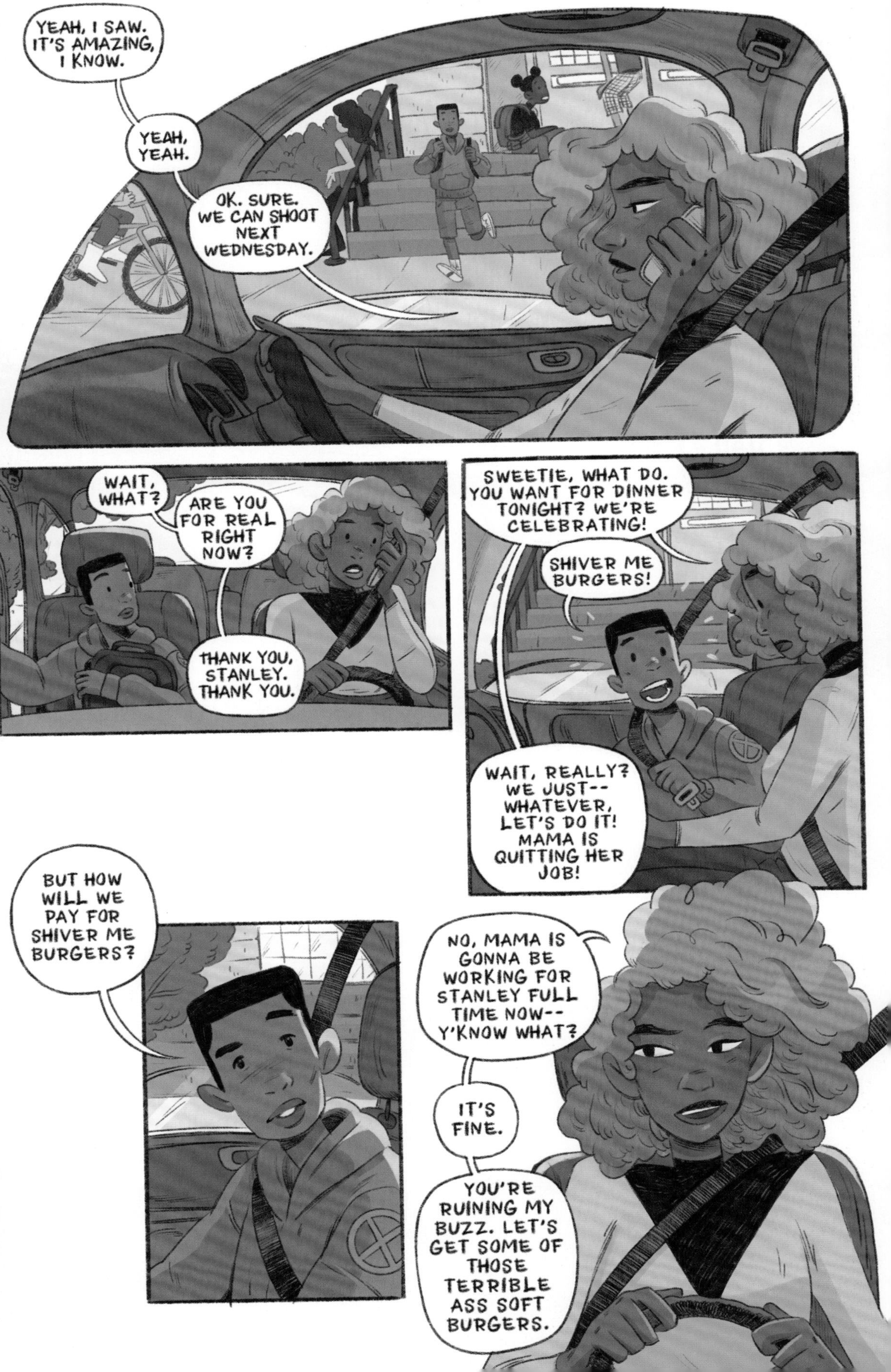
YEAH, I SAW. IT'S AMAZING, I KNOW.
YEAH, YEAH.
OK. SURE. WE CAN SHOOT NEXT WEDNESDAY.
WAIT, WHAT?
ARE YOU FOR REAL RIGHT NOW?
THANK YOU, STANLEY. THANK YOU.
SWEETIE, WHAT DO. YOU WANT FOR DINNER TONIGHT? WE'RE CELEBRATING!
SHIVER ME BURGERS!
WAIT, REALLY? WE JUST-- WHATEVER, LET'S DO IT! MAMA IS QUITTING HER JOB!
BUT HOW WILL WE PAY FOR SHIVER ME BURGERS?
NO, MAMA IS GONNA BE WORKING FOR STANLEY FULL TIME NOW-- Y'KNOW WHAT?
IT'S FINE.
YOU'RE RUINING MY BUZZ. LET'S GET SOME OF THOSE TERRIBLE ASS SOFT BURGERS.

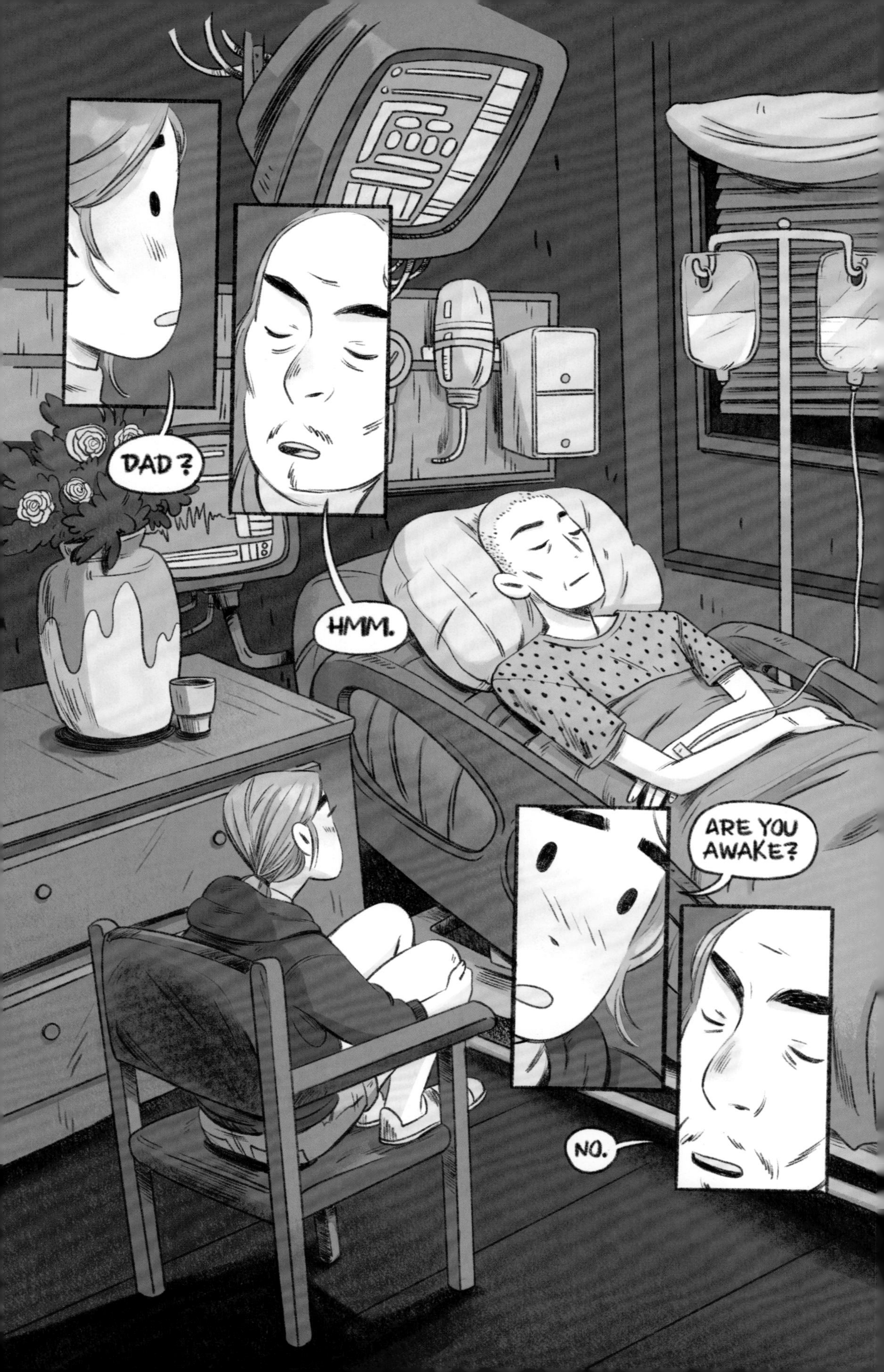
DAD?
HMM.
ARE YOU AWAKE?
NO.

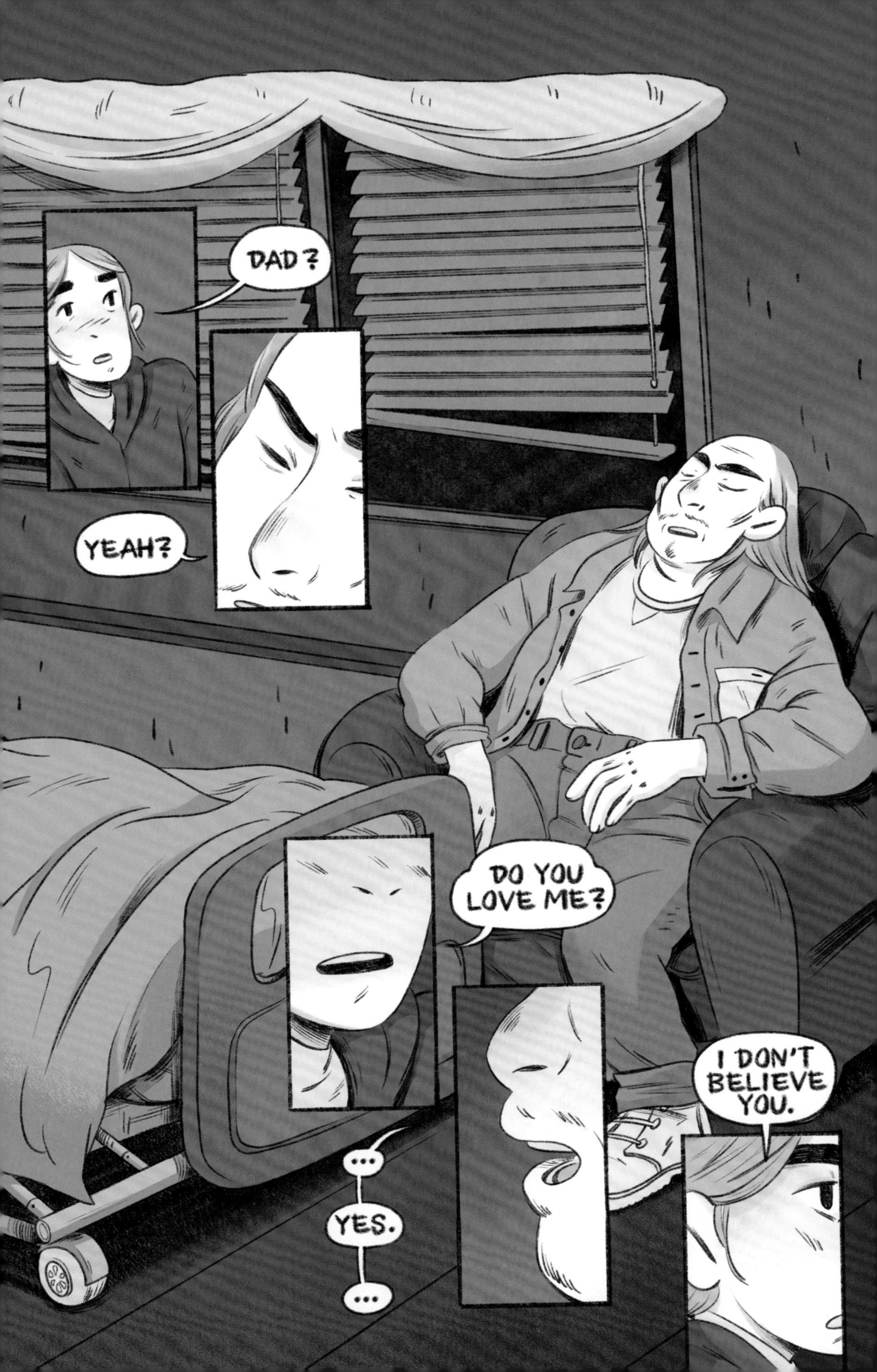
DAD?
YEAH?
DO YOU LOVE ME?
...
YES.
...
I DON'T BELIEVE YOU.

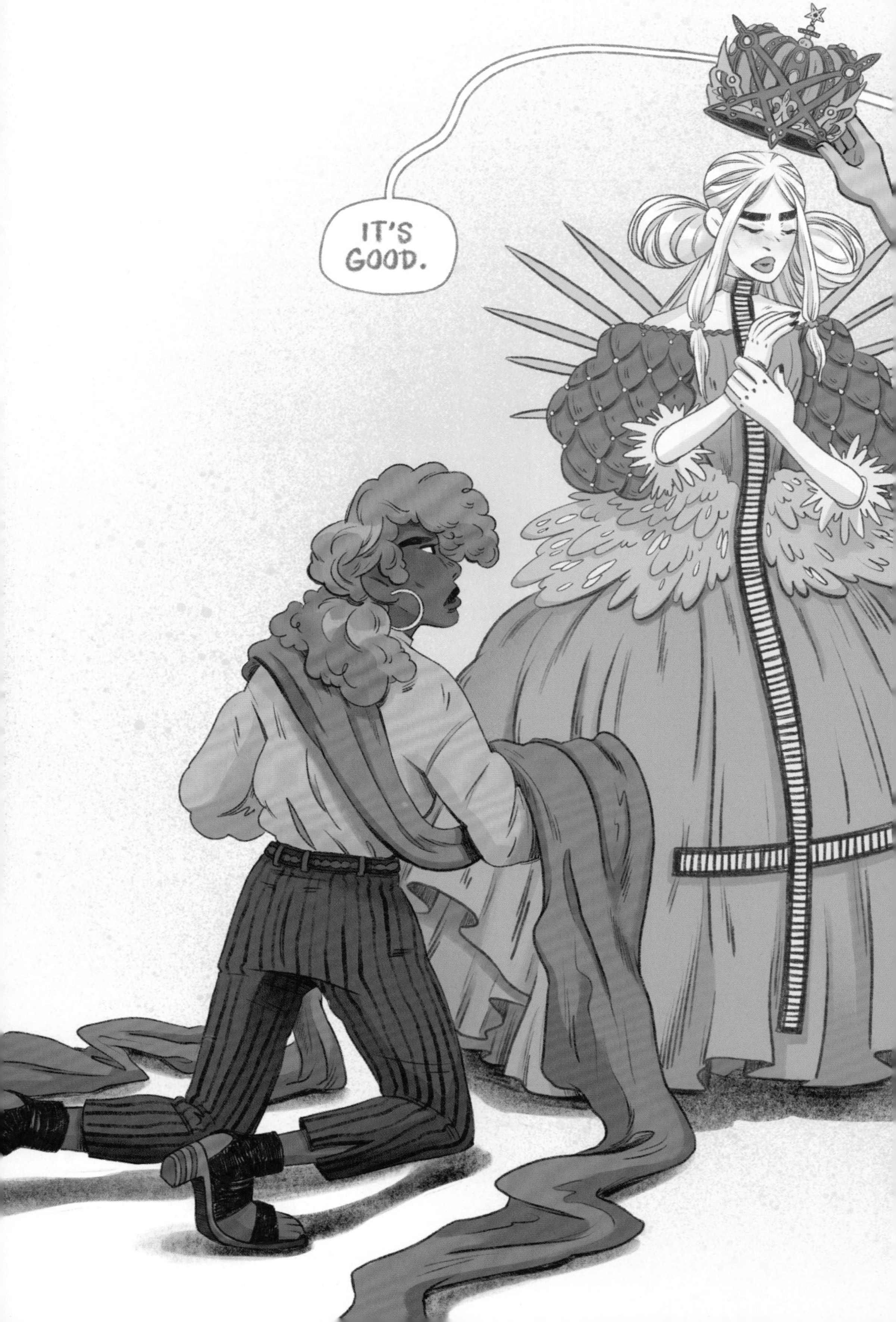
IT'S GOOD.

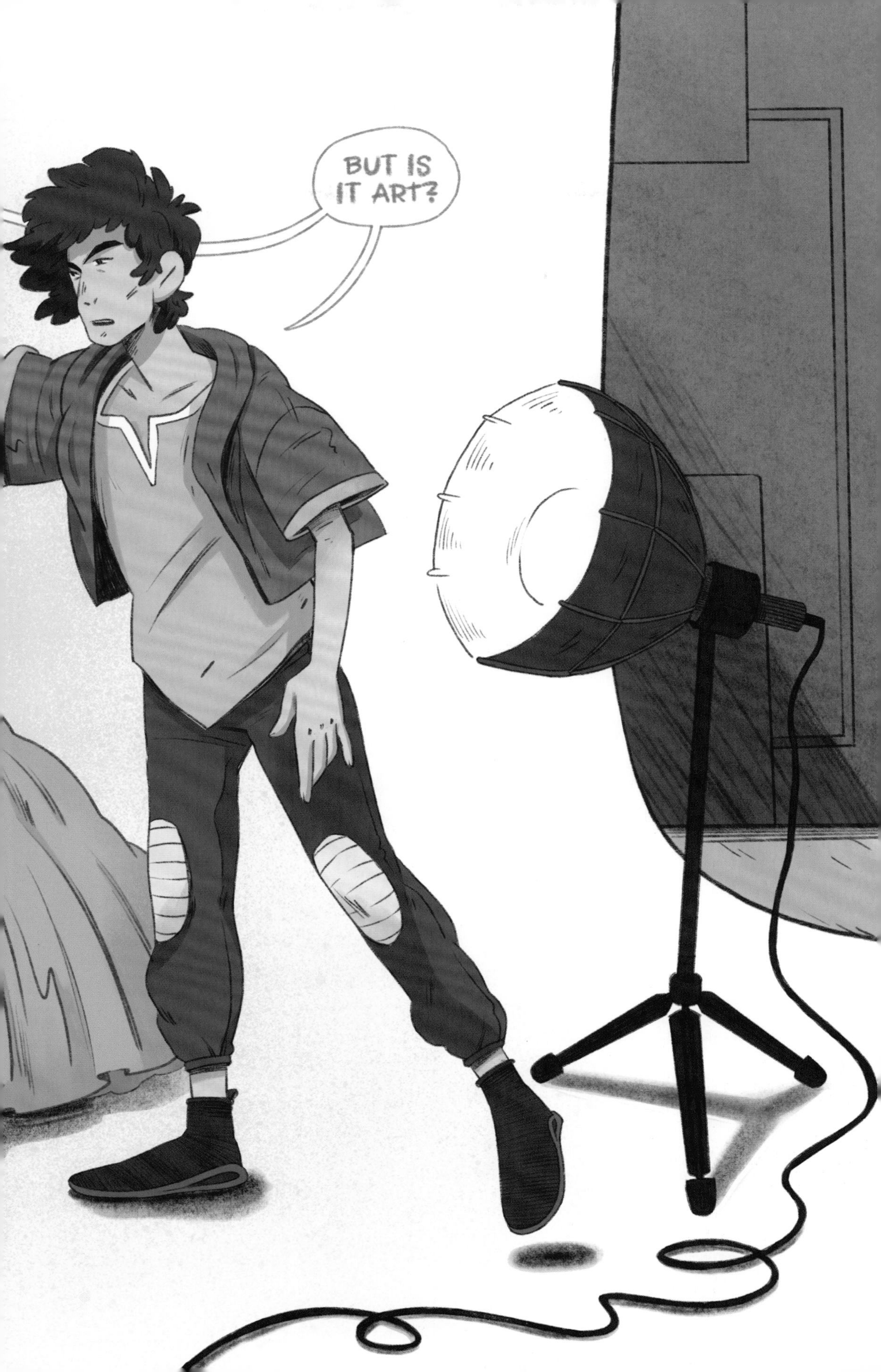
BUT IS IT ART?

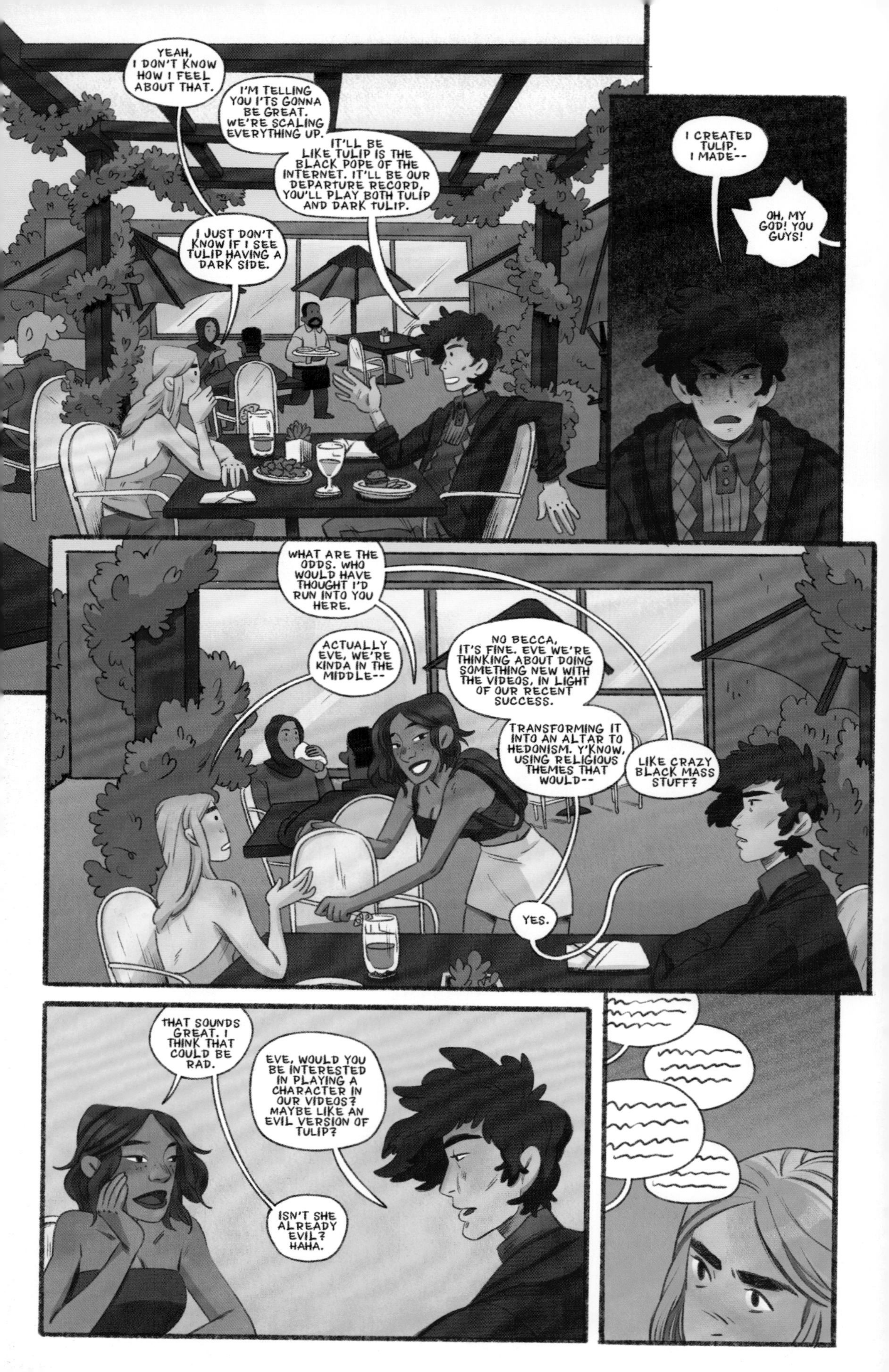
YEAH, I DON'T KNOW HOW I FEEL ABOUT THAT.
I'M TELLING YOU IT'S GONNA BE GREAT. WE'RE SCALING EVERYTHING UP.
IT'LL BE LIKE TULIP IS THE BLACK POPE OF THE INTERNET. IT'LL BE OUR DEPARTURE RECORD, YOU'LL PLAY BOTH TULIP AND DARK TULIP.
I JUST DON'T KNOW IF I SEE TULIP HAVING A DARK SIDE.
I CREATED TULIP. I MADE--
OH, MY GOD! YOU GUYS!
WHAT ARE THE ODDS. WHO WOULD HAVE THOUGHT I'D RUN INTO YOU HERE.
ACTUALLY EVE, WE'RE KINDA IN THE MIDDLE--
NO BECCA, IT'S FINE. EVE WE'RE THINKING ABOUT DOING SOMETHING NEW WITH THE VIDEOS, IN LIGHT OF OUR RECENT SUCCESS.
TRANSFORMING IT INTO AN ALTAR TO HEDONISM. Y'KNOW, USING RELIGIOUS THEMES THAT WOULD--
LIKE CRAZY BLACK MASS STUFF?
YES.
THAT SOUNDS GREAT. I THINK THAT COULD BE RAD.
EVE, WOULD YOU BE INTERESTED IN PLAYING A CHARACTER IN OUR VIDEOS? MAYBE LIKE AN EVIL VERSION OF TULIP?
ISN'T SHE ALREADY EVIL? HAHA.

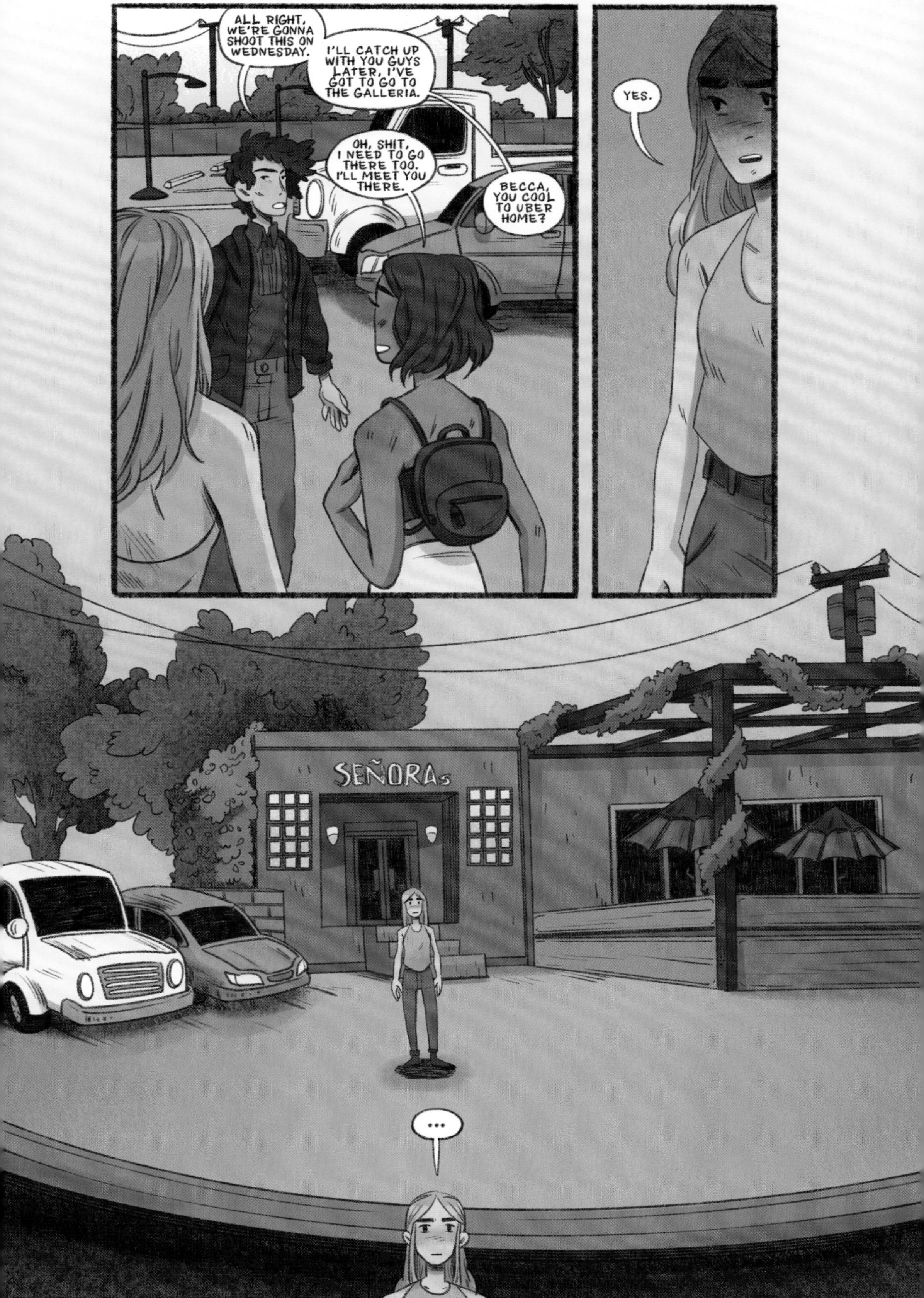
ALL RIGHT, WE'RE GONNA SHOOT THIS ON WEDNESDAY.
I'LL CATCH UP WITH YOU GUYS LATER, I'VE GOT TO GO TO THE GALLERIA.
OH, SHIT, I NEED TO GO THERE TOO. I'LL MEET YOU THERE.
BECCA, YOU COOL TO UBER HOME?
YES.
SEÑORAs
...

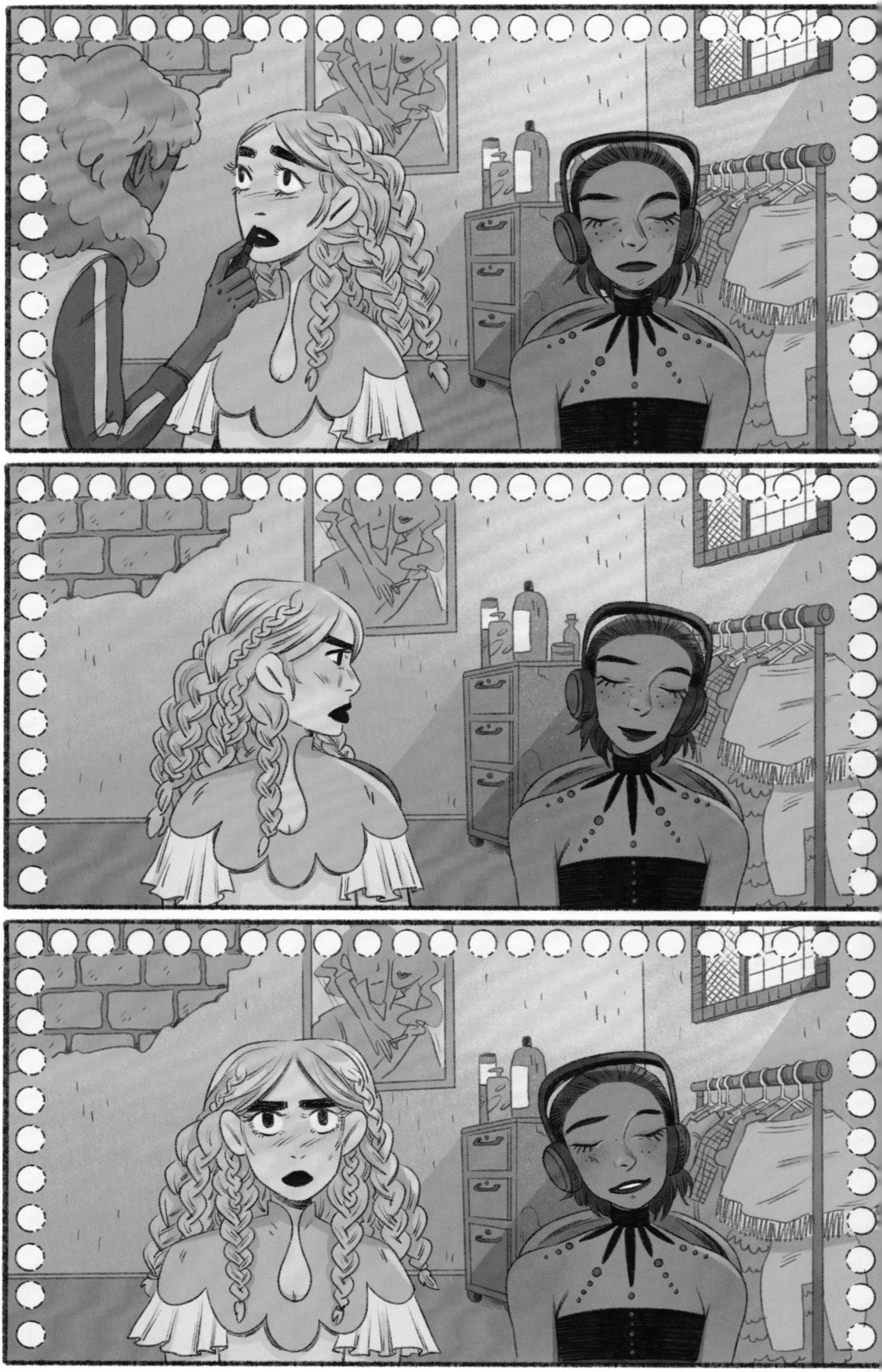

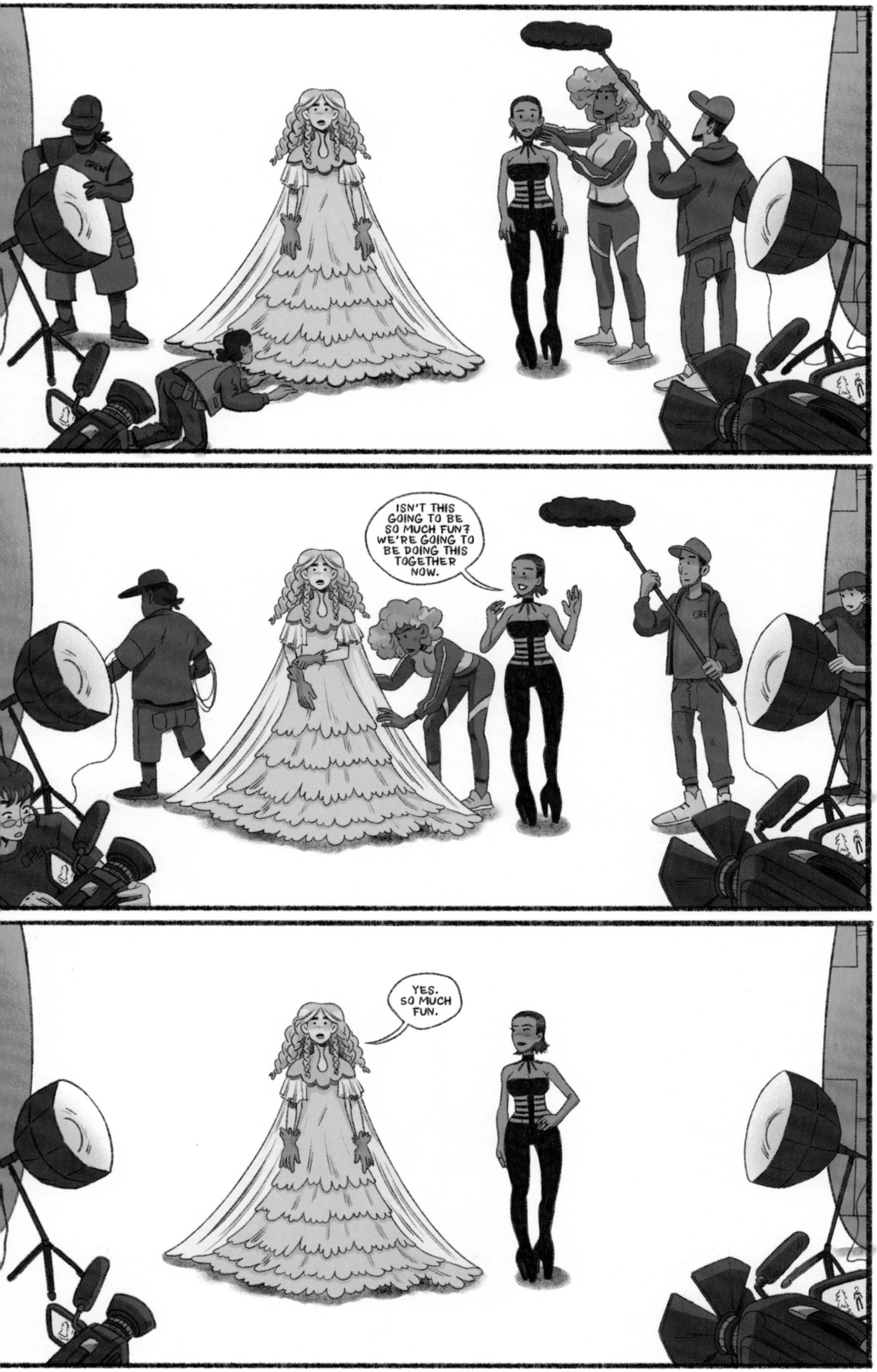
ISN'T THIS GOING TO BE SO MUCH FUN? WE'RE GOING TO BE DOING THIS TOGETHER NOW.
YES. SO MUCH FUN.

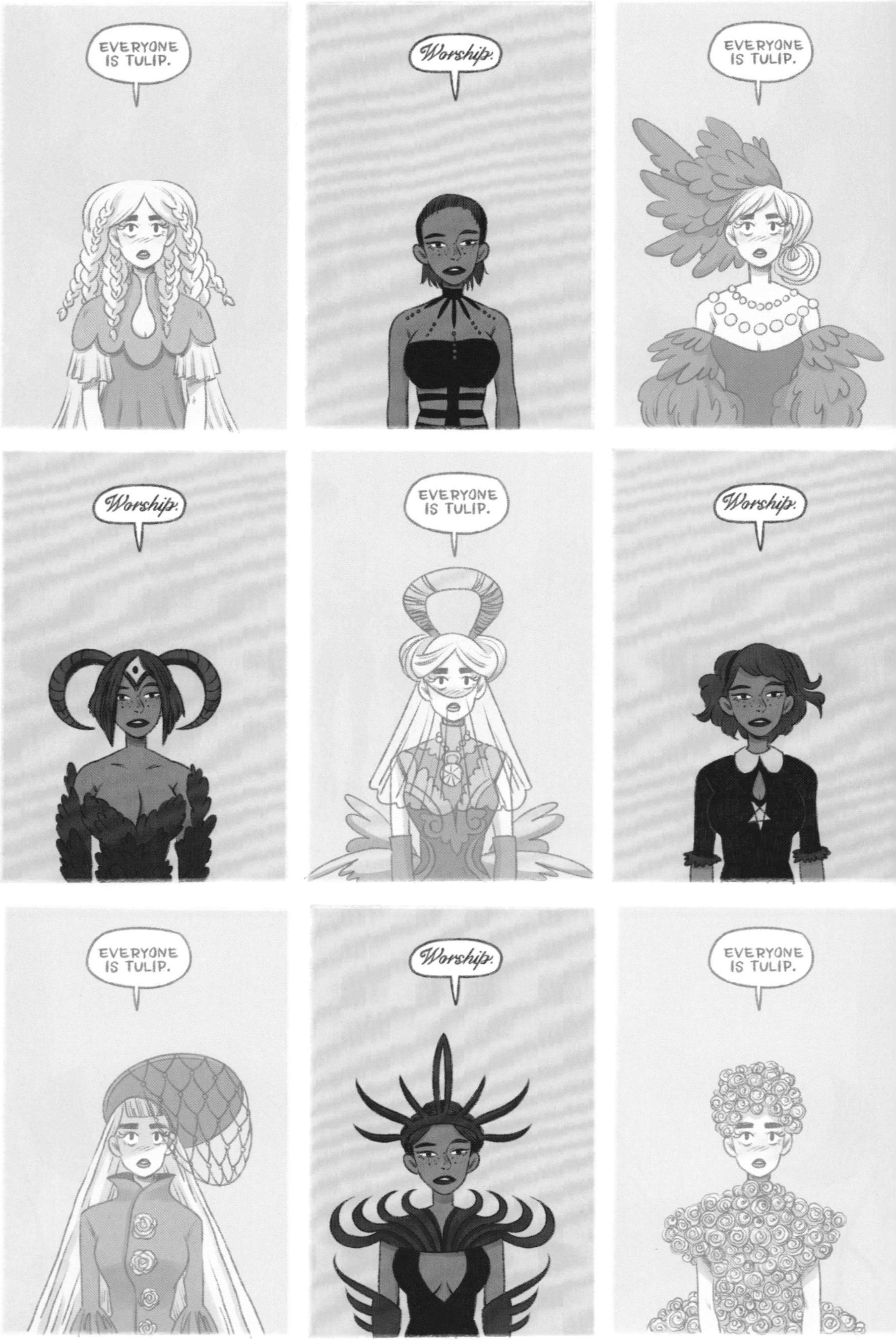
EVERYONE IS TULIP.
Worship.
EVERYONE IS TULIP.
Worship.
EVERYONE IS TULIP.
Worship.
EVERYONE IS TULIP.
Worship.
EVERYONE IS TULIP.

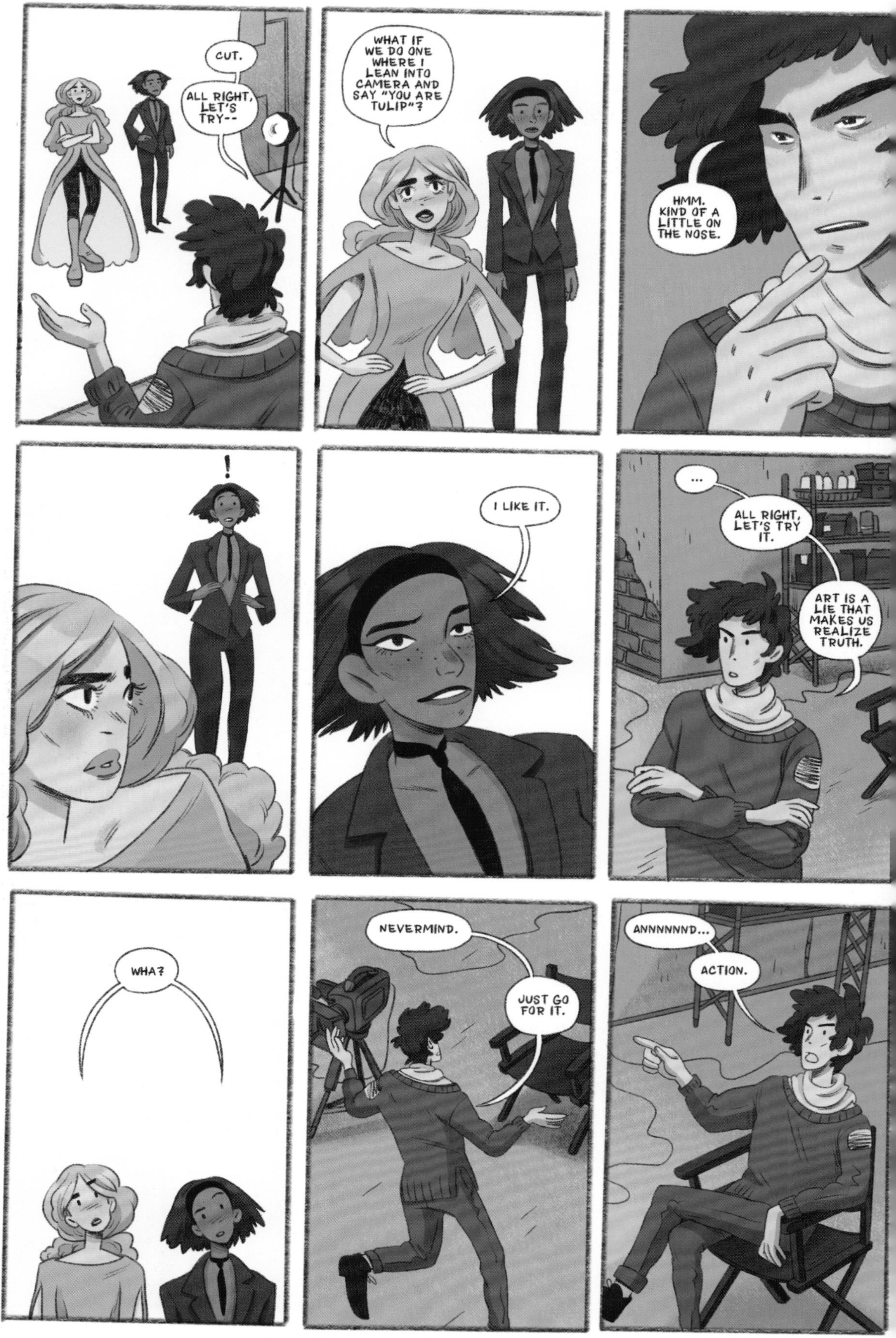
CUT.
ALL RIGHT, LET'S TRY--
WHAT IF WE DO ONE WHERE I LEAN INTO CAMERA AND SAY "YOU ARE TULIP"?
HMM. KIND OF A LITTLE ON THE NOSE.
!
I LIKE IT.
...
ALL RIGHT, LET'S TRY IT.
ART IS A LIE THAT MAKES US REALIZE TRUTH.
WHA?
NEVERMIND.
JUST GO FOR IT.
ANNNNNND...
ACTION.

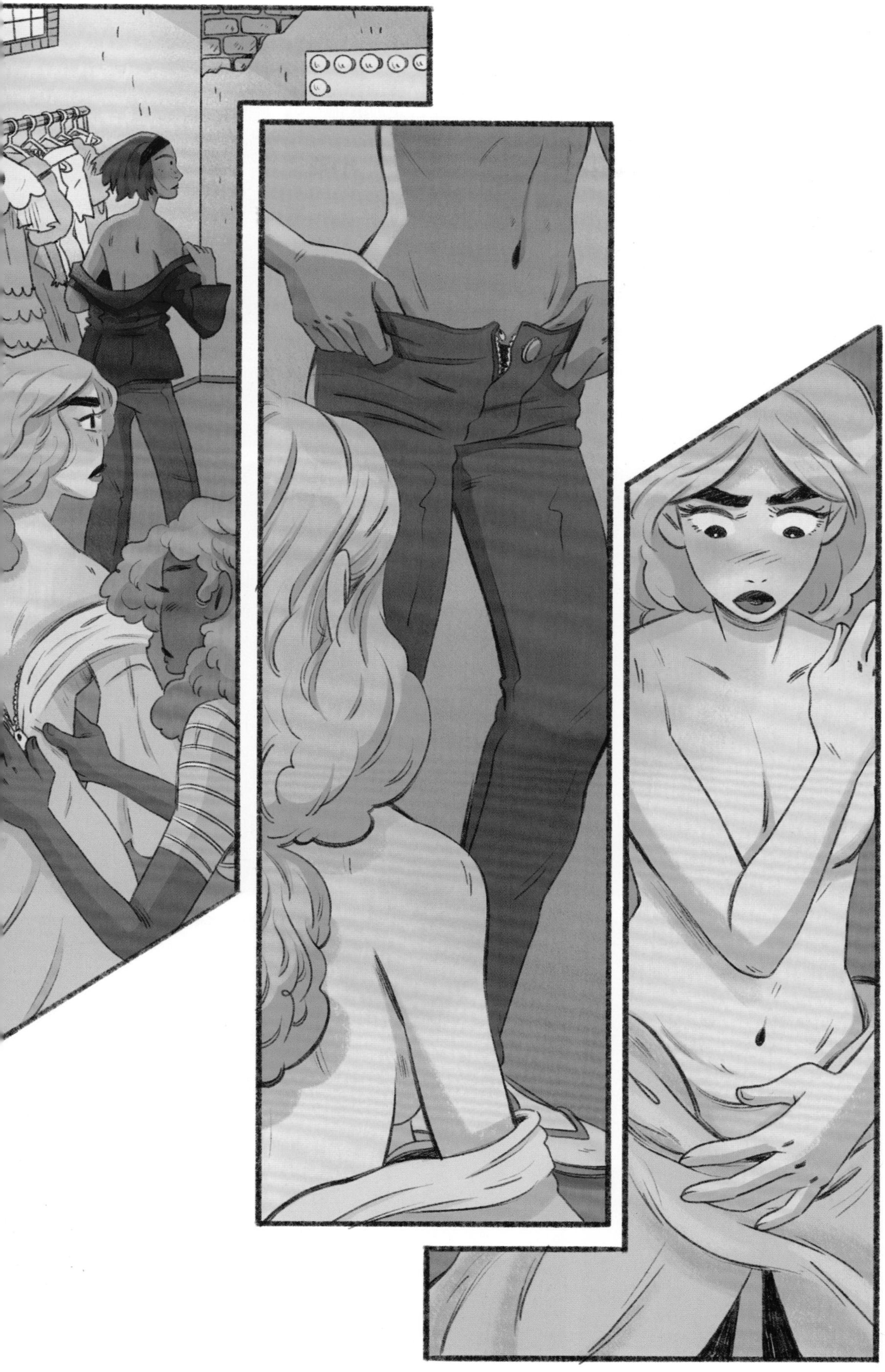

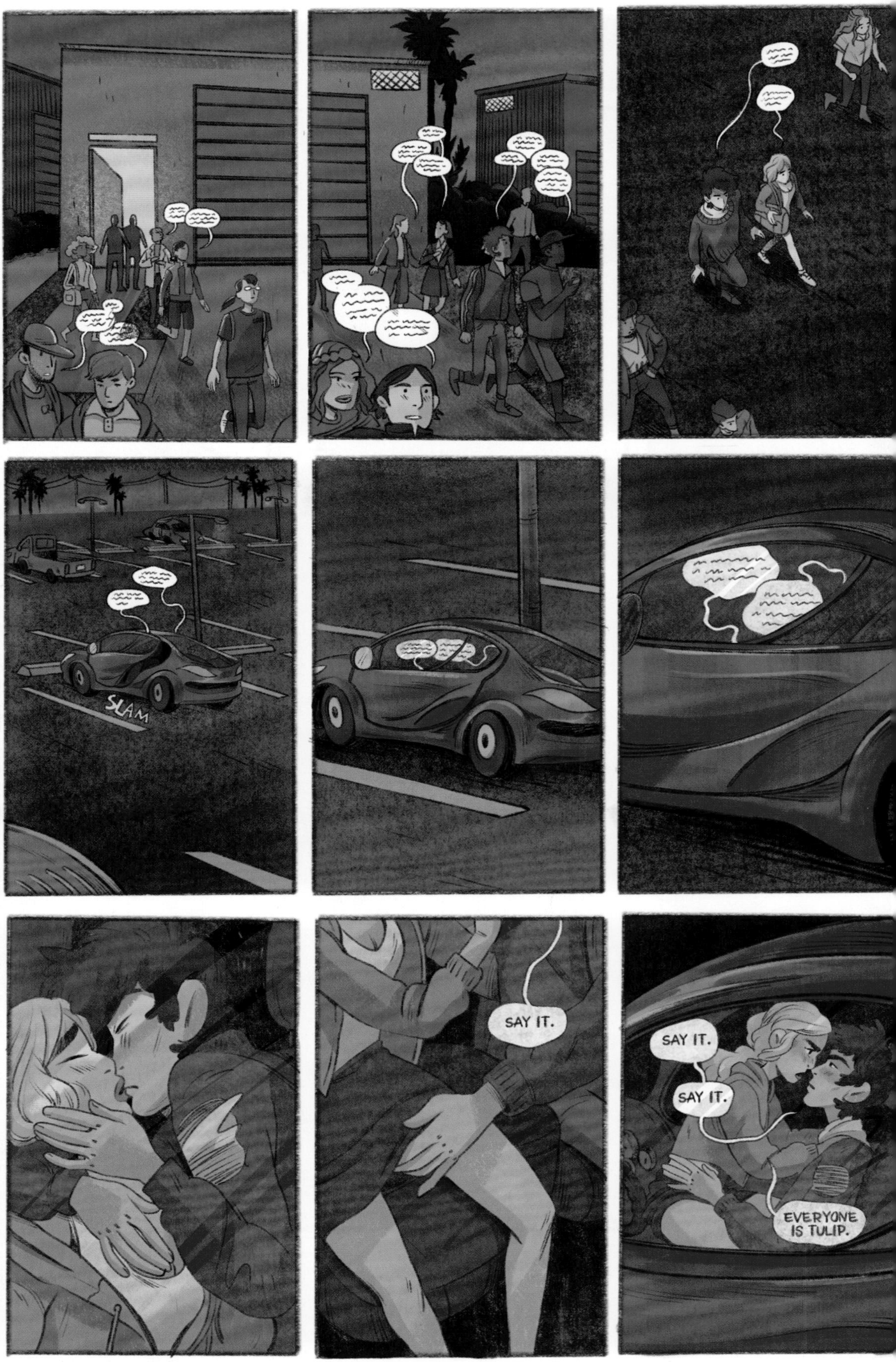
SLAM
SAY IT.
SAY IT.
SAY IT.
EVERYONE IS TULIP.

CHAPTER 5

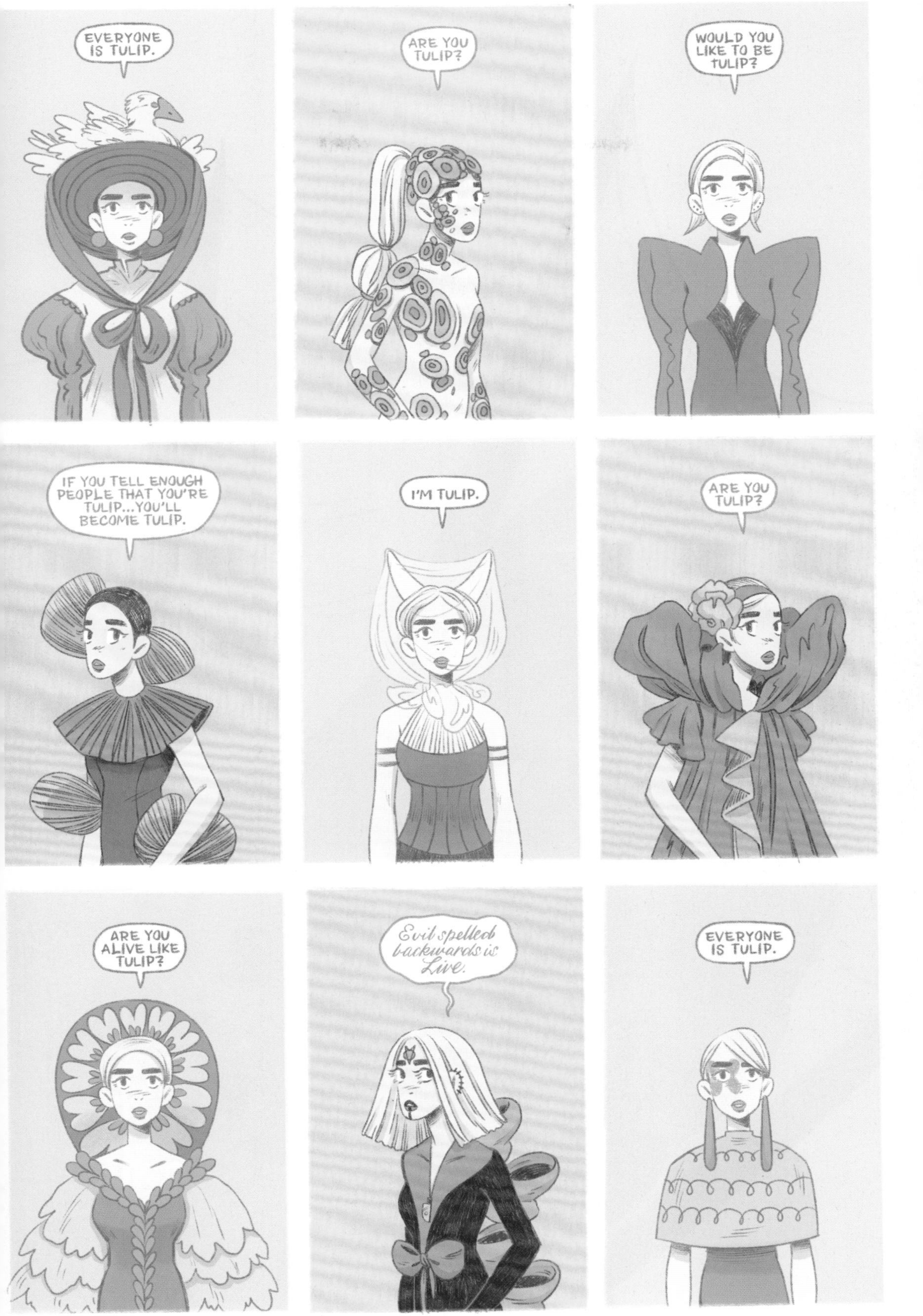
EVERYONE IS TULIP.
ARE YOU TULIP?
WOULD YOU LIKE TO BE TULIP?
IF YOU TELL ENOUGH PEOPLE THAT YOU'RE TULIP...YOU'LL BECOME TULIP.
I'M TULIP.
ARE YOU TULIP?
ARE YOU ALIVE LIKE TULIP?
Evil spelled backwards is Live.
EVERYONE IS TULIP.

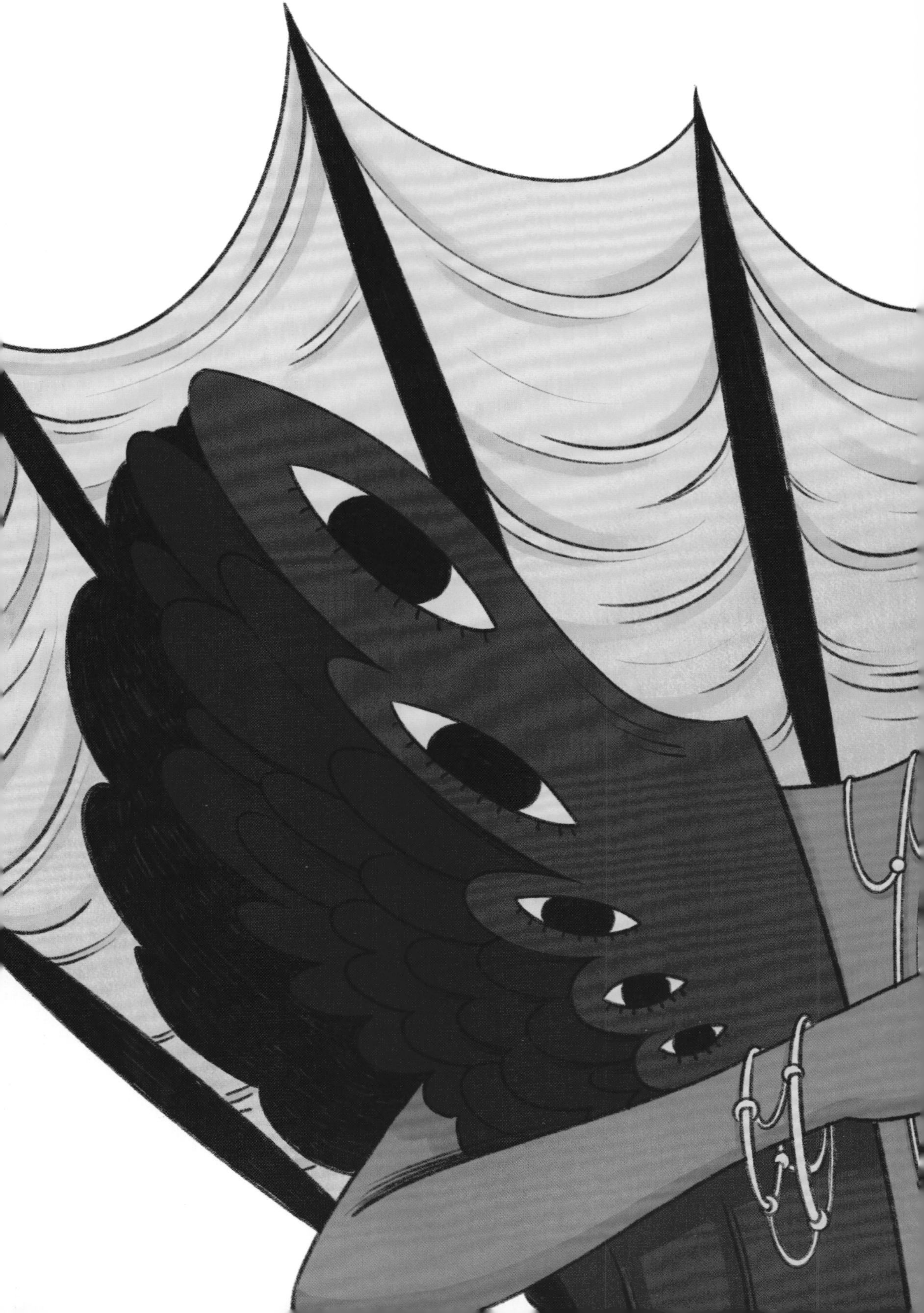

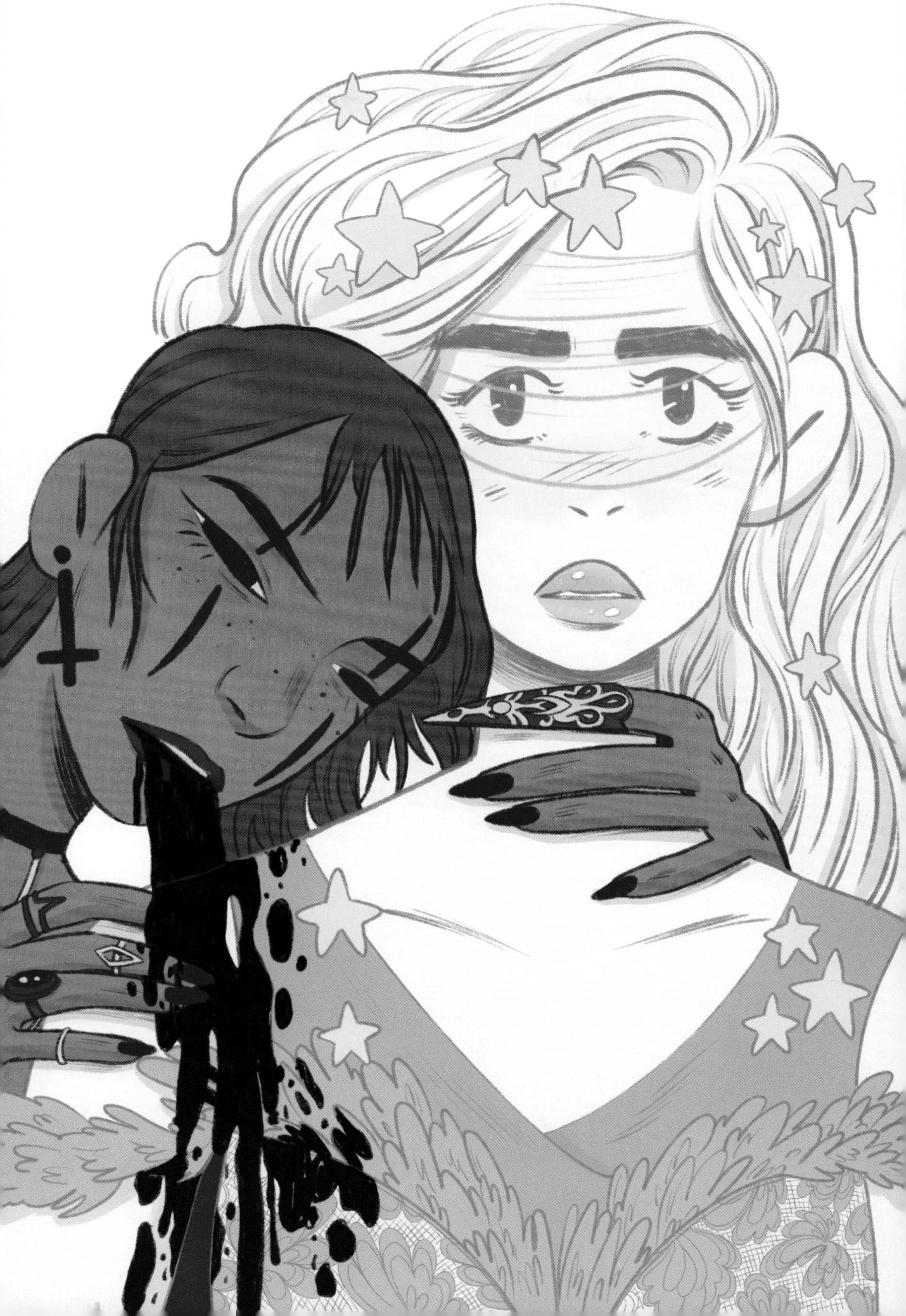

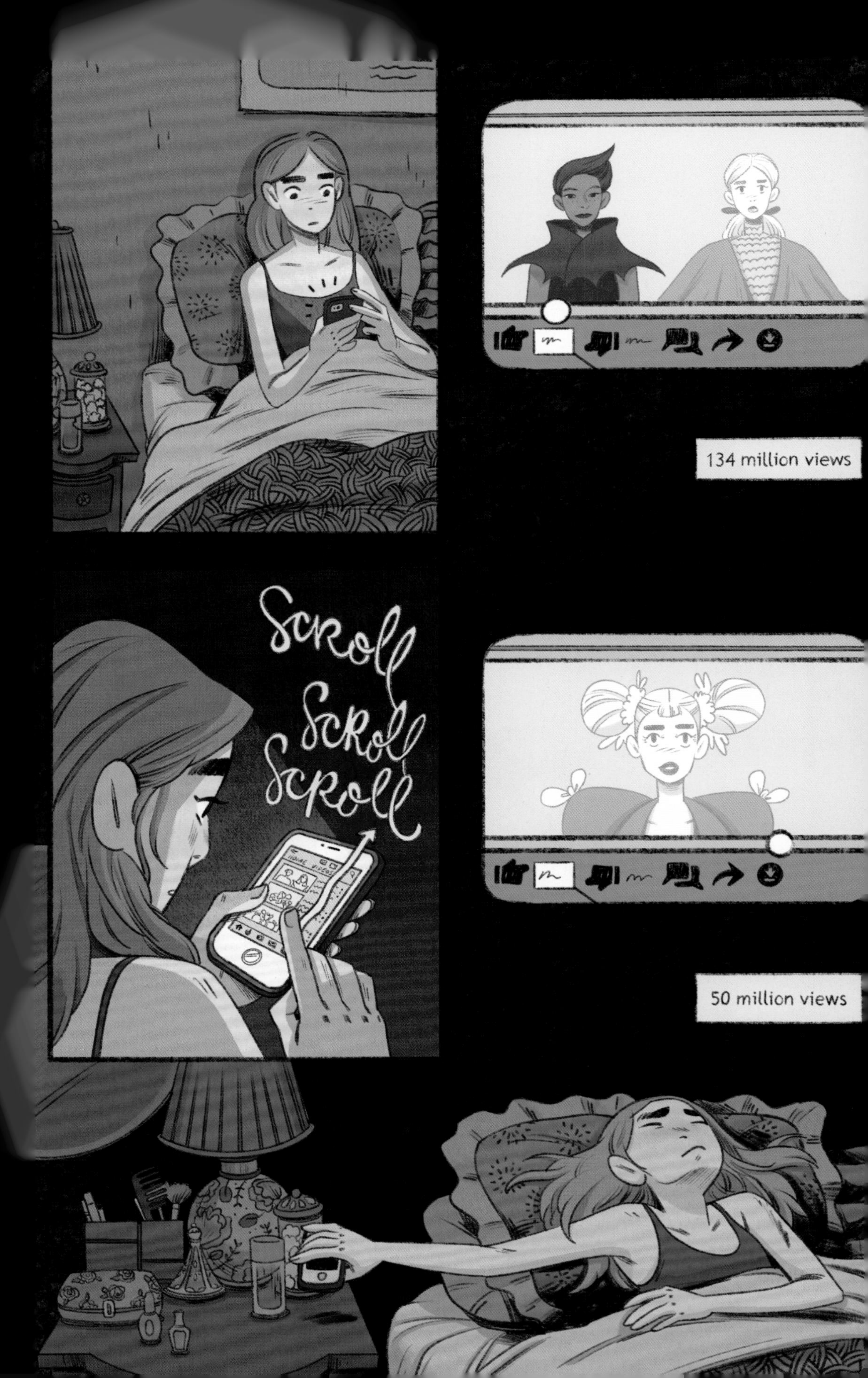
134 million views
scroll
scroll
scroll
50 million views

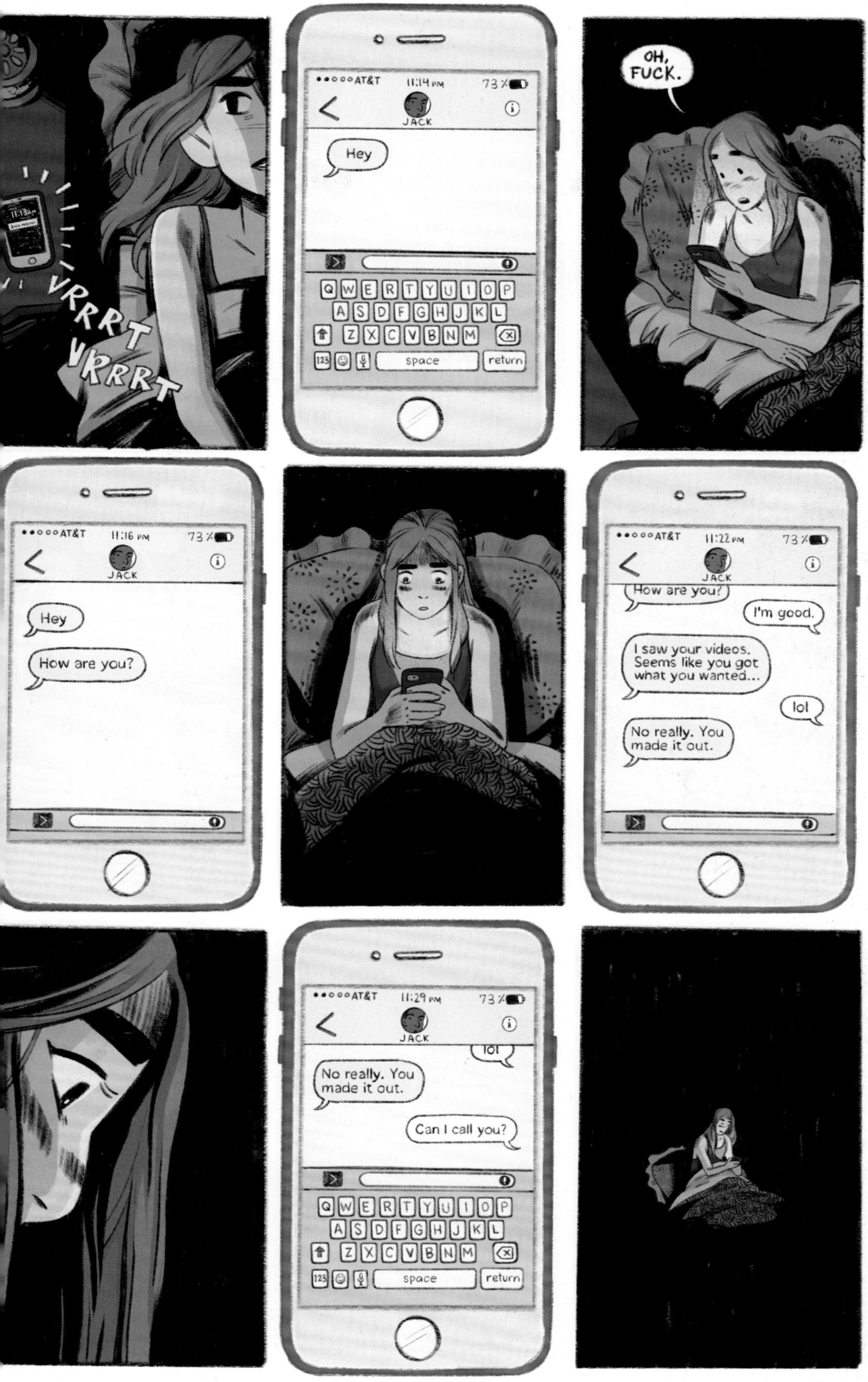
VRRRT
VRRRT
●●○○○AT&T 11:14 PM 73%
JACK
Hey
OH, FUCK.
●●○○○AT&T 11:16 PM 73%
JACK
Hey
How are you?
●●○○○AT&T 11:22 PM 73%
JACK
How are you?
I'm good.
I saw your videos. Seems like you got what you wanted...
lol
No really. You made it out.
●●○○○AT&T 11:29 PM 73%
JACK
lol
No really. You made it out.
Can I call you?

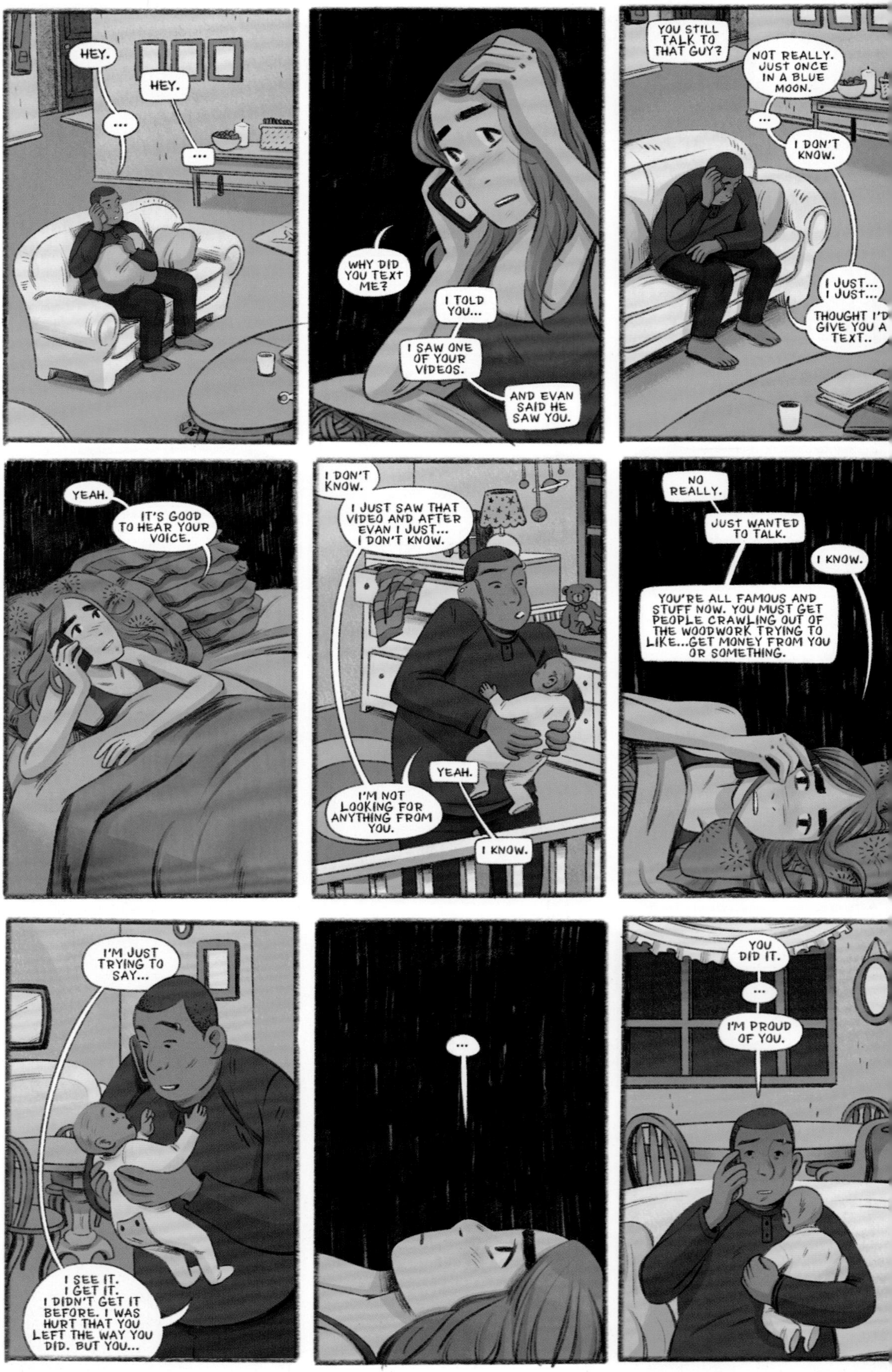
HEY.
HEY.
...
...
WHY DID YOU TEXT ME?
I TOLD YOU...
I SAW ONE OF YOUR VIDEOS.
AND EVAN SAID HE SAW YOU.
YOU STILL TALK TO THAT GUY?
NOT REALLY. JUST ONCE IN A BLUE MOON.
...
I DON'T KNOW.
I JUST... I JUST...
THOUGHT I'D GIVE YOU A TEXT..
YEAH.
IT'S GOOD TO HEAR YOUR VOICE.
I DON'T KNOW.
I JUST SAW THAT VIDEO AND AFTER EVAN I JUST... I DON'T KNOW.
YEAH.
I'M NOT LOOKING FOR ANYTHING FROM YOU.
I KNOW.
NO REALLY.
JUST WANTED TO TALK.
I KNOW.
YOU'RE ALL FAMOUS AND STUFF NOW. YOU MUST GET PEOPLE CRAWLING OUT OF THE WOODWORK TRYING TO LIKE...GET MONEY FROM YOU OR SOMETHING.
I'M JUST TRYING TO SAY...
I SEE IT. I GET IT. I DIDN'T GET IT BEFORE. I WAS HURT THAT YOU LEFT THE WAY YOU DID. BUT YOU...
...
YOU DID IT.
...
I'M PROUD OF YOU.

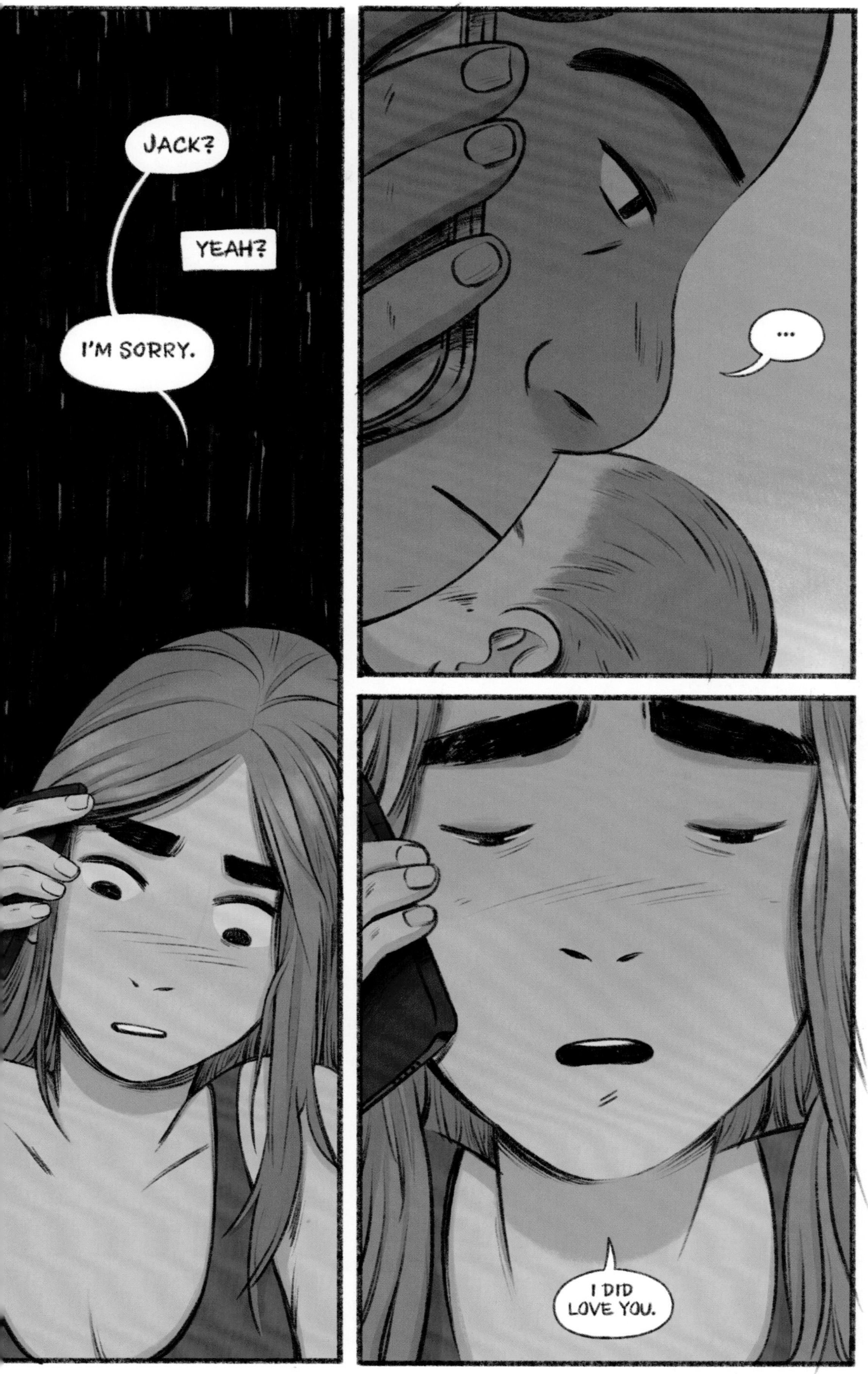
JACK?
YEAH?
I'M SORRY.
...
I DID LOVE YOU.

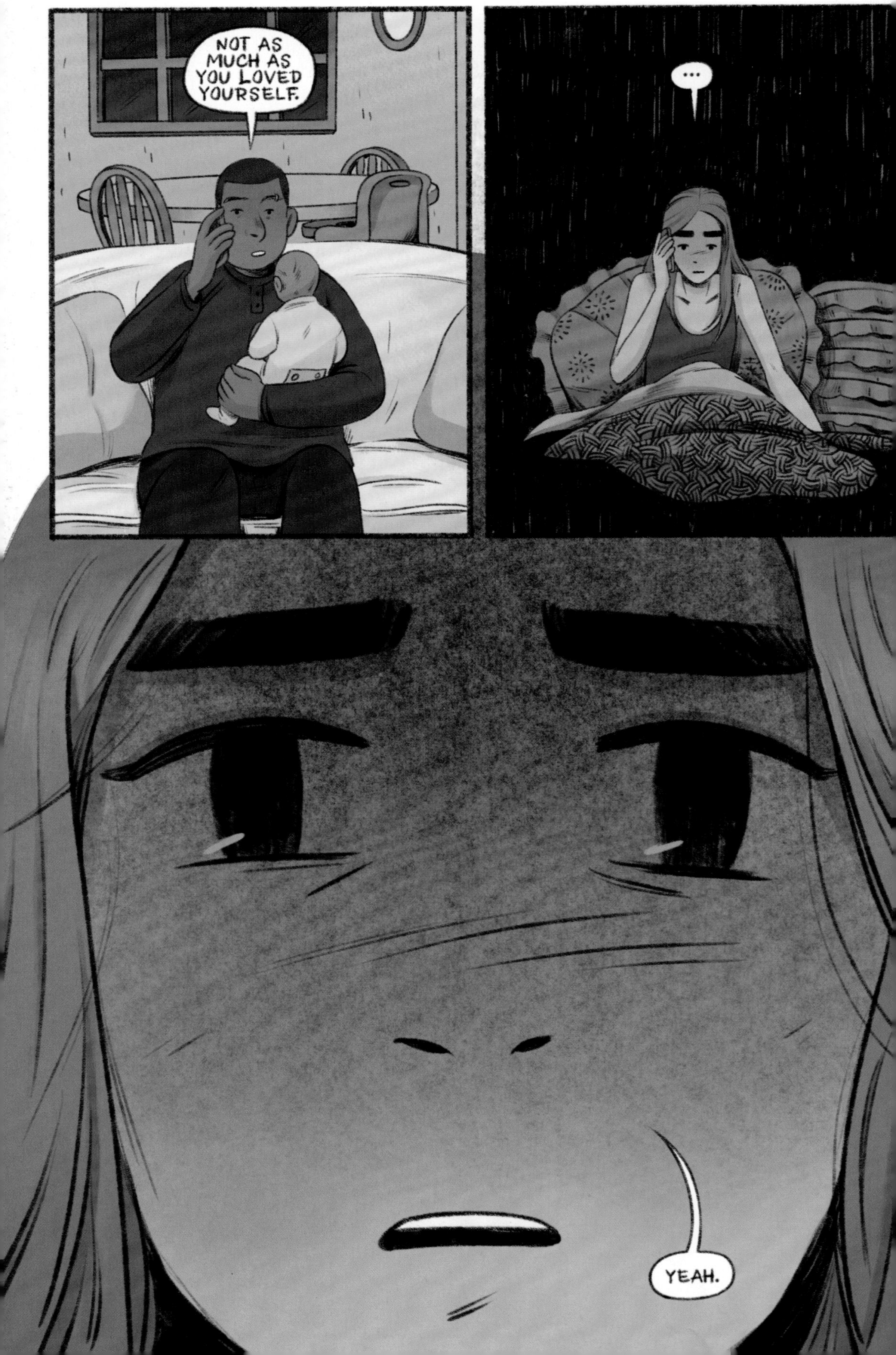
NOT AS MUCH AS YOU LOVED YOURSELF.
...
YEAH.

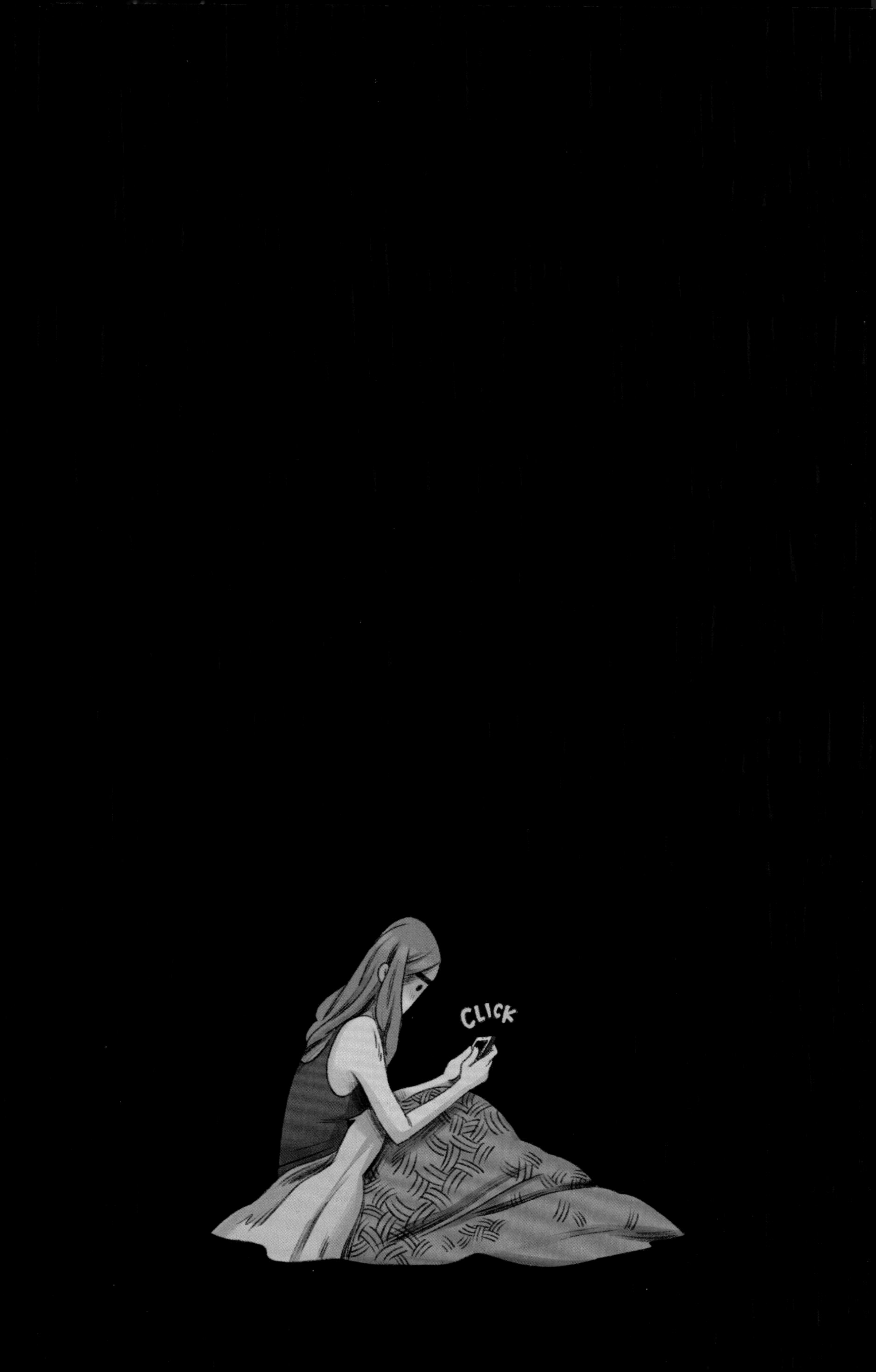
CLICK

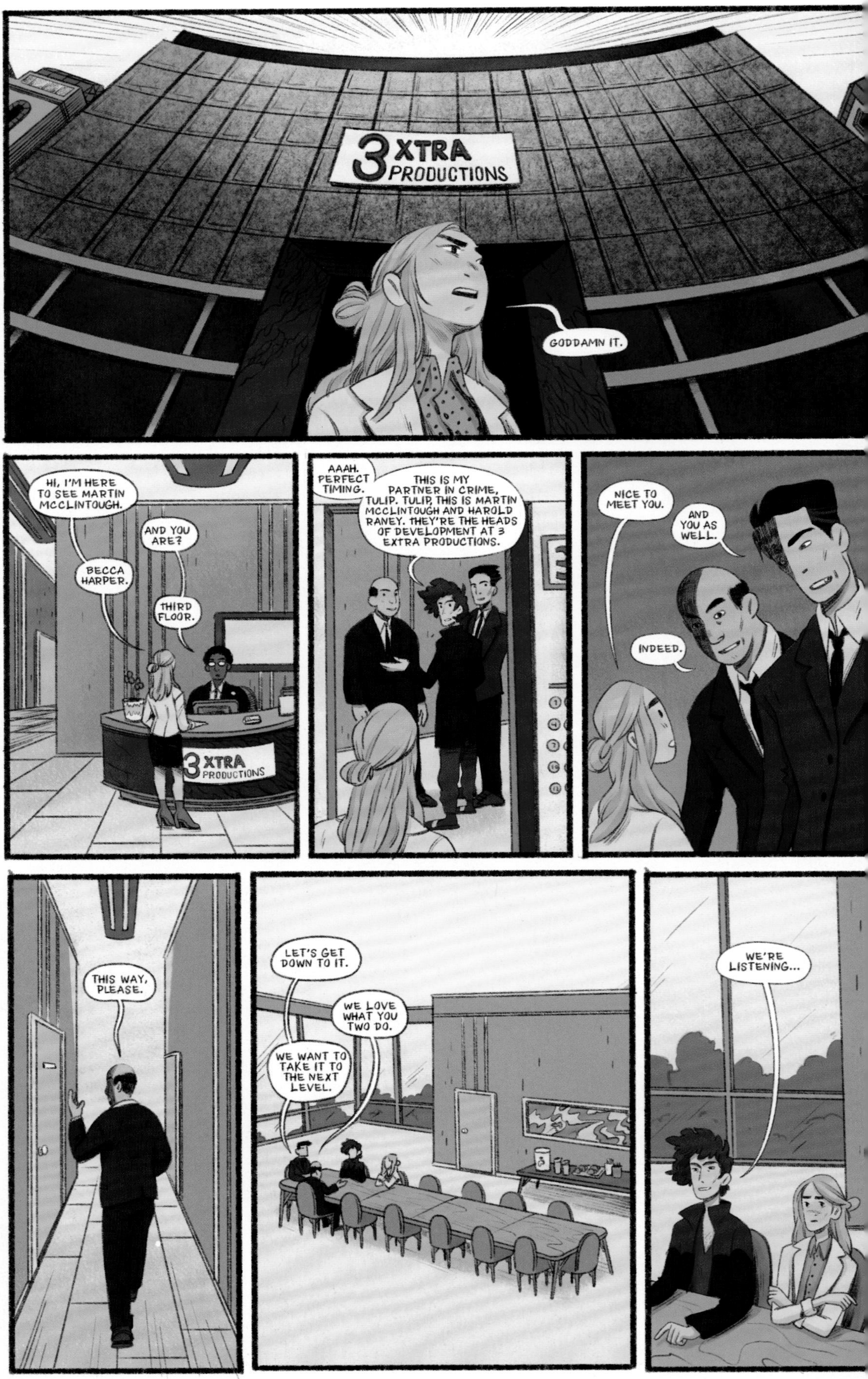
3 XTRA PRODUCTIONS
GODDAMN IT.
HI, I'M HERE TO SEE MARTIN MCCLINTOUGH.
AND YOU ARE?
BECCA HARPER.
THIRD FLOOR.
3 XTRA PRODUCTIONS
AAAH. PERFECT TIMING.
THIS IS MY PARTNER IN CRIME, TULIP. TULIP, THIS IS MARTIN MCCLINTOUGH AND HAROLD RANEY. THEY'RE THE HEADS OF DEVELOPMENT AT 3 EXTRA PRODUCTIONS.
NICE TO MEET YOU.
AND YOU AS WELL.
INDEED.
THIS WAY, PLEASE.
LET'S GET DOWN TO IT.
WE LOVE WHAT YOU TWO DO.
WE WANT TO TAKE IT TO THE NEXT LEVEL.
WE'RE LISTENING...

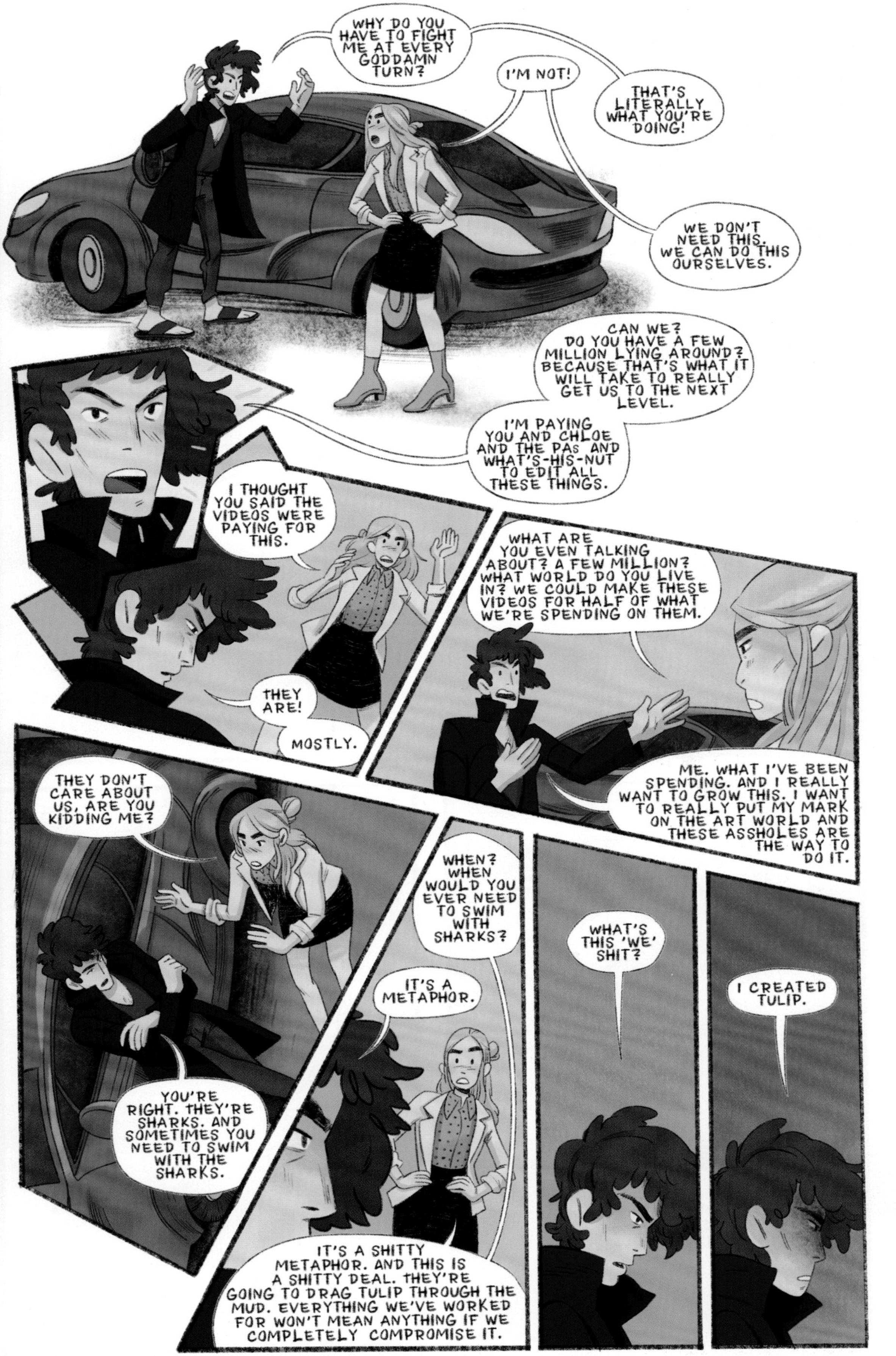
WHY DO YOU HAVE TO FIGHT ME AT EVERY GODDAMN TURN?
I'M NOT!
THAT'S LITERALLY WHAT YOU'RE DOING!
WE DON'T NEED THIS. WE CAN DO THIS OURSELVES.
CAN WE? DO YOU HAVE A FEW MILLION LYING AROUND? BECAUSE THAT'S WHAT IT WILL TAKE TO REALLY GET US TO THE NEXT LEVEL.
I'M PAYING YOU AND CHLOE AND THE PAs AND WHAT'S-HIS-NUT TO EDIT ALL THESE THINGS.
I THOUGHT YOU SAID THE VIDEOS WERE PAYING FOR THIS.
THEY ARE!
MOSTLY.
WHAT ARE YOU EVEN TALKING ABOUT? A FEW MILLION? WHAT WORLD DO YOU LIVE IN? WE COULD MAKE THESE VIDEOS FOR HALF OF WHAT WE'RE SPENDING ON THEM.
ME. WHAT I'VE BEEN SPENDING. AND I REALLY WANT TO GROW THIS. I WANT TO REALLY PUT MY MARK ON THE ART WORLD AND THESE ASSHOLES ARE THE WAY TO DO IT.
THEY DON'T CARE ABOUT US, ARE YOU KIDDING ME?
YOU'RE RIGHT. THEY'RE SHARKS. AND SOMETIMES YOU NEED TO SWIM WITH THE SHARKS.
WHEN? WHEN WOULD YOU EVER NEED TO SWIM WITH SHARKS?
IT'S A METAPHOR.
IT'S A SHITTY METAPHOR. AND THIS IS A SHITTY DEAL. THEY'RE GOING TO DRAG TULIP THROUGH THE MUD. EVERYTHING WE'VE WORKED FOR WON'T MEAN ANYTHING IF WE COMPLETELY COMPROMISE IT.
WHAT'S THIS 'WE' SHIT?
I CREATED TULIP.

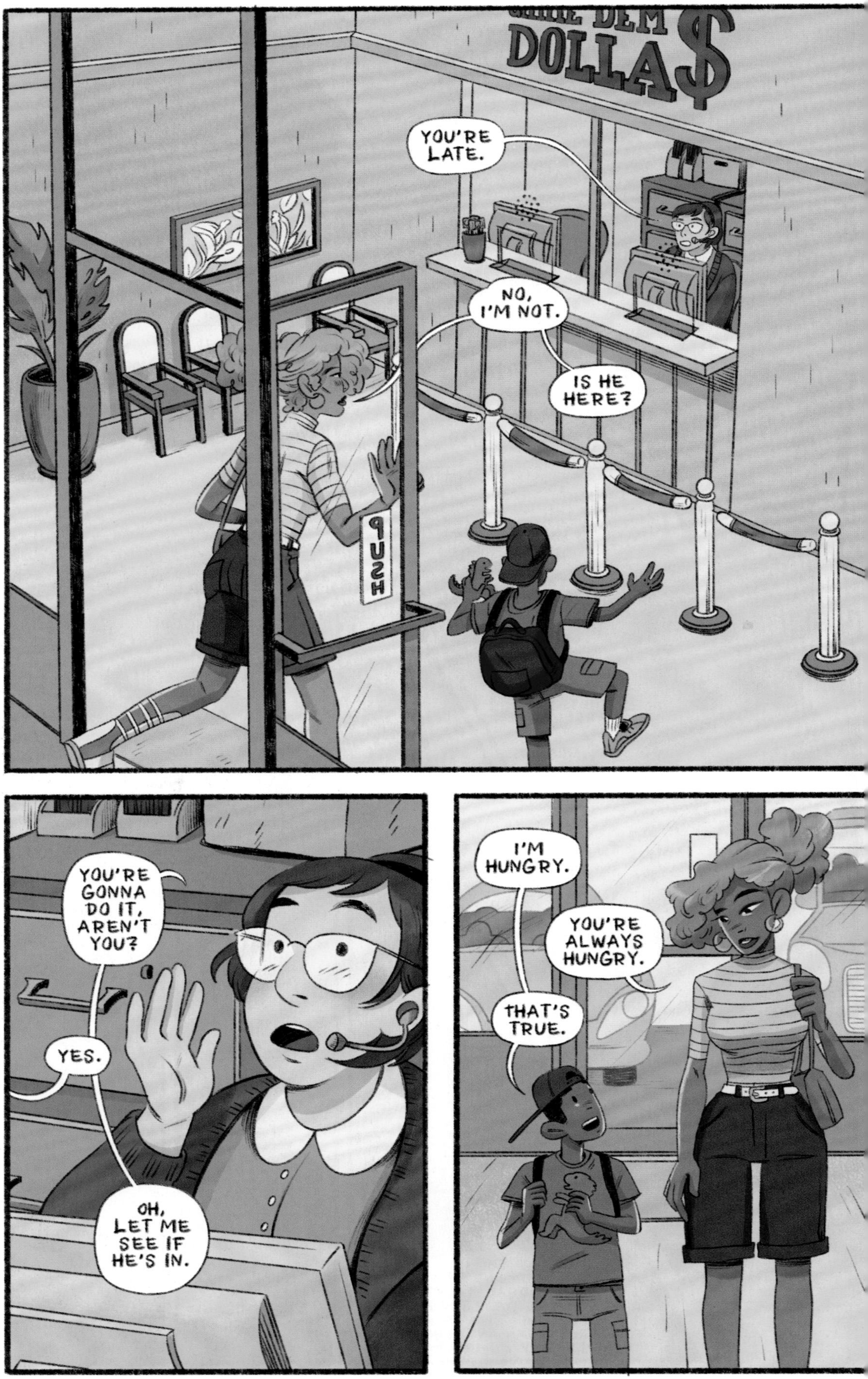
DOLLA$
YOU'RE LATE.
NO, I'M NOT.
IS HE HERE?
YOU'RE GONNA DO IT, AREN'T YOU?
YES.
OH, LET ME SEE IF HE'S IN.
I'M HUNGRY.
YOU'RE ALWAYS HUNGRY.
THAT'S TRUE.

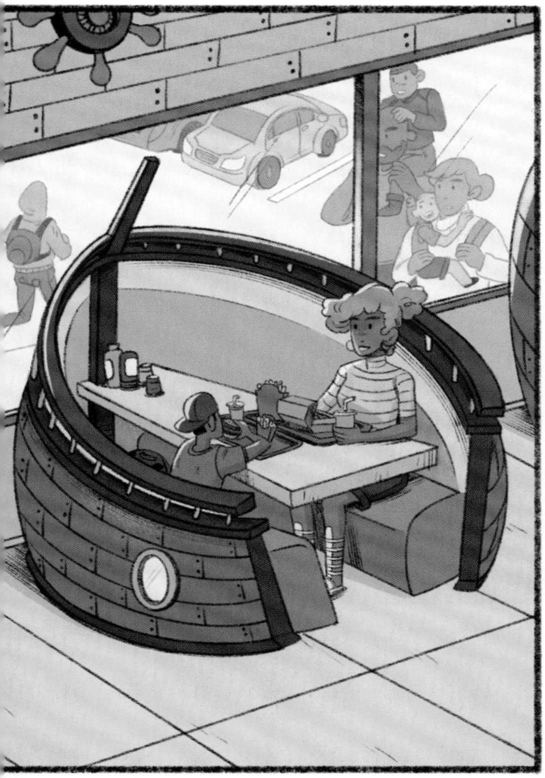

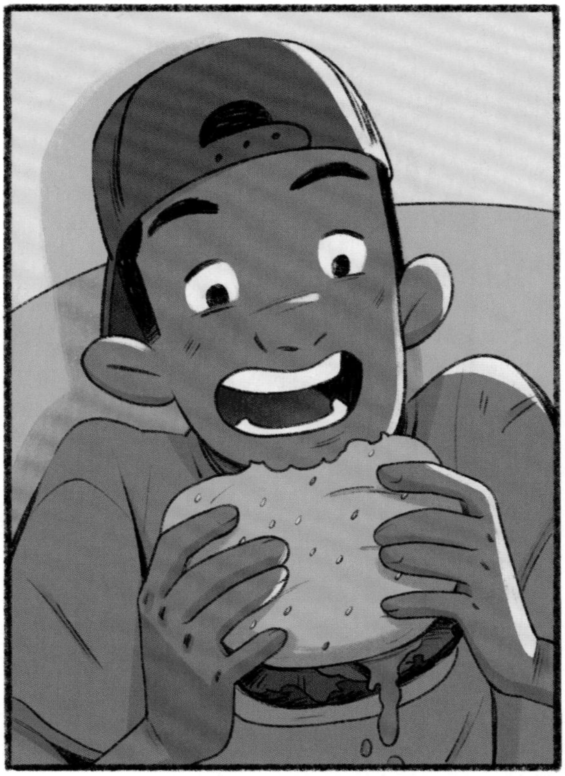

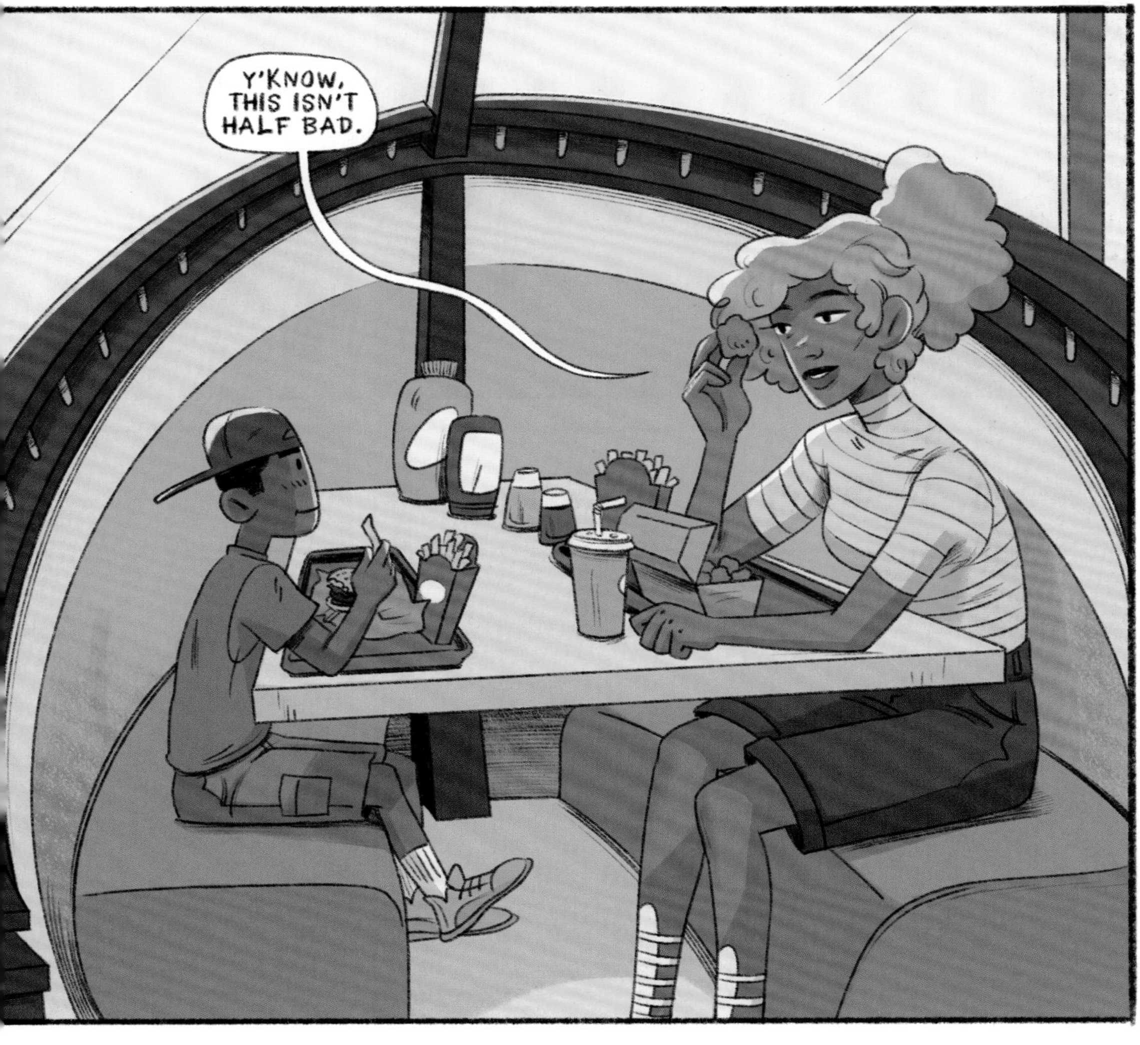
Y'KNOW, THIS ISN'T HALF BAD.

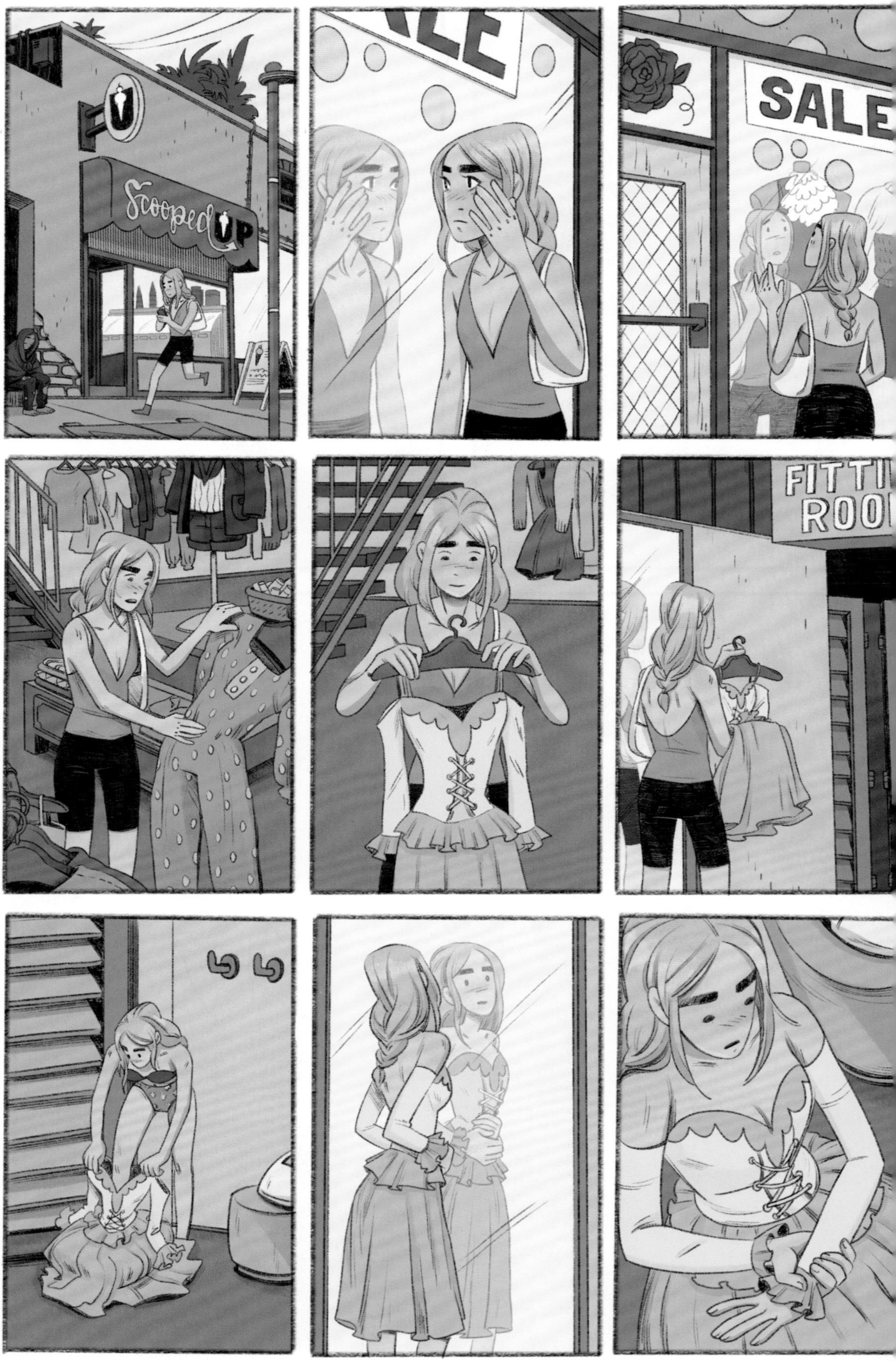
Scooped UP
ALE
SALE
FITTI
ROO

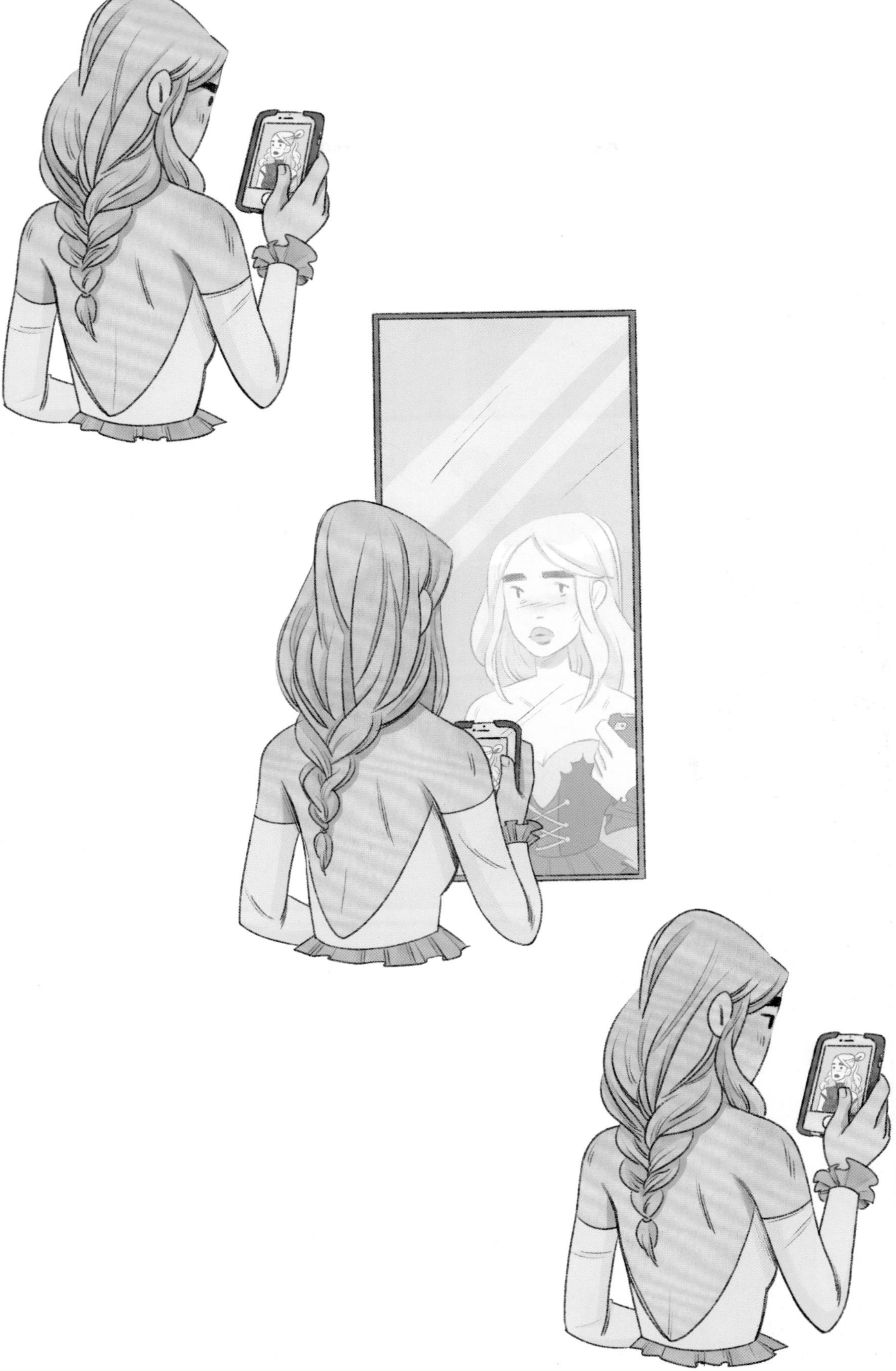

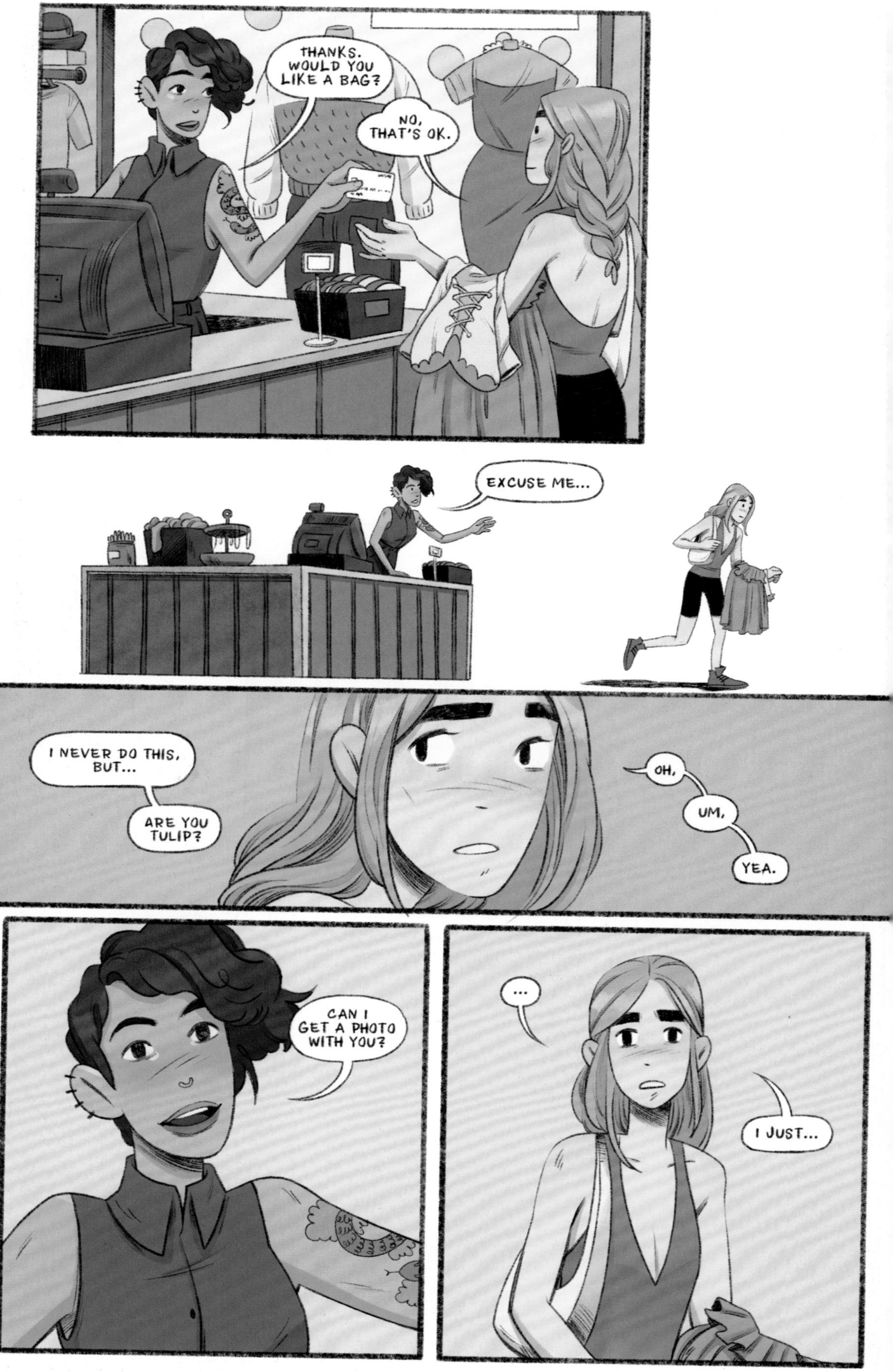
THANKS. WOULD YOU LIKE A BAG?
NO, THAT'S OK.
EXCUSE ME...
I NEVER DO THIS, BUT...
ARE YOU TULIP?
OH,
UM,
YEA.
CAN I GET A PHOTO WITH YOU?
...
I JUST...

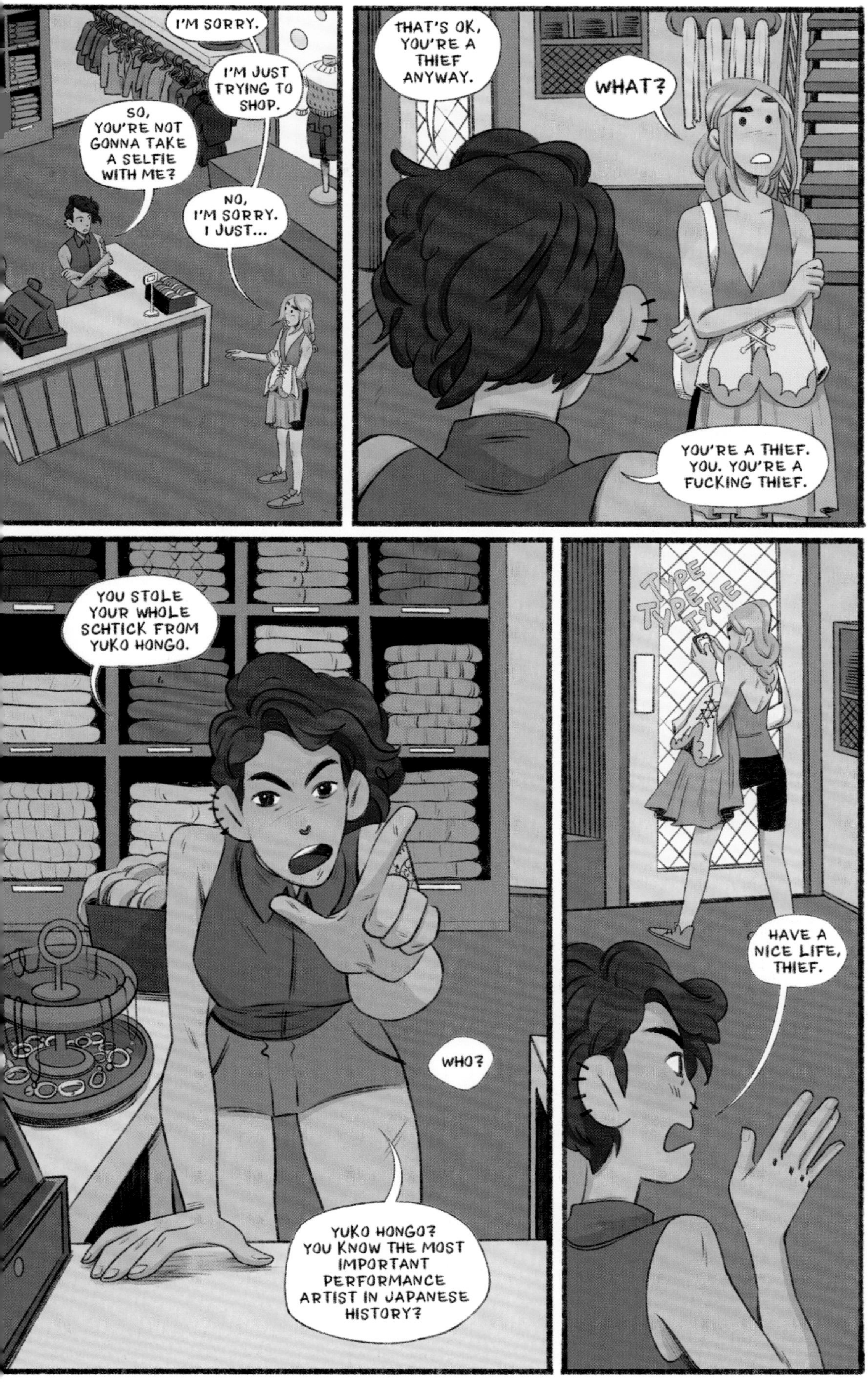
I'M SORRY.
I'M JUST TRYING TO SHOP.
SO, YOU'RE NOT GONNA TAKE A SELFIE WITH ME?
NO, I'M SORRY. I JUST...
THAT'S OK, YOU'RE A THIEF ANYWAY.
WHAT?
YOU'RE A THIEF. YOU. YOU'RE A FUCKING THIEF.
YOU STOLE YOUR WHOLE SCHTICK FROM YUKO HONGO.
WHO?
YUKO HONGO? YOU KNOW THE MOST IMPORTANT PERFORMANCE ARTIST IN JAPANESE HISTORY?
TYPE TYPE TYPE
HAVE A NICE LIFE, THIEF.

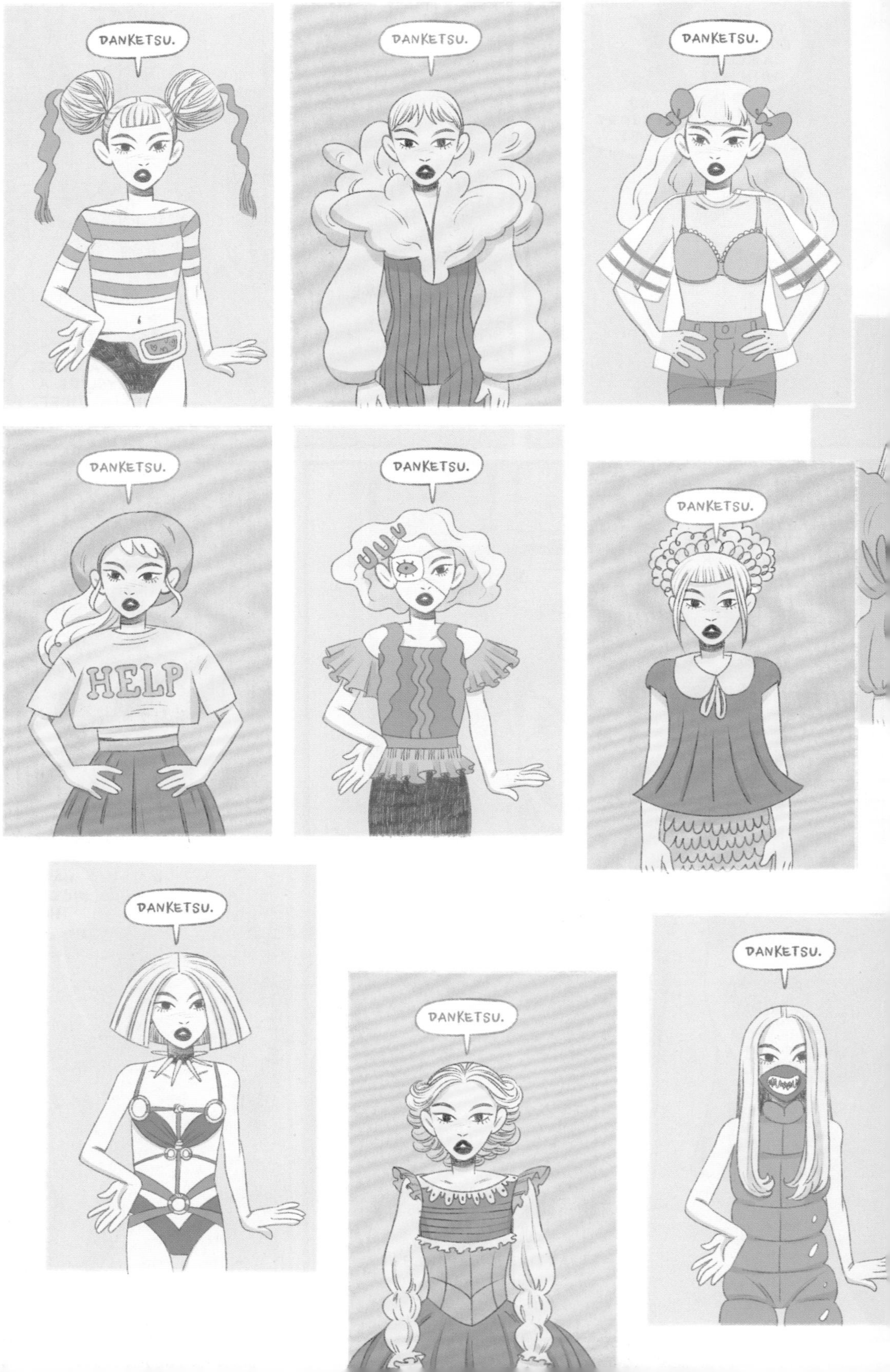
DANKETSU.
DANKETSU.
DANKETSU.
DANKETSU.
DANKETSU.
DANKETSU.
DANKETSU.
DANKETSU.
DANKETSU.

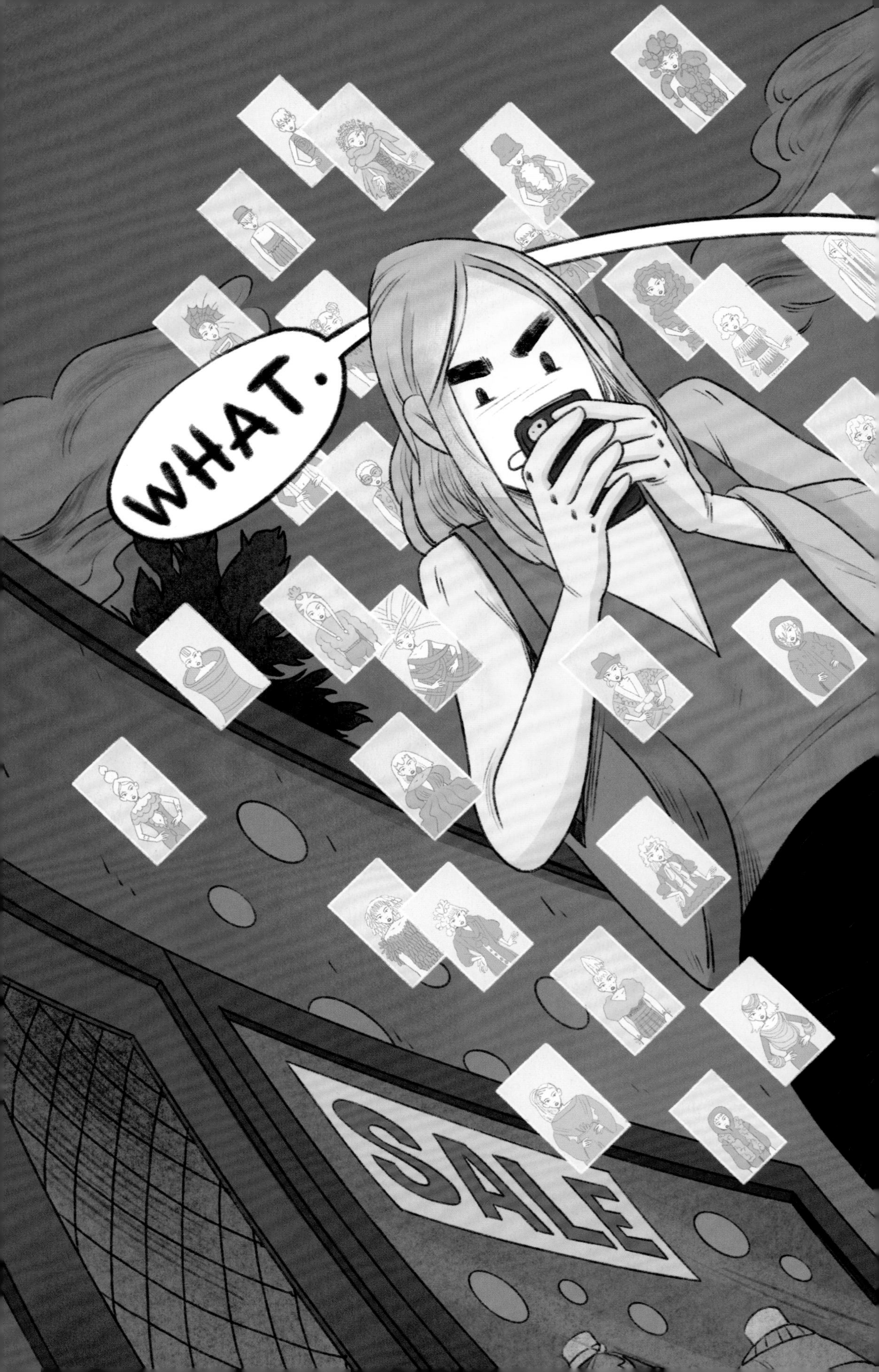
WHAT.
SALE

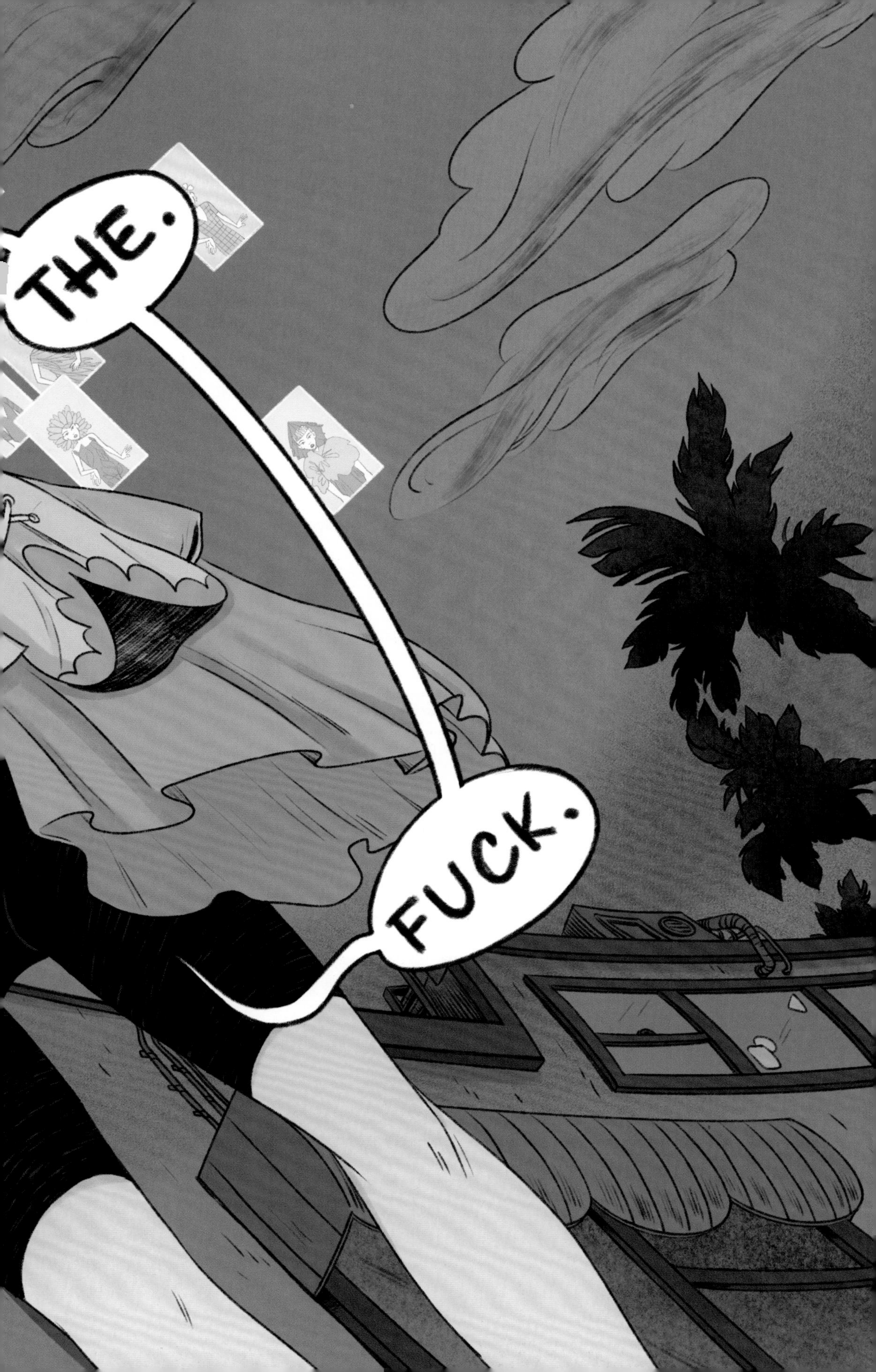
THE.
FUCK.

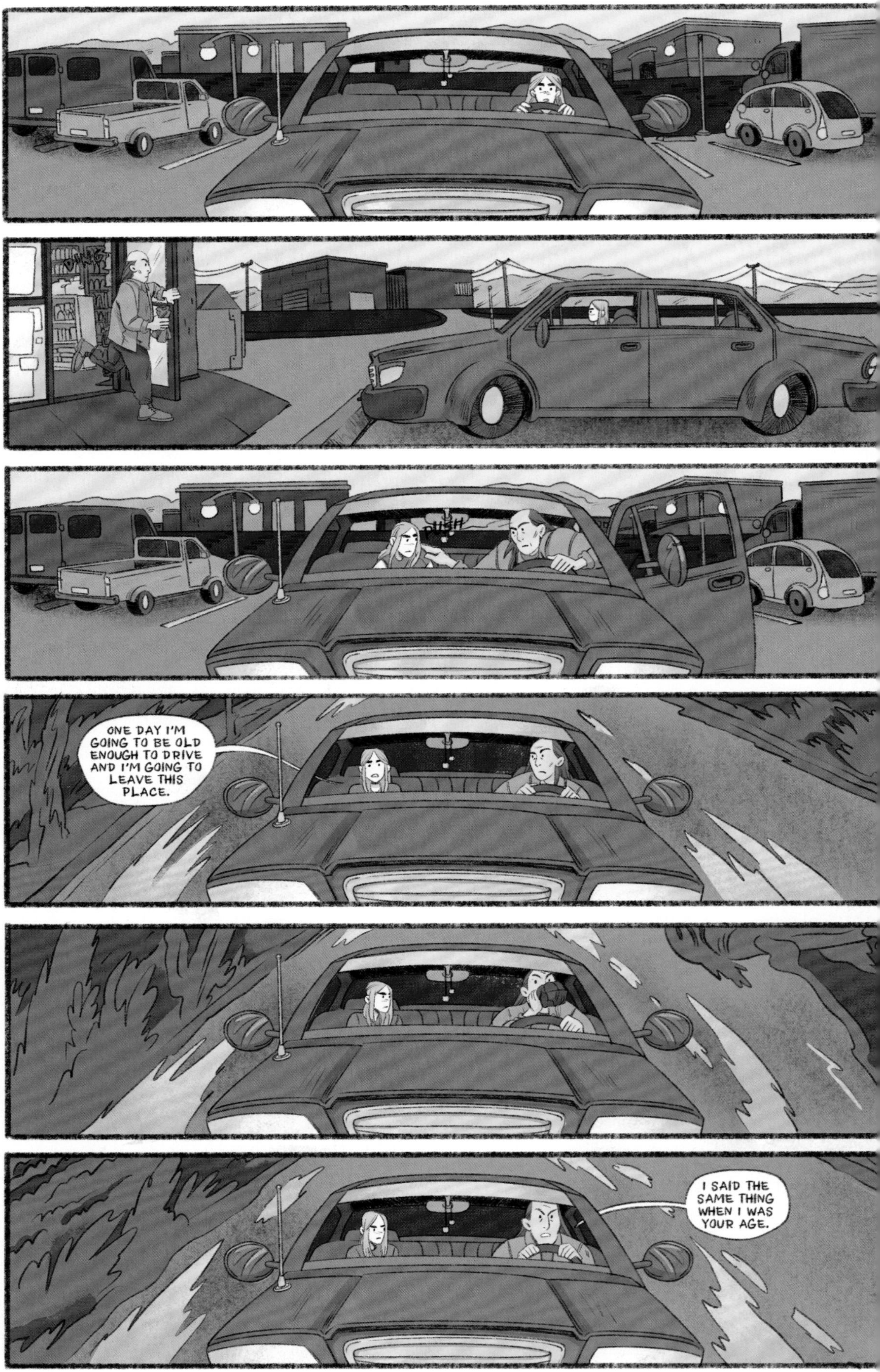
DING!
PUSH!
ONE DAY I'M GOING TO BE OLD ENOUGH TO DRIVE AND I'M GOING TO LEAVE THIS PLACE.
I SAID THE SAME THING WHEN I WAS YOUR AGE.

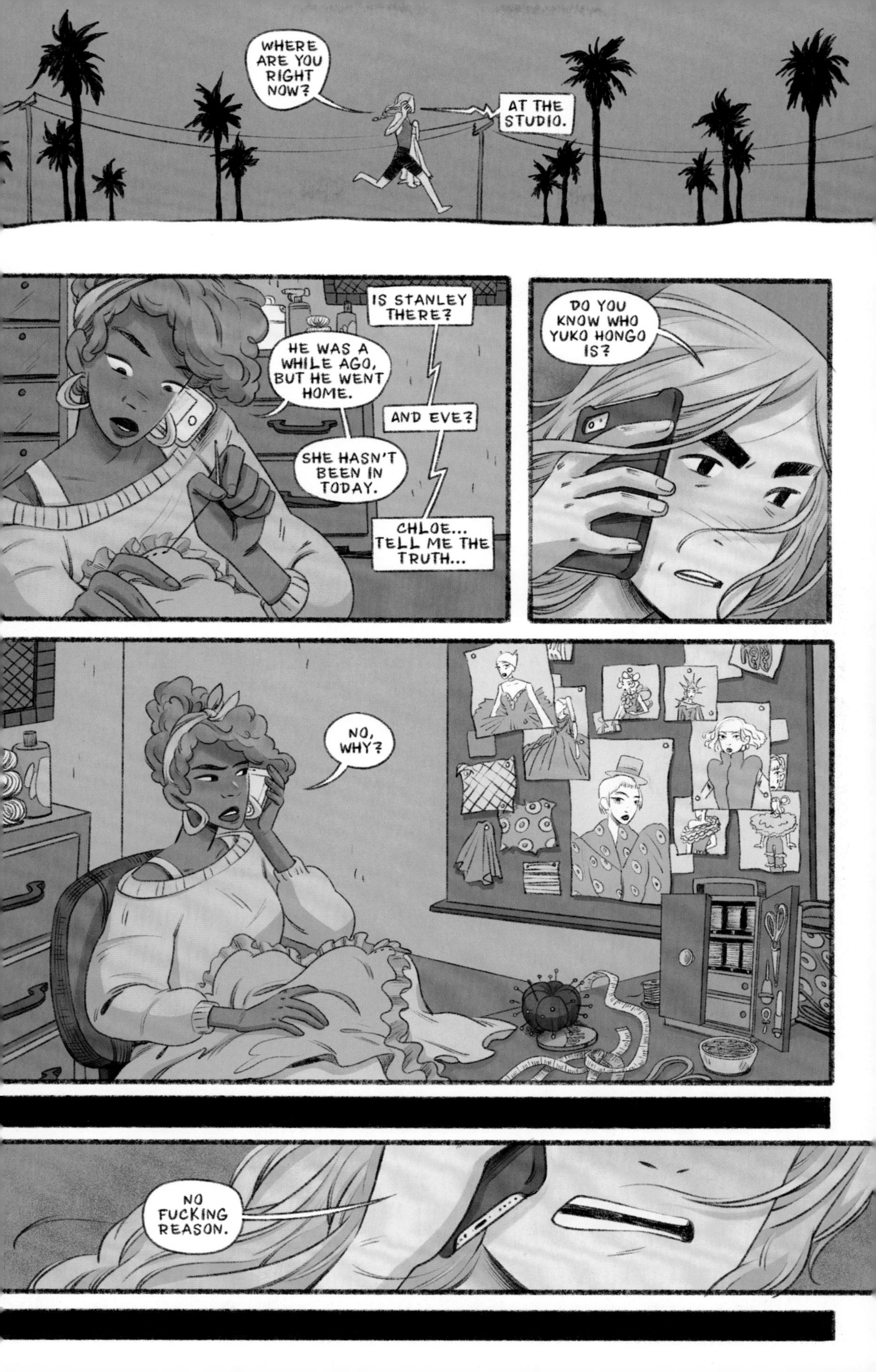
WHERE ARE YOU RIGHT NOW?
AT THE STUDIO.
IS STANLEY THERE?
HE WAS A WHILE AGO, BUT HE WENT HOME.
AND EVE?
SHE HASN'T BEEN IN TODAY.
CHLOE... TELL ME THE TRUTH...
DO YOU KNOW WHO YUKO HONGO IS?
NO, WHY?
NO FUCKING REASON.

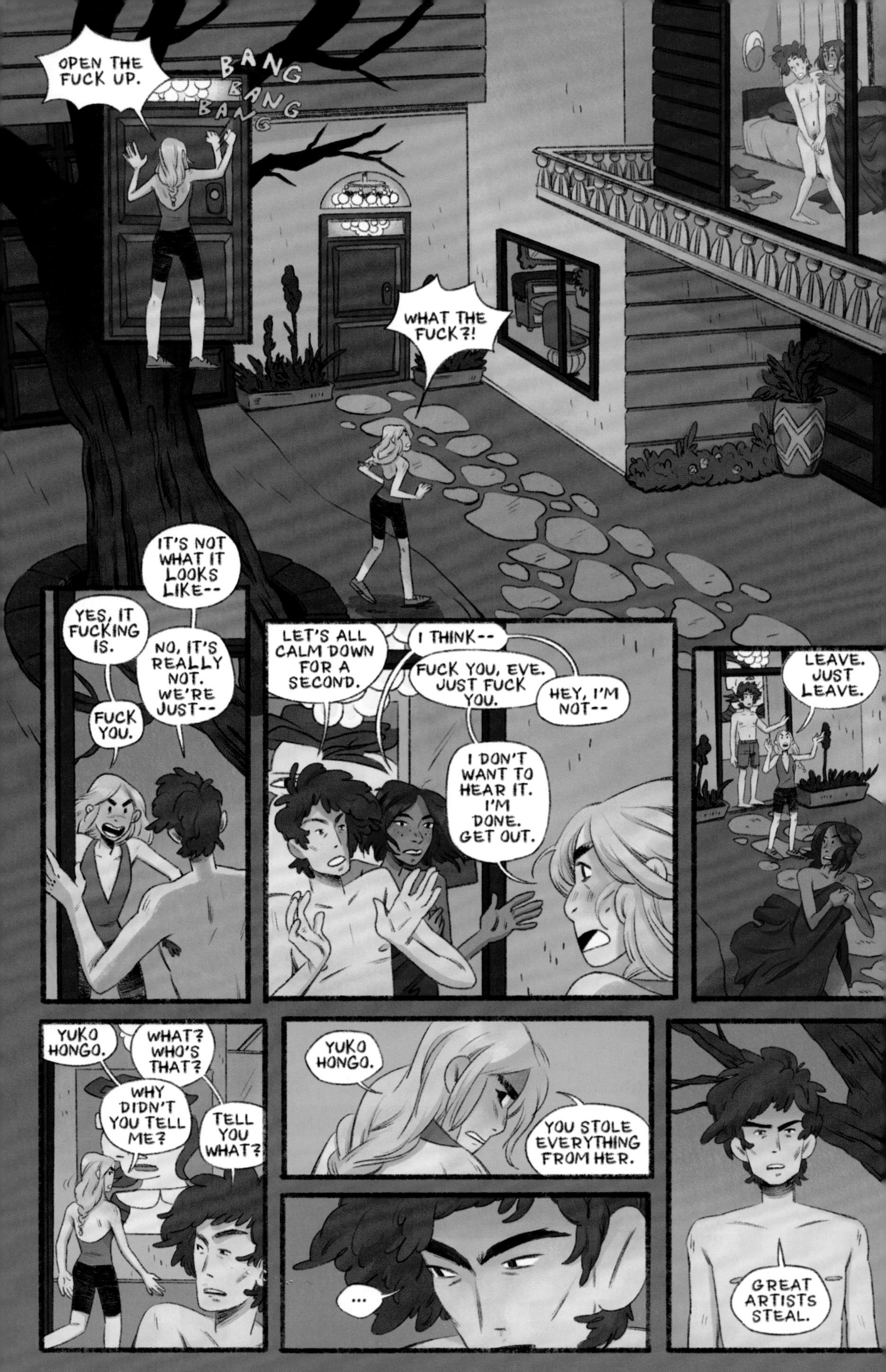
OPEN THE FUCK UP.
BANG BANG BANG
WHAT THE FUCK?!
IT'S NOT WHAT IT LOOKS LIKE--
YES, IT FUCKING IS.
NO, IT'S REALLY NOT. WE'RE JUST--
FUCK YOU.
LET'S ALL CALM DOWN FOR A SECOND.
I THINK--
FUCK YOU, EVE. JUST FUCK YOU.
HEY, I'M NOT--
I DON'T WANT TO HEAR IT. I'M DONE. GET OUT.
LEAVE. JUST LEAVE.
YUKO HONGO.
WHAT? WHO'S THAT?
WHY DIDN'T YOU TELL ME?
TELL YOU WHAT?
YUKO HONGO.
YOU STOLE EVERYTHING FROM HER.
...
GREAT ARTISTS STEAL.

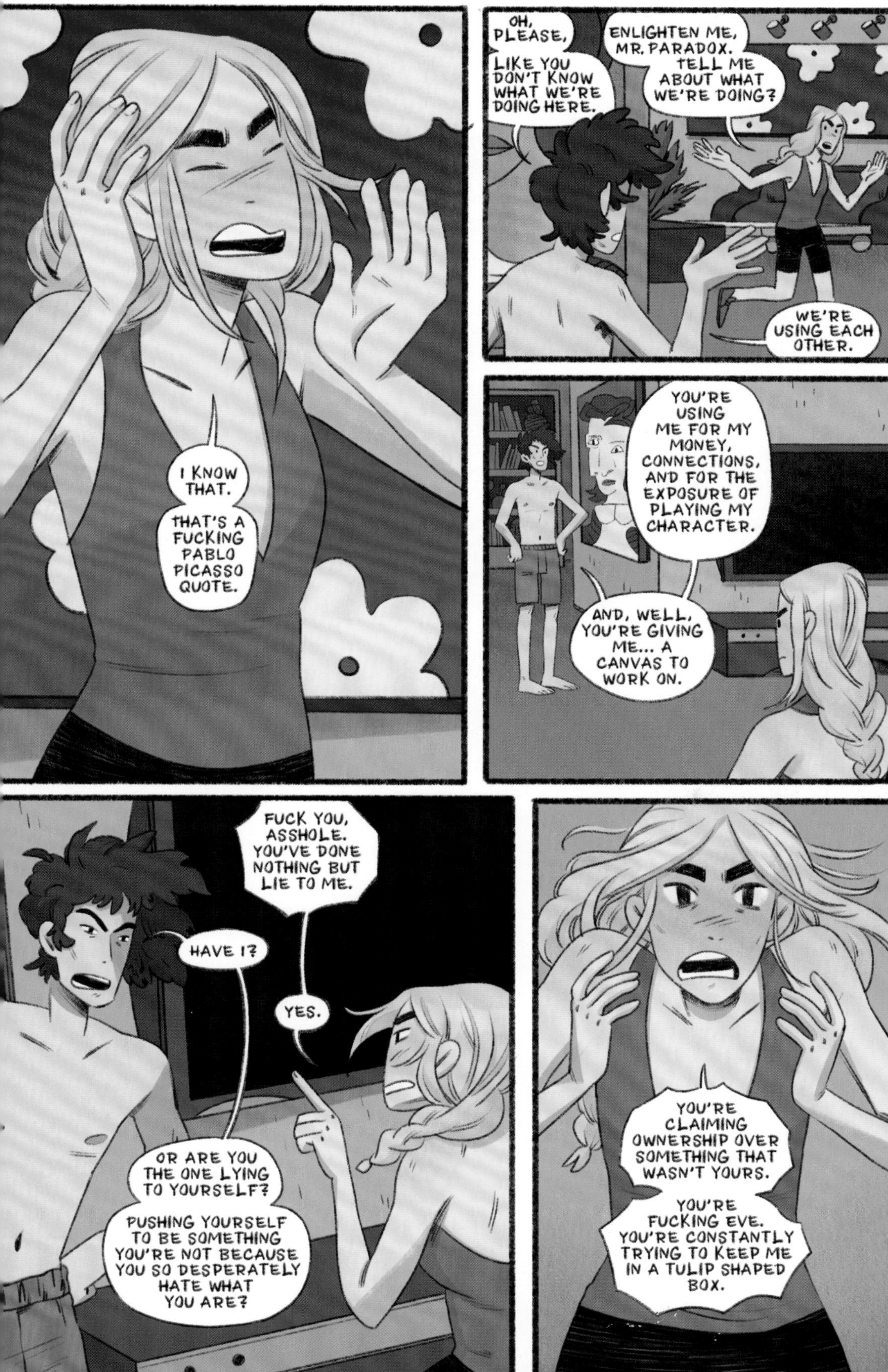
I KNOW THAT.
THAT'S A FUCKING PABLO PICASSO QUOTE.
OH, PLEASE,
LIKE YOU DON'T KNOW WHAT WE'RE DOING HERE.
ENLIGHTEN ME, MR. PARADOX.
TELL ME ABOUT WHAT WE'RE DOING?
WE'RE USING EACH OTHER.
YOU'RE USING ME FOR MY MONEY, CONNECTIONS, AND FOR THE EXPOSURE OF PLAYING MY CHARACTER.
AND, WELL, YOU'RE GIVING ME... A CANVAS TO WORK ON.
FUCK YOU, ASSHOLE. YOU'VE DONE NOTHING BUT LIE TO ME.
HAVE I?
YES.
OR ARE YOU THE ONE LYING TO YOURSELF?
PUSHING YOURSELF TO BE SOMETHING YOU'RE NOT BECAUSE YOU SO DESPERATELY HATE WHAT YOU ARE?
YOU'RE CLAIMING OWNERSHIP OVER SOMETHING THAT WASN'T YOURS.
YOU'RE FUCKING EVE. YOU'RE CONSTANTLY TRYING TO KEEP ME IN A TULIP SHAPED BOX.

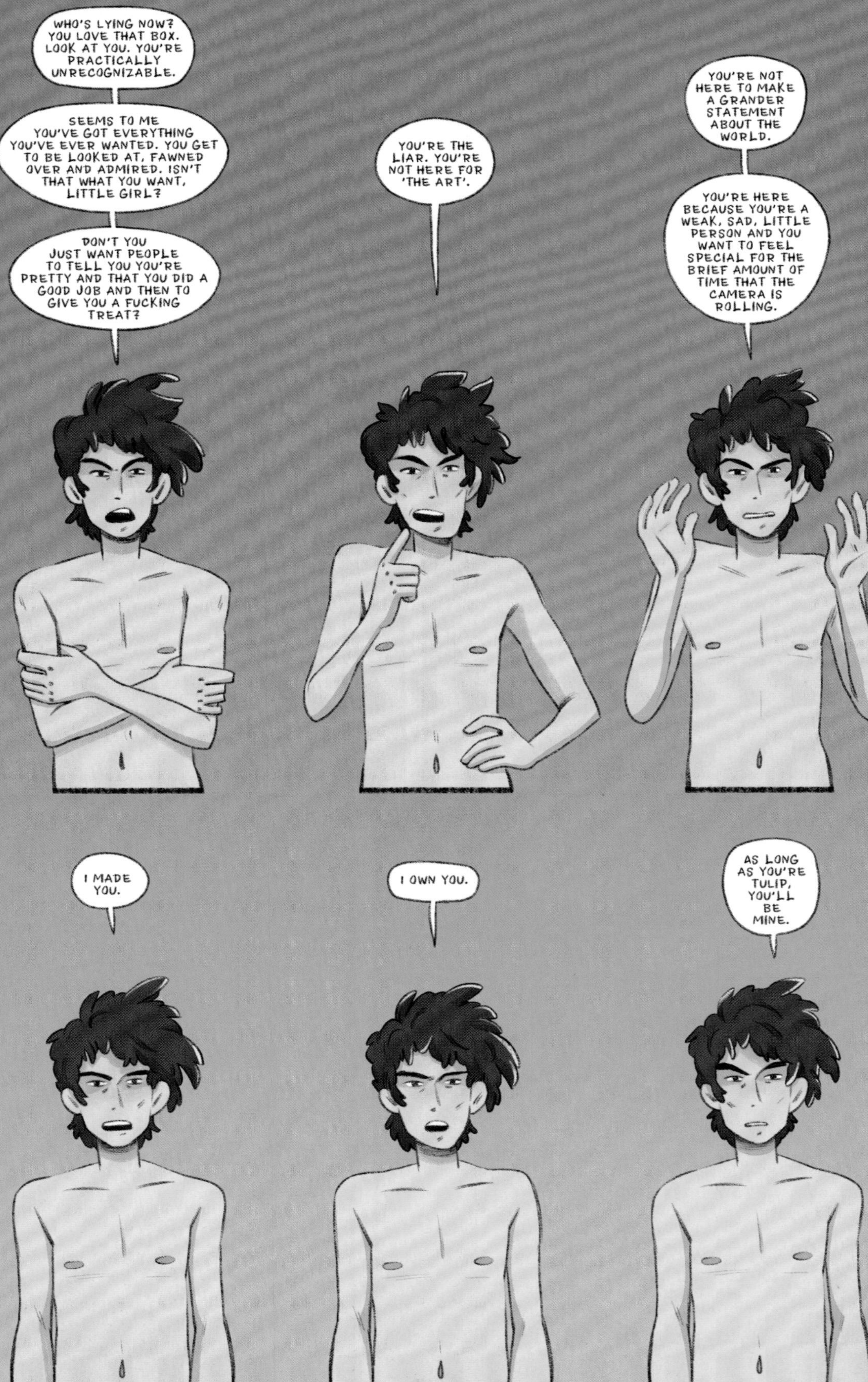
WHO'S LYING NOW? YOU LOVE THAT BOX. LOOK AT YOU. YOU'RE PRACTICALLY UNRECOGNIZABLE.
SEEMS TO ME YOU'VE GOT EVERYTHING YOU'VE EVER WANTED. YOU GET TO BE LOOKED AT, FAWNED OVER AND ADMIRED. ISN'T THAT WHAT YOU WANT, LITTLE GIRL?
DON'T YOU JUST WANT PEOPLE TO TELL YOU YOU'RE PRETTY AND THAT YOU DID A GOOD JOB AND THEN TO GIVE YOU A FUCKING TREAT?
YOU'RE THE LIAR. YOU'RE NOT HERE FOR 'THE ART'.
YOU'RE NOT HERE TO MAKE A GRANDER STATEMENT ABOUT THE WORLD.
YOU'RE HERE BECAUSE YOU'RE A WEAK, SAD, LITTLE PERSON AND YOU WANT TO FEEL SPECIAL FOR THE BRIEF AMOUNT OF TIME THAT THE CAMERA IS ROLLING.
I MADE YOU.
I OWN YOU.
AS LONG AS YOU'RE TULIP, YOU'LL BE MINE.

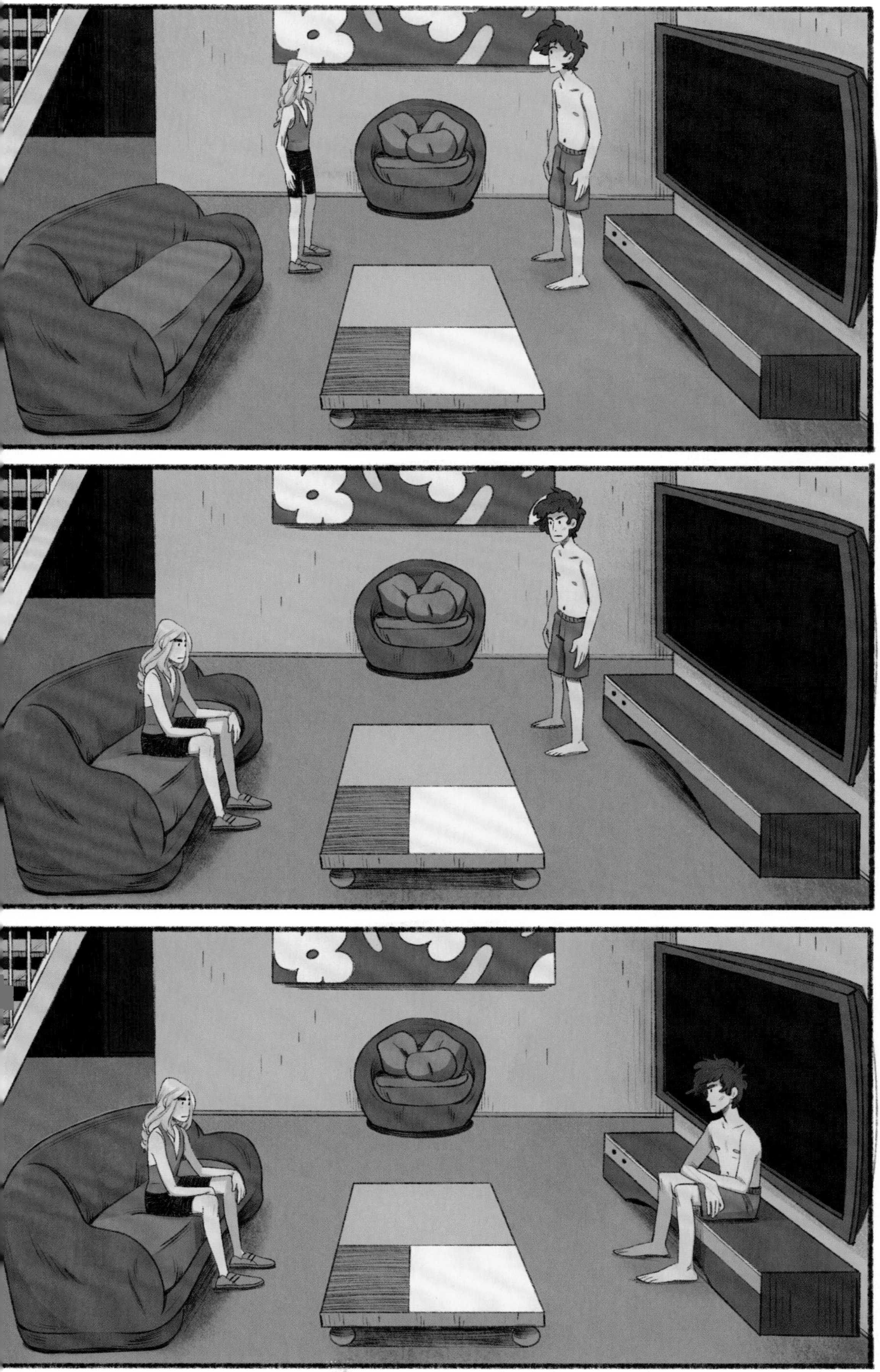

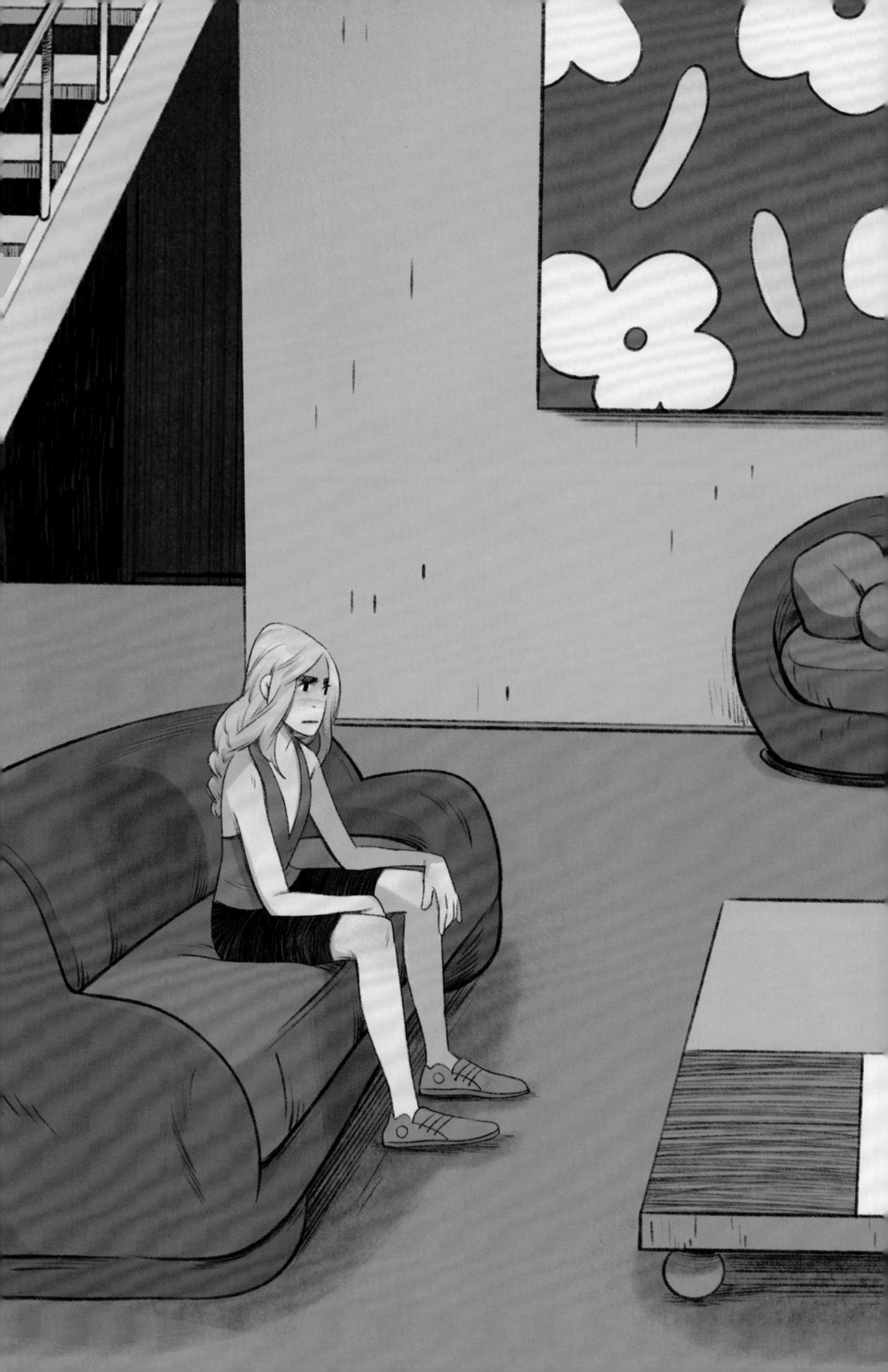

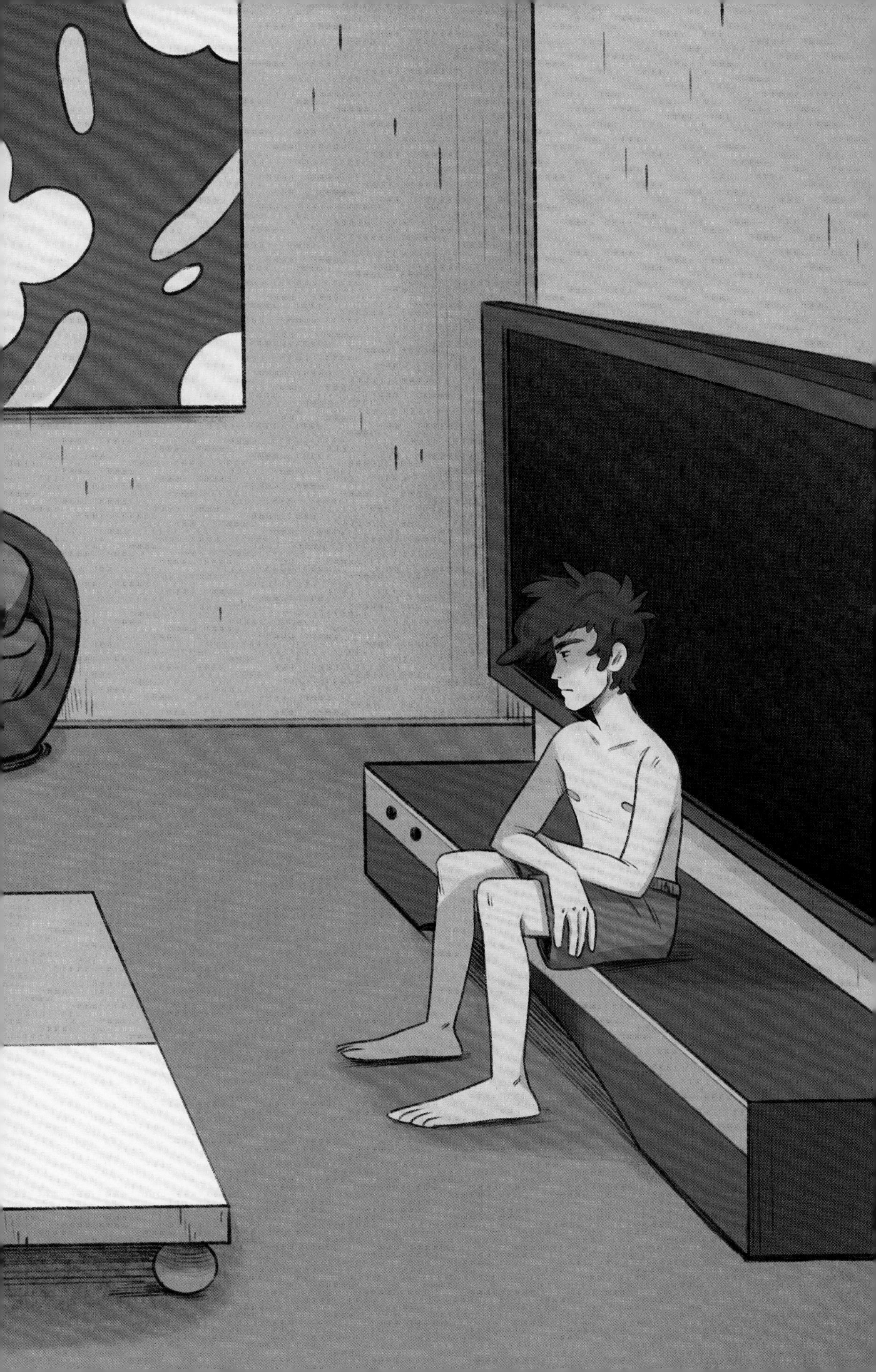

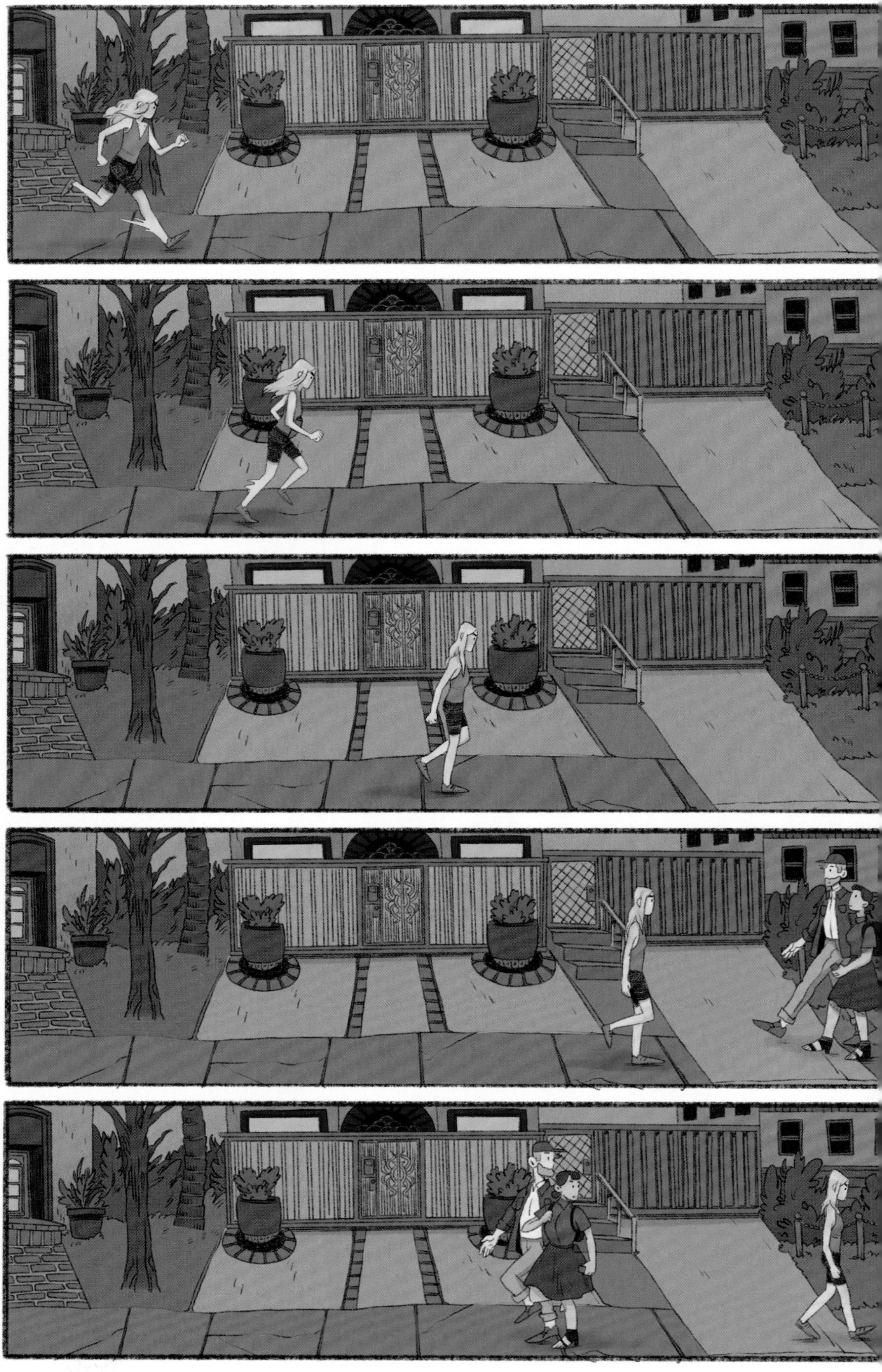

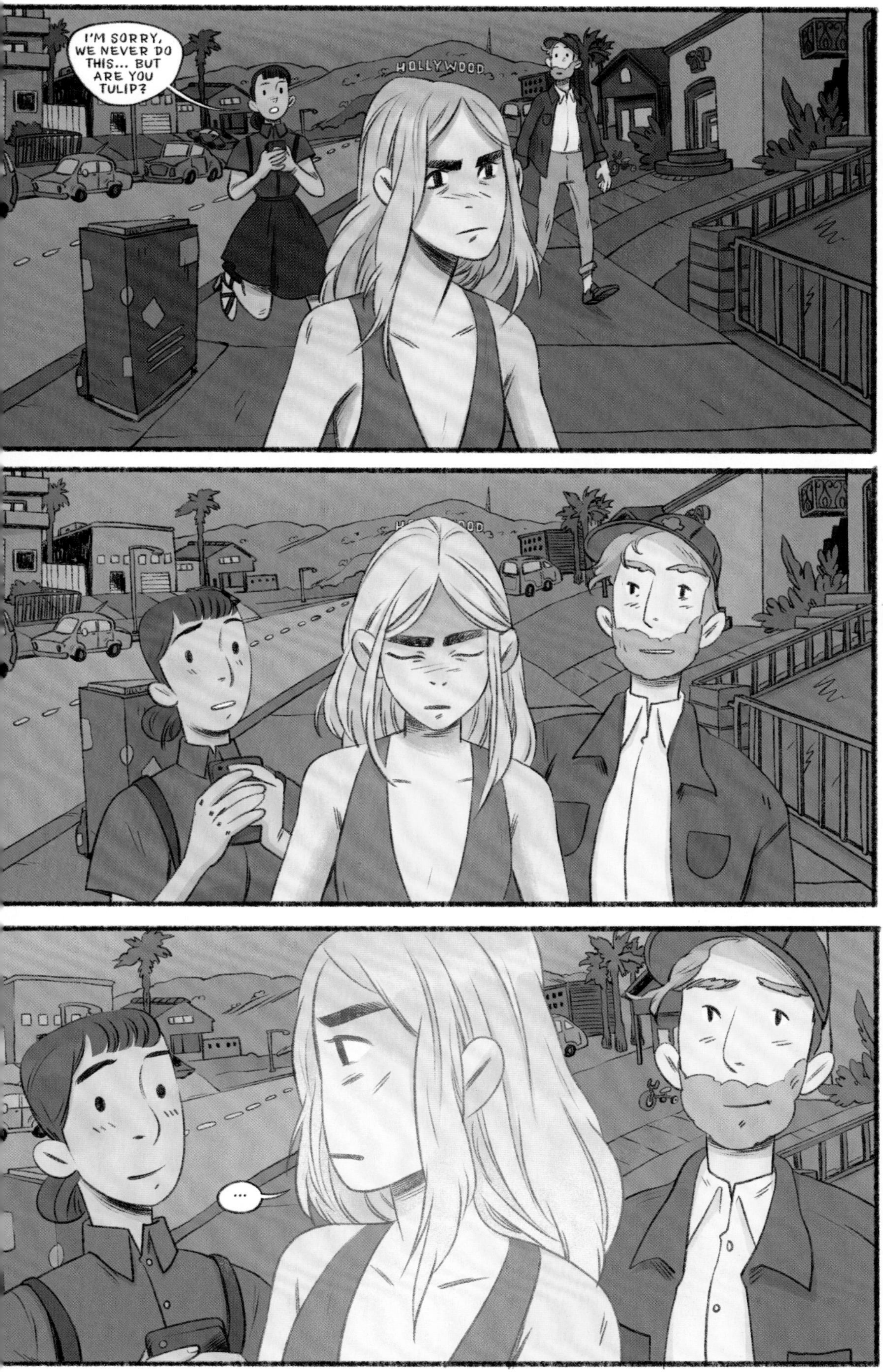
I'M SORRY, WE NEVER DO THIS... BUT ARE YOU TULIP?
HOLLYWOOD
...

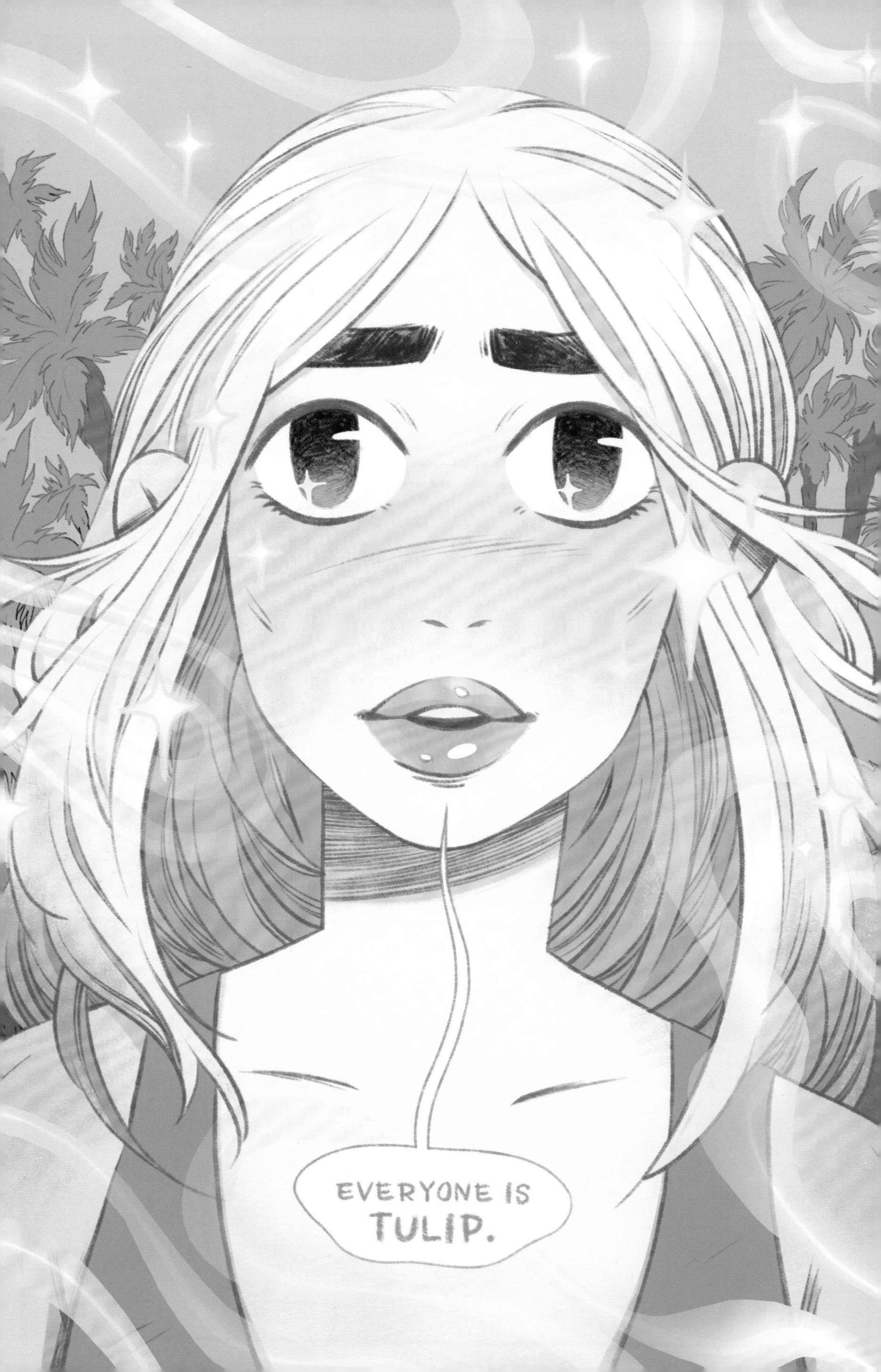
EVERYONE IS TULIP.

LIVING IN THE PAST, WORKING IN THE FUTURE

Art is time travel.
No matter how you want to spin it . . .
All art.
No matter the medium . . .

It's a simple truth but at the same time a seemingly universal constant, from what I can tell. It's a small fact that sneaks into the corners of your mind when phrases like "what if we did a book about . . . " and "y'know what would be cool . . . " are uttered in the harsh stillness before creative entropy takes hold.

Sure, it's a bit pretentious, but in the back of a book about the never-ending struggle of pursuing your art, it feels fitting to me. To be honest, it's also just the unblinking cold reality of attempting to make things. I wish it wasn't true, more often than not. But it is . . . even when you will it otherwise . . .

Art is time travel.

I know this might sound strange. But let me explain.

This book started in 2017. Nicole and I were obsessed with two things around that time: Internet-based performance artists and not dying from exhaustion in Europe. The life of a perennially impoverished cartoonist exists in harmony with a fairly discordant atonal frequency. You're constantly trying to balance living[1] and being able to work[2].

---

[1] This is typically defined by most functioning members of the subgenus *comixa cartoonisto independia* as existing well below the poverty line, owning only one pair of black jeans, and typically never eating more than one meal a day. Alternative definitions include: only feeling like you have friends while you're standing on a convention floor, and constantly uttering the phrases like "My hand is starting to hurt again from swiping right so much on Tinder, in a futile attempt to meet someone."

[2] Also known as somehow being able to afford to not get paid in order to pour years of your life into a creative project that will more than likely not yield you any significant monetary gain, but will still be worth it for that three seconds when you see your book on the shelf at your local comic book store in between *Batman* and *Some Weird Titty Book* starring Copyright Free Female Tarzan.

You see, we had just traveled to Thought Bubble in Leeds, England. The reputedly indie comix friendly show that had a killer line-up of guests, and a "No, you should totally do Thought Bubble" running endorsement from almost every one of our cartoonist friends. So, we decided to table at the show, and then afterward go on a mini vacation, running around Europe. This was a seemingly perfect way to shirk the ever-present specter of the drawing table, slowly beaconing me back towards it as both work and fun.

Nicole is better about unplugging than I am. For better or worse, I'm very much someone who has internalized the hellish status quo of a Kirby-esque work-life balance. That is to say . . . within the phrase "work life balance", I can only really internalize one of the words. And it sure as fuck ain't life or balance.

I'm sure armchair psychologist/comic book aficionados everywhere are diagnosing me as a workaholic from their leather bound lazy boys, as we speak[3]. After tabling at the show, selling all our books, and literally throwing our excess suitcases away so we wouldn't have to lug them around,

we traveled up to Edinburgh, Scotland and then over to Paris, France. Yes, it sounds glamorous, in hindsight. But what isn't easily understood about this time, was neither of us could work, so . . . in true cartoonist fashion, what did we do? We talked about work. An irony that is as potent as it is sharp.

This is really where Tulip began.

On trains, buses, and in nippy fall parks, Nicole and I started casually discussing what our next project would be. If you haven't read our other books like *Fuck Off Squad* or her lovely *Shadow of the Batgirl* with Sarah Kuhn, you should. They're pretty spiffy.

At the time, Nicole and I were in between longform projects. We had just come off of finishing *Fuck Off Squad*, which had been picked up and re-released for publication by Silver Sprocket. To say that we felt like we were leveling up our comics would have been an understatement. We'd been grinding away, producing work, and talking to various publishers for the previous three or four years, however we weren't finding an ownership deal we were happy with[4]. Simply put,

"ART IS TIME TRAVEL"

---

[3] And, honestly, they're probably right. It's something that I'm working on. It's something that will probably be with me forever. I think it's something that most creatives, who are actually driven to achieve something substantial, grapple with on one level or another. I'm someone who loves comics more than anything else. They're my religion. And the Purveyors of the Highest Art in the Land are, to me, like the anointed street preachers cursed with a futility-laden holy purpose and grand mission. A cynic would be existentially frustrated by the inborn cultural irrelevancy that their medium of mission has had foisted upon it, but in this specific area, I'm an optimist. I count myself lucky enough be a stalwart soldier in the Army of Poorly Dressed Crazed Proselytites standing on street corners, barking gibberish at the passing throngs in the vain hopes that one soul might be converted. That is to say, we all are suffering from a shared delusion. We're all supremely committed, and we're all intimately aware that everyone in Comics History has been fucked over seven ways from Sunday. The only solution that we've silently agreed upon, as a means of self-protection, is to just work harder and longer hours. Is it healthy? No. But you don't get your name on the Mount Rushmore of Comics by taking naps and going on walks, unfortunately.

[4] Word to the wise: most comic book companies that say they publish creator owned comics...don't. They publish comics that the creators own a percentage of. However, looking back at the long line of creators like Siegel and Shuster, Kirby, Moore and Gibbons, Starlin, and Ditko, I'm very aware of what happens when creators don't actually own and control their work. Basically, what I'm saying is: if I can help it, I'd much rather be Eastman and Laird, than Moore and Gibbons. If you know the details of their stories, you'll know what I'm talking about.

thanks to *Fuck Off Squad* being published we were feeling pretty good about things, but as is the case with creative minds . . . it's very difficult to sit still for too long.

As we roamed around, the ideas for what our next project would be would pop up during idle talk. Maybe a sorta-vampire kinda-roadtrip comic? An undead pirate comic? A book about a young woman running a bar and struggling with ghosts of her past?

They all sounded cool, but nothing was really clicking with both of us. The fun thing about having a long term creative collaborator is that you have such an understood sense of communication that when you come across that small nugget of gold that excites you both, it's instantly apparent what the next thing is gonna be.

Being as my short term memory is pretty shitty, I don't quite remember where we were, Scotland or France, but over the course of attending art museums and eating in pubs and open air cafes, we started talking about this growing trend of YouTube and Instagram performance artists.

If you're unaware, they're a real thing. The digital ecosystems that we currently live in are getting weirder and weirder, by the day. The fact that there are major conspiracy theories that have gotten people killed and changed the course of political careers that were spawned off the backs of people just ostensibly just LARPing on anonymous message boards is all the proof you need.

You could even make the case that since the invention of usernames and the rise in artificially cultivated online personas that we're all just YouTube Performance Artists[5]. We were both struck by the simultaneously bizarre and completely transparent nature of these artists' work. Which then led to Nicole and I having long in depth discussions about the nature of art, the definition of success, and the

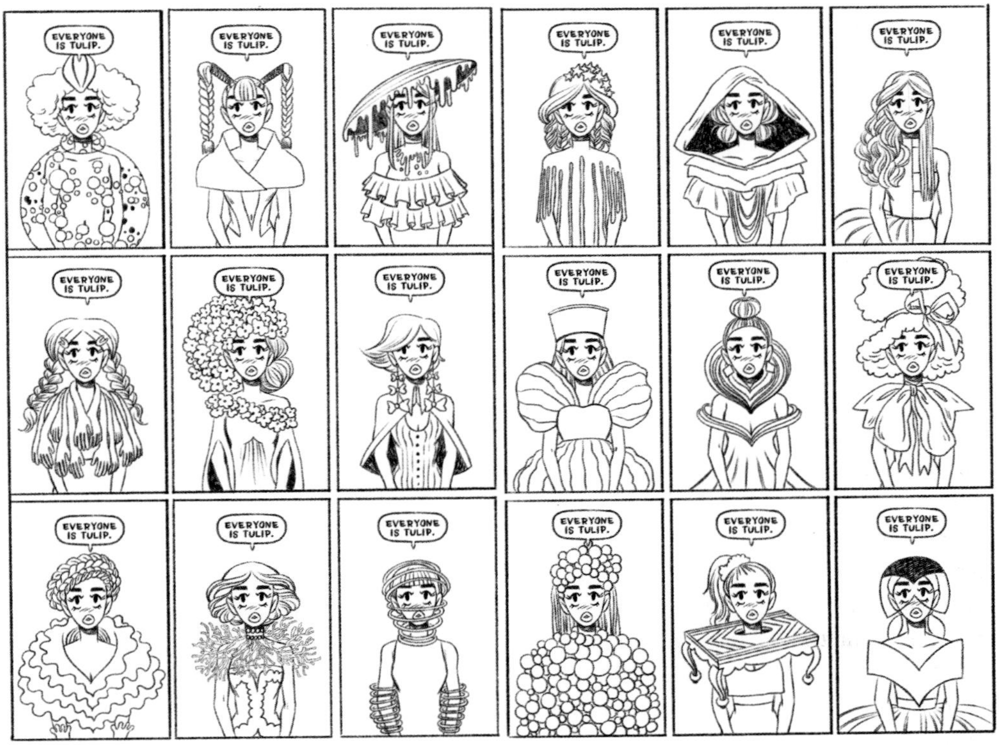
EVERYONE IS TULIP.
EVERYONE IS TULIP.
EVERYONE IS TULIP.
EVERYONE IS TULIP.
EVERYONE IS TULIP.
EVERYONE IS TULIP.
EVERYONE IS TULIP.
EVERYONE IS TULIP.
EVERYONE IS TULIP.
EVERYONE IS TULIP.
EVERYONE IS TULIP.
EVERYONE IS TULIP.
EVERYONE IS TULIP.
EVERYONE IS TULIP.
EVERYONE IS TULIP.
EVERYONE IS TULIP.
EVERYONE IS TULIP.
EVERYONE IS TULIP.

sacrifices that every creator has to make in order to chart their winding path towards recognition and success[6].

These conversations were juxtaposed against something that we had both been grappling with for the past few years. The eternal war raging inside your favorite pieces of art. The issue that's at the core of almost every artist's life. Artistic expression vs. commercial viability. Every person who wakes up in the morning and says to themselves, "I'm going to create something that didn't exist yesterday. I'm going to bring it to life today" has had to stare this grey-eyed grinagog in the face every waking moment.

Art, much like politics, is about compromise. How much time do you have? How much money do you have? What's your natural ability? How many gatekeepers do you need to get through in order to achieve your goal? Each one of these ideological hurdles must be reconciled with.

And to make it even more frustrating, the more personal, the more individualistic, or the more unique you make something? The more people you will have to push through in order to bring the idea to fruition. It's almost enough to make you understand why people like Michael Bay and Bret Ratner operate in the hermetically sealed, completely safe, artistic fingerprint free way they do. You don't have to navigate art vs. commerce when you're only attempting to do cocaine and have a beach house in Malibu.

We were both extremely excited by these ideas. We started thinking that we could make this book into a definitive statement. Into a story that would say what every artist wants to say. THIS IS WHO THE FUCK I AM. That was simultaneously exciting and terrifying to both of us. Which meant one thing.

We had to make this book.

The ultimate destination that all these conversations gave us was Tulip. Not the

---

[5] The future we're currently in feels so much more bizarre and bleak than we were warned it would be. It's filled with so much incredible stupidity and neon garnished bigotry that it feels like something from a Paul Verhoeven movie. Where the exploitation of the subject matter is so earnest and over the top that it becomes a parable. It's almost like we're not living in a dystopia; we're just living inside Verhoeven's Toupee.

[6] What does success even mean, anymore? In a world where babies have millions of followers for just showing up and burping, is there space for craft? When you're an artist who works in a style that is labor intensive, how do you maintain an audience that is expecting you to post three pieces of finely honed content every 3-4 hours? What does craft even mean anymore? Do we live in a Duchampian parallel world where all art is made just by a recontextualization of previously existing, and more often than not diametrically opposed, objects or intellectual properties?

book, but the character. Becca. The joint persona that we could both live through.

Eventually, all of these heady themes and existential frustration were boiled down into a simple and clean core question: "How far would you go to get what you want?[7]"

Surprisingly, the completed *Everyone Is Tulip* adhered fairly closely to our initial idea. Occasionally, we've started projects and they've significantly evolved over the course of creation, but for whatever reason Tulip remained pure, frozen in amber. The irony of this is not lost on either of her creators.

Nicole's initial exploratory drawings of lavish couture fashion and elaborate costumed regalia sealed the deal for us. As soon as I saw her first few drawings of Tulip created it was crystal clear what we had to do. We needed to build a world for Becca and Tulip to live in. We need to manufacture a pocket reality so that our collective voyeurism would have somewhere to live. A manicured existence where our obsessions and proclivities could manifest. A dark

timeline for us to play god with . . . to excise our deepest creative fears. A Butterfly Effect Dimension that we could role play Grand Inquisitor and Heretic in an attempt to gain entrance into the unknowable.

Which brings me back to my initial point.

Art is time travel.

It's simultaneously a means by which to observe ourselves from the fourth dimension and placate our futile need for control.

It's ultimately pointless, and literally the point of existence.

For me, as cheesy or pretentious as it sounds, there's nothing more concrete or unarguable.

Art is time travel.

When I look at these pages they pull me back to a time when this project that we've spent hundreds of thousands of hours breathing life into was just a glimmer in our minds.

On some undefined point in the near future timeline you're going to be reading this book, reading these words, and you're going to have a reaction to them[8]. You're going to come into the world that we've constructed

[7] This question is hopefully relatable to readers who are artistic and readers who aren't. It's something I'm constantly plagued by, in my everyday life. Does this book answer that shrieking howl? No, I don't think so. Does it provide a parable of just what happens when an individual sacrifices everything? Maybe. That's not for me to decide. I can only create the work that's the thing I wished existed and then go from there.

[8] Hey, what's up. Nice to meet you. I hope we can become friends. And not passing each other in the hallway on the way to Chemistry friends. I'm talking It's 11:17 On A Tuesday, Fuck It -- Let's Skip School And Go Throw Rocks Into The Ravine Out Behind The Blockbuster friends.

> ## *"Who knows what amazing events or opportunities or connections this book will make. It will have a life all its own."*

and you're going to live in it . . . you might love it . . . you might hate it . . . but it'll evoke a response . . . hopefully.

In the distant future who knows what alternate timeline this project could spawn. Who knows where this will lead. Who knows what amazing events or opportunities or connections this book will make. It will have a life all its own. Beyond me and beyond Nicole.

This book is our little message in a bottle sent out through the seas of time.

Perhaps it'll find you, sitting on a dusty bookshelf in the back of a used bookstore hundreds of years from now, when books are rare objects that only the super rich can afford.

Or perhaps it will just languish in the back of a dollar bin in a comic book store in Arizona . . . which would be a fitting fate, in my opinion. A higher honor, I can't think of. It's the destiny of most of the work produced in this medium, if we're all being honest with ourselves.

This book is constructed from the past versions of Nicole and I. This book was built by current versions of Nicole and I. This book was packaged for the old versions of Nicole and I, when we're too emotionally broken and physically unable to hold drawing utensils anymore. But most of all, this book was grown from the joint experiences that Nicole and I had. It was made from our collective vision. Honestly, I wish I could now send it back in time to those two artists who met in a crowded bar and started playing a drawing game on a cocktail napkin and show them what their frivolous dalliance would one day bring into being.

One more time, for the cheap seats . . .

Art is time travel . . .

Hopefully I'll run into you at some point in the future . . .

Your friend,
—Davey
Los Angeles, 2020

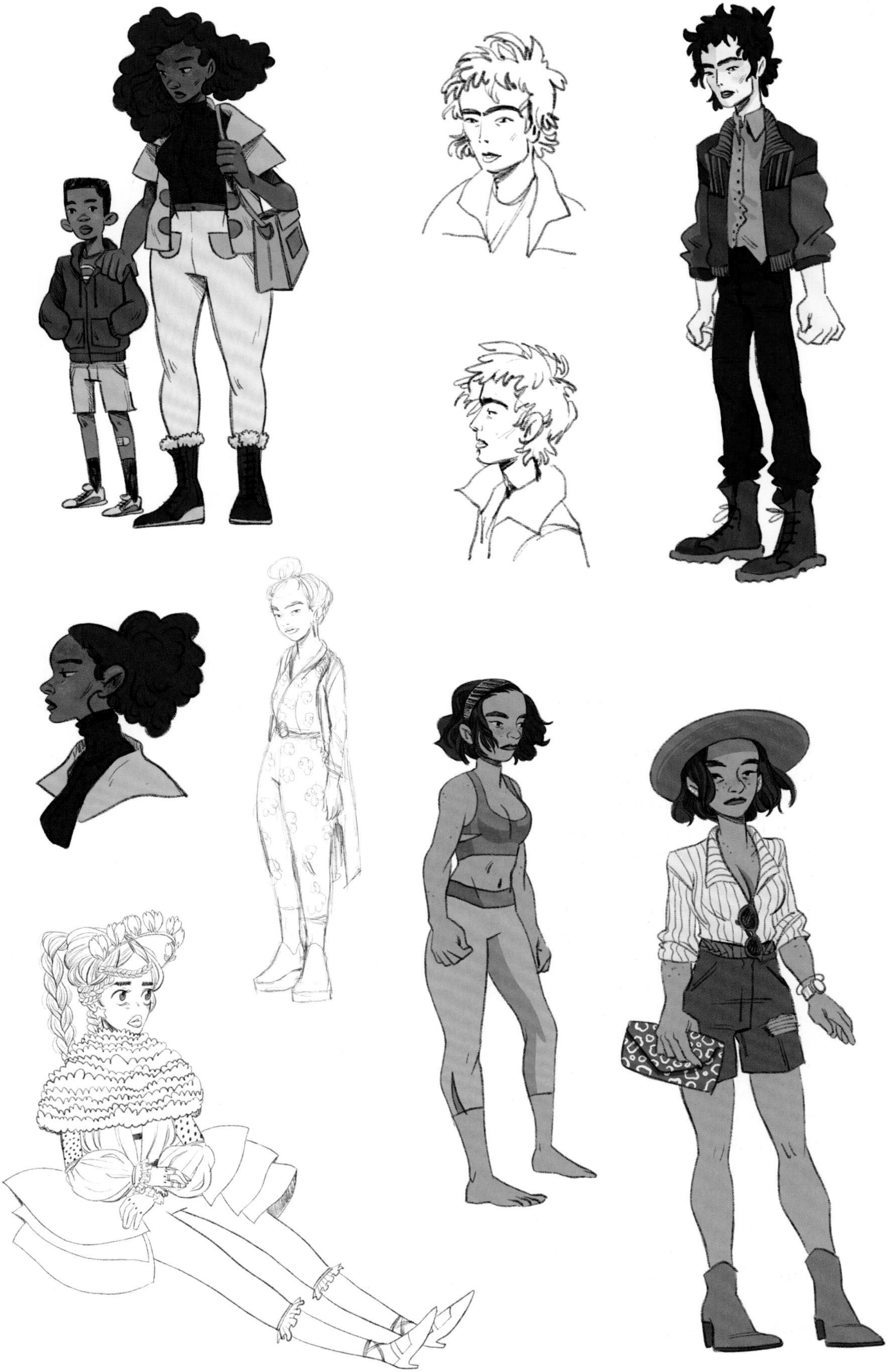

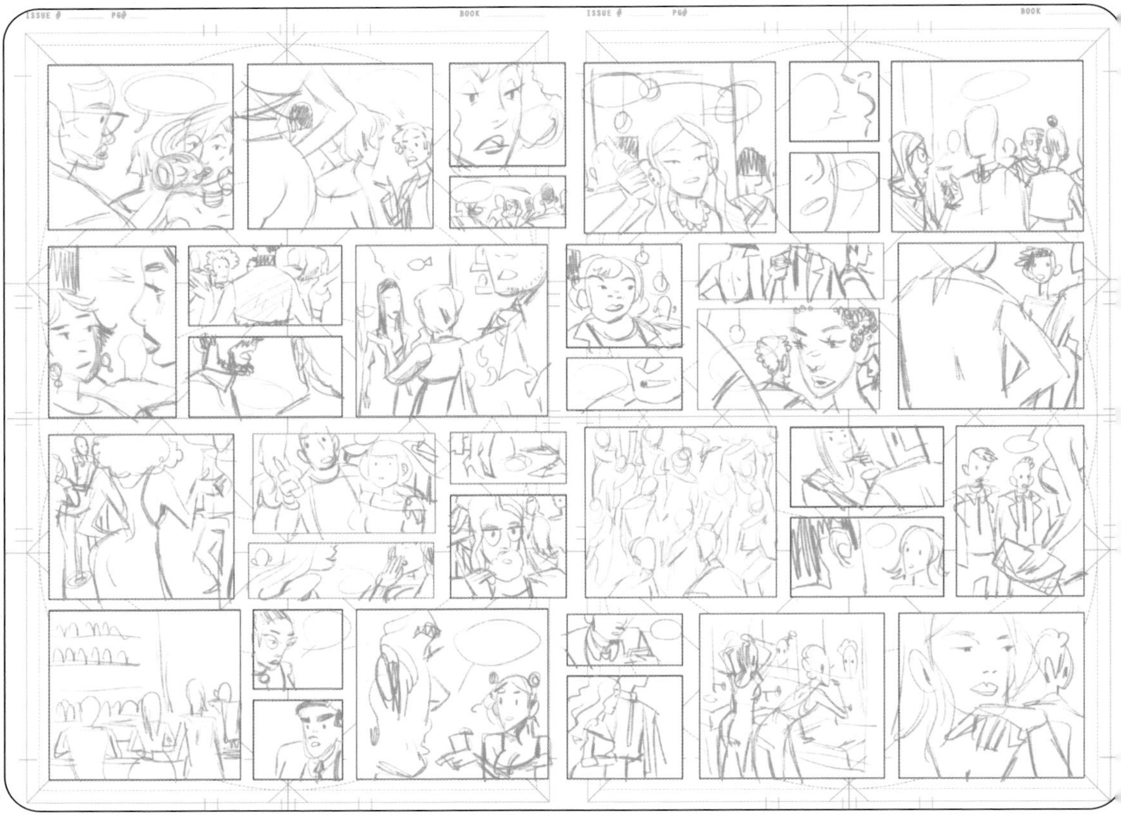
ISSUE # PG#
BOOK
ISSUE # PG#
BOOK

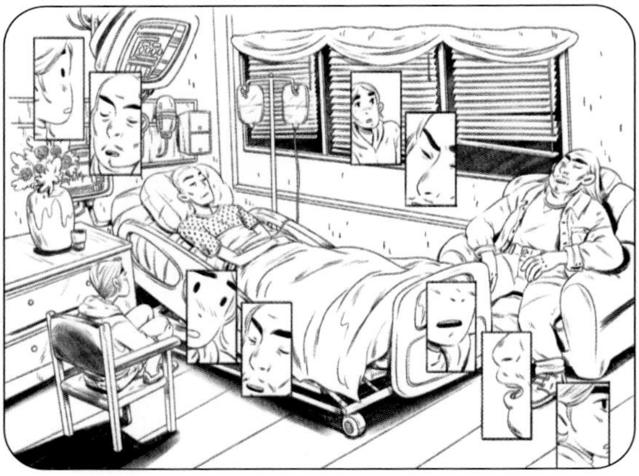

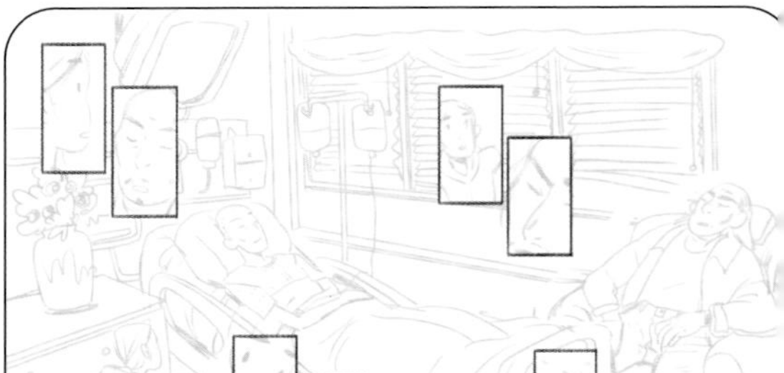

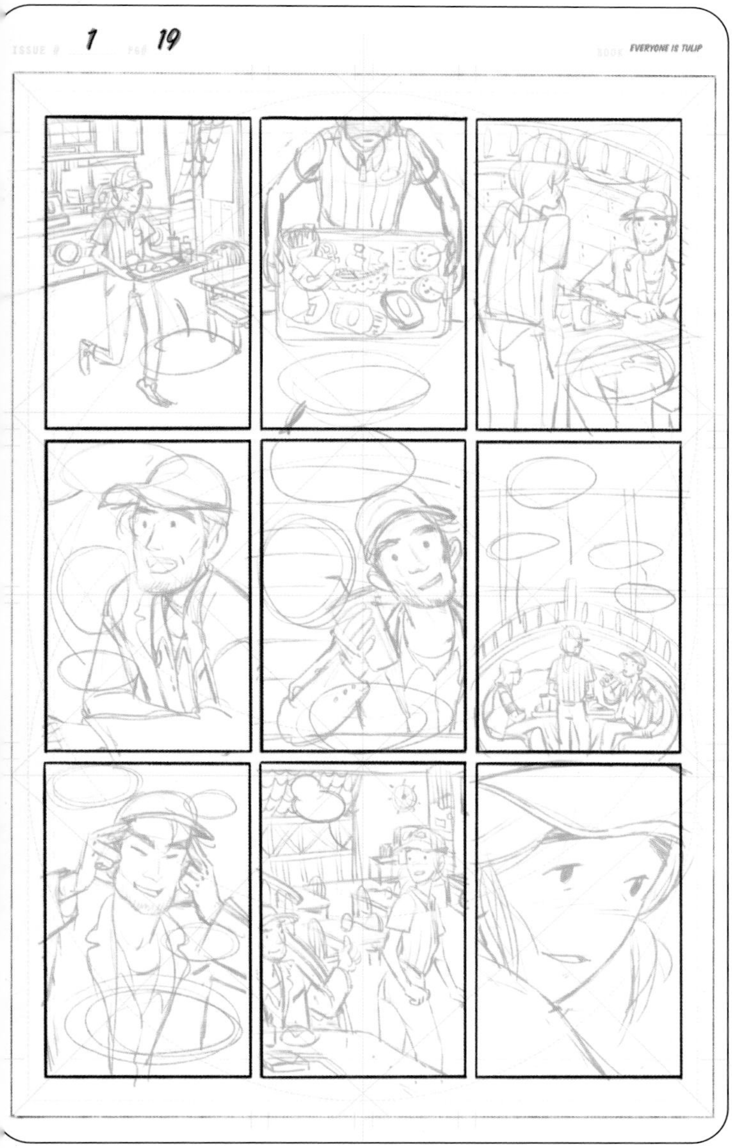
1
19
EVERYONE IS TULIP

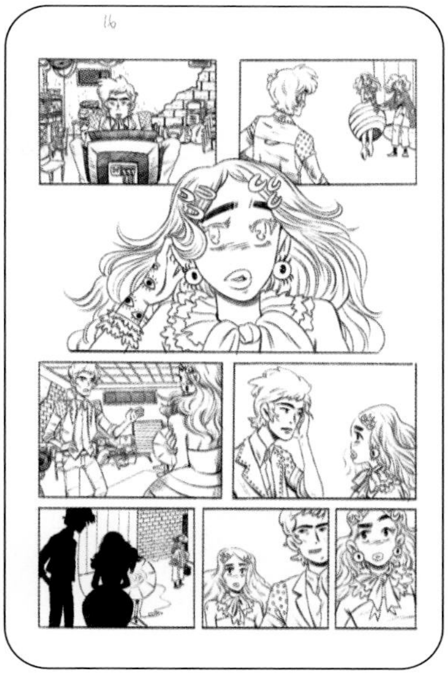
16

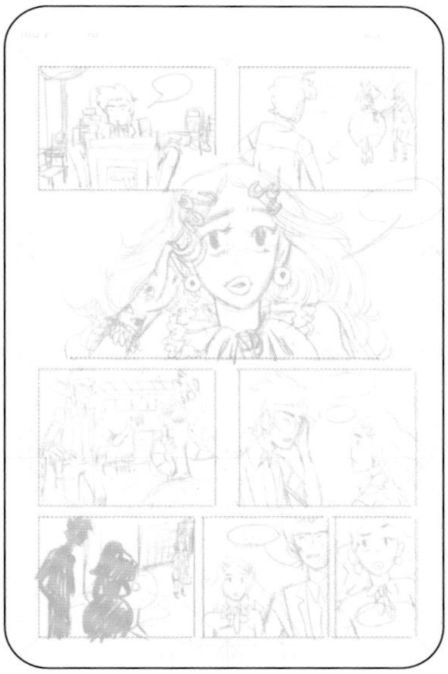

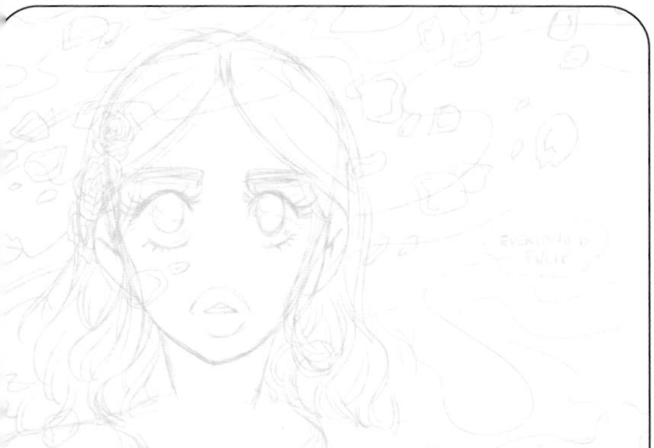

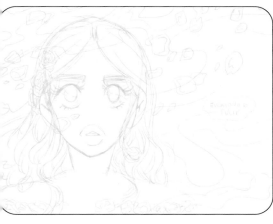

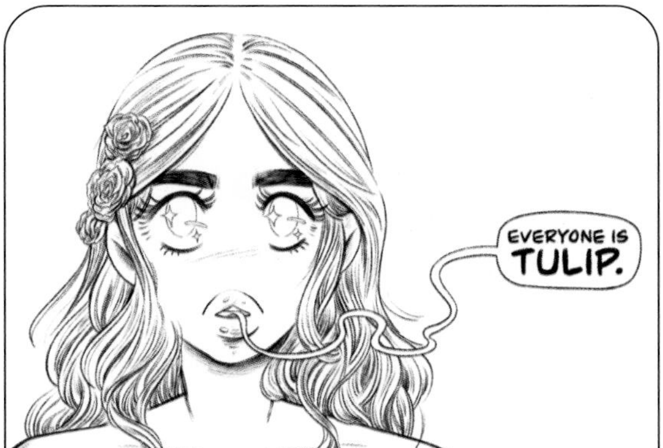
EVERYONE IS TULIP.

DAVE BAKER IS A WRITER AND ILLUSTRATOR BASED IN LOS ANGELES, CALIFORNIA. HIS MOST RECENT WORKS, *ACTION HOSPITAL*, *FUCK OFF SQUAD*, *NIGHT HUNTERS*, AND *STAR TREK VOYAGER: SEVEN'S RECKONING*, HAVE BEEN WELL RECEIVED BY COMIC BOOK READERS EVERYWHERE. HE ALSO CO-WROTE THE FEATURE FILM *ALIEN WARFARE*, NOW STREAMING ON NETFLIX. DAVE AND NICOLE'S NEXT COLLABORATION, THE HIGHLY ANTICIPATED YA GRAPHIC NOVEL *FOREST HILLS BOOTLEG SOCIETY*, DEBUTS FROM SIMON AND SCHUSTER IN 2022. HE HAS ALSO WRITTEN FOR 20TH CENTURY FOX, UNIVERSAL, AND CARTOON NETWORK.

WWW.HEYDAVEBAKER.COM
IG & TWITTER: @XDAVEBAKERX

NICOLE GOUX IS A CARTOONIST AND ILLUSTRATOR WORKING IN LOS ANGELES. SHE'S THE CO-CREATOR OF *FUCK OFF SQUAD* AND THE ARTIST OF DC'S *SHADOW OF THE BATGIRL*. SHE'S ALSO WORKED WITH DC COMICS, SILVER SPROCKET BICYCLE CLUB, IDW, AND LIONFORGE, AND SELF PUBLISHED VARIOUS WORKS. HER NEXT UPCOMING WORK WITH DAVE IS THE YA GRAPHIC NOVEL *FOREST HILLS BOOTLEG SOCIETY* FROM SIMON & SCHUSTER: ATHENEUM IN 2022.

YOU CAN FIND HER TOOLING AROUND ON IG AND TWITTER, POSTING IN BOXES, DRAWING THINGS IN BOXES, LIVING IN BOXES, LIKE YOU DO.

WWW.NICOLEGOUX.COM
IG @NGOUX
TWITTER @NICOLEGOUX

ELLIE HALL HAS DONE WORK FOR STARBURNS INDUSTRIES AND NICKELODEON AS A BACKGROUND PAINTER AND COLOR STYLIST.

END